# Genetic Discrimination

As genetic technologies advance, genetic testing may well offer the prospect of detecting the onset of future disabilities. Some research also forwards that certain behavioural profiles may have a strong genetic basis, such as the determination to succeed, or the propensity for risk-taking. As this technology becomes more prevalent, there is a danger that genetic information may be misused by third parties and that particular genetic profiles may be discriminated against by employers, by providers of social goods and services, such as insurance companies and even by educational facilities.

This book explores the different forms and potential uses of genetic testing. Drawing together leading experts in disability law, bioethics, health law and a range of related fields, it highlights the ethical and legal challenges arising as a result of emerging and rapidly advancing genetic science. On examining transatlantic perspectives on the matter, chapters in the book ask whether the US Genetic Information Nondiscrimination Act (GINA) is proving to be an effective tool in addressing the issue of genetic discrimination and alleviating fears of discrimination. The book also reviews what insights may be gained from GINA within employment and health insurance contexts, and asks how the UN Convention on the Rights of Persons with Disabilities (CRPD) may impact similar debates within the European Union. The book focuses particularly on the legislative and policy framework in the European Union, with an emphasis on the gaps in protection and the scope for specific legislative action in this area.

This book will be of great interest to scholars and students of discrimination law, bioethics and disability law, and will be of considerable use to legal practitioners, medical practitioners and policy-makers in this area.

**Gerard Quinn** is University Professor and Director of the Centre for Disability Law and Policy, National University of Ireland, Galway.

**Aisling de Paor** is Lecturer in Law at Dublin City University.

**Peter Blanck** is University Professor and Chairman of the Burton Blatt Institute at Syracuse University, USA.

# Genetic Discrimination

## Transatlantic perspectives on the case for a European-level legal response

**Edited by Gerard Quinn, Aisling de Paor and Peter Blanck**



Routledge
Taylor & Francis Group
LONDON AND NEW YORK

First published 2015
by Routledge
2 Park Square, Milton Park, Abingdon, Oxon, OX14 4RN

and by Routledge
711 Third Avenue, New York, NY 10017

*Routledge is an imprint of the Taylor & Francis Group, an informa business*



*British Library Cataloguing in Publication Data*
A catalogue record for this book is available from the British Library

*Library of Congress Cataloging-in-Publication Data*
Genetic discrimination : transatlantic perspectives on the case for a European level legal response / edited by Gerard Quinn, Aisling de Paor, Peter Blanck.
pages cm
Includes bibliographical references and index.
ISBN 978-0-415-83693-7 (hardback) — ISBN 978-0-203-69429-9 (ebk)
1. Genetic screening—Law and legislation—United States.
2. Genetic screening—Law and legislation—European Union countries.
3. United States. Genetic Information Nondiscrimination Act of 2008.
4. Discrimination in employment—Law and legislation. 5. Discrimination in insurance—Law and legislation. 6. Human chromosome abnormalities—Diagnosis—Law and legislation—United States. 7. Human chromosome abnormalities—Diagnosis—Law and legislation—European Union countries. 8. Convention on the Rights of Persons with Disabilities and Optional Protocol (2007) I. Quinn, G. (Gerard), editor. II. De Paor, Aisling, editor. III. Blanck, Peter, editor.
K3611.G46G43 2015
344.2404'36—dc23
2014025060

ISBN: 978-0-415-83693-7 (hbk)
ISBN: 978-0-203-69429-9 (ebk)

Typeset in Baskerville
by FiSH Books Ltd, Enfield

MIX
Paper from responsible sources
FSC® C013604

Printed and bound by CPI Group (UK) Ltd, Croydon, CR0 4YY

# Contents

# Notes on contributors

**Peter Blanck** (editor) is University Professor at Syracuse University, New York, and Chairman of the Burton Blatt Institute at Syracuse University, one of the leading disability law and policy institutes in the United States. Professor Blanck holds appointments at the Syracuse University Colleges of Law, and Arts and Sciences, David B. Falk College of Sport and Human Dynamics, School of Education, and the Maxwell School of Citizenship and Public Affairs. He is Honorary Professor at the Centre for Disability Law and Policy, at the National University of Ireland, Galway. Professor Blanck received a Bachelor of Arts from the University of Rochester, a Juris Doctorate from Stanford University, where he was President of the Stanford Law Review, and a PhD from Harvard University. Blanck has written articles and books on the Americans with Disabilities Act (ADA) and related laws, and received grants to study disability law and policy.

**Harold J. Bursztajn** MD is an Associate Clinical Professor of Psychiatry and a co-founder of the Program in Psychiatry and the Law at the Massachusetts Mental Health Center and the Beth Israel Deaconess Medical Center, Department of Psychiatry at Harvard Medical School. He also serves as President and Co-founder of the American Unit of the UNESCO Bioethics Chair and its American Bioethics Culture Institute. He has authored numerous peer-reviewed publications, five books and a variety of educational materials on medical decision making, bioethics, psychiatry and the law for public and the professions. He has an active clinical and forensic neuropsychiatric practice. Dr. Bursztajn has been qualified as a testifying expert in clinical and forensic neuropsychiatry. He has received a variety of awards and honors for his work as a clinician, teacher and clinical decision-making researcher, including being a recipient of the Clifford A. Barger Excellence in Mentoring Award of Harvard Medical School.

**James Davey** has been Professor of Insurance Law at the University of Southampton since September 2014. He was previously Senior Lecturer in Law at Cardiff University. He writes primarily on insurance contract theory, but with a particular interest in the regulation of (potentially) discriminatory underwriting practices in UK, EU and US regulatory systems.

**Aisling de Paor** (editor) is a Lecturer in Law at Dublin City University (DCU). She is a former Irish Research Council Scholar and former PhD candidate at the Centre for Disability Law and Policy at NUI Galway. In 2013 Aisling defended her PhD, entitled 'Advancing Science and Controlling the Misuse of Genetic Information in Employment and Insurance – Towards an Effective European Union Regulatory Framework'. Aisling graduated from National University of Ireland, Galway with a law degree (BCL) in 2005 and graduated from University College Cork with a masters in law (LLM) in 2006. She is a qualified Solicitor and trained in a large commercial law firm in Dublin (from 2006 to 2009), having specialised in Employment Law and Commercial Litigation for the majority of her traineeship. She has also worked as a Research Assistant at the Centre for Disability Law and Policy (2009–2010), working on a project entitled 'The New Transatlantic Agenda and the UN Convention on the Rights of Persons with Disabilities – Taking the US/EU Dialogue to a New Level'. From 2009 to 2014 she was a part-time Lecturer in Law at the School of Law, NUI Galway, lecturing modules including Health Law and Policy, and Genetics, Disability and the Law. Aisling is an affiliated researcher of the Burton Blatt Institute, Syracuse University and was a visiting scholar at this Institute in October 2012 and May 2014.

**Delia Ferri** holds a Master in Law *magna cum laude* from the University of Verona, an LLM in International and European Business Law 1st Hons with Distinction from Trinity College Dublin, and a PhD in European and Italian Constitutional Law from the University of Verona. Delia is a Lecturer in Law at National University of Ireland, Maynooth. Delia was a former Research Associate at the Centre for Disability Law and Policy, National University of Ireland Galway. She has previously lectured a module on 'The European Union and Human Rights' at the Irish Centre on Human Rights (NUIG), and a module of EU law at the University of Trento (Italy). Delia is also attorney at law enrolled at Verona Bar and, since 2006, has worked as independent consultant in several EU-funded projects. Most recently, she has been appointed international expert in a project 'Partnership for Change – Institutionalizing Access to Justice for Persons with Disabilities in Albania'.

**Yann Joly**, PhD (DCL), AdE is a Lawyer Emeritus from the Quebec Bar and the Research Director of the Centre of Genomics and Policy. He is an Assistant Professor at the Faculty of Medicine, Department of Human Genetics and at the Bioethics Unit at McGill University. He is a research fellow from the Fonds de recherche du Québec-Santé (FRQS) and an associate researcher at the Centre de Recherche en Droit Public (University of Montreal). He also works as an ethics and legal consultant in the private sector. Prof. Joly is the Data Access Officer of the International Cancer Genome Consortium (ICGC). His research activities lie at the interface of the fields of intellectual property, health law (biotechnology and other emerging health technologies) and bioethics. He has served as a legal advisor on several ethics committees in the public and private sectors. Prof. Joly is a member of the Scientific Committee of the legal journal *Lex Elextronica* and an Advisory Board member of the *Current Pharmacogenomics and Personalized Medicine Journal.* He recently received the Quebec Bar Award of Merit (Innovation) for his work on the right to privacy in the biomedical field.

**Janet E. Lord** is an international human rights lawyer who is currently Senior Vice President for Human Rights and Inclusive Development at the Burton Blatt Institute (BBI) at Syracuse University College of Law where she oversees international legal research and global programming. She is also senior research associate at the Harvard Law School project on Disability and teaches human rights at the University of Maryland and at American University. Prior to BBI, Lord served as senior partner and director of human rights and inclusive development at BlueLaw International LLP, where she worked in more than thirty countries, designing, managing, implementing, and evaluating human rights and inclusive development projects. She has worked with a variety of international organisations and donors, including the UN Office of the High Commissioner for Human Rights, the UN Disability Program, UNAIDS, UNDP, and the United States Agency of International Development. Prior to joining BlueLaw, Lord served as legal advisor and advocacy director at an international landmine survivor organisation, participating in all of the negotiations for the UN Convention on the Rights of Persons with Disabilities, serving as legal advisor to several lead governments, expert to the UN and legal advocacy advisor to Disabled Peoples International. She worked as an attorney at the World Bank Group at the start of her international law career. Lord holds an LLB and LLM in law from the University of Edinburgh (Scotland), an LLM in international and comparative law from George Washington University Law School, and a BA in History from Kenyon College. She is a member of the New York Bar and is currently serving on the Board of Amnesty International USA.

**Noel Lowndes**, BA (Mod) PhD is Chair of Biochemistry and Director of the Centre for Chromosome Biology, NUI Galway. Professor Lowndes graduated with a degree in Genetics from Trinity College Dublin in 1983. His post-graduate studies were completed at the Beatson Institute for Cancer Research, Glasgow and Columbia University, New York. He was awarded a PhD in Molecular Pathology by the University of Glasgow in 1987 for his work on the transcriptional regulation of the c-Ha-*ras* proto-oncogene. His post-doctoral work on the regulation of cell cycle-regulated gene transcription was conducted in Lee Johnston's laboratory at the National Institute for Medical Research (NIMR) in London. He is the founding director of the Centre for Chromosome Biology, where his laboratory focuses on genetic and biochemical analyses of genome stability pathways.

**Ida Ngueng Feze** is an attorney admitted to practice in the State of New York. She holds a Bachelor of Arts degree (BA) in Law and Society with a minor in Psychology from Ramapo College of New Jersey and a Juris Doctor degree (JD) from Howard University School of Law in Washington. DC. She recently completed a Master's degree in International Public and Private Law at the University of Montreal and a certificate in Chinese Law at the China University of Political Science and Law. Before joining the Centre of Genomics and Policy, she worked at a law firm in the US and at several not-for-profit organisations including the Environmental Law Institute and the Law Development Service of the United Nations Food and Agriculture Organization in Rome. Her main projects at the Center include genetic discrimination and the ethical and legal duties of health professionals, pharmacogenomics, biotechnologies (health and environmental law) and intellectual property. She has been a guest lecturer on legal and ethical issues of genetics, genomics and pharmacogenomics at the University of Montreal and Laval University since 2013. Ms. Ngueng Feze is also a member of the Quebec Bar Working Group for a more inclusive legal profession and a member of the Montreal General Hospital's Research Ethics Board.

**Robert S. Olick**, JD, PhD, is Associate Professor, Center for Bioethics and Humanities, SUNY Upstate Medical University, Syracuse, New York, where he teaches bioethics and health law for medical students and allied health professional students, chairs the hospital ethics committee and provides ethics consultations. He is a senior fellow at the Burton Blatt Institute, Syracuse University. Dr. Olick's previous positions include serving as Executive Director of the New Jersey Bioethics Commission. His publications and research interests include the areas of genetic privacy and discrimination, research ethics, intellectual disability, advance directives, end-of-life decisions, the limits of informed consent and confidentiality, and the intersection of law and ethics in health policy and at the bedside.

**Anya Prince,** JD, MPP, is a Post-Doctoral Research Fellow at the Center for Genomics and Society at University of North Carolina, Chapel Hill. She received her JD and Masters of Public Policy at Georgetown University. She recently worked at the Cancer Legal Resource Center, where she focused on discrimination and privacy concerns for those with genetic predispositions to cancer. Her research explores the implementation and practical considerations of state and federal laws regarding genetic testing and whether emerging genetic rights laws effectively protect individual interests.

**Gerard Quinn** (editor) is the Director of the Centre for Disability Law and Policy at the NUI Galway School of Law. Called to the Irish Bar in 1983, he holds a masters (LLM) and doctorate in law (SJD) from Harvard Law School. His specialisation is international and comparative disability law and policy. He is a member of the Irish Human Rights Commission and helps co-ordinate the work of National Human Rights Institutions worldwide on disability issues. He led the delegation of Rehabilitation International (RI) during the UN Working Group that elaborated the basis for the new Convention on the Rights of Persons with Disabilities.

He has worked in the European Commission (as a civil servant) and held a number of posts such as Director of Research for the Irish Government's Law Reform Commission and Vice President of the European Committee of Social Rights (Council of Europe). He sits on various advisory boards dealing with disability law and policy issues such as the Commonwealth Secretariat, SOROS-OSI (Washington, DC), Disability Rights Fund (Boston, MA), European Foundation Centre Consortium on Disability (Brussels), European Coalition for Community Living (London) and Interights (London). In January 2012 President Michael D. Higgins appointed Professor Quinn to the Republic of Ireland's Council of State.

**Javier Romañach Cabrero** is a social activist, philosopher and writer. He has developed a new theoretical model on functional diversity (disability), based on dignity and diversity and rejecting ability as a way to value human beings: 'the diversity model'. He is an expert in the area of bioethics and author of the book 'Bioethics From the Other Side of the Looking-glass' (in Spanish). He is co-author of the new ethical proposal, 'diversity ethics', as an alternative to Peter Singer ethics. He is a member of the Independent Living and Diversity Forum, an Internet-based network to promote Independent Living and Human Rights for functionally diverse (disabled) people in Spain.

**Henriette Roscam Abbing** is one of the pioneers of Dutch and European Health Law. She has worked for the Council of Europe (Public Health Department) and combined her professoriates (Universities of Maastricht and Utrecht) with a position as a legal counsel (health law) to the Minister of Health. She has been a member of the editorial board of the Dutch *Journal for Medicine* and served over 25 years as one of the editors of the Dutch *Journal on Health Law*. She was a co-founder of the *European Journal of Health Law*, of which she is still a co-editor. She is the vice-president of the European Association of Health Law, which she initiated. She also acts as an advisor to (European) research projects and gives lectures and expert opinions in her field of expertise. The present focus of her publications is on European health law.

**J. Rosel Kim** is currently enrolled in the joint civil law and common law (BCL/LLB) programme at McGill University. She has worked as a legal intern at the Canadian HIV/AIDS Legal Network, a non-profit organisation that advocates for human rights-based approaches for people living with HIV, where her research focused on human rights and health, particularly in HIV prevention and treatment. At the Centre of Genomics and Policy at McGill University, her research focused on the issues of stem cell research policies and genetic discrimination. Prior to her law degree, she completed a Master of Arts degree in English Literature at McGill University, which was funded by the Social Science and Humanities Research Council of Canada. She is a 2014 Summer Law Student at Goodmans LLP in Toronto, Canada.

**Shahad Salman** is a lawyer, member of the Quebec Bar. She is a University of Montreal (LLB) graduate and holds a Juris Doctorate (JD) degree in Common Law. She has also studied international law in Europe with the University of San Diego's summer Institute of International and Comparative Law. Ms Salman is a master's in law candidate at McGill University's Institute of Comparative Law. She practised in civil litigation before joining the Centre of Genomics and Policy. Her work is concentrated in the fields of genetic discrimination, legal duties and liability of health care professionals.

**Michael Ashley Stein** holds a JD from Harvard Law School and a PhD from Cambridge University. Co-founder and Executive Director of the Harvard Law School Project on Disability, he has taught at Harvard, New York University, Stanford, and William and Mary law schools. An internationally recognised expert on disability law and policy, Stein participated in the drafting of the UN Convention on the Rights of Persons with Disabilities, works with disabled persons organisations around the world, actively consults with governments on their disability laws and policies, and advises a number of UN bodies. Stein has received numerous awards for his work (most recently, the inaugural Henry Viscardi Achievement Award and the inaugural Morton E. Ruderman Prize for Inclusion) and was appointed by President Obama to the United States Holocaust Council.

**Mark Taylor** is a Senior Lecturer in the School of Law, and Deputy Director of the Sheffield Institute of Biotechnology, Law and Ethics (SIBLE), at the University of Sheffield. He specialises in health information law, privacy and legal and ethical conceptions of the public interest. Author of *Genetic Data and the Law* (CUP, 2012), he is a mid-career Fellow of the British Academy, and a Research Associate at the HeLEX Centre for

Health, Law and Emerging Technologies at the University of Oxford. He has either led or otherwise contributed towards a number of research projects, including currently an EU FP7 project to make policy recommendations for open access to Research Data in Europe (RECODE). He is the establishing Chair of the Confidentiality Advisory Group (CAG). This is an independent expert group providing advice to the Health Research Authority and the Secretary of State for Health on access to confidential health information without patient consent in England and Wales. The contribution to this collection is made in a personal capacity.

**Ine Van Hoyweghen** is Research Professor at the Centre for Sociological Research (CeSO) at KU Leuven. Her work focuses on the societal, regulatory, and ethical dimensions of biomedicine. She holds a PhD in Social Sciences (2004, KU Leuven), which was published as a book, *Risks in the Making. Travels in Life Insurance and Genetics* (Amsterdam University Press, 2007). Currently she is the PI in the project 'Postgenomic Solidarity. European Life Insurance in the Era of Personalized Medicine' funded by the Research Foundation – Flanders (FWO). She is a Member of the Young Academy of the Royal Flemish Academy of Belgium for Science and the Arts (KVAB).

**Michael Waterstone** is Associate Dean for Research and Academic Centers, J. Howard Ziemann Fellow and Professor of Law at Loyola Law School, Los Angeles. He joined Loyola's faculty in the fall of 2006. Previously, Waterstone clerked for the Honorable Richard S. Arnold on the United States Court of Appeals for the Eighth Circuit, then worked as an associate in the Los Angeles law firm of Munger, Tolles, & Olson for three years. In 2003–2006, Waterstone taught at the University of Mississippi Law School. Waterstone is a nationally recognized expert in disability and civil rights law. He is one of the co-authors of a leading casebook on disability law and his recent articles are in the *Harvard Law Review, Notre Dame Law Review, Minnesota Law Review, Duke Law Journal, Vanderbilt Law Review, William & Mary Law Review,* and *Northwestern Law Review,* amongst others. He is an associated colleague with the Harvard Law School Project on Disability, an affiliated researcher with the Burton Blatt Institute and has consulted on projects with the Human European Consultancy, the National Council on Disability, the World Bank and the Vietnam Assistance for the Handicapped. In 2012, Professor Waterstone received a grant from the Japan Foundation to work on shared understandings of US and Japanese Disability Law. He was also elected to the American Law Institute in 2012.

**Rebecca Wolf** holds a Juris Doctorate from American University Washington College of Law and a Master of Public Health degree from the Harvard School of Public Health. During her time at American University Washington College of Law, she served as a Dean's Fellow for the Health Law and Justice Initiative, and the Program on Informational Justice and Intellectual Property. In recognition of her scholarship during her time at American University, she received the Award for Outstanding Scholarship at the Graduate Level. During her time at Harvard, she served as a visiting researcher at the Harvard Law School Project on Disability. Prior to her graduate studies, Rebecca founded and directed the Helping Hands Medical Fellowship, which brings Israeli physicians to Uganda to provide volunteer medical services to impoverished communities. Rebecca has published academic papers and presented at international conferences on topics related to global health, legal issues in public health, disability rights, social justice and bioethics. She has conducted research for and served as a consultant to several global health organisations, such as the World Health Organization, the Israeli Medical Association, Unite for Sight, Global Youth Partnership for Africa and Naturopaths Without Borders.

**Michael Joseph Young** is an MD Candidate at Harvard Medical School and a Fellow at the Petrie-Flom Center for Health Law Policy, Biotechnology and Bioethics at Harvard Law School. His research examines the ethical dimensions and philosophical framework underlying standards of care in medicine and public health. Prior to arriving at Harvard, Michael completed an MPhil in philosophy at the University of Cambridge as a Gates Cambridge Scholar, where he focused on philosophical issues relating to medicine and the mind. In the past he has worked as a Patient-Family Advocate in the Emergency Department at Johns Hopkins Hospital and as a research assistant in the Division of Medical Ethics and Health Policy at the University of Pennsylvania, where he studied resource strain and decision procedures surrounding allocation of scarce resources in intensive care units. Most recently, Michael was awarded the Henry K. Beecher Prize in Medical Ethics from Harvard Medical School.

# Preface

I am delighted to write a preface for this informative and timely book. Throughout time, much scholarly activity ranging from philosophy, psychology, neuroscience and now genetic science has focused on what it means to be human. Our understandings of the nature of man are undergoing profound adjustments and further scientific advances are fully expected in the decades ahead.

Sometimes these great scientific advances lead to a form of social determinism – a belief that the human can be reduced to a set of determinants and that freedom itself is an illusion. This is both wrong and dangerous. We, in Europe, can learn from how the US has taken legislative and regulatory steps to ensure that genetic information is not abused by third parties which includes employers, insurance companies and Government. After all, our EU Charter on Fundamental rights explicitly protects our citizens against discrimination based on 'genetic features'.

I welcome the book for its contribution to a necessary debate in Europe. I also welcome its transatlantic focus since it provides an opportunity for mutual learning. And I especially welcome the debate it should stimulate on this side of the Atlantic about how we should embrace scientific advances while, at one and the same time, protecting our citizens against potential harms such as loss of privacy as well as the discriminatory use of information about their personal genetic make up.

Human rights are ultimately about the human person. As we face into the twenty-first century we have an unparalleled opportunity to grow our scientific understandings of the person. But we also have an ongoing ethical as well as legal imperative to ensure that potential abuses are dealt with. I commend this book as a contribution to a debate that has yet to happen at European level but which is inevitable as the science advances.

Emily O'Reilly
European Ombudsman

# Acknowledgements

Firstly, the editors acknowledge the transatlantic teamwork and collaboration of the Centre for Disability Law and Policy at National University of Ireland, Galway, and the Burton Blatt Institute (BBI), at Syracuse University, New York, USA. We thank our colleagues who have supported this book and with the preceding conferences from which this book evolved.

We greatly appreciate the work and scholarship of the authors who have contributed to this book. The diversity of the perspectives contributed provides a multifaceted insight into the complex ethical, legal, and regulatory issues arising in this field.

The editors also thank Emily O'Reilly, European Ombudsman who has supported this publication and who has kindly written the Preface.

The editors wish to recognise the support of the Irish Members of the European Parliament, particularly Marian Harkin MEP and Phil Prendergast (former MEP), who facilitated the organisation of a major conference (in March 2012) in this field, from which this publication evolved.

The editors also wish to acknowledge the funding and support of the Irish Research Council and Atlantic Philanthropies. Professor Blanck's participation also was supported in part by the National Institute on Disability and Rehabilitation Research (NIDRR) and the Rehabilitation Services Administration (RSA), both in the US Department of Education, as well as by Syracuse University. Additional information on grant support to Professor Blanck for this and related projects may be found at the Burton Blatt Institute website: bbi.syr.edu.

Finally, the editors extend their sincere thanks and appreciation to their families, for all of their love, patience, and support throughout the completion of this book.

Aisling de Paor, Gerard Quinn and Peter Blanck
September 2014

# 1 Introduction

*Aisling de Paor, Gerard Quinn and Peter Blanck*

## 1. Introduction and background

Revolutionary scientific and technological advances have led to a dramatic increase in the practice of genetic testing for medical and non-medical purposes. Genetic science and technology is advancing at a significant pace, with scientists continuing to make genetic discoveries as to the make-up of the human body and the cause and effect of disease, disability and other conditions. These discoveries are facilitating technological innovation and development of a range of genetic tests that are becoming increasingly refined and sophisticated. Therefore, as genetic science continues to advance, genetic technologies inevitably become more accessible and available, in the medical context, in third-party contexts and in society in general.

In addition to providing details about an individual's health, personality and behavioural traits, genetic testing technology provides insights into future health and offers the prospect of being able to detect the onset of future illnesses and disabilities. Therefore, advancing genetic science, in conjunction with an ageing population, is resulting in more individuals being exposed as having putative disabilities. The increasing availability of genetic information, together with the insights it offers into an individual's future health and predisposition to disability, is valuable to a range of third parties (including employers), as well as providers of social goods and services (such as insurers).

In light of the potential for new uses and misuse of this information, the need arises to consider the flow and use of genetic information, and whether an adequate regulatory framework may be proposed to address ethical and legal issues and to protect an individual's fundamental human rights. It is also necessary to address the evident conflict of competing interests and rights that may arise. In the absence of an appropriate regulatory framework, it is anticipated that more individuals will be excluded unnecessarily and inappropriately from a range of social and economic goods and services, potentially leading to the creation of a 'genetic underclass.' The absence of an appropriate regulatory framework also has the potential to stifle scientific and technological progression, with adverse implications for public health and economic growth. Accordingly, there are compelling reasons to decipher the ethical and legal issues presented and explore options available in regulation.

## 2. Aims and objective of book

To date, there is no European Union (EU)-level regulation protecting the privacy of genetic information or protecting against the discriminatory use of such information. Against the backdrop of rapidly advancing genetic technologies, this book aims to bring together different facets of this debate, including theoretical questions arising, challenges presented in the clinical context and conflict of rights evident in third-party contexts. This volume extrapolates the ethical and legal issues arising and examines the need for an EU-level regulatory framework.

The main focus of this book is on the regulatory questions arising, and on the need to consider the uses and misuses of genetic information, with the objective of advancing genetic science and acknowledging competing interests at stake. Although the focus is primarily on the contexts of employment and insurance, we also offer insights into additional scenarios where genetic information and genetic testing may cause concerns, such as immigration and criminal justice, and indeed in the general clinical setting. This book offers tentative suggestions as to the appropriate shape and content of a potential EU-level regulatory response.

On examining transatlantic perspectives, this book further offers insights into the United States experience and the regulatory framework in place. This will be the first United States/European Union publication examining the need for a EU response (to protect the privacy of genetic information and prevent the discriminatory use of genetic information) and exploring options available for regulating this issue at EU level, as well as the challenges with regulation. The US and the EU are grappling with similar ethical and legal dilemmas stemming from advancing genetic technology, albeit against the backdrop of different social, economic and political settings. In the US and throughout Europe (and indeed throughout the world), genetic science and technology is advancing at a rapid pace. This book highlights the merits of engaging in a transatlantic dialogue and learning from the experience of the US in addressing these ethical and legal issues, of course in consideration of other national perspectives.

This publication takes an interdisciplinary approach towards addressing genetic discrimination by engaging scientific, ethical and legal perspectives in looking towards the regulation of genetic discrimination and genetic privacy across commercial fields, primarily insurance and employment. It includes a section on genetic science and technology, the objective of which is to provide scientific context to this discussion and highlight the state of the art of genetic science, as well as the future orientation of such technologies. This book recognises the necessity of engaging in discussion that is informed of the realities and limitations of science and technology, by all stakeholders. This publication also highlights the ethical perspectives arising, which present complex challenges in the medical and non-medical contexts.

This publication includes contributions from an array of leading experts across a spectrum of interdisciplinary areas, such as science, ethics, law and public policy. The collection of contributions represents the multifaceted and interdisciplinary nature of this field, as well as different perspectives and diverse issues arising. It includes contributions from experts in Europe and the US, to reflect the transatlantic perspective. The range of authors from a variety of disciplines and the diversity of topics covered reflect the topical and cutting-edge nature of this area.

## 3. Origins of the book

This publication evolved from two major international conferences that the editors developed and organised on this topic. The first conference took place on 19th November 2011, at National University of Ireland, Galway. It was entitled 'Genetic Discrimination – Transatlantic Perspectives on the Case for a European Level Legal Response' and was organised by the Centre for Disability Law and Policy, National University of Ireland, Galway, in conjunction with the Burton Blatt Institute at Syracuse University. The conference brought together leading experts in the area, with the objective of exploring the case for a European Union-level response to protect the privacy of genetic information and to prevent genetic discrimination.

The editors were subsequently invited to organise and hold a further conference on this topic (of the same title), which took place on 6th March 2012, at the European Parliament, Brussels. This event was funded, in part, by a New Ideas Scheme Award from the Irish Research Council (awarded to Aisling de Paor, co-editor). The objective was to highlight this issue and spark the debate at EU level, as well as to explore the case for an EU-level response with the relevant stakeholders in the area. This conference brought together multidisciplinary experts in areas including disability law and policy, bioethics, medicine and insurance, in Europe and the United States. This conference engaged actively with politicians, the media and other interested parties and stakeholders. The editors collated the conference papers from these two events to form this volume.

## 4. Structure of book

This book includes five sections.

### *4.1 Section 1*

Section 1 is entitled 'Advances in genetic science and technology'. It comprises one chapter, written by Aisling de Paor and Noel Lowndes, which is entitled 'Tracing the history, evolution and future orientation of genetic science and technology'. In providing a scientific and technological context to this discussion, this chapter details the history of genetic science and the future of advancing genetic technology, such as whole genome sequencing and direct-to-consumer genetic testing. The objective is to illustrate the reality and speed at which genetic science and technological innovation is advancing, resulting in benefits for health care and facilitating personalised medicine. It also examines the limitations of genetic science and technology, with reference to the predictive value of genetic technologies. This chapter provides a background for examining the myriad of ethical and legal issues arising as a result of the deluge of genetic information that is increasingly becoming available to individuals and third parties.

### *4.2 Section 2*

Section 2 is entitled 'Ethical and legal dilemmas arising from emerging technologies' and comprises three chapters. This section focuses on emerging and challenging bioethical and legal issues presented as genomic science proliferates and as these cutting-edge technologies are used frequently in health care and other settings. It explores the use of genetic information and genetic testing in the clinical setting, as well as in other third-party contexts. It highlights societal implications of increased use of such technologies. The first chapter is written by Javier Romañach Cabrero and is entitled 'Diversity ethics and the impact of genetic technologies'. It explores the theoretical framework of 'diversity ethics' and how this concept translates with the advent of developing genetic technologies. This chapter examines the rationale and merits of a genetically diverse society and anticipates the potential for a form of 'new eugenics' developing in Europe.

The next chapter is entitled 'Genes, identity and clinical ethics under conditions of uncertainty' by Rebecca Wolf, Michael Joseph Young, Michael Ashley Stein and Harold J. Bursztajn. This chapter examines the application of genetic science in a clinical setting. It provokes consideration of the bioethical issues arising from the use, misuse and misinterpretation of genomic medicine and technology. This chapter looks at complex issues in this area such as informed consent and the challenges presented by use of genetic technologies in this regard. It examines issues arising in the reproductive context. This chapter identifies the future landscape in health care and medicine in this new genomic era.

The final chapter in Section 2 is entitled 'The use of genetic information outside of the therapeutic health relationship: An international perspective' and is written by Yann Joly, J. Rosel Kim and Shahad Salman. This chapter explores the use and misuse of genetic information by third parties, from an ethical, social and legal perspective. It takes a comparative approach to present an international legal and ethical overview of the scenarios involving the use and misuse of genetic information outside of the therapeutic relationship, such as in employment and insurance. It also examines the use of genetic information in challenging scenarios such as the criminal justice context as well as its use in the immigration setting. This chapter provides an overview of some of the regulatory responses in this area at a national and an international level. It highlights evidence of genetic discrimination and other misuse of genetic information, as well as emerging case law in this field. This chapter provides practical insight into the regulatory concerns, which are further developed in Sections 3, 4 and 5.

### *4.3 Section 3*

One objective of this publication is to examine transatlantic perspectives in this area and to highlight the merits of engaging in a transatlantic dialogue and learning from the approaches taken in comparative jurisdictions, such as the US. The US is an early entry into this field, enacting genetic-specific, federal-level legislation in the Genetic Information Nondiscrimination Act (GINA) in 2008. Section 3 focuses on the US position and the legislative response and experience. It highlights how the protection of genetic information fits within the civil rights framework of the United States and how the issue gathered momentum over the past twenty years. In examining the US legal and policy response, this section details past and current legal frameworks and offers insight into the effectiveness of the existing legal protections in practice. It examines how the US has tackled challenging ethical and legal contours of this debate. It provides historical and social context and documents the US experience of the eugenics movement, which is a key consideration in examining the current regulatory framework of GINA.

This section contains three chapters from leading experts in this area. The first chapter, by Peter Blanck and Aisling de Paor is entitled 'US legislative and policy response: Some historical context to GINA'. With a focus on the historical and cultural background preceding the US legislative framework, this chapter explores the stark history of eugenics in the US and how it has shaped current perspectives on advancing genetic science in today's society. This chapter introduces the Genetic Information Nondiscrimination Act 2008 (GINA).

The second chapter in this section is entitled 'The Genetic Information Nondiscrimination Act (GINA) 2008' by Michael Waterstone and Anya Prince. This chapter discusses the nature of GINA as a preemptive law, as well as its objective in the fields of employment and health insurance. It overviews the main provisions of the legislation, exceptions and enforcement mechanisms contained therein. In line with recent developments in the field of health care, this chapter also highlights the introduction of the Patient Protection and Affordable Care Act and its impact in this area and in health care generally.

The final chapter in this section is entitled 'Genetic discrimination in the workplace after GINA' and is written by Robert Olick. This chapter examines the issue of genetic discrimination in the aftermath of GINA. It looks at the effect of GINA in practice and highlights claims of genetic discrimination and the cases taken under the legislation. With a particular focus on the employment context, it explores the effectiveness of the legislation and identifies some of the challenges and evident gaps in the legislative protection offered in the US.

### *4.4 Section 4*

Upon exploring the scientific context, background issues and in consideration of transatlantic perspectives, Section 4 focuses on the European context and details the current regulatory framework. Unlike in the US, there is no concrete EU-level regulation to protect the privacy of genetic information or to prevent the discriminatory use of such information. Section 4 is entitled 'Building the case for a European Union regulatory response' and contains six chapters, the objective of which is to highlight the current position in Europe and build the background to examining the potential need for an EU-level regulatory response.

This section provides a comprehensive overview of the perspectives and stakeholders in this area, including employers and insurance companies. It focuses on existing regulatory frameworks and benchmarks at international level, Council of Europe level and European Union level. It highlights the patchwork of national-level protections. In highlighting relevant stakeholders and perspectives, this section details the more nuanced issues that arise in the employment and insurance contexts. It draws attention to the tension arising between the competing rights, particularly highlighting the conflict between commercial interests and fundamental human rights.

In highlighting the position of interested stakeholders in this area, James Davey's chapter is entitled 'Genetic discrimination in insurance: Lessons from *Test Achats*' and focuses on the field of insurance. The focus of this chapter is on the landmark *Test Achats* case, a seminal case in insurance law which tested the boundaries of equality in the EU and highlighted the conflict arising between the foundational principles of insurance and fundamental human rights such as equality. This chapter examines the impact of this decision on use of genetic information as a risk factor in insurance.

In further highlighting the position of interested stakeholders in this area, Aisling de Paor's chapter focuses on the employment context and is entitled 'Employment practices in a new genomic era: Acknowledging competing rights and striking a balance'. This chapter elaborates upon the use of genetic information in employment and concerns arising, as highlighted in earlier chapters. It examines the use and misuse of genetic information from the perspective of employers and employees, highlighting the inevitable conflict between commercial interests and fundamental human rights. With a focus on the current EU position, it also provides a brief overview of the legislative framework in the EU and considers whether it approaches balance.

Henriette Roscam Abbing's chapter focuses on the Council of Europe norms in this area. This chapter is entitled 'Medical (genetic) examinations for non-health purposes: The relevance of European legal standard setting'. In particular, it examines the Council of Europe legal framework in this area, with a focus on the European Convention on Human Rights, the Convention on Human Rights and Biomedicine and the Additional Protocol to this Convention, and explores the extent to which these frameworks protect genetic information. In highlighting a fundamental human rights framework, this chapter overviews core rights provided for, such as privacy and the right to equality.

Section 4 draws attention to the existing patchwork of protection amongst the EU Member States and the variety of legislative approaches evident, as is reflected in the chapter entitled 'National legal and policy responses to genetic discrimination in Europe: The difficulties of regulation' by Ine Van Hoyweghen. The objective of this chapter is to document regulatory approaches and diverging levels of protection offered in different jurisdictions. It highlights the difficulties with regulating this complex area and the practical challenges presented.

With a focus on the EU data protection framework and its application in this area, Mark Taylor's chapter is entitled 'Genetic discrimination and the draft European Union General Data Protection Regulation'. This chapter addresses genetic discrimination and genetic privacy from the perspective of data protection law. It examines the data protection legal framework in the EU and focuses on the proposed data protection reform process taking place in the EU. This examination includes an overview of the draft European Union General Data Protection Regulation and the scope of the protections proposed. In this regard, it assesses the proposed legislative changes and the extent to which this new framework will protect genetic information in third-party contexts.

This book acknowledges the connection between genetics and disability, and highlights potential for emerging genetic technologies to challenge traditional concepts of disability and personhood. This book also draws on the United Nations Convention on the Rights of Persons with Disabilities (CRPD), as an anchoring international instrument and as an important forum for discussion. Janet Lord's chapter in Section 4 is entitled 'Accommodating genes: Disability, discrimination and international human rights law'. This chapter analyses the concept of genetic discrimination from a disability perspective. It examines the challenges presented in the reproductive context with emerging genetic technologies. It examines the impact of such genetic screening technologies on the concept of disability.

### *4.5 Section 5*

On consideration of the current regulatory framework in the EU, the evident gaps in protection and the insights offered into the US experience, Section 5, 'Considering the way forward for the EU', provides further evaluation of the scope of EU legislation and presents proposals for reform. This section addresses the hypothesis that, in light of the unprecedented advances in genetic technology and the corresponding potential for misuse of genetic information, comprehensive and uniform legislation is preferable at EU level, perhaps in the form of a new genetic information non-discrimination directive.

This section contains one chapter entitled 'Genetic discrimination: Is it time for the EU to take on a new challenge?' by Delia Ferri. It focuses on the EU regulatory framework from the perspective of privacy and non-discrimination. It examines the legal basis for action by the EU and the scope for EU intervention, as well as presenting the challenges in this regard. By highlighting factors compelling action, this chapter offers a way forward for the EU in the form of a proposed new genetic information non-discrimination directive.

The final chapter of this book draws together findings from each contribution and presents overarching conclusions. It offers insights as to the broader context. It also highlights and anticipates the future orientation of genetic science and technology and associated ethical and legal issues.

# Section 1

# Advances in genetic science and technology

Section 1 of this book provides a scientific and technological framework from which to view and contextualize the issues arising in this area. It chronicles the history of genetic science and highlights the potential for advancing genetic technologies to enhance health care and medicine, by offering insights into genetic profiles. It also offers the potential of detecting potential future disabilities and disease, which is key to this discussion. This section highlights the increasing accessibility to and availability of genetic information, for medical and non-medical purposes.

This section comprises one chapter, 'Tracing the history, evolution and future orientation of genetic science and technology', by Aisling de Paor and Noel Lowndes.

# 2 Tracing the history, evolution and future orientation of genetic science and technology

*Aisling de Paor and Noel Lowndes*

## 1. Introduction

Genetics is the science of inheritance, and the study of how particular traits and characteristics are passed on from parents to offspring, from physical traits such as height or eye colour to complex disease susceptibilities such as heart disease and certain types of cancer (Guttman *et al.*, 2011; Gelehrter *et al.*, 1998). It focuses on genes and their effects on disease and heredity (Guttman *et al.*, 2011; Gelehrter *et al.*, 1998). Medical genetics is therefore concerned with gaining a greater understanding of disease and the interaction between disease and genes in the human body. In the context of this discussion, it is necessary to provide a conceptual framework of the science of genetics and formulate a debate that is fully informed of advancing genetic technologies.

The aim of this paper is to explore the reality (as well as limitations) of advancing genetic science and the rapid pace of technological innovation. This raises questions as to the implications of the resulting deluge of genetic information becoming widely available and accessible. We will chronicle the evolution of genetic science and technology, including the history of genetics, with a view to providing a basic insight into the various elements of genetic science. The paper will outline the endeavours of the Human Genome Project (HGP) as a major international scientific project in this area, and its success in accelerating the pace of genetic science. The HGP was instrumental in the rapid pace of genetic discovery and the development of genetic technologies.

This paper will also explain the potential of genetic testing to detect the onset of future disabilities and to offer the possibility of personalised medicine, and the possible treatment and even cures for diseases at an early stage. Genetic testing and other genetic technologies are becoming more accessible and sophisticated, and such technologies are being increasingly used for both medical and non-medical purposes. The increasing availability of genetic information produces a myriad of emerging ethical and legal dilemmas, creating a minefield of problems if not appropriately addressed.

## 2. The history of genetic science

Since ancient times humanity has been exploiting genetics for the breeding of both plants and animals. However, in tracing the history of genetic science it is normally considered that the proper study of heredity began in the mid-nineteenth century with the work of the Austrian monk, Gregor Mendel (Hartl and Orel, 1992; Marantz Henig, 2001). Mendel (Sorsby, 1965) endeavoured to uncover the process of inheritance and observed that organisms inherit characteristics through units of inheritance, now referred to as genes (Charlesworth and Charlesworth, 2009). Mendel engaged in the practice of pea breeding, with a view to learning more about the inheritance patterns in peas (Morgan *et al.*, 1915). He observed that different factors indicated the different elements of the pea's appearance, for example, the colour and shape of the pea (Morgan *et al.*, 1915).

Around the same time Charles Darwin pioneered the concept of natural selection, based on his theory of evolution (Darwin, 1859; Darwin, 1871). His theory postulated that all plants and animals had evolved from a few common ancestors by means of natural selection (Charlesworth and Charlesworth, 2009: 758–762). Natural selection works at the level of the naturally occurring variations that occur within whole populations of a species: some variants within a population are better adapted to their environment and therefore most likely to proliferate successfully. On the other hand, those members of the population least well adapted to their environment are less likely to contribute their genes to the subsequent generations. This is often termed 'survival of the fittest' (Charlesworth and Charlesworth, 2009: 758) While Darwin's theory of natural selection is an important concept in genetics, the discovery of the individual units of inheritance was the work of Gregor Mendel. Subsequently, a Danish botanist, Wilhelm Johannsen, termed these individual units of heredity genes (Johannsen, 1909).

Importantly, Mendel discovered that the individual units of inheritance, the genes, occurred in pairs, with one member of the pair being passed on from each parent. This provides the theoretical basis for dominant and recessive conditions (Allen, 2003: 65–66). He discovered that the two factors which determine a trait may have contradicting instructions and in these circumstances it is the dominant form which determines the appearance or phenotype observed in the individual (Allen, 2003: 65–66). However, Mendel's key observation was that 'the other factor would persist in latent form, and its effects could reappear in later generations in predictable ratios' (Lander and Weinberg, 2000: 1778). The principles of inheritance were put forward for the first time in Mendel's 1865 paper 'Experiments in Plant Hybridization' (Mendel, 2008 [1865]). Although Mendel's theories were largely ignored during his lifetime, after his death the concept of Mendelian genetics was rediscovered and is now the central concept in genetic science (Koonin, 2012). It is a concept with many applications in all organisms, not just human beings.

Subsequent important genetic discoveries were made throughout the twentieth century. In 1910, Thomas Morgan's research on fruit flies indicated that genes sit on chromosomes, resulting in the theory of the linear arrangement of genes on chromosomes (Morgan *et al.*, 1915). His work also demonstrated the important insight that random mutations appeared in flies, indicating that random mutations should also occur in human genes (Haldane, 1931; Drake, 1998). Alfred Sturtevant, who worked with Morgan, was also instrumental in the understanding of chromosomes and used the concept of genetic linkage to illustrate how genes are situated in a linear manner on the chromosome (Sturtevant, 2001). He proposed that genes were linked because they were arranged in sequence along the same chromosome and in 1913 he presented the first map of a chromosome (Sturtevant, 2001).

Following initial genetic discoveries in the late nineteenth century and early twentieth century, the modern study of genetics began in 1953 when Crick and Watson discovered the double helix structure of deoxyribonucleic acid (DNA) and published an explanation of the structure of DNA also which suggested how genes could be replicated (Watson and Crick, 1953). This discovery accelerated interest in the science of genetics and, as it promised a greater understanding of the basis of many diseases, resulted in the awarding of the Nobel Prize in Medicine or Physiology in 1962 to both Watson and Crick (Watson and Crick, 1953; Watson, 1998). The discovery of the double helix structure of DNA laid the foundation for the subsequent genetic revolution in our understanding of the human genome (Crick, 1974). Further scientific discoveries and technological innovations in the 1970s, in particular the ability to join different DNA molecules together and propagate them at will, the so-called recombinant DNA technologies (Maxim and Gilbert, 1977; Sanger and Coulson, 1975), added greatly to our ability to identify and characterise new genes. Importantly, these developments also provided the basis and the foundations for the HGP and subsequent genetic testing. Before highlighting the potential of genetic technology, the next section will briefly explore the biology underlying genetic science.

## 2.1 The biology behind genetic science

In order to provide a more detailed description of the science of genetics, this section will illustrate the mechanisms that contribute towards our understanding of the human genome and the framework within which current and future genetic advances are based. A starting point for exploring genetic science is by explaining the concepts of DNA and genes. Each gene is part of a large molecule of DNA, the structure of which was discovered in 1953 (Watson and Crick, 1953). The usual model of DNA is in the form of a double helix and resembles a twisted ladder, termed a helix (Dervan, 1986: 464). The rungs of the ladder suggest the base pairs: the binding of two of the four molecules, known as nucleotides, each one from an opposing strand of DNA (Gelehrter *et al.*, 1998: 10–11). Specifically, this double helix structure is partially composed of four related nucleotides that differ only in the bases, guanine (G), cytosine (C), adenine (A) and thymine (T), that define each one (Gelehrter *et al.*, 1998: 10–11). The bases occur in pairs, A always binds to T and C always to G, and the arrangement of these pairs along one strand is called the DNA sequence. The sequential arrangement of nucleotides along one strand of DNA encodes the genetic information that in total defines the individual (Weinberg, 1991: 44). In the human genome there are forty-six thread-like DNA molecules, each one packaged in chromosomes that are numbered according to size and are found in every cell in the human body (Weinberg, 1991: 44).

A gene can be described as 'a piece of DNA, the chemical responsible for storing and transferring all hereditary information in a cell' (Casey, 1997: 14). Genes achieve this 'by containing recipes for making proteins, described as the true workhorses of all our trillions of cells' (Casey, 1997: 14). Therefore, all living organisms consist of proteins, which supply the internal workings of all cells 'as well as specialized enzymes for all essential chemical reactions' (Casey, 1997: 14). Through these proteins, genes establish bodily structures and functions, as well as how the body operates, for example, the metabolism of food. Genes dictate the production of proteins which, in turn, determine the function of each cell, as well as physical traits, characteristics, predisposition to disease and disability, which are all passed on through the generations (Holmes 1996–1997: 520). Disease generally occurs when mutations, or genetic flaws arise (in conjunction with external influences) (Smith and Burns, 1994–1995; Singer and Berg, 1991). Genes vary slightly from individual to individual, which, together with external factors such as environmental influences, lifestyle choices and diet, influence the expression of an individual's traits (Lewis, 2011).

Chromosomes are also a crucial element to understanding the science of inheritance. Genes are grouped together sequentially along the DNA molecule and packaged with specialist proteins to form the chromosomes (Gelehrter *et al.*, 1998: 9). An individual has two copies of each chromosome, one inherited from their mother and the other from their father (Holmes, 1996–1997: 521–522). Together the complete set of genes for a human being is collectively called the human genome, being effectively the sum of the genetic information that is stored in each cell and passed from one generation to the next via egg and sperm, the specialist sex cells (Holmes, 1996–1997: 520).

Highlighting the various biological elements which constitute the human genome provides a scientific framework within which to further explore the intricacies of genetic science and to illustrate the reality and the potential of advancing technology.

### *2.2 Genetic conditions and disorders*

The discoveries in genetic science made throughout the twentieth century contributed towards a greater understanding of the genetic make-up of human beings, as well as our understanding of the connection between disease and genes and the influence of external factors. In order to fully understand the science of genetics and its potential to improve our knowledge of genes and disease, it is necessary to review the different types of genetic conditions. Together with general characteristics that determine an individual's physical appearance, such as height, eye colour and hair colour, one may also inherit diseases and disorders, such as predispositions to heart disease, diabetes and different types of cancer. Certain hereditary diseases can be explained by a single gene, or monogenic defect. However, the majority of hereditary diseases are multifactorial and are caused by the interaction of environmental factors and numerous variant forms of each gene that exist within the population of individuals. The following section will give an overview of the different types of genetic disorders. It is generally acknowledged that there are four classes of genetic disorders: chromosomal disorders, single-gene disorders, multifactorial disorders and mitochondrial disorders (Riba, 2007: 473).

Chromosomal genetic disorders can occur when an individual possesses the incorrect number of chromosomes (Gelehrter *et al.*, 1998: 3). Chromosomal disorders therefore arise if the number or structure of any of an individual's forty-six chromosomes is abnormal, which leads to physical or mental disorders. The prototypical example of a chromosomal genetic disorder is Down's Syndrome in which affected individuals are born with three, as opposed to two, copies of chromosome 'twenty-one' (Antonarakis, 2004). Chromosomal abnormalities arise from mistakes during the division of cells, resulting in additional or reduced numbers of chromosomes. In addition, sometimes the chromosomal material might be reorganised, resulting in parts of one chromosome being fused to another to form hybrid chromosomes, which again can result in perturbed cellular function and disease (Holmes 1996–1997: 528).

Mitochondrial genetic disorders are genetic disorders caused by mutations in DNA molecules that exist outside of the chromosomes in cellular structures termed mitochrondria (Falk and Sondheimer, 2010). Mitochondria 'are a subcompartment of the cell bound by a double membrane' (Chinnery and Schon, 2003: 1189), are found specifically in each cell's cytoplasm and are required to convert energy obtained from food into a chemical form that cells can use. Mitochondria have a small amount of their own DNA, termed mitochondrial DNA or mtDNA (Taylor and Turnbull, 2005). Being outside the nucleus where the chromosomes reside, mitochondria are inherited only from the mother as sperm delivers only chromosomes to the fertilised ovum which contains mitochrondria inherited down the maternal lineage. Thus, disorders of mitochrondrial function are inherited through the mother to all offspring, male or female (Chial and Craig, 2008). Mitochondrial disorders vary in terms of nature and severity, and some may express at any age. Some mitochondrial disorders even affect just a single organ, for example, the eye in Leber hereditary optic neuropathy (Man *et al.*, 2002; Wallace, 1988: 1427), but most affect several organs (Nissenkorn *et al.*, 1999).

Single gene disorders result from a single gene mutation, which causes the gene to be damaged, missing or incorrectly expressed. This type of genetic disorder is characterised by a pattern of inheritance termed Mendelian after Gregor Mendel's pioneering work with peas (Gelehrter *et al.*, 1998: 4). A dominant single gene disorder arises if an abnormality is evident when only one of the chromosomal pair contains the variant gene (Chial, 2008). Any individual affected by a dominant single gene disorder had one parent who carried the mutant gene inherited from one of their own parents (Holmes, 1996–1997: 528). While dominantly inherited single gene disorders only require one mutant copy of the gene to result in disease, recessive gene disorders occur when an affected individual inherits an abnormal gene from each parent. Typically each parent does not have the disease as they have one good copy of the gene, but one in four of their offspring will inherit the bad copy from each parent resulting in disease (Holmes, 1996–1997: 528). Single gene disorders include muscular dystrophy, cystic fibrosis, sickle-cell anaemia and Huntington's disease.

Multifactorial (or polygenic) genetic disorders are the largest group of genetic disorders. They are caused by complex genetic interactions involving variations in very many genes and tend to have equally complex interactions with environmental factors, such as diet and lifestyle (Gelehrter *et al.*, 1998: 4-5). Common multifactorial genetic disorders include heart disease, diabetes and different types of cancer. Testing for multifactorial genetic disorders will indicate only that a person has a higher than average probability of developing a disease, but it is not certain if and when the condition will manifest. Discussion of multifactorial genetic conditions therefore provokes consideration of the interaction between genes and the environment with respect to disease expression (Deodutta and Teyfile, 2010).

### *2.2.1 Interaction between genes and environment*

Research has shown that an individual's identity and indeed an individual's predisposition to disease is a complex interaction between both genes and external environmental factors. Although genes can dictate disease and disability, they also arise as a result of external factors and lifestyle choices, and the interaction of these factors (Diver and Maslow Cohen, 2000–2001: 1451). Therefore, it is necessary to highlight the impact of environmental factors upon disease expression.

While human diseases that are caused by mutations in single genes operating in isolation are numerous, they tend not to correspond to the major disease burden within the human populations. Disorders involving multiple genes are more common, although the genetic basis is often much less well understood. Examples of multiple gene disorders include asthma, diabetes and heart disease, which cause much morbidity. These common disorders arise from an intricate interaction among multiple genes and between genes and factors in the environment. An individual's lifestyle choices and access to health care are some of the environmental factors that can impact upon the expression of a genetic-based disorder. It is important to be aware of the interaction between genes and environment, particularly in considering the predictive value of genetic tests in certain circumstances (Roy and Tevfik Dorak, 2010).

### 2.2.2 *Behavioural traits*

Advances in genetic science are also revealing the potential to detect certain behavioural traits and predispositions to certain lifestyle activities. Behaviour manifests as a result of complex traits involving multiple genes that are influenced by a number of other factors, including environment (Garcia Coll *et al.*, 2004). Researchers have discovered a genetic basis for various types of behaviour. Recent research indicates the existence of the risk-taking gene (Alleyne, 2009; Shane, 2010; Kreek *et al.*, 2005) and predisposition towards determination and success (Hsu, 2012). Similarly, in recent times, scientists have detected at least one genetic contribution towards leadership. The so-called 'leadership genotype', known as rs4950, results from a single nucleotide polymorphism (SNP) that is associated with individuals taking charge (De Neve *et al.*, 2013). As leadership qualities are also learned, the genetic contribution to leadership from this SNP is estimated at only 25 per cent indicating that, even for the re4950 genotype, the individual's environment has very significant impact upon the expression of leadership skills. Researchers discovered the leadership SNP gene following analysis of DNA samples from around 4,000 individuals and linking them with details of employment and relationships (De Neve *et al.*, 2013). The discovery of this SNP and potentially many others may one day reveal interesting insights into those most likely to become successful managers and those most likely to remain in a more subordinate role. While such information may ultimately provide potentially valuable information for employment purposes, it comes with some ethical considerations.

The field of behavioural genetics has the potential to reveal both genetic and environmental influences on normal and abnormal behaviour. In addition, this research can yield benefits in various fields of medicine, in finding the most effective treatment options available, based on an individual's unique genetic make-up.

### 2.3 Genetic testing

The above analysis provided a basis to discuss genetic testing and what such tests can reveal. The success of the HGP (discussed below) has accelerated the pace of genetic discoveries and resulted in an increase in the practice of genetic testing (for medical and non-medical purposes). Genetic tests can be broadly categorised into predictive and diagnostic tests. For the purposes of this publication, the majority of the ethical and legal issues arise out of predictive genetic tests and what they can reveal about an individual's predisposition to disease, disability and behavioural tendencies.

Technologies that 'identify genetic variations' are known as genetic tests (Holmes, 1996–1997: 523–524). Genetic testing has been defined as 'the analysis of a specific gene, its product or function, or other DNA and chromosome analysis, to detect or exclude an alteration likely to be associated with a genetic disorder' (Harper, 1997: 749). In other words, genetic testing (or screening) is the process of scanning an individual's genetic make-up to ascertain if the individual has a genetic predisposition to developing or passing on a genetic defect or disease (Kaufman, 1999: 397–398). Genetic monitoring focuses on the workplace itself or other environments as potentially provoking the expression of certain genetic conditions. It follows that certain genetic conditions are exacerbated by exposure to carcinogens or other toxic chemicals. Genetic monitoring is utilised to improve the working environment and therefore protect employees (Weaver, 1997: 246). Such testing can be carried out to monitor workplace exposure to hazardous substances, which could predict increased predisposition to future illness or disability (Kaufman, 1999: 398–399).

The technique of genetic testing 'involves examining a person's DNA for some anomaly that flags a disease or disorder' (Miller, 2000: 229; Casey, 1997: 16). Genetic testing involves cells from the individual being tested and, generally, the cells used come from blood, saliva, the inside of the cheek or any other human tissue. Suspected mutations and predisposition to disease can be confirmed by genetic testing before symptoms appear (Harper, 1997: 749). The objective is that suspected genetic abnormalities and predisposition to disease can be confirmed or denied by genetic testing, before the expression of symptoms. There are a number of different types of genetic tests, used in a variety of scenarios.

First, there are genetic tests that can be used to identify carriers of certain diseases or disorders. Carrier screening, to detect Mendelian diseases, involves identifying asymptomatic individuals who carry just one copy of a disease associate variant form of a gene for a disease that requires two copies for the disease to be expressed (Holtzman *et al.*, 1997: 603). Individuals who carry one copy of the disease-associated gene do not themselves have a particular disease or disorder and usually never develop the disease or disorder, but they nevertheless possess these recessive genes and pass them along to future generations. Individuals may therefore decide to undergo such genetic testing where there is a family history of a particular disease, if they have symptoms of a genetic disorder or if they are concerned about passing on genetic disorders to their children. These genetic tests are therefore particularly relevant in the area of reproduction (Bell *et al.*, 2011).

Preimplantation genetic diagnosis is another type of genetic technology which is particularly relevant in reproduction and which involves screening embryos. It is a technique used to identify genetic abnormalities in embryos created through in vitro fertilisation (Sermon *et al.*, 2004; Braude *et al.*, 2002). It is noted that this practice potentially produces many ethical concerns in deciding in what circumstances to continue with pregnancy and arguably provokes ethical issues such as the value and dignity of all individuals.

Additional genetic tests are used in the context of reproduction. Prenatal diagnostic testing involves testing the foetus before birth to determine whether the foetus has certain abnormalities, including inherited or random genetic mutations. Genetic disorders such as cystic fibrosis can be tested at this stage. Newborn screening is a technique used on newborn babies to test for a range of genetic disorders, such as the 'heel prick test' (Timmermans and Muchbinder, 2013: 7). These technologies generally identify treatable genetic disorders in babies, usually prior to the manifestation of conditions, many of which are metabolic disorders (Timmermans and Muchbinder, 2013: 7). These tests are advantageous from the perspective of earlier diagnosis, with the potential of earlier intervention and prevention.

There are also many predictive genetic tests available for adult-onset disorders. Presymptomatic testing is a type of test for predicting adult-onset disorders, such as Huntingtons's disease and other monogenic genetic conditions (Harper, 1997: 750). There is also presymptomatic testing for predicting the risk of developing adult-onset disorders such as Alzheimer's disease or different types of cancer. These are multifactorial genetic conditions and such genetic testing detects the presence of genes indicating a probability of an individual expressing the condition. As well as predictive genetic-testing technologies, genetic testing can also be used as an effective diagnostic mechanism. Confirmational diagnosis of a symptomatic individual may be carried out following the suspected presence of a genetic condition or disease (Harper, 1997: 750). In these circumstances, a family history of a genetic condition may be confirmed by undergoing a genetic test.

Forensic or identity testing is another type of genetic test that is generally utilised as an investigative tool from a legal and criminal justice perspective. Such testing is also used in the context of paternity and maternity suits, as confirmation of genetic lineage (Harper, 1997: 750).

In terms of accessibility, the cost of genetic testing can range from hundreds to thousands of dollars or euros, depending on the nature of the genes and the numbers of mutations tested. Currently, more than 1,000 genetic tests are available, which can test for a range of genetic-based illnesses and predisposition to potential illnesses. In the clinical context, it is generally advisable that an individual undergo genetic counselling, which will assist the individual, (and the family) understand genetic disorders, the implications of genetic testing and the various options available (Harper, 1997: 751). Most genetic tests provide only an estimated risk for developing the disorder and therefore it is acknowledged that the accuracy of genetic testing is limited.

### *2.3.1 Accuracy of genetic testing*

It is important to refer to the accuracy of genetic testing and the general perception of such testing. There is a common belief that genetic technologies 'are always accurate, highly predictive and capable of identifying an individual's or offspring's inevitable pre-destination of future disability. The facts are diametrically opposed to this common belief' (Gostin, 1991: 113). Although science is advancing rapidly, the majority of genetic tests are still uncertain and lack accuracy. Predicting the nature and severity of disease based upon an identified gene is challenging (Holtzman *et al.*, 1997: 604). The probability that a genetic flaw will manifest in a particular disease or disorder in the future is dependent on a variety of complex factors. Therefore the scientific accuracy and validity of genetic tests is limited.

On considering the accuracy of genetic testing it is important to refer to the distinction between multifactorial genetic conditions and monogenic conditions. In the case of the majority of genetic conditions (for example, multifactorial genetic conditions), the time of onset, severity of the condition and impact of treatment varies greatly (Gostin, 1991: 114). For example, individuals who are diagnosed with the gene for Huntington's disease will develop, with a 'chilling certainty', the fatal disorder generally around middle age (Miller, 2000: 231). On the other hand, the detection of the breast cancer gene (BRCA1 mutation) has a more uncertain predictive value. An individual who is diagnosed with the breast cancer gene has a reasonably high probability of developing breast cancer. This probability is also influenced by possible history of breast cancer in the family. Similarly, a genetic test result indicating a predisposition to heart disease is dependent upon a number of external factors such as lifestyle, diet and other potential genetic markers (Cambien and Tiret, 2007).

Therefore, the predictive value of genetic tests is somewhat limited because, generally, they reveal merely the possibility that the person may develop the trait, disease or disorder in the future and are not certain indicators that symptoms will develop. Therefore, possessing a genetic mutation does not necessarily lead to the expression of the disease or disorder (Miller, 2000: 229; National Cancer Institute United States Department of Health and Human Services, 1995). In the future, it is anticipated that genetic tests will become more sophisticated and will be able to predict the expression and onset of disease more accurately, as well as the degree to which environmental factors contribute towards disease. It is necessary to be aware of, not only the potential benefits of genetic technologies, but also the limitations of such technologies at this stage.

### *2.3.2 Genetic information*

In terms of clarifying the concept of genetic information, it is important to highlight that an individual's genetic information can also be revealed without the use of genetic tests. For example, one may discover such information through insights obtained from their medical history, as well as details of family medical history (Miller, 2000: 231). Family medical history has traditionally been a reliable source of genetic information, and individuals can obtain considerable knowledge from analysis of the medical history of their blood-relatives. Therefore, when discussing the concept of genetic information and use of such information, it is necessary to refer to both the results of genetic tests as well as information gained from family medical history. As will be highlighted throughout this publication, genetic information, gained from test results, as well as from family history, can potentially be misused.

### *2.3.3 Benefits of genetic testing*

These technologies may potentially enhance health care and medical treatment (Rajiv *et al.*, 2011; Lamberts and Uitterlinden, 2009: 431–442). By taking a genetic test, an individual can discover what genes he/she may have that may potentially indicate predisposition to a range of conditions and diseases. Genetic technology may offer the prospect of being able to detect the onset of future disabilities, thereby highlighting genetic predispositions to disability. In addition to identifying genetic markers for disease and disability, genetic testing can also identify potential behavioural and personality traits in individuals, with potentially vast benefits in the medical field.

Genetic testing offers opportunities for individuals to be fully informed as to their genetic status, so that they can effectively manage their health care and treatment plans. This facilitates the practice of personalised medicine, a concept which effectively tailors health care to an individual, based on his/her unique genetic make-up (Francis, 2010: 188; Hamburg and Collins, 2010). These technologies also improve the health care profession generally, by providing health care professionals with detailed information about a patient's genetic make-up, thereby enabling more effective diagnosis and treatment. Genetic technologies can offer the treatment and possible cures for diseases at an earlier stage (Batty, 2012). Genetic testing and its potential arguably enhances patient autonomy and self-determination, increasing self-awareness and ultimately enabling patients to make more informed decisions in relation to their health care and the health care of family members. From a societal perspective, genetic technologies offer significant public health benefits.

Genetic testing and other genetic technologies advanced throughout the twentieth century. The modern genetic revolution began in the twenty-first century and was accelerated significantly with the success of the HGP. The next section will examine the HGP in further detail.

## 3. The Human Genome Project

Although the twentieth century witnessed extraordinary discoveries in the field of genetics, there was still a great deal that was unknown. In exploring the history of genetic science, it is necessary to highlight the importance of the HGP as a key milestone in the genetic science revolution. This section will provide an overview of the HGP, highlighting its relevance in this area. The HGP was a 13-year quest to sequence the human genome, with a view to gaining a greater understanding of disease and genes. It has been the first significant endeavour of the biological and medical research communities into what has been described as 'big science' (Collins *et al.*, 2003: 286). The HGP was one of the largest and most significant scientific projects embarked upon in both the US and internationally. The following sections will look more closely at the reasons behind the HGP, its goals and its impact in the field of genetics.

### *3.1 Motivation behind the Human Genome Project*

In response to the need to develop genetic technologies and to help tackle genetic disease, there was a recognised need for a concerted international effort to unravel the human genome. In 1988 the US Congress funded the National Institutes of Health (NIH) and the Department of Energy (DOE) for a project to explore the human genome. In 1988 James Watson took the lead in a new NIH component of the effort, which became a joint NIH-DOE project (Collins *et al.*, 2003: 286). The HGP officially began in 1990.

Additionally, many other countries and the EU established human genome research programmes (Collins *et al.*, 2003: 286). The general objective of this multi-disciplinary global initiative was to discover fundamental information needed to further scientific understanding of human genetics and of the role of genes in health and disease (National Human Genome Research Institute, 1990). This $3 billion project was expected to take fifteen years to complete, but rapid technological advances, together with competition from private endeavours, accelerated the process, and the completion date was brought forward by two years (Chial, 2008: 1).

### *3.2 Goals of the Human Genome Project*

The HGP had a number of very specific goals (the majority of which were achieved ahead of schedule and under budget). In April 1990 the NIH and DOE published a five-year plan ('The United States Human Genome Project, The First Five Years: Fiscal Years 1991–1995', National Human Genome Research Institute, 1990). The principal goal was to map and sequence the twenty-four chromosomes that contain the complete genetic contents of a human cell – in other words, the aim was to sequence the entire human genome (National Human Genome Research Institute, 1990). The basic idea of the map is that it establishes specific markers throughout the genome that can be used as reference points to pinpoint specific genes on chromosomes. The project effectively creates a map of the entire genetic structure of the human species. The map is then used to develop new ways to treat, cure and prevent diseases and disorders. According to Collins and Monsura, the objective of the HGP was 'to unravel some of the mysteries of disease by unravelling the thread of DNA present in nearly every cell in our bodies' (Collins and Monsura, 2001: 222).

One of the most important goals was to identify and address the potential ethical, legal and social issues (Collins *et al.*, 2003: 289). The HGP therefore recognised its responsibility to consider how the data generated will impact society. The group that worked on these issues is referred to as the Ethical, Legal and Social Implications (ELSI) Program. Indeed, one of the HGP's main goals was to 'develop programs addressed at understanding the ethical, legal and social implications of the Human Genome Project, identify and define the major issues, and develop initial policy options to address them' (National Human Genome Research Institute, 1990). This segment of the HGP had a number of purposes, including, anticipating the consequences for individuals and society in general of undertaking this project, addressing the ethical and legal dilemmas of sequencing the human genome, engaging the public in this debate and formulating policy options to ensure the appropriate use of these new technologies (National Human Genome Research Institute, 1990). The inclusion of a budget to address these issues is recognition that, although scientific advances have enormous potential benefit, there is also a potential for misuse.

Collectively, these goals would act to contribute towards a greater understanding of the genetic basis of disease, for the medical and scientific community and for society as a whole, as well as recognising the need to acknowledge the corresponding ethical and legal dilemmas. In 1993, rapid advancements in the HGP led the NIH and the DOE to amend their initial goals (Collins and Gallas, 1993). Following unprecedented success at the end of the revised five-year plan, a new plan was introduced in 1998 that further refined the HGP's goals (Collins *et al.*, 1998).

### *3.2.1 Private versus public human genome sequencing*

As highlighted, the HGP was completed ahead of schedule and under budget. A major contributing factor behind this success was the private endeavour to sequence the human genome. The private effort was spearheaded by Celera Genomics (co-founded by Applera Corporation and Dr. J. Craig Venter), which began competing against the public HGP in 1998. Celera's mission was to generate and commercialise genomic information. (Shampo and Kyle, 2011: 26). Specifically, it aimed to sequence the human genome and provide its future clients with early access to the resulting data. The firm aimed to complete the sequencing of the human genome quicker and at a lower cost than the public project ($300 million versus $3 billion) (Huang and Murray, 2010: 567–582). The private versus public competition provoked the publicly funded project to alter its strategy in order to accelerate progress. Indeed, the private element to this competition was applauded by those in the public project, as enhancing the completion of the endeavours (Collins, 2000).

## *3.3 The completion of the Human Genome Project*

In June 2000, it was confirmed that a rough draft of the human genome was completed a year ahead of schedule, which was described as 'the most wondrous map ever produced by mankind' (Clinton *et al.*, 2000). In 2003 it was announced that they had successfully mapped the human genome. In April 2003 researchers publicly released the results of the HGP. GenBank holds all of the genetic information deposited by the international contributors to the HGP, in a publically available and accessible forum. As a publically available resource, the information provided by GenBank is a valuable tool in promoting genetic discoveries and facilitating knowledge sharing.

## *3.4 Consequences of the Human Genome Project*

The HGP culminated in the successful sequencing and publication of the draft sequence of the human genome in 2001 and the complete sequence in 2003. The HGP has generated great interest in the scientific and medical communities. This is due primarily to the promise of facilitating knowledge that could revolutionise the manner in which disease is diagnosed and treated. Following the sequencing of the human genome and the many genetic puzzles which the HGP solved, scientists have been provided with information that is proving vital to developing an enhanced understanding of genetics. The HGP was applauded as having 'three main advantages, namely improved diagnostics, new approaches to the prevention of disease, and gene enhancement therapy' (Madden, 2011: 292).

As a result of the success of the HGP and subsequent advancing technology, genetics is playing an increasingly important role in the diagnosis, prevention and treatment of diseases. Genetic advances will help facilitate the preferable approach to health care, from a preventative, diagnostic or therapeutic perspective. Genomics, the study of the genomes of organisms, including the application of genetic science, is emerging as a key area of science in clinical medicine and diagnosis, highlighting the practical application of this research (Lander, 1996: 536). It has also resulted in a greater understanding of human disease and disability, and the influence of genes, environment and other factors. The success of the HGP offers great opportunities to predict an individual's propensity to develop certain diseases and disabilities (Gostin, 1991: 113). This has led to more sophisticated genetic tests and an increase in the number of tests available.

In illustrating the success of the HGP, it is observed that genetic advances have revolutionised the diagnosis and treatment of different types of cancer, particularly breast cancer. The discovery of the BRCA1 and BRCA2 genes associated with breast cancer and ovarian cancer have led to earlier diagnosis and further treatment options (Narod and Foulkes, 2004: 665). An individual's risk of developing breast and/or ovarian cancer is greatly increased if they have the BRCA1 or BRCA2 mutation. In addition, individuals who carry these mutations may be at increased risk of developing other certain cancers (Narod and Foulkes, 2004: 665). Genetic tests have been designed to test for BRCA1 and BRCA2 mutations, and several options are therefore available for monitoring risk in individuals (and family members) who test positive for the BRCA1 or BRCA2 mutation (Narod and Foulkes, 2004: 665). One option is surveillance (including mammograms and breast exams), with a view to detecting cancer early, when it is most treatable. Another, more radical option available to those who test positive with these genes is prophylactic surgery, with a view to reducing the risk of developing cancer (Narod and Foulkes, 2004: 665).

In addition, there have been major advances in recent years enhancing the diagnosis of breast cancer and also the potential for reoccurrence of breast cancer. Based on recent research, it is thought that, in the future, a simple blood test could be a more effective way to test for the early signs of breast cancer than using mammograms. This research indicates that a blood test can detect the early signs of cancer, meaning that individuals could have a regular blood test rather than breast screening (Cancer Research UK Press Release, 2012).

Further, recent research is indicating that a simple blood test could predict if certain types of breast cancer are likely to reoccur following treatment (Sapkota *et al.*, 2013). By facilitating an advance warning this would avoid unnecessary treatment with anti-cancer drugs. Scientists claim they discovered a 'genetic marker' that could be the key to predicting which patients' cancer will reoccur at a later stage (Sapkota *et al.*, 2013). Reflecting the aim of personalised medicine, treatment strategies could be tailor-made for individuals based on their genetic make-up and their susceptibility to breast cancer recurrence ascertained.

The discovery of these genes, the genetic tests that have been developed and the treatment options available have contributed towards more effective diagnosis and treatment of breast and ovarian cancer. The result is a higher rate of survival and an overall improvement in public health. It is anticipated that, in the future, certain types of cancer will no longer be described as fatal, life-threatening diseases, but as chronic illnesses that are easily detected, treated or prevented. The success of the HGP has led to a significant increase in the practice of genetic testing, for medical and other reasons. The HGP laid the foundations for a twenty-first-century revolution in genetic research that offers longer, healthier futures for all individuals. The next section will explore these advances in greater detail and illustrate the potential for the future of genetics.

## 4. The future of genetic technology

The success of the HGP has led to unprecedented advances in the understanding of disease (Collins and McKusick, 2001: 540). Genetic discoveries and technological advances have introduced a new age in genetic exploration. These advances have resulted in an increase in the practice of genetic testing, for diagnostic, predictive and other purposes (Terhune, 2012). Such advances have facilitated the development of more sophisticated genetic tests, as well as drug treatments and diagnostic techniques. These technologies facilitate the practice of personalised medicine, which is likely to become a routine element of health care in the future. This section will explore recent advances in genetic technologies and illustrate the potential to improve health care.

### *4.1 Whole genome sequencing*

Whole genome sequencing is quickly developing as technology advances. Whole genome sequencing is a process that determines the complete DNA sequence of an organism's genome at a single time (Ng and Kirkness, 2010: 215). To recap, a genome can be described as the sum of the genetic information that is contained in cells and passed from one generation to the next. This process involves sequencing all of an organism's chromosomal DNA as well as the DNA contained in the mitochondria (Sapkota *et al.*, 2013). This practice provides a whole picture of an individual's genome, including susceptibility to disease and disability.

It is anticipated that this technology will offer great benefits that will be used in medicine, by facilitating more effective diagnostics for genetically based disease (Shendure *et al.*, 2004: 342). Using genetics as a diagnostic tool (for example, in children and infants) will provide for earlier diagnosis, earlier intervention and consequently better treatment and options for the individual, thereby enhancing quality of life and patient choice (Morrison, 2012). In addition, this technology can also be used in identifying individuals who might be sensitive to certain drugs (Morrison, 2012). This is effectively a form of pharmacogenetics, (discussed below). It is also anticipated that genomes will be sequenced to identify the best and most effective treatment regimes for different types of cancers (Kolata, 2012; Mardis and Wilson, 2009). Whole genome sequencing therefore facilitates personalised medicine. In addition, whole genome sequencing may be used for reproductive purposes. Couples may decide to sequence their genomes before having children, to gain insights into potential genetic abnormalities before making an informed reproductive decision.

With the decreasing cost of whole genome sequencing, it is likely that this technology will become more routine in health care in the future (Kolata, 2012). In January 2012, Life Technologies announced that it had developed technology that could sequence the whole genome for just over $1,000 (Herper, 2012). It was also reported recently that the human genome can now be sequenced for $1,000, and inevitably this will continue to decrease in price (Markoff, 2012; Rincon, 2014). It is anticipated that it will one day be a powerful diagnostic tool and a means for effective health care management.

The benefits of advancing technology are quickly being realised, not only for individuals, but also for the medical industry and companies specialised in genetic testing and human genome sequencing, for example Complete Genomics and Illumina. It is also important to point out the corresponding challenges that will inevitably arise in the application of whole genome sequencing. This technique results in a huge amount of information being created about an individual's genetic make-up. Accordingly, a great deal of expertise and knowledge is needed to read and interpret the results, as well as acknowledgement of the inevitable challenges of this practice (Ormond *et al.*, 2010). Whole genome sequencing may raise practical considerations, particularly where the technique reveals more information than an individual wishes to know, as will be explored in subsequent chapters.

### *4.2 Pharmacogenetics*

Scientific advances are also facilitating the development of pharmacogenetics (Lemmens, 2000: 351; Evans and Relling, 2004: 464). Pharmacogenetics is based on the premise that individuals respond differently to drugs and often vary in their response to the same drug (Roscam Abbing, 2006: 28). Variation in response to medicines can be based on genetic factors; for example, the genetic make-up of a person influences the process by which and rate at which medicines pass through an individual body (Roscam Abbing, 2006: 28). As another example of personalised medicine, pharmacogenetics involves tailoring drug treatments to an individual's genetic make-up.

Pharmacogenetics may facilitate greater efficiency as regards expenditure in health care (Lemmens, 2000: 351), as well as safer and more effective use of drugs (Buchanan *et al.*, 2002: 3). The technique can offer benefits, not only for an individual and for the medical fields, but also for the pharmaceutical industry, with the potential to develop more accurate drug treatments with more effective results, thereby promoting efficiency. Indeed, pharmacogenetics is already being used successfully in clinical practice, and this practice has been particularly effective in the treatment of certain cancers (Nagasubramanian *et al.*, 2003: 437; Ansari and Krajinovic, 2007: 15).

As with other types of genetic technology, it is noted that drug response depends not only on an individual's genetic structure, but upon a number of other factors as well, including environment and current health (Buchanan *et al.*, 2002: 4). Therefore, sophisticated clinical judgment is necessary to determine the practical implications of the test results (Buchanan *et al.*, 2002: 4). Education is also key to fully understanding the benefits and limitations of this technology. Advances in pharmacogenetic research and the resulting information it produces also raise a variety of ethical and legal dilemmas that need to be addressed in order to facilitate further developments in the technology. These issues will be discussed further in subsequent chapters.

### *4.3 Direct-to-consumer genetic testing*

In recent years, there has also been a surge in the availability of direct-to-consumer (DTC) genetic testing, illustrating the speed at which genetic science is advancing and the increasing accessibility of genetic testing. DTC genetic tests are genetic tests that are accessible directly to the consumer. Such genetic tests facilitate access to an individual's genetic information, for example, through mail, or over the Internet. Traditionally, genetic tests have been available only through medical professionals. These tests effectively bypass the requirement for a medical professional in the process of discovering one's genetic status.

Relying on the power of the Internet and recent genetic advances, 'an increasing number of companies are starting to offer health-related genetic testing services directly to the public' (Hogarth *et al.*, 2008: 162; Lynch *et al.*, 2011: 486). It is observed that the growing market for DTC genetic testing may promote awareness of genetic diseases, allowing consumers to take control of their genetic health and take a more proactive role in their health care. In this regard, it is observed that these tests 'enhance autonomy and free choice, in that any person who wishes to know about his or her health risks can learn about them, in an accessible manner' (Hoedemaekers, 2000: 284; Kishore, 2009–2010). This pattern in health care has 'shifted the central role physicians have traditionally played in making medical decisions towards a balance that favours the patient's particular risk and value preferences' (Kapp, 2006: 2; Modra, 2006: 263).

However, such genetic tests have significant risks and limitations. Indeed, DTC genetic tests are a prime example of advancing genetic technology giving rise to a range of ethical and legal issues. Consumers may make important health care decisions on the basis of inaccurate test results. In the absence of medical guidance and genetic counselling, this may result in psychological and emotional distress for the individual. Consumers may also experience an invasion of privacy and discrimination if DTC genetic testing companies use their genetic information in an unauthorised manner or if test results are available to third parties. Inadequate regulation in the DTC genetic testing industry may further exacerbate the possibility of risk of harm and abuse of genetic information. Indeed, these issues recently came to the fore in the United States, with the Food and Drug Administration ordering the company, 23andMe to cease advertising DTC genetic tests (Loftus, 2013). This development illustrates the challenges presented with DTC genetic testing and the need to regulate such services.

These technologies and new discoveries highlight the speed at which science is developing and the potential benefits for individuals and for society. The speed at which science is advancing also highlights how genetics is increasingly becoming a part of medical practice (Cohen, 2011). DTC genetic testing, and the emergence of other types of genetic technologies, increases the accessibility of genetic tests and contributes towards the avalanche of genetic information that is quickly becoming available to individuals, family members and interested third parties. Legal and ethical issues therefore arise when genetic information is used and misused by third parties, and these issues need to be addressed if science is to continue to flourish.

## 5. Conclusion

The past century has witnessed great progress in genetics, from the discovery of the DNA double helix to the successful completion of the HGP. These and subsequent scientific developments have provoked a worldwide interest in genetics and prompted increasing efforts to learn more about the genetic make-up of human beings, as well as the reasons behind disease and disability. Advancing genetic technology offers the possibility of personalised medicine, which, in the future, may potentially transform health care – through earlier diagnosis, more effective prevention and treatment of disease and avoidance of drug side effects. It also offers the potential of being able to detect the onset and possible severity of future disabilities. The technology is becoming more prevalent and is being used increasingly in mainstream health care practice, as highlighted by developments in the field of breast cancer diagnosis and treatment. The speed at which science is advancing becomes clear, as does the speed at which genetic technologies are becoming more sophisticated and cheaper. This results in greater availability of genetic testing and genetic information.

This chapter also highlights some of the limitations of genetic technologies, from the perspective of predicting future disease and disability. It found that the majority of conditions are caused by the complex interaction of genes and environmental factors. In addition, it therefore concludes that the majority of genetic tests available yield limited accuracy and statistical validity in terms of predictive value. This may lead to misinterpretation and misuse of such technologies.

As illustrated in this chapter, genetic science and technology is therefore advancing at a rapid pace. Although the HGP and subsequent advances in science have provided the impetus for a revolution in genetic science, it has also therefore generated concerns. Indeed, it is submitted that 'technology is advancing far more rapidly than our ability to legislate or otherwise deal with the moral ramifications of our newfound expertise' (McLochlin, 2001: 615).

These advances in genetic science require an innovative approach towards law and regulation, taking into consideration the reality and speed of technological advances and the subsequent ethical and legal issues that arise from potential misuse of genetic information. The following chapters will look at the various ethical and legal dilemmas arising from use of genetic science, by exploring the various competing and conflicting interests in genetic information and public policy issues arising, from the perspective of the individual and family members, third parties and society as a whole.

## References

Allen, G. E. (2003) 'Mendel and modern genetics: the legacy for today' *Review Endeavour* 27(2): 63.

Alleyne, R. (2009) 'Why risk taking runs in the family – scientists find gene that makes you gamble' *The Telegraph* 6 May. Available at www.telegraph.co.uk/news/newstopics/howaboutthat/5279222/Why-risk-taking-runs-in-the-family-scientists-find-gene-that-makes-you-gamble.html [accessed 15 April 2014].

Ansari, M. and Krajinovic, M. (2007) 'Pharmacogenomics in cancer treatment defining genetic bases for inter-individual differences in responses to chemotherapy' *Current Opinion in Pediatrics* 19(1): 15.

Antonarakis, S. E. (2004) 'Chromosome 21 and Down Syndrome: from genomics to pathophysiology' *Nature Reviews: Genetics* 5: 725.

Batty, D. (2012) 'Breast cancer treatment gets boost' *The Guardian* 19 April. Available at www.guardian.co.uk/science/2012/apr/19/breast-cancer-treatment-boost [accessed 15 April 2014].

Bell, C. J. *et al.* (2011) 'Carrier testing for severe childhood recessive diseases by next-generation sequencing' *Science Translational Medicine* 3(65): 1.

Braude, P. *et al.* (2002) 'Preimplantation genetic diagnosis' *Nature Reviews* 3: 941.

Buchanan, A. E. *et al.* (2002) 'Pharmacogenetics: ethical issues and policy options' *Kennedy Institute of Ethics Journal* 12(1): 3–4.

Cambien, F. and Tiret, L. (2007) 'Genetics of cardiovascular diseases – from single mutations to the whole genome' *Circulation* 116: 1717.

Cancer Research UK (2012) 'A simple blood test could be used to detect breast cancer' Press Release 2 October. Available at www.cancerresearchuk.org/cancer-info/news/archive/pressrelease/2012-10-02-breast-cancer-blood-test [accessed 15 April 2014].

Casey, D. K. (1997) 'What can the new gene tests tell us?' *The Judges Journal* 36(14): 14.

Charlesworth, B. and Charlesworth, D. (2009) 'Anecdotal, historical and critical commentaries on genetics: Darwin and genetics' *Genetics Society of America* 183: 757.

Chial, H. (2008a) 'Mendelian genetics: patterns of inheritance and single gene disorders' *Nature Education* 1(1).

Chial, H. (2008b) 'DNA sequencing technologies key to the human genome project' *Nature Education* 1.

Chial, H. and Craig, J. (2008) 'mtDNA and mitochondrial' *Nature Education* 1(2).

Chinnery, P. F. and Schon, E. A. (2003) 'Mitochondria: neuroscience for neurologists' *Journal of Neurology and Neurosurgery Psychiatry* 74: 1188, 1189.

Clinton, W., Blair, T., Collins, F. and Venter, C. (2000) Remarks by the Presidents on the completion of the first survey of the entire Human Genome Project, White House Press Release 26 June, White House website. Available at http://clinton3.nara.gov/WH/EOP/OSTP/html/00628_2.html [accessed 15 April 2014].

Cohen, J. (2011) 'The human genome, a decade later', *Technology Review* January/February. Available at www.technologyreview.com/featured-story/422140/the-human-genome-a-decade-later [accessed 15 April 2014].

Collins, F. (2000) Testimony before the Health, Education, Labor and Pensions Committee, United States Senate, Hearing on Genetic Information in the Workplace (20 July).

Collins, F. and Gallas, D. (1993) 'A new five year plan for the US human genome program' *Science* 262: 43.

Collins, F. *et al.* (1998) 'New goals for the U.S. Human Genome Project: 1998–2003' *Science* 282(5389): 682.

Collins, F. S. and McKusick, V. A. (2001) 'Implications of the Human Genome Project for medical science' *Journal of the American Medical Association* 285(5): 540.

Collins, F. S. and Monsura, M. K. (2001) 'The Human Genome Project: revealing the shared inheritance of all humankind', 7th Biennial Symposium on Minorities, The Medically Undeserved and Cancer, p. 222.

Collins, F. S., Morgan, M. and Patrinos A. (2003) 'The Human Genome Project: lessons from large scale biology' *Science* 300(5617): 286–289.

Crick, F. (1974) 'The double helix: a personal view' *Nature* 248: 766.

Darwin, C. (1859) *On the Origin of Species.* London: John Murray.

Darwin, C. (1871) *The Descent of Man.* London: D. Appleton & Co.

De Neve, J. E. *et al.* (2013) 'Born to lead? A twin design and genetic association study of leadership role occupancy' *Leadership Quarterly* 24(1): 45.

Dervan, P. B. (1986) 'Design of sequence specific DNA – binding molecules' *Science, New Series* 232(4749): 464.

Diver, C. S. and Maslow Cohen, J. (2000–2001) 'Genophobia: What is wrong with genetic discrimination?' *University of Pennsylvania Law Review* 149: 1440, 1451.

Drake, J. W. (1998) 'Rates of spontaneous mutation' *Genetics* 148(4): 1667.

Evans, W. E. and Relling, M. V. (2004) 'Moving towards individualized medicine with pharmacogenomics' *Nature* 429: 464.

Falk, M. J. and Sondheimer, N. (2010) 'Mitochondrial genetic disease' *Current Opinion in Pediatrics* 22(6): 711.

Francis, L. P. (2010) 'You are born with your genes: justice and protection against discrimination in the use of genetic information' *Mount Sinai Journal of Medicine* 77: 188.

Garcia Coll, C. T. *et al.* (2004) *Nature and Nurture: The Complex Interplay of Genetic and Environmental Influences on Human Behaviour and Development.* New York: Erlbaum.

Gelehrter, T. D., Collins, F. S. and Ginsburg D. (1998) *Principles of Medical Genetics.* 2nd edition. Baltimore, Maryland: Williams & Wilkins.

Gostin, L. O. (1991) 'Genetic discrimination: the use of genetically based diagnostic and prognostic tests by employers and insurers' *American Journal of Law and Medicine* 17(1 and 2): 109.

Guttman, B. *et al.* (2011) *Genetics: The Code of Life.* New York: The Rosen Publishing Group, Inc.

Haldane, J. B. S. (1931) 'The rate of mutation of genes' *Journal of Genetics* 31(3): 317.

Hamburg, M. A. and Collins, F. S. (2010) 'The path to personalized medicine' *New England Journal of Medicine* 363(4): 301.

Harper, P. S. (1997) 'What do we mean by genetic testing?' *Journal of Medical Genetics* 34: 749–751.

Hartl, D. L. and Orel, V. (1992) 'What did Gregor Mendel think he discovered?' *Genetics* 131: 245.

Herper, M. (2012) 'Not quite the $1000 genome, but maybe close enough' *Forbes* 10 January. Available at www.forbes.com/sites/matthewherper/2012/01/10/not-quite-the-1000-genome-but-maybe-close-enough [accessed 15 April 2014].

Hoedemaekers, R. (2000) 'Commercial predictive testing: the desirability of one overseeing body' *Journal of Medical Ethics* 26: 282, 284.

Hogarth, S. *et al.* (2008) 'The current landscape for direct-to-consumer genetic testing: legal, ethical and policy issues' *Annual Review of Human Genomics and Human Genetics* 9: 161.

Holmes, E. M. (1996–1997) 'Solving the insurance/genetic fair/unfair discrimination dilemma in light of the human genome project' *Kentucky Law Journal* 85(3): 503.

Holtzman, N. A. *et al.* (1997) 'Predictive genetic testing: from basic research to clinical practice' *Science* 278: 602.

Hsu, C. (2012) 'New findings suggest that winners are born, not bred' *Medical Daily* 16 May. Available at www.medicaldaily.com/news/20120516/9908/success-genes-dna-characteristics-failure-twins.htm [accessed 15 April 2014].

Huang, K. G. and Murray, F. E. (2010) 'Entrepreneurial experiments in science policy: analyzing the Human Genome Project' *Research Policy* 39(95): 567–582.

Johannsen, W. (1909) Elemente der exakten Erblichkeitslehre. Jena: Gustav Fischer

Kapp, M. B. (2006) 'Patient autonomy in the age of consumer-Driven health care: informed consent and informed choice' *Journal of Health and Biomedical Law* 2(1): 2.

Kaufman, M. B. (1999) 'Genetic discrimination in the workplace: an overview of existing protections' *Loyola University Chicago Law Journal* 30: 393.

Kishore, D. (2009–2010) 'Test at your own risk: your genetic report card and the direct-to-consumer duty to secure informed consent' *Emory Law Journal* 159: 553.

Kolata, G. (2012) 'In gene sequencing treatment for leukemia, glimpses into the future', *New York Times* 7 July. Available at www.nytimes.com/2012/07/08/health/in-gene-sequencing-treatment-for-leukemia-glimpses-of-the-future.html?pagewanted=all [accessed 15 April 2014].

Koonin, E. V. (2012) *The Logic of Chance: The Nature and Origin of Biological Evolution.* New Jersey, USA: FT Press Science.

Kreek, M. J. *et al.* (2005) 'Genetic Influences on impulsivity, risk-taking, stress, responsibility and vulnerability to drug abuse and addiction' *Nature Neuroscience* 8(11): 1450.

Lamberts, S. W. J. and Uitterlinden, A G. (2009) 'Genetic testing in clinical practice' *Annual Review of Medicine* 60: 431.

Lander, E. S. (1996) 'The new genomics: global views of biology' *Science* 274(5287): 536.

Lander, E. S. and Weinberg, R. A. (2000) 'Pathways of discovery – genomics: journey to the center of biology' *Science* 5287(459): 1777–1778.

Lemmens, T. (2000) 'Selective justice, genetic discrimination, and insurance: Should we single out our genes in our laws?' *McGill Law Journal* 45: 347.

Lewis, R. (2011) *Human Genetics: The Basics.* New York: Routledge.

Loftus, P. (2013) 'Genetic test service 23andMe ordered to halt marketing by FDA' *Wall Street Journal* 25 November. Available at http://online.wsj.com/news/articles/SB10001424052702304281004579219893863966448 [accessed 9 March 2014].

Lynch, J. *et al.* (2011) 'Media coverage of direct-to-consumer genetic testing' *Journal of Genetic Counselling* 20(5) 486.

Madden, D. (2011) *Medicine, Ethics and the Law.* 2nd edition. Dublin: Bloomsbury Professional.

Man, P. Y. W. *et al.* (2002) 'Leber hereditary optic neuropathy' *Journal of Medical Genetics* 39: 162.

Marantz Henig, R. (2001) *The Monk in the Garden: The Lost and Found Genius of Gregor Mendel, the Father of Genetics.* Boston/New York: Mariner Books.

Mardis, E R. and Wilson, R K. (2009) 'Cancer genome sequencing: a review' *Human Molecular Genetics Review* 18(2): 163.

Markoff, J. (2012) 'Cost of gene sequencing falls, raising hopes for medical advances' *New York Times* 7 March. Available at www.nytimes.com/2012/03/08/technology/cost-of-gene-sequencing-falls-raising-hopes-for-medical-advances.html?pagewanted=all&_r=0 [accessed 9 March 2014].

Maxim, A. M. and Gilbert. W. (1977) 'A new method for sequencing DNA' *Proceedings of the National Academy of Science* 74: 560.

McLochlin, D. L. (2001) 'Whose genetic information is it anyway? A legal analysis of the effects that mapping the human genome will have on privacy rights and genetic discrimination' *John Marshall Journal of Computer and Information Law* 19: 609–615.

Mendel, G. (2008) *Experiments in Plant Hybridization.* First published 1865 and 1909. New York: Cosimo Inc.

Miller, P. S. (2000) 'Is there a pink slip in your genes? Genetic discrimination in the workplace' *Journal of Health Care Law and Policy* 3(2): 225.

Modra, L. (2006) 'Prenatal genetic testing kits sold at your local pharmacy: promoting autonomy or promoting confusion? *Bioethics* 20: 254.

Morgan, T. *et al.* (1915) *Mechanism of Mendelian Heredity.* London: Henry Holt and Company.

Morrison, C. (2012) 'The evolution of genetic science and technology', Genetic Discrimination – Transatlantic Perspectives on the Case for a European Level Legal Response. 6 March. Brussels, Belgium.

Nagasubramanian, R. *et al.* (2003) 'Pharmacogenetics in cancer treatment' *Annual Review of Medicine* 54(1): 437.

Narod, S. A. and Foulkes, W. D. (2004) 'BRCA1 and BRCA2: 1994 and beyond' *Nature Reviews Cancer* 4: 665.

National Cancer Institute United States Department of Health and Human Services (1995) 'Understanding gene testing', pp. 4–5.

National Human Genome Research Institute (1990) 'Understanding our genetic inheritance: The United States Human Genome Project, the first five years: fiscal years 1991–1995'. Available at www.genome.gov/10001477 [accessed 9 March 2014].

Ng, P. C. and Kirkness, E. F. (2010) 'Whole genome sequencing' *Genetic Variation – Methods in Molecular Biology* 628: 215.

Nissenkorn, A. *et al.* (1999) 'Multiple presentation of mitochondrial disorders' *Archives of Disease in Childhood* 81(3): 209.

Ormond, K. E. *et al.* (2010) 'Challenges in the clinical application of whole-genome sequencing' *The Lancet* 375: 9727.

Rajiv, S. *et al.* (2011) 'Genetic screening: the vista of genomic medicine' *Journal of Pharmacy and Bioallied Sciences* 3(1): 109.

Riba, S. C. (2007) 'The use of genetic information in health insurance: who will be helped, who will be harmed and the possible long-term effects' *Review of Law and Social Justice* 16(2): 470, 473.

Rincon, P. (2014) 'Science enters $1,000 genome era' BBC News 15 January. Available at www.bbc.com/news/science-environment-25751958 [accessed 9 March 2014].

Roscam Abbing, H. (2006) 'Pharmacogenetic data: mapping the subject's rights' *Good Clinical Practice Journal* 13: 28.

Roy, D. and Tevfik Dorak, D. (2010) *Environmental Factors, Genes and Development of Human Cancers.* New York: Springer.

Sanger, F. and Coulson, A. R. (1975) 'A rapid method of determining sequences by primed synthesis with DNA polymerase' *Journal of Molecular Biology* 94(3): 441.

Sapkota, Y. *et al.* (2013) 'Germline DNA copy number aberrations identified as potential prognostic factors for breast cancer recurrence' *Public Library of Science* ONE 8(1): e53850.

Sermon, K. *et al.* (2004) 'Preimplantation genetic diagnosis' *The Lancet* 363: 1633.

Shampo, M. A. and Kyle, R. A. (2011) 'J. Craig Venter – The Human Genome Project' *Mayo Clinic Proceedings* 86(4): 26.

Shane, S. (2010) 'Explaining innate risk-takers' *Bloomberg Businessweek* 12 February. Available at www.businessweek.com/smallbiz/content/feb2010/sb20100211_567240.htm [accessed 9 March 2014].

Shendure, J. *et al.* (2004) 'Advanced sequencing technologies: methods and goals' *Nature Reviews: Genetics* 5: 335–342.

Singer, M. and Berg, P. (1991) *Genes and Genome: A Changing Perspective.* California: University Science Books.

Smith, G. P., II and Burns, T J. (1994–1995) 'Genetic determinism or genetic discrimination' *Journal of Contemporary Health Law and Policy* 11: 23.

Sorsby, A. (1965) 'Gregor Mendel' *British Medical Journal* 1: 333.

Sturtevant, A. H. (2001) *A History of Genetics*. Cold Spring Harbor, NY: Cold Spring Harbor Laboratory Press. First published 1965.

Taylor, R. W. and Turnbull, D. M. (2005) 'Mitochondrial DNA mutations in human disease' *Nature Reviews: Genetics* 6: 389.

Terhune, C. (2012) 'Spending on genetic tests is forecast to rise sharply by 2021' *Los Angeles Times* 12 March. Available at: http://articles.latimes.com/2012/mar/12/business/la-fi-genetic-test-20120312 [accessed 9 March 2014].

Timmermans, S. and Buchbinder, M. (2013) *Saving Babies – The Consequences of Newborn Genetic Screening*. Chicago: University of Chicago Press.

Wallace, D. C. (1988) 'Mitochondrial DNA mutation associated with Leber's hereditary optic neuropathy' *Science, New Edition* 242(4884): 1427.

Watson, J. D. (1998) *The Double Helix (A Personal Account of Watson and Crick's Discovery of the Structure of DNA)*. New York: Scribner.

Watson, J. D. and Crick, F. (1953) 'Molecular structure of nucleic acids: a structure for deoxyribose nucleic acid' *Nature* 737.

Weaver, K. D. (1997) 'Genetic screening and the right not to know' *Issues in Law and Medicine* 13: 243–246.

Weinberg, R. A. (1991) 'The dark side of the genome' *Technology Review* 91 (3): 44.

# Section 2

# Ethical and legal dilemmas arising from emerging technologies

Section 2 focuses on the emerging and challenging bioethical and legal issues presented as genomic science proliferates and as these cutting-edge technologies are used more frequently in healthcare and other settings. It explores the use of genetic information and genetic testing in the clinical setting, as well as in other third party contexts, particularly employment and insurance.

This section comprises three chapters. Javier Romañach Cabrero writes the first chapter, 'Diversity ethics and the impact of genetic technologies'. The next chapter is entitled 'Genes, identity and clinical ethics under conditions of uncertainty', by Rebecca Wolf, Michael Joseph Young, Michael Ashley Stein and Harold J. Bursztajn. The final chapter in Section 2 is entitled 'The use of genetic information outside of the therapeutic relationship: An international perspective' and is written by Yann Joly, J. Rosel Kim and Shadad Salman. These three chapters draw together the myriad of complex ethical and legal concerns arising in this area in a variety of different fields, and provide a background before addressing the challenging regulatory and policy questions that arise.

# 3 Diversity ethics and the impact of genetic technologies

*Javier Romañach Cabrero*

## 1. Introduction

Public opinion in Western countries considers health as one of the key issues for the quality of life of any citizen. Scientific and medical advances, and especially those related to genetics, such as genetic embryo selection, gene therapy, and genetic testing, are considered to be good for society, as we hope that they will prevent humans from suffering from illness, and from disability. Little thought is given to the type of society we are heading for, and to the deep economical, philosophical and sociological roots, and consequences, of the advances in biomedicine and genetics. Our society is becoming utilitarian and ableist, and quality of life and comfort act as anaesthetics for a humanity that rejects aging and disability, in a quest for the unfulfilled promise of eternal youth and absolute health.

During the last few years, a new ethical and bioethical voice has been raised by the most fragile, unseen and undervalued people: people with disabilities or, as proposed by diversity ethics and the diversity model, functionally diverse people. The term 'functional diversity' (more functionally diverse people) as a substitute of 'disability' was first proposed by Romañach and Lobato (2005) and it is a part of the diversity model (Romañach and Palacios, 2007). It should be noted that it is the first non-negative description on this reality that evades the ability concept. This voice rises from the deepest fragility of human beings, and escapes from ableism, proposing that what used to be thought of as disability is just a part of human diversity, a part that affects not only those who are thought to be disabled, but all humans. This new voice proposes a paradigm shift, from ability and disability to dignity and diversity, and a new theoretical framework, to unveil the secret deep implications of biomedicine and genetics origins and advances, and their consequences for the type of society in which we want to live in the future.

This chapter will analyse and develop a new point of view on genetic technologies and their implications in society, the point of view that observes society 'through the looking glass'; the point of view of those who will not be allowed to be born in the future because they are nowadays considered to be genetically incorrect and, or, unhealthy.

## 2. A choice for the future society

When we reflect and write about genetic discrimination in this book, we are undoubtedly reflecting about the type of society we expect for the future: our future and the future of our descendants. What is really at stake is the type of human being we expect to fit in that society and which, if any, will suffer discrimination in the European Union.

The acceptance of every kind of human diversity, including age, race, religion, origin, gender, sexual orientation, disability or functional diversity ('functional diversity' is the term that will be used in this text in conjunction with 'diversity ethics') seems to be quite well established in EU legislation, but it hides subtle inconsistencies derived from our deepest and unquestioned beliefs.

As stated on the European Commission, Directorate-General of Justice's website:[1]

> The EU acts on behalf of EU citizens to prevent them being discriminated against on grounds of racial or ethnic origin, religion or belief, disability, age or sexual orientation and sex.
>
> The European Commission takes action to:
>
> - improve knowledge of discrimination by raising awareness among the population of their rights and obligations and also of the benefits of diversity;
> - support intermediary actors such as NGOs, social partners and equality bodies to improve their capacity to combat discrimination;
> - support the development of equality policies at national level and encourage the exchange of good practices between EU countries;
> - achieve real change in the area of anti-discrimination through anti-discrimination training activities;
> - push for business-oriented diversity management as part of a strategic response to a more diversified society, customer base, market structure and workforce.

In achieving these objectives, the EU directives concerning the subject of discrimination are: Directive of 29 April 2004 on the right of citizens of the Union and their family members to move and reside freely within the territory of the Member States; Council Directive of 27 November 2000 establishing a general framework for equal treatment in employment and occupation; Council Directive of 29 June 2000 implementing the principle of equal treatment between persons irrespective of racial or ethnic origin;

1 http://ec.europa.eu/justice/discrimination/index_en.htm.

Proposal for a directive of 2 July 2008 against discrimination based on age, disability, sexual orientation and religion or belief beyond the workplace (although after five years, this proposal has not been approved). These directives will be discussed in greater detail in Section 4 of this book.

In relation to bioethics, in addition to the Nuremberg Code and the Helsinki Declaration, the most relevant framework is the Oviedo Convention, (Convention on Human Rights and Biomedicine, 1997) approved by the Council of Europe in 1997, which is discussed further by Roscam Abbing in Section 4. In relation to the Oviedo Convention, its content still raises ethical and human rights issues, if analysed in the light of diversity ethics (Devandas, 2008).

Regarding functionally diverse people, the United Nations Convention on the Rights of Persons with Disabilities 2006, approved by the EU in 2010, is also a reference document. The theory of diversity ethics points out that the UN Convention leaves some unresolved theoretical questions, as it does not completely overcome ableism in its conception (Romañach and Palacios, 2007).

As can be read in the preceding list, there is a clear strategic attitude towards building an EU in which diversity is accepted and respected. The freedom of movement, employment and racism have already been addressed, and age, functional diversity, religion and sexual orientation have yet to be addressed. The author proposes that this happens not by chance, as productivity requires the first three, but not the four latter. It is further observed that, philosophically, productivity is related to ableism (Wolbring, 2008).

We therefore face a choice for our future society: Do we want a future non-discriminatory society in which every individual, no matter how capable, or smart, or productive or skilled, or able to run and walk, able to speak, or able to hear, etc. has a chance to live and enjoy life at any age? Or do we want a discriminatory society in which only people who are useful, capable, smart, skilled, with good sight and hearing, for example, will be welcome and allowed to live and enjoy what society provides?

## 3. Diversity ethics

*Diversity ethics* (Guibet-Lafaye and Romañach, 2010) is an ethical proposal that faces this challenge, providing a dynamic theoretical framework that gathers different ethical approaches from different sources and is open to future contributions and evolutions.

It proposes a powerful extension of recognition and redistribution ethics (Fraser and Honneth, 2003). Diversity ethics broadens prior approaches, as it includes functional diversity as part of human diversity to be accounted for in moral philosophy; it addresses the need to break social domination logics (Foucault, 1975; Romañach *et al.*, 2009) and *habitus* (Bourdieu, 1991) and the need to analyse redistribution at the end of the process, to ensure it will account for self-respect and self-esteem (Guibet-Lafaye, 2007).

The inclusion of functional diversity in recognition and redistribution ethics proposes the idea of auto-recognition of fragility and diversity in all humans, as we are all functionally diverse and risk personal discrimination on those grounds. In fact, any discrimination that starts with functionally diverse people today is most likely going to affect all members in society some time in the future.

Furthermore, a pragmatic approach of dignity, that proposes giving the same value for all human lives, and the same rights and opportunities to all persons, is included in diversity ethics, providing tools to face bioethical challenges and human rights issues (Romañach and Palacios, 2007). Diversity ethics relies on mutual recognition, because both value of life and rights are 'given' by society, but it also relies on self-recognition, on self-diversity through time and self-recognition of fragility for all human beings.

Together with the feminine approach to ethics, known as 'care ethics' (Noddings, 1984), the diversity model also contributes to provide a new ethical approach to different human realities and challenges such as the 'inDependency' or care situations, as care ethics diminishes the traditional asymmetry between the functionally diverse people and the rest of society, and it proposes a two-way relation between subjects.

Diversity ethics is proposed as a choice for future society, as we are to choose now whether, in the future, we will live in a non-discriminatory society in which all human diversity is welcome and every individual regardless of her or his differences, abilities and productivity has a chance to live and enjoy life at any age; or whether we will live in a society in which not all diversity is accepted, a discriminatory society.

Diversity ethics makes a clear choice of the first option, and confronts Peter Singer's utilitarian proposal (Singer, 2002), which prefers and promotes the second option, by showing its weakness and incoherencies. Diversity ethics provides alternative bioethical positions that are coherent with the choice of a future society, a society in which all humans will have the right to justice and equality, a society in diverty,[2] a society that should be different from the one we have today, in which inequalities are reproduced through generations.

## 4. Science and modern mythology

From a diversity ethics point of view, recognition is prior to distribution, and therefore the absence of recognition of functionally diverse people's lives as having the same value as those of 'healthy' people is a crucial issue

2 Diverty stands for dignity and liberty in diversity. It is a translation from the Spanish 'divertad' (Romañach Cabrero, 2009).

at stake. Today, the consequence of this differing value of lives is that humans socially considered to be 'not healthy' are not welcome in society and are discriminated against in every present or future human form.

In the research of the roots of this lack of recognition, the ethical proposal *diversity ethics* frequently gathers ideas from reflections on non-mainstream approaches; it challenges the established power, science and thought, as it considers them a part of the domination logics developed and described by Foucault. As stated by the French philosopher, we have built a disciplined surveillance society that pursues the practical control and measurement and training of useful forces and bodies that can be productive; this discipline characterises, classifies, specialises; they distribute along a scale, around a norm, hierarchise individuals in relation to one another and, if necessary, disqualify and, if necessary, invalidate (Foucault, 1975).

From this point of view, the science that is used to invalidate or prevent some types of human beings is just another human activity submitted to institutional forces and contemporary social views. For example, Stephen Jay Gould has been accused of bringing Marx's revolutionary ideas into biology; in the same way, Darwin's evolution was influenced by Malthus's ideas. As any human activity or institution, science is full of errors, unfulfilled promises and uncertainty. This does not imply a position against science, but a position for true solid science that does not transmit to society a certainty and absolute knowledge that it has not. It should be stressed that the goal is not to diminish science's value for progress, but to break the traditional dominant view on functional diversity as just medical, or an ability issue; the goal is to promote a shift towards a diversity and dignity social approach.

Scientific myths persist nowadays; the modern Promethean myth claims today's fusion of biomedicine and biotechnology to explain, manipulate and transform the lives of the wealthy global minority government. Indeed it has become part of everyday assumptions and social perception. Evolutionary theory proposes to explain human origins, genomics offers to define similarity and difference of genetics, and stem cell therapies offer to cure or prevent disease, and even enhance bodies and minds; the neurosciences' promise to predict behaviour, to explain consciousness and, with brain organisation theory, to re-essentialise gender difference genetics, this time with benign intent, if not with benign consequences, has sought to reracialise human difference (Rose and Rose, 2013).

Modern science and society ignore Korzybski's analysis, 'the map is not the territory', that describes the relationship between an object and a representation of that object (Korzybski, 1933). Society and science confuse models of reality and reality itself. For example, the chemical elements, the proteins, the genes or the cells may be a map of a human being, but they are not his or her entire territory. They do not fully describe his or her feelings, thoughts, dreams, ideas, desires or behaviour, or even his or her health. Furthermore, natural and social environment are ignored too.

This type of confusion seems to be especially true regarding the scientific and medical discourse, a discourse that has great influence on social construction and beliefs, and that rarely speaks about the economic interests of the pharmaceutical companies and their shareholders.

As Brock has described, there is a coercive potential of medicalising people's departure from typical customary functioning: 'generally it is when we have noticed an adverse effect or change in normal functional capacity that we go to healthcare professionals and begin the process which can result in our being labeled as sick or diseased'. Anita Silvers's view is that 'Brock accurately describes the impact of medicalised discourse. Designating an anomaly, difference, or change in anyone's customary functioning as sick, diseased, or a defect or deviance in health is potentially coercive' (Silvers *et al.*, 1998). In this regard, gene diversity is scientifically named as genetic malformation or disease, regardless of the views of 'genetically incorrect' people (Journet, 2007) and their political organisations (Disabled People's International, 2000).

Science-dominant paradigms are not neutral. The case of Jérôme Lejeune, is exemplifying. Lejeune discovered in 1958 that individuals with Down's Syndrome have three copies of the twenty-first chromosome, instead of two. It should be noted that this implies difference or diversity. Calling it a disease or genetic fault is a social construct. Lejeune dedicated his life to research for cure and care for those with Trisomy 21, declaring, 'because every new human belongs to our species from the moment of conception, each new human being is entitled to life, and, if she is sick to the care and to our devotion' (Coulter *et al.*, 2012). Regardless of his personal religious beliefs, his discovery led to the concept that this type of human being is genetically incorrect. Prenatal screening is now routinely performed to detect Down's syndrome in many countries in Europe, and in 88 per cent of the cases results in termination (Boyd *et al.*, 2004). Although this is a clear indicator of new eugenics, prenatal screening is considered a good scientific advance and social progress all over the world. What Lejeune conceived as illness has proven to have a simple cure: eugenics. In this way, the new eugenics is socially promoted as a cure for genetically incorrect people.

Despite the influence of positivism in modern science, humanity in science should change the view of scientists; it would be better to regard scientists as being somewhat like artists who produce quite different paintings of the same sitter. Each scientific theory will be capable of painting a unique insight which is aesthetically satisfying to a given person in some ways and not in others. Some interpretations may show creative originality, while others may be mediocre. Yet they will not be the final truth about the subject (Bohm and Peat, 1987).

As an example, the history of genetics can be described as a series of miscalculations and unfulfilled promises of cure. The human genome was estimated to have 100,000 genes, but it turned out that there were only around 30,000 genes. Out of these 30,000, only 3 per cent were supposed to carry valid genetic information. Then the existence of hox genes (or homeotic genes) was discovered; these are genes that control and help lay out the basic body forms (morphogenesis) of many animals, including humans. The genome was supposed to give us all the information needed to cure every genetic disease, but now, as has been learned, this is mostly not the case; we are now moving on to the proteome.

Embryo stem cells were supposed to be the panacea and cure for everything, but that has not been proven yet. Gene therapy has promised a cure for many diseases for over 15 years, and we are still at the starting point. In fact, the more we have learned in recent years, the more complicated matters have tended to become. Even thinking, it turns out, affects the way genes work. How fast a man's beard grows, for instance, is partly a function of how much he thinks about sex, because thinking about sex produces a testosterone surge.

The genome is like a parts list for the human body: it tells us what we are made of, but says nothing about how we work. What is needed now is the operating manual, instructions for how to make it go. We are not close to that point yet (Bryson, 2010). So now the quest is to crack the human proteome, and the proteome is much more complicated than the genome (*Scientific American*, 2002: 44–45; cited by Bryson, 2010).

Only a few disorders, for example haemophilia, Parkinson's disease, Huntington's disease and cystic fibrosis, are caused by single dysfunctional genes. But, as a rule, disrupted genes are weeded out by natural selection long before they can become commonly troublesome to a species or population. The greatest part of our fate and comfort, and even eye colour, is determined not by individual genes but by complexes of genes working in alliance (Bryson, 2010). Furthermore, genes and environment interact in unimaginably complex patterns (Engleman, 2011).

But even single gene diseases had a disruptive behaviour. For example, a deletion on the fifteenth chromosome can be expressed in two completely different human results: Prader-Willy and Angeline syndromes, as depicted by Marcus Pembrey (Clayton-Smith *et al.*, 1993: 683–686). Furthermore, and thanks to the Överkalix study, (Pembrey *et al.*, 2006: 159–166), the research on this subject led to the concept of genetic imprinting, which means that genes have the memory of where they came from, an unknown feature for many years. This led to the discovery of switches that turn on and off determined genes, and to epigenetics; and now we have to understand the epigenetics code.

All of these mistakes, trials and errors in the quest for scientific knowledge and theories are routine in science and would not matter too much if they did not lead to social behaviour based on a scientific certainty that never existed. That is, genetic discrimination is based on the social belief of genetic determinism and the illusion of our powerful understanding of the genes. On those grounds, functionally diverse people are, for example, not allowed by law to access certain IVF procedures, and genetic selection is performed with a brand of health 'guarantee', and insurance companies are ready to use genetic information to modify their policies. Scientific research should not be stopped on these grounds, but transposition to public opinion and legal systems must be based on scepticism, not on non-existent scientific certainty.

## 5. Diversity ethics and genetic technologies' ethical challenges

Diversity ethics is born 'on the other side of the looking glass' and breaks the traditional conceptualisation of part of human diversity as 'dis-ability.' It acts like a mirror of every human being's fragility and diversity. It helps in performing an analysis from another point of view, the point of view in which oppression mechanisms, productivity and economic issues, and scientific and medical uncertainty are disclosed. It provides a clear view on what type of society we are building nowadays and a theoretical framework to build a different one. Therefore, the ethical challenges of genetic technologies can be described in a different way.

Diversity ethics shows that we are pursuing and developing eugenics in the quest for the Promethean myth of a perfect human being that never existed and is, most probably, not going to exist, at least, in the next centuries. New genetic technologies have ethical implications in many aspects, but the most relevant one is the promotion of new eugenics.

### *5.1 New eugenics in Europe*

Scientific eugenic ideas started in Europe in 1907 with Sir Francis Galton. In his book *Inquiries into human faculty and its development* he wrote:

> The easiest direction to which a race can be improved is towards a central type, because nothing new has to be sought out. It is only necessary to encourage as far as practicable the breed of those who conform most nearly to the central type, and to restrain as far as may be the breed of those who deviate widely from it.

This famous sentence seems far away in time and place, and the deadly consequences that this type of thinking had all over the world during the twentieth century are well known, as is further highlighted by Blanck and de Paor later in this book.

In the quest for a superior race for humanity, elimination, experimentation and sterilisation of functionally diverse people was firstly developed (Evans, 2004); others followed. Millions were killed and hundreds of thousands sterilised pursuing the superior race, all over the Western world. After this catastrophe of explicit and brutal eugenics, the word 'eugenics' fell into disgrace. But, from 1945, in Europe and the US the vocabulary of eugenics slowly disappeared from respectable scientific research, to be replaced by that of genetics and molecular biology (Rose and Rose, 2013).

Nevertheless, the idea of breeding healthy, 'normal'[3] human beings, using the science and technology available, has remained untouched in modern society, as could be read in 1989 in the editorial of the well-known *Science* magazine:

> The benefits to science of the genome project are clear. Illness such as manic depression, Alzheimer's, schizophrenia, or heart disease are probably all mutagenic and even more difficult to unravel than cystic fibrosis. Yet these diseases are at the root of many current social problems. The costs of mental illness, the difficult civil liberties problems they cause, the pain to the individual, all cry out for a solution that involves prevention, not caretaking. To continue the current warehousing or neglect of these people, many of whom are in the ranks of the homeless, is it the equivalent of providing iron lungs to polio victims at the expense of working on vaccine.
>
> (Koshland, 1989: 189)

These stark eugenic ideas are also spread through legislation, and have been supported by contemporary philosophers such as Peter Singer (Singer, 2002). Many others are not that explicit and have approached genetic challenges with ancient but more subtle concepts: negative and positive euthanasia (Camps, 2002). The Promethean myth persists.

Diversity ethics shows that the challenges that emerge from contemporary genetics are not derived from scientific knowledge, but from social institutions that control the social perception of science and the actual or potential use of that scientific knowledge.

New eugenics can be detected in many related issues such as genetic determinism, prenatal screening, abortion, embryo genetic selection and disease prediction. In all of them, the values of the lives of functionally diverse human beings are considered to be inferior to 'normal', 'healthy' human beings, productive human beings. The goal of many of these practices is to 'cure' by elimination of genetic diversity. Society does not accept the same value for all human beings' lives, and human beings who are expected to grow as capable and productive are selected to be born. Wealth in human society groups appears to be more important than humanity itself.

3 It should be noted that 'normal' is a mathematical concept equivalent to Galton's 'central type'.

It is quite clear that selecting an embryo that has different human characteristics from others means discrimination of the value of specific human lives, and that is called eugenics. Diversity ethics is opposed to eugenics, as we have a firm historical knowledge of what those ideas and facts lead to, and their disastrous consequences. Furthermore, if we want to be coherent with the social choice of not giving the same value to all human lives, other characteristics (for example eye colour and gender) should be allowed to be selected. Of course that should only happen in the case that we want to be a coherent society, and act according to how we think.

Another sign that shows the way we think is that new abortion laws consider eugenic-based abortion as progress in the fight for women's rights, as is the case in Spain (Law on sexual and reproductive health on a voluntary interruption of pregnancy, 2010). Furthermore, recent attempts to avoid eugenics in abortion are strongly contested by feminists and political parties who view themselves as defending social progress. We can therefore assume that, in Europe, there is a general social ethical view around functional diversity that still considers this human reality is the source of sufferance, lack of quality of life, lack of happiness, lack of productivity, etc. and, as consequence, its existence should be avoided.

The approval of the United Nations Convention on the Rights of Persons with Disabilities in 2006, its formal ratification by the European Union on 5 January 2011 and the individual ratifications of several European countries (Finland, Ireland and Netherlands are the only ones that have not ratified it yet) should help change this eugenic mentality, but its effect has not reached the general population and political parties yet.

### *5.2 Other issues*

There are many other issues at stake regarding genetic technologies not directly linked with eugenics, such as human cloning, inheritable genetic modification, informed consent, stem cells, genetic privacy, genetic determinism, gene patents, decease prediction, in vitro fertilisation, gene therapy, non-discrimination, equal access to basic services, the right to know, stem cell tourism and gender selection. Stein *et al.* and Joly *et al.* explore some of these issues in later chapters of this book.

In-depth discussion of these issues is outside the scope of this chapter, but the concept of self-recognition of fragility is useful to analyse some of them. That is, the idea of being conscious of our own fragility, and therefore realising that, whatever attitude is taken towards those considered today to be genetically incorrect, will come back and be applied to ourselves in a boomerang behaviour in the future. In this way, disease prediction, the right to know, genetic determinism and genetic privacy are issues that will concern all human beings sooner or later and can provide a mirror image of what we are really doing with genetically incorrect people.

Accepting genetic determinism for those considered to be genetically incorrect, even before they were born, will most likely have as a consequence the acceptance of our own genetic determinism. If we accept the premise, we will slowly go down the slope of losing our own genetic privacy, to prove to society that we are genetically correct. Therefore, companies will be allowed to access our genetic data and details of our disease prediction or our probability of acquiring a genetic default in the future. That will affect our insurance policies, our access to employment and to health and social services, etc.

The concept of diversity ethics rejects this notion of genetic determinism and biological reductionism of a human being, not because they are incorrect, but because they are incomplete. A human being is not just a biological machine; feelings, dreams, behaviours, social relations and environment are more important in determining what makes us human.

There is no more scope to analyse the rest of the issues related to genetic technologies, but some of the relevant points concerning the construction of a future society have been addressed, and diversity ethics has shown some aspects that should be revised and rethought.

## 6. Conclusion

Human genetic science is a human activity, with its simplifications, failures, incoherencies and minor effective advances. Furthermore, it has been shown that science is not neutral and is subject to domination logics and social economic pressures. Nevertheless, science has been used to reinforce Galton's view of society, regardless of its historically adverse consequences. Although we now know that our genetic knowledge and its connection with disease is very small, and not very reliable, this insufficient knowledge is enough to undermine the value of genetically diverse individuals' lives and has consequently led to discrimination against some individuals who are thought to be ill, instead of being considered as different.

This type of approach to human functional diversity (also known as disability) has been overridden by the United Nations Convention on the Rights of Persons with Disabilities, which is now part of the legislation of most European countries.

Diversity ethics is an ethical proposal originating in Europe that provides new theoretical tools to approach the subject in a deep innovative way and in which illness and disability are replaced by functional diversity; functional diversity affects all people through their lives, whilst discrimination only affects some of them; but if the full time period of life of a human being is considered, sooner or later almost all persons will be affected by that discrimination.

This theoretical approach shows that what is at stake is the type of the future society we want for ourselves and for our descendants: Do we want to build a society in which every human being will be welcome and granted the same rights, regardless of their health status or capabilities? Or do we prefer a society in which only the healthy and capable will be suited to live?

The analysis provided in this chapter on issues such as new eugenics, and genetic determinism, shows that we are heading towards the paradigm of a productive, able, healthy society; but as there is no human being that has a life that is consistently productive, healthy and full of ability, robots or machines are probably best suited for that future than human beings. We should be aware of the fact that the choices we make now are the building blocks for our future society. Diversity ethics is an ethical proposal that might be useful if we choose to build a future society in which diversity, dignity and liberty are to be the guidelines of our future – a future in diversity.

## References

Bohm, D. and Peat, F. D. (1987) *Science Order and Creativity. A Dramatic New Look to Creative Roots of Science and Life.* Toronto, New York, London, Sydney, Auckland: Bantam Books.

Bourdieu, P. (1991) *El sentido práctico.* Madrid: Taurus.

Boyd, P., DeVigan, C., Khoshnood, B., Loane, M., Garne, E., Dolk, H. and the EUROCAT working group (2004) 'Survey of prenatal screening policies in Europe for structural malformations and chromosome anomalies, and their impact on detection and termination rates for neural tube defects and Down's syndrome'.

Bryson, B. (2010) *A Short Story of Nearly Everything.* Kindle version.

Camps, V. (2002) 'Qué hay de malo en la eugenesia?', in AAVV (2002) *Los problemas morales de la biogenética, Revista ISEGORÍA. Revista de Filosofía Moral y Política* 27 (December). Madrid: Consejo Superior de Investigaciones Científicas (CSIC), Instituto de Filosofía.

Clayton-Smith, J., Driscoll, D. J., Waters, M. F., Webb, T., Andrews, T., Malcolm, S., Marcus E. Pembrey, M. E. and Nicholls, R. D. (1993) *American Journal of Medical Genetics* 47(5): 683–686.

Coulter, M. L., Myers, R. S. and Varacalli, J. A. (2012) *Encyclopedia of Catholic Social Thought, Social Science, and Social Policy: Supplement.* Lanham, MD: Scarecrow Press.

Devandas, C. (2008) 'El Convenio de Asturias de Bioética: Protección o desprotección para las personas con discapacidad intelectual y psico-social?'. Research paper for the Carlos III University, in Getafe, Spain.

DPI (Disabled People's International) (2000) 'Disabled people speak on new genetics, DPI position statement on bioethics and human rights'. Available at: www.codex.vr.se/texts/bioethics%20statement.pdf.

Engleman, D. (2011) *Incognito: The Secret Lives of the Brain.* Edinburgh: Canongate Books Ltd.

Evans, S. E. (2004) 'Forgotten crimes. The holocaust and people with disabilities'. *Disability Rights.* Chicago: Ivan R. Dee.

Foucault, M. (1975) *Surveiller et punir.* Paris: Editions Gallimard.

Fraser, N. and Honneth, A. (2003) *Redistribution or Recognition? A Political-Philosophical Exchange.* London, New York: Verso.

Guibet-Lafaye, C. and Romañach Cabrero, J. (2010) 'Diversity ethics. An alternative to Peter Singer's ethics', *Dilemata* (International Magazine in Applied Ethics) 3: 95–116. Madrid.

Journet, N. (2007) *Génétiquement Incorrect*. Paris: Danger Public.

Korzybski, A. (1933) *Science and Sanity. An Introduction to Non-Aristotelian Systems and General Semantics*. New York: Institute of General Semantics (2000). The full sentence is 'If words *are not* things, or maps *are not* the actual territory, then, obviously, the only possible link between the objective world and the linguistic world is found in *Structure, and Structure Alone*.'

Koshland, D. (1989) 'Sequences and consequences of the human genome', *Science* 246: 189.

Noddings, N. (1984) *Caring: A Feminine Approach to Ethics and Moral Education*. Berkeley and Los Angeles: University of California Press.

Pembrey, M. E., Bygren, L. O., Kaati, G., Edvinsson, S., Northstone, K., Sjöström, M. and Golding, J. (2006) 'Sex-specific, male-line transgenerational responses in humans', *European Journal of Human Genetics* 14(2): 159–166.

Romañach Cabrero J. (2009) *Bioética al otro lado del espejo*. Diversitas ediciones.

Romañach, J. and Lobato, M. (2005) 'Diversidad funcional, un nuevo término para la lucha por la dignidad del ser humano'. Available at: http://centrodocumentaciondown.com/uploads/documentos/1dcb1a899435d2b2806acdf5dbcf17aa941abd8d.pdf.

Romañach Cabrero, J. and Palacios, A. (2007) 'Diversity approach: A new view on bioethics from the functionally diverse (disabled) people'. Available at: http://diversocracia.org/docs/Diversity_approach_overview.doc.

Romañach, J., Palacios, A., Ferreira, M. A. V. and Ferrante, C. (2009) 'Functional diversity, bioethics and sociological theory: A new approach to disability' *Intersticios: Revista Sociologica de Pensamiento Critico* 6(1): 115.

Rose, H. and Rose, S. (2013) *Genes, Cells and Brains. The Promethean Promises of the New Biology*. London: Verso.

*Scientific American* (2002) 'More over, human genome', pp. 44–45.

Silvers, A., Wasserman, D. T. and Mahowald, M. B. (1998) *Disability, Difference, Discrimination: Perspectives on Justice in Bioethics and Public Policy*. Oxford: Rowman & Littlefield Publishers, Inc.

Singer, P. (2002) *Unsanctifying Human Life: Essays on Ethics*. Helga Khuse (ed.). Oxford: Blackwell.

—— (2002) Desacralizar la vida humana. Ensayos de ética. Colección Teorema. Madrid: Cátedra. 2003. Spanish translation of P. Singer, *Unsanctifying Human Life*.

Wolbring, G. (2008) 'The politics of ableism'. *Development* 51: 252, 288. Society for International Development.

## Legislation

Convention for the Protection of Human Rights and Dignity of the Human Being with Regard to the Application of Biology and Medicine: Convention on Human Rights and Biomedicine 1997.

Ley Orgánica 2/2010, de 3 de marzo, de salud sexual y reproductiva y de la interrupción voluntaria del embarazo. (Law on Sexual and Reproductive Health on a Voluntary Interruption of Pregnancy).

United Nations Convention on the Rights of Persons with Disabilities 2006 G.A. Res 61/106.

# 4 Genes, identity and clinical ethics under conditions of uncertainty

*Rebecca Wolf, Michael Joseph Young, Michael Ashley Stein and Harold J. Bursztajn*

## 1. Introduction

Completion of the Human Genome Project has made it possible to more accurately assess some risks of disease prior to the presentation of clinical symptoms and to better evaluate responses that individuals might have to particular therapeutics. Consequently, the age of genetic medicine has enormous potential for improving individual well-being as well as collective public health (US Department of Health and Human Services, 2010). As with any technological advance, and especially one that can quite easily influence conceptions of what it means to be human, it is vital to be mindful of potential misuses, misunderstandings and pitfalls so that the promise of the genetic revolution in progress can be realised without undue costs and risks.

Despite the transformative promise of genetic-based medicine, public perceptions of its utility are often unrealistic, and many doctors lack knowledge and clinical expertise regarding the application of genomics. Popular media, coupled with natural propensities toward psychological essentialism (Gelman, 2004: 404–9) foments a determinist notion that personal genetic tests are a foolproof tool for accurately predicting individuals' biological and social futures premised on the presence of specific genes (Gould and Heine, 2012; Dar-Nimrod, 2012: 362–3; Dar-Nimrod *et al.*, 2012: 132–8). Such a Mendelian conception of genetics faithfully reflects the nature of some simple conditions with one-to-one genetic correspondences such as phenylketonuria (Scriver, 2007: 831–45), Tay-Sachs disease (McKusick and Hamosh, 2011), sickle cell anemia (Bhagat *et al.*, 2012: 36–9) and Huntington's disease (Chial, 2008). However, much of what has been learned about the heritable dimensions of complex traits indicates that the relationship of genotype to phenotype is highly polygenic, and not fully penetrant, with no single gene exhibiting a major phenotypic effect (interview with Briere, Beth Israel Deconess Medical Center, 2012; interview with Briere, Beth Israel Deconess Medical Center, 2013); experts, moreover, have found that these interrelationships may be strongly altered by environment, social context and personal behavior (Briere, Beth Israel

Deconess Medical Center, 2012; Briere, Beth Israel Deconess Medical Center, 2013; Champagne, 2012: 33). Concurrently, policymakers and public health experts are concerned that most physicians do not receive adequate training in genetics, and that the medical profession as a whole has struggled to keep pace with many of the implications raised by the genomics revolution (Fulda and Lykens, 2006: 143–7). As a result, all too many physicians are not adequately trained to effectively counsel their patients even as genetic testing becomes increasingly prevalent.

Especially without comprehensive and continuing medical education on how to understand and integrate scientific evidence arising from genomic assessments, the growing body of genetic tests and information available in clinical practice raises serious ethical issues for medical providers. This is particularly so regarding fulfilment of the basic fiduciary duty to provide adequate information to patients in order to genuinely elicit informed consent. Full discussion with patients about the implications of genomic tests, including their potential risks and benefits, is crucial to pre-test counselling and the process of informed consent. So, too, is an honest disclosure of the uncertainty about results derived from personalised medicine. Yet, fulfilment of these goals may prove elusive in the absence of comprehensive training for clinicians on how to do so.

Additional concerns arise because genetic material, present from conception, can influence how patients view themselves and how clinicians counsel them. Ultimately, the increasing use of genetics compels greater social self-awareness regarding our individual and collective desires for genomic testing and treatment, and the fact that genetic information speaks to our earliest childhood tendencies to be essentialists about ourselves. While philosophically some existentialists argue that existence proceeds essence, there is a striking tendency present from childhood to claim, quite to the contrary, that essence precedes existence (Herrmann *et al.*, 2013: 198–220). Whether such essentialism entails genetic determinism, or even fatalism, remains to be explored, as does the sustainability of intuitive dualism. Can the distinction between mind and body – with the former being a matter of indeterministic free will, even while the latter is deterministic – be maintained (Bloom, 2006)?

This chapter raises fundamental bioethical issues arising from the use, misuse and under-comprehension of genomic medicine. In doing so, it addresses the core matter of informed consent, the determination of whether to test genetically, the special case of prenatal testing and the tension between disclosing results of genetic testing and the right not to know such information. The chapter then presents a best practice case study of how clinicians are currently being trained to properly assess genetic-based information and advise their patients. Although often drawn from an American context, the issues and prospects we raise have global implications.

## 2. Informed consent

Advances in genomic information and treatments raise ethical challenges in relation to the principle of informed consent, especially when the counselling clinician lacks substantive or current knowledge.

Informed consent is best considered as an ongoing process rather than as a fleeting formality. The process should involve a conversation between clinician and patient in which the clinician honestly and thoroughly explains the benefits and risks to the patient. In turn, the patient should be empowered to ask questions and to express concerns. Ideally, informed consent plays both a preventative and constructive role. The principle serves not only to protect patients, but also to affirm the autonomy of patients; to ensure reasonable expectations; to protect the integrity of the medical profession; to foster trust between patients and providers; and to forestall abuses of power among providers (American Medical Association, 2013; Coy, 1989: 826–33; Eyal, 2012). It also can serve the heuristic function of making salient for both clinician and patient the subtle but substantial uncertainty that may remain even post genetic testing. When properly conducted, informed consent likewise makes salient the interaction between nature and nurture and between genetic endowment and the environment, rather than obscuring these connections by an undue focus on the biological presented as genetic determinism.

In the context of genomic tests and corresponding treatments – much as in other medical contexts – informed consent entails affirmative and educated agreement to participate in clinical assessments and, possibly, related subsequent therapies. Gaining adequate knowledge is at the heart of informed consent (Gutheil *et al.*, 1984: 49–51). Thus, if a physician lacks information to fully inform a patient, it is that physician's responsibility to either find such information or explain to a patient when information is unknowable. Moreover, interpreting the results of a genetic test is a complicated process, in which a practitioner must also consider the reliability and accuracy of the genetic test, confounding environmental factors and limited knowledge about the expression of a particular gene mutation, among other factors.

With regard to genetic testing, the traditional understanding of and approach to informed consent may need to be modified to comport with ambiguity associated with genetic testing. Questions that arise over informed consent in the particular context of genetic testing revolve around four key issues: (1) providing meaningful information that informs consent despite the indeterminacy and uncertainty of genetic data, including information that highlights rather than obscures genetic and environmental interaction; (2) creating criteria for disclosure or nondisclosure of primary and incidental genetic test results for patients, surrogates and others, including genetically related kin; (3) preventing misconceptions about the predictive value and significance of genetic information which, in the realm of behavioral genetics, also includes safeguarding the extent to which human choices can still be understood as autonomous, authentic and at times conflicted; and (4) mitigating potential stigma (including internalisation) and discrimination occasioned by disclosing genetic information while simultaneously protecting patients' autonomy and right to informed consent.

## 3. Determining whether to test

The advent of genetic testing as an increasingly common procedure has engendered myriad concerns for medical professionals and policymakers alike. As an initial matter, the determination of whether to test genomically has become more complex. Physicians must ask themselves whether to order a particular test based upon pre-test probability (which itself might be empirically questionable), the sensitivity and specificity of the test, and the clinical actionability of test results (again, a crucial issue on which certainty is in doubt) (Reyna and Lloyd, 2001: 2406–8). These features do not substantially differentiate genetic tests from non-genetic tests; however, given the tendency to misconstrue genomics as Mendelian, and in the absence of clinician familiarity with the discipline, determining whether to test a patient has become more fraught with external and unscientific influences. For example, physicians may fear litigation for failing to inform a patient that he has a genetic predisposition to a disease that is said to be clinically actionable in the future, or moral censure for refraining from informing a family member who may have a similar genetic predisposition to a currently clinically actionable disease or condition (interview with Saffitz, Beth Israel Deaconess Medical Center, 2012; interview with Saffitz, Beth Israel Deaconess Medical Center, 2013). Moreover, genetic testing and consequent over-explanation via reference to genetics may serve to bolster the clinical tendency to 'hang crepe' as a way of avoiding patient disappointment by lowering expectations.

Before conducting a genetic test, a physician should initially determine whether there is sufficient pre-test probability to warrant ordering a particular genetic test, the manner in which that likelihood was assessed and the way in which the results should be interpreted (Lea *et al.*, 2005: 234–40; Reyna and Lloyd, 2001: 2406–8). To avoid needlessly alarming the patient and a battery of additional unnecessary tests, a physician should consider whether a patient has unexplained symptoms that may be attributed to a genetic disease, or whether the patient has a family history of a particular disease. In the absence of guidelines or national standards, clinicians might find these tasks particularly burdensome.

Physicians must also consider their degree of responsibility for informing patients with predispositions to particular diseases that are not clinically actionable at the time tests were conducted, but become clinically actionable at some point in the future (Saffitz, Beth Israel Deaconess Medical Center, 2012; Saffitz, Beth Israel Deaconess Medical Center, 2013). As a growing field, results from genetic results may only be partially clinically actionable at a given time. In the future, as technology and knowledge of genetics progress, certain aspects of a person's genetic information may become clinically actionable (Saffitz, Beth Israel Deaconess Medical Center, 2012; Saffitz, Beth Israel Deaconess Medical Center, 2013). When adjudicating this issue, clinicians and patients should jointly consider the possibility that in some cases the outcomes of genetic testing, rather than mitigating uncertainty, might occasion even more uncertainty. Consequently, it is imperative for clinicians to consider how to optimise psychological adjustment among patients and families in settings where new genetic information may disrupt perceptions by patients and families of their identities and lives (Gilbert, 2006).

## 4. Non-invasive prenatal testing

Ethical concerns with respect to whether any particular genetic test ought to be conducted weigh heavily in the area of prenatal testing. Prenatal testing for women of advanced maternal age (i.e. above the age of 35), such as a maternal serum screening and amniocentesis, has been commonplace for decades (Schwartz-Cowan, 1994). Recent advances in technology have allowed for very early detection of genetic abnormalities:

> Massively parallel genomic sequencing, which uses a highly sensitive assay to quantify millions of DNA fragments in biological samples in a span of days and has been reported to accurately detect trisomy 13, trisomy 18, and trisomy 21 as early as the tenth week of pregnancy.
>
> (The American College of Obstetricians and Gynecologists Committee on Genetics and The Society for Maternal-Fetal Medicine Publications Committee, 2012)

While many individuals and groups celebrate such advances, such early detection has raised ethical concerns for both the medical community and disability rights advocates (Mills and Erzikova, 2012).

Non-invasive prenatal testing/non-invasive prenatal diagnosis (NIPT/NIPD) involves testing cell-free DNA from the mother's plasma to determine whether the most common aneuploidies are present. Empirical evidence has shown high levels of sensitivity with a false positive rate of less than 1 percent (Devers *et al.*, 2013: 291–5). Such testing provides opportunities for mothers to obtain information very early in pregnancy regarding potential genetic abnormalities. Such testing may also be used to determine foetal sex and foetal RhD genotype (Devers *et al.*, 2013: 291–5). Before undergoing such testing, however, it is crucial that a qualified clinician fully informs and educates patients so that patients can give genuine informed consent, and so that patients will receive the best information possible about their test results.

The National Society for Genetic Counselors (NSGC) takes the stance that NIPT/NIPD is an important and useful tool for women whose pregnancies are at an increased risk for genetic abnormalities (Devers *et al.*, 2013: 291–5). Similarly, in December 2012, The American College of Obstetricians and Gynecologists (ACOG) Committee on Genetics and The Society for Maternal-Fetal Medicine Publications Committee published a Committee Opinion about such issues. The ACOG recommends that women with an increased risk of aneuploidy, regardless of maternal age, be offered cell-free foetal DNA testing as a primary screening test. The Committee Opinion provided that cell-free foetal DNA testing should be offered to

> women aged 35 years or older, fetuses with ultrasonographic findings that indicate an increased risk of aneuploidy, women with a history of a child affected with a trisomy, or a parent carrying a balanced robertsonian translocation with increased risk of trisomy 13 or 21. It can also be used as a follow-up test for women with positive first-trimester or second-trimester screening test result.
>
> (The American College of Obstetricians and Gynecologists Committee on Genetics and The Society for Maternal-Fetal Medicine Publications Committee, 2012)

The Committee does not recommend cell-free DNA testing to low-risk women. Additionally, the Committee noted that, before undergoing such testing, it is important that a treating physician engage in an open conversation regarding informed consent and that such testing should not be routine for all pregnant women (The American College of Obstetricians and Gynecologists Committee on Genetics and The Society for Maternal-Fetal Medicine Publications Committee, 2012).

Nevertheless, disability rights, reproductive rights and justice groups have expressed concern that, if NIPT/NIPD testing is offered to an increasing number of pregnant women, then women may feel unduly coerced to undergo these examinations even if they may not have otherwise chosen to do so (Devers *et al.*, 2013: 291–5). They argue that, if genetic testing is widely available and offered to an increasing number of pregnant women, then women who otherwise may have let nature take its course will end up terminating their pregnancies due to early knowledge of a foetal chromosomal abnormality (de Jong *et al.*, 2010: 272–7; Benn and Chapman, 2010: 131–4). This is because, in their view, it is possible that parents in the very early stages of pregnancy may feel less attached to a foetus and, therefore, may feel more inclined to abort a foetus with a genetic abnormality than they would feel towards a later-term foetus (Hall *et al.*, 2009: 14–16). Conversely, this concern may be allayed by the position that early termination is generally less ethically, psychologically and physically taxing.

In addition, some disability rights advocates assert that disability is a natural matter of human variation (United Nations Convention on the Rights of Persons with Disabilities, 2006). Thus, one concern with an increased number of selective abortions based upon genetic abnormalities is that long term there may be fewer infants born with particular genetic variations, ultimately decreasing the number of individuals with specific congenital disabilities both generally and as potential counsellors to parents deciding whether to have children with those disabilities (Buckley and Buckley, 2008: 79–84; Lord, 2013). Such decrease of particular disabilities may reduce research aimed at treating such disabilities. In addition, parents who elect to carry to term a foetus with a genetic abnormality may be stigmatised by those who chose the alternative, and may struggle to access crucial services to assist a child with special needs, as has been the case in some countries with Deaf individuals who have Deaf children (Wolbring, 2002: 209–10; Tucker, 1998: 6–14; Sparrow, 2002). Therefore, simply offering early-term genetic testing to all pregnant women, as recommended by the ACOG, could result in an increased number of selective abortions, make it even more difficult for parents and individuals born with disabilities to access crucial services from insurance providers and increase stigma of individuals with disabilities in society. On the other hand, it may be argued that an appropriate response to these concerns would be to heighten public education efforts and augment the availability of disability services as a counter-balance to the use of genetic testing.

## 5. Disclosure versus the right not to know

By way of general principle, the American Medical Association has stressed that '[w]ithholding medical information from patients without their knowledge or consent is ethically unacceptable' (American Medical Association, 2006). The American College of Physicians Ethics Manual similarly recommends that '[i]nformation should be disclosed whenever it is considered material to the patient's understanding of his or her situation, possible treatments, and probable outcomes' (American Medical Association, 2006). Consequently, disclosure of information relevant to the health and well-being of patients has been regarded as ethically obligatory in clinical and research settings.

Similarly, disclosing the nature and implications of genetic tests to patients, and making shared decisions about what will be done with information garnered from those examinations, are essential parts of informed consent. Yet, the precise parameters of the obligation to disclose in these settings have been a source of debate among ethicists and practitioners. The uncertainty that exists over the boundaries of disclosure in the arena of genetic knowledge stems largely from the high prevalence of incidental and secondary findings and the indeterminacy and variable utility of genetic information, including 'variants of unknown significance' (Grist *et al.*, 2008: 199–217; Fogel, 2011: 347–52). These matters have been amplified as whole-exome sequencing and genome-wide association studies have become more prevalent in research and clinical practice (Aronson *et al.*, 2012: 713–19; Katsanis and Katsanis, 2013; 415–36).

Genome-wide association studies, which seek to correlate particular phenotypes (observable traits) with particular genetic variants, rely on comparison of sequenced whole-genome information from individuals with a particular trait of interest to whole-genome information from individuals without that trait. The goal in such studies is to identify a particular genetic variant that may be associated with a trait of interest (Katsanis and Katsanis, 2013; 415-26). Since such tests scan thousands of genetic loci, there exists a distinct possibility of incidentally discovering particular genetic variants that correspond to risks of developing a disease, such as *BRCA1*, a strong risk-factor for breast cancer (Krier and Green, 2013: 23).

This raises the question of whether such results should be disclosed to participants in a study, even if the findings in question lie far afield of the intended scope of the study. How should the possibility of such incidental findings be conveyed prior to testing? Given the patterns of inheritance of genetic variants, is there a duty to disclose information with the possibility of associated risks to family members? Additionally, given the sheer volume of information obtained in such genetic tests, complete disclosure of all information might seem impossible. This places practitioners in the difficult position of having to decide not only whether and when genetic information ought to be reported, but also how to do so while balancing other practical obligations.

Incidental findings have been defined as those with potential clinical significance that arise 'unrelated to the purpose or variables of the study' or genetic test utilised (Illes *et al.*, 2006: 783–4). However, knowledge of such information might be important for the health or knowledge of the patient. Recognising the lack of clinical consensus over how to handle such information, the American College of Medical Genetics and Genomics appointed a working group to examine this issue (Green *et al.*, 2013: 565–74). The Working Group recommended in March 2013 that genomic information ought to routinely be provided to the 'ordering clinician who can place them into the context of that patient's medical and family history, physical examination and other laboratory testing' and 'be reported without seeking preferences from the patient and family' (Green *et al.*, 2013: 565–74).

The Working Group recommendations, which advise clinicians to request and disclose genetic information about specific conditions that may be beyond the explicit purpose of a given test, raise a host of ethical and social questions. First, are the Working Group recommendations themselves at odds with clinicians' responsibility to respect and protect patient preferences? Suppose a patient undergoes testing for genes associated with familial hypercholesterolemia (*LDLR*; *APOB*; *PCSK9* genes) and wishes not to know if she is a carrier of a genetic variant associated with hereditary breast and ovarian cancer (*BRCA1*; *BRCA2* genes). Does the recommendation to override the patient's preference not to know, and to disclose this information nonetheless, constitute an affront to the patient's autonomy? Second, which criteria are to be used to determine which genetic variants merit or do not merit disclosure?

Full explication of what level of risk ought to be regarded as the threshold for reporting deserves further analysis. Given the rapid pace at which the field of clinical genetics is advancing, clinicians may consider maintaining a dynamic database of patients' genetic information, which can be used for ongoing monitoring and reporting of felt risks should a particular variant be found to have clinical utility many years after initial testing. Yet, this possibility raises the question of how patients might justifiably consent to this type of monitoring without advanced knowledge of the nature and scope of the conditions that will warrant further tests. Another issue raised by these recommendations is whether the practice of mandatory reporting ought to extend to family members as well. Carried out to its full conclusion, it would seem that the 'prevention of harm' motive behind disclosure would argue in favor of such reporting. Others may argue that concerns for patient privacy should override this possibility.

In a preface to their recommendations, the Working Group specifically addressed the first of these points, explaining that the fiduciary duty by clinicians to prevent harm 'supersedes concerns' about violating patient preferences and autonomy (Green *et al.*, 2013: 565–74). The underlying concern here is that patients might be viewed as bearing ethical obligations to find out information that may allow for otherwise inevitable harms to be prevented and which may significantly enrich decisions about health and well-being. Given the inherent subjectivity in determining what constitutes harm, however, questions remain regarding the ethical valence of forcing information on patients who may have expressed wishes not to receive that information. The theoretical bases for these recommendations thus warrant further investigation.

## 6. Training tomorrow's health care team in genomics

To maximise clinicians' familiarity and ability to deal effectively with these issues, introducing clinicians to the practical uses and ethical complexities of genetic technologies should ideally begin during training. The approaches taken by different medical schools, specialty societies and residency/post-graduate training programmes toward these ends have varied in scope and substance. While some medical schools have taken it upon themselves to incorporate such knowledge into their curricula, generally speaking, the extent to which medical students are educated about genomics is not sufficient for practical use in the clinical setting. Almost all programmes teach molecular pathology (genetics), but most do not teach genomics. Indeed, several studies have found that medical schools and residency training programmes do not include adequate training in genomics, (Haspel, 2013: 125–9) and that future physicians in medical schools and residency programmes lack 'practical training' in medical genetics or rate their knowledge of genetics as poor, and identify that they need more training in genomics (Bell *et al.*, 2007: 441–5).

Nevertheless, there are a number of promising initiatives underway in medical training and practice design to address these limitations. The field of pathology has been among the leaders in adapting and redefining its role in light of the ascendance of genomic technologies. This goal was underscored at the October 2012 Banbury Conference, which aimed to define the future of pathology within the context of genetic medicine (Tonellato *et al.*, 2011: 668–72). Participants identified 'the need to introduce next-generation sequencing and whole-genome technologies topics into medical student and pathology resident education' (Tonellato *et al.*, 2011: 668–72).

Leaders in the field of pathology argue that pathologists are best equipped to serve as experts in genetic medicine because pathologists are adroit in clinical laboratory testing, and also have better access to patient samples (Tonellato *et al.*, 2011: 668–72). Further, pathologists are generally trained in principles of quality control and assurance, as well as method validation, all of which are instrumental in genomic testing (Tonellato *et al.*, 2011: 668–72). Interpretation of such genetic testing and diagnosis of the results of genetic testing fits squarely within the purview of pathology, which traditionally has interpreted medical tests and has diagnosed illness. Geneticists also specialise in interpretation of genetic testing, but because there are more pathologists than there are geneticists currently practising in the United States, training pathologists to interpret genetic tests can augment the limited supply of clinicians qualified in this area (Uscher, 2013; Klein and Kant, 2006: 1603–4; Cooksey *et al.*, 2005: 439–43).

Beth Israel Deaconess Medical Center (BIDMC) is one of the pioneer pathology programmes instituting a mandatory genetics curriculum. BIDMC developed a series of three lectures – a general overview of genomics, genomic testing methods and a discussion of ethical concerns (Haspel, 2013: 125–9). Additionally, participating residents were required to conduct their own research in the medical literature and to present their findings. Residents were also given the opportunity to undergo genetic testing themselves. The purpose of such an exercise was to provide an appreciation to residents of the emotional effects that genetic testing has on a patient. BIDMC trainers found the above exercises to be quite effective in educating pathology residents about the technicalities of genetic testing and additionally in providing residents with an appreciation for the ethical, social and emotional concerns associated with genetic testing (Haspel, 2013: 125–9). Although physicians who choose pathology as a specialty are better known for being research-focused than patient-centered, this innovative programme potentially could provide knowledge while also nurturing empathy for what genetic information may mean for the clinicians with whom the pathologist consults and to the patient whose genetic information is at issue.

Another pioneer in this area, Stanford University, created a training programme for residents in genomics. Faculty at Stanford developed a series of ten lectures about genomic pathology, which were made available on YouTube in 2012 (Schrijver *et al.*, 2013: 141–8). Lectures touch upon subjects such as methods for measuring and manipulating DNA, next-generation sequencing (NGS) methods and microarrays, application of molecular pathology and genomics, and policy concerns, such as ethical, regulatory and commercial issues (Haspel *et al.*, 2012: 287–93).

Despite the efforts of BIDMC, Stanford University and other such pathology residency programmes, the majority of pathology residency training programmes do not provide comprehensive training in genomics to residents. One survey demonstrated that, as of spring 2010, approximately 70 per cent of pathology residency programmes did not include genomics as a component of their training programmes (Klitzman *et al.*, 2013). Pathology residency programmes surveyed about their desire to provide such training to their residents explained that the absence of such training is primarily due to financial barriers and lack of faculty with adequate knowledge of genomics (Haspel *et al.*, 2012: 287–93). Directors of such residency programmes indicated that online modules would be the most effective tool in helping to train pathology residents in genomics.

In 2010, BIDMC pathologists published *A Call to Action* in an effort to raise awareness of the need for medical genetics training in the pathology community and the importance of incorporating genetics into the medical curricula (Haspel *et al.*, 2010: 832). The paper argues that the medical profession lags behind the technology and business communities in the field of genomics (Haspel *et al.*, 2010: 832).

An outcome from the *Call to Action* paper was the establishment of a national working group – Training Residents in Genomics (TRIG) (Haspel *et al.*, 2012: 287–93). Created through the Pathology Residency Directors Section (PRODS) of the Association of Pathology Chairs (APC), the TRIG Working Group was established in the summer of 2010 to facilitate the education of pathology residents in genomics and consists of experts in molecular pathology, genetic counselling and medical education (TRIG Working Group, 2012). The group involves numerous organisations related to residency training, genetics and pathology, including the Academy of Clinical Laboratory Physicians and Scientists, American Society for Clinical Pathology, American Society for Investigative Pathology, Association for Molecular Pathology, Association of Pathology Chairs, Pathology Residency Program Directors Section, Undergraduate Medical Educators Section, College of American Pathologists, Intersociety Council for Pathology Information, National Coalition for Health Professional

Education in Genetics, National Society of Genetic Counselors, and US and Canadian Academy of Pathology (Haspel *et al.*, 2012: 287–93).

The first major goal of the TRIG Working Group is to broaden and improve pathologists' knowledge of genomics through expanding training for pathology residents and for practising pathologists. A second major goal of the TRIG Working Group is to educate those in the field about the importance of training pathology residents in genomics. A third goal of the TRIG Working Group is to incorporate questions pertaining to genetics in the pathology resident in-service exam (RISE) (Haspel *et al.*, 2012: 287–93). TRIG aims to increase training of genomics testing among pathologists so that the medical specialty of pathology can serve as leaders in the area of genomic testing (interview with Haspel, 2012; interview with Haspel, 2013). The TRIG Working Group initially created a series of lectures that can be used by training programmes to supplement an already existing molecular pathology curriculum for residents, to teach pathology residents about genomics (American Society for Clinical Pathology, 2013). Such projects have helped to advance developing, implementing and evaluating genomics training for pathology residents at the national level.

TRIG was recently awarded a grant from the National Cancer Institute for $1.3 million over five years beginning in September 2012. This sizable grant will provide the TRIG Working Group with the resources necessary to expand the TRIG programme. In collaboration with the American Society for Clinical Pathology (ASCP), TRIG is currently in the process of developing day-long workshops, which comprise team-based learning and small lectures, online modules and a 'train the trainer' book, which will assist attending physicians to educate pathology residents in genomics (American Society for Clinical Pathology, 2013). Training modules and workshops will be designed and led by an interdisciplinary team, which will include genetic counselors, medical geneticists and pathologists so that the content of the workshops and courses will include a variety of professional perspectives. TRIG utilises Knowles's principles of adult learning, which focus on a 'need to know' approach, emphasising the importance of such knowledge for future clinical application. RISE will continue to be a helpful tool for the TRIG Working Group to determine the efficacy of their training programme and will be used to evaluate the degree to which the training has been implemented effectively on a national level (Haspel *et al.*, 2012: 287–93). Perhaps a next step would be to examine whether the BIDMC approach, which integrates knowledge with empathy, can be expanded upon internationally and can include an emphasis on increasing clinicians' self-awareness of potential pitfalls and misunderstandings inherent in genomic information.

## 7. Conclusion

It is worth noting that, when it comes to informed consent, as clinicians implement processes relative to genetic information, we cannot assume that effective communication of genetic testing information is simply a function of the doctor knowing enough about genetics to communicate. Since even as children we are essentialists, it is not surprising that we identify ourselves with our genes, with our core fantasies of who we are, and with our visions of who our children will be. These tendencies are intertwined with what we imagine about the relationship between our genes and ourselves. When it comes to identity, insecurity is not tolerated, and uncertainty and complexity tend to be avoided via denial and reductionism. Thus, the ethical problem arises – are we mature enough, and do we know ourselves well enough, to be able to use the fruits of the bountiful harvest of genetic information? Can we maintain doubt and make responsible choices in the face of our desires for certainty about our genes and ourselves? Perhaps also for our own denial of death, genetic determinism may be misunderstood as providing a *via regia* for our own immortality.

The rapidly expanding role of genetic information in health care and society underscores the great need for further empirical work on how clinicians and patients can speak freely, effectively and honestly about what we know about genes, what our ideals about and desires for genetic certainty and reductionism may be, and why uncertainty may nonetheless persist. Any comprehensive solution to the problems posed in this chapter will be multidimensional, involving not only physicians acting at the bedside, but also policymakers, medical educators, public health officials and other stakeholders who are empowered to enact structural changes that can reinforce proper uses of genetic tools and to encourage sound interpretations of genetic information in the face of continued innovation and daunting complexity.

## References

The American College of Obstetricians and Gynecologists Committee on Genetics and The Society for Maternal-Fetal Medicine Publications Committee (2012) *Committee Opinion* 545.

American Medical Association (2013) 'Informed Consent', available at: www.ama-assn.org//ama/pub/physician-resources/legal-topics/patient-physician-relationship-topics/informed-consent.page [accessed 20 July 2013].

American Medical Association (2006) 'Opinion 8.082 – Withholding Information from Patients', available at: www.ama-assn.org//ama/pub/physician-resources/medical-ethics/code-medical-ethics/opinion8082.page [accessed 8 July 2013].

American Medical Association, American College of Physicians (2006) 'The Physician and the Patient', available at: www.ama-assn.org/ama/pub/physician-resources/medical-ethics/about-ethics-group/ethics-resource-center/education al-resources/federation-repository-ethics-documents-online/american-college-physicians/acp-physician-and-patient.page [accessed 11 July 2013].

American Society for Clinical Pathology (2013) 'Training Residents in Genomics', National Institutes of Health, available at: www.ascp.org/TRIG [accessed 19 August, 2013].

Aronson, S. J. *et al.* (2012) 'Communicating New Knowledge on Previously Reported Genetic Variants' *Genetics in Medicine* 14(8): 713.

Bell, M. A. *et al.* (2007) 'The Current Status of Medical Genetics Instruction in US and Canadian Medical Schools' *Academic Medicine* 82: 441.

Benn, P. A. and Chapman, A. R. (2010) 'Ethical Challenges in Providing Noninvasive Prenatal Diagnosis' *Current Opinion in Obstetrics and Gynecology* 22(2): 131–4, available at: www.med.upenn.edu/timm/documents/Benn2012 DISCUSSION.pdf [accessed 17 July 2013].

Bhagat, S., Patra, P. K. and Thakur, A. S. (2012) 'Association between XmnI Polymorphism and HbF Level in Sickle Cell Disease Patients from Chhattisgarh' *International Journal of Biomedical Sciences* 8(1): 36–9.

Bloom, P. (2006) 'My Brain Made Me Do it' *Journal of Culture and Cognition* 6: 1–2.

Interview with Briere, L. MS, Genetic Counselor, Beth Israel Deaconess Medical Center (20 February 2012 and 24 April 2013).

Buckley, F. and Buckley, S. (2008) 'Wrongful Deaths and Rightful Lives – Screening for Down Syndrome', *Down Syndrome Research and Practice* 12(2): 79–84, available at: www.down-syndrome.org/editorials/2087/editorials-2087.pdf [accessed 17 July 2013].

Champagne, F. A. (2012) 'Interplay Between Social Experiences and the Genome: Epigenetic Consequences for Behavior' *Advances in Genetics* 77: 33.

Chial, H. (2008) 'Mendelian Genetics: Patterns of Inheritance and Single-gene Disorders' *Nature Education* 1(1).

Cooksey, J. A., Benkendorf, J. and Blitzer, M. G. (2005) 'The State of the Medical Geneticist Workforce: Findings of the 2003 Survey of American Board of Medical Genetics Certified Geneticists' *Genetics in Medicine* 7(6): 439.

Coy, J. A. (1989) 'Autonomy-Based Informed Consent: Ethical Implications for Patient Noncompliance' *Physical Therapy* 69(10): 826–33, available at: www.physther.org/content/69/10/826.full.pdf [accessed 20 July 2013].

Dar-Nimrod, I. (2012) 'Postgenomics and Genetic Essentialism' *Behavioral and Brain Sciences* 35(05): 362.

Dar-Nimrod, I., Zuckerman, M. and Duberstein P. R. (2012) 'The Effects of Learning about One's Ogenetic Susceptibility to Alcoholism: A Randomized Experiment' *Genetics in Medicine* 15(2): 132.

de Jong, A. *et al.* (2010) 'Non-invasive Prenatal Testing: Ethical Issues Explored' *European Journal of Human Genetics* 18(3): 272–7, available at: www.ncbi.nlm.nih.gov/pmc/articles/PMC2987207 [accessed 17 July 2013].

Devers, P. L. *et al.* (2013) 'Noninvasive Prenatal Testing/Noninvasive Prenatal Diagnosis: The Position of the National Society of Genetic Counselors' *Journal of Genetic Counseling* 22(3): 291.

Eyal, N. (2012) 'Informed Consent', *The Stanford Encyclopedia of Philosophy* (Fall), Zalta, S. N. (ed.), available at: http://plato.stanford.edu/entries/informed-consent [accessed 20 July 2013].

Fogel, B. L. (2011) 'Interpretation of Genetic Testing: Variants of Unknown ignificance' *Continuum* 17: 347.

Fulda, K. G. and Lykens, K. (2006) 'Ethical Issues in Predictive Genetic Testing: A Public Health Perspective' *Journal of Medical Ethics* 32(3): 143.

Gelman, S. A. (2004) 'Psychological Essentialism in Children' *Trends in Cognitive Sciences* 8(9): 404.

Gilbert, D. (2006) *Stumbling on Happiness.* London: Vintage.

Gould, W. A. and Heine, S. J. (2012) 'Implicit Essentialism: Genetic Concepts Are Implicitly Associated with Fate Concepts', *PLoS ONE* 7(6): e38176.

Green, R. C. *et al.* (2013) 'ACMG Recommendations for Reporting of Incidental Findings in Clinical Exome and Genome Sequencing' *Genetics in Medicine* 15: 565.

Grist, S. A., Dubowsky, A., and Suthers, G. (2008) 'Evaluating DNA Sequence Variants of Unknown Biological Significance' *Methods in Molecular Medicine* 141: 199.

Gutheil, T. G. Bursztajn, H. and Brodsky, A. (1984) 'Malpractice Prevention through the Sharing of Uncertainty: Informed Consent and the Therapeutic Alliance' *New England Journal of Medicine* 311: 49.

Hall, A., Bostanci, A. and John, S. (2009) 'Ethical, Legal and Social Issues Arising from Cell-free Fetal DNA Technologies', In: Appendix III to the report, *Cell-free Fetal Nucleic Acids for Noninvasive Prenatal Diagnosis.* Cambridge: PHG Foundation 14–6, available at: www.phgfoundation.org/download/ffdna/ffDNA_appendix.pdf [accessed 17 July 2013].

Interview with Haspel, R., MD (23 March 2012 and 4 June 2013).

Haspel, R. L. *et al.* (2010) 'A Call to Action: Training Pathology Residents in Genomics and Personalized Medicine' *American Journal of Clinical Pathology* 133: 832.

Haspel, R. L. *et al.* (2012) 'TRIG on TRACK: Educating Pathology Residents in Genomic Medicine' *Personalized Medicine* 9(3): 287.

Haspel, R. L. (2013) 'Teaching Residents Genomic Pathology: A Novel Approach for New Technology' *Advances in Anatomic Pathology* 20(2): 125.

Herrmann, P. A., French, J. A., DeHart, G. B. and Rosengren, K. S. (2013) 'Essentialist Reasoning and Knowledge Effects on Biological Reasoning in Young Children' *Merrill-Palmer Quarterly* 59(2): 198.

Illes, J. *et al.* (2006) 'Ethics: Incidental Findings in Brain Imaging Research' *Science* 311: 783.

Katsanis, S. H. and Katsanis, N. (2013) 'Molecular Genetic Testing and the Future of Clinical Genomics' *Nature Reviews Genetics* 14(6): 415.

Klein, R. D. and Kant, J. A. (2006) 'Opportunity Knocks: The Pathologist as Laboratory Genetics Consultant' *Archives of Pathology and Laboratory Medicine* 130(11): 1603.

Klitzman, R. *et al.* (2013) 'Attitudes and Practices Among Internists Concerning Genetic Testing' *Journal of Genetic Counseling* 22: 90.

Krier, J. B. and Green, R. C. (2013) 'Management of Incidental Findings in Clinical Genomic Sequencing' *Current Protocols in Human Genetics*, Chapter 9, Unit 9: 23.

McKusick, V. A. and Hamosh, A. (2011) 'Online Mendelian Inheritance in Man', United States National Institutes of Health [accessed 10 July 2013].

Lea, D. H., Williams, J. and Donahue, M. P. (2005) 'Ethical Issues in Genetic Testing' *Journal of Midwifery and Women's Health* 50(3): 234.

Lord, J. E. (2013) 'Screened Out of Existence: The Convention on the Rights of Persons with Disabilities and Selective Screening Policies' *International Journal of Disability, Community and Rehabilitation* 12(2), available at: www.ijdcr.ca/VOL12_02/articles/lord.shtml [accessed 17 July 2013].

Mills, C. B. and Erzikova, E. (2012) 'Prenatal Testing, Disability, and Termination: An Examination of Newspaper Framing' *Disability Rights Quarterly* 32(3).

Reyna, V. F. and Lloyd, F. J. (2001) 'Genetic Testing and Medical Decision Making' *Archives of Internal Medicine* 161: 2406.

Interview with Saffitz, J., MD, PhD, Pathologist, Beth Israel Deaconess Medical Center (6 March 2012 and 15 May 2013).

Schrijver, I., Natkunam, Y., Galli, S. *et al.* (2013) 'Integration of Genomic Medicine into Pathology Residency Training: The Stanford Open Curriculum' *Journal of Molecular Diagnostics* 15(2): 141–8.

Schwartz-Cowan, R. (1994) 'Women's Roles in the History of Amniocentesis and Chorionic Villus Sampling', in Rothenberg, K. and Thomson, E. (eds) *Women and Prenatal Testing: Facing the Challenges of Genetic Technology*. Columbus: Ohio State University Press.

Scriver, C. R. (2007) 'The PAH Gene, Phenylketonuria, and a Paradigm Shift' *Human Mutation* 28(9): 831.

Sparrow, R. (2002) 'Culture and Choice: Two Models of Culture and the Cochlear Implant Controversy' *Proceedings of the 2nd Victorian State Deaf Conference*, 'Different Views... One Vision', Victorian Council of Deaf People, 4–5 May. Note 32, available at: http://profilesarts.wpengine.netdna-cdn.com/rob-sparrow/files/2012/10/rsparrow-vcod-paper.pdf [accessed 20 July 2013].

Tonellato, P. J. *et al.* (2011) 'A National Agenda for the Future of Pathology in Personalized Medicine: Report of the Proceedings of a Meeting at the Banbury Conference Center on Genome-era Pathology, Precision Diagnostics and Preemptive Care: A Stakeholder Summit' *American Journal of Clinical Pathology* 135: 668–72.

TRIG Working Group (2012) 'Lecture Materials from the TRIG Working Group: Training Residents in Genomics', available at: www.pathologytraining.org/pdfs/uscap_trig/TRIGcompiled.pdf [accessed 11 July 2013].

Tucker, B. P. (1998) 'Deaf Culture, Cochlear Implants, and Elective Disability' *Hastings Center Report 00930334*, 28(4): 6–14. Hastings: Blackwell Publishing, available at: JSTOR.

United Nations Convention on the Rights of Persons with Disabilities, (2006) G.A. Res. 61/106, Article 3(d), *Publishing on the Internet*, available at: www.un.org/disabilities/documents/convention/convention_accessible_pdf.pdf [accessed 17 July 2013].

Uscher, J. (February 2013) 'Increasing the Ranks of Medical Geneticists', *Association of American Medical Colleges Reporter*, available at: www.aamc.org/newsroom/reporter/feb2013/329004/geneticists.html [accessed 21 July 2013].

US Department of Health and Human Services (2010) 'Genetics Education and Training of Health Care Professionals, Public Health Providers and Consumers: Draft Report of the Secretary's Advisory Committee on Genetics, Health, and Society', available at: http://oba.od.nih.gov/oba/sacghs/sacghs%20draft%20genetics%20education%20and%20training%20report.pdf [accessed 21 July 2013].

Wolbring, G. (2002) 'Science and Technology and the Triple D (Disease, Disability, Defect)', in Rocco, M. C. and Bainbridge, W. S. (eds) *Converging Technologies for Improving Human Performance*, 209–210. Arlington, VA: WTEC, Inc., available at: http://wtec.org/ConvergingTechnologies/1/NBIC_pre_publication.pdf#page=220 [accessed 20 July 2013].

## Note

For critical readings, comments and suggestions, we thank Oren Asman, Lauren Briere, Richard Haspel, Mona Indargiri, Sydney Levine, Jeffrey Saffitz, Tom Shakespeare and Anita Silvers; we thank Karel Mazanec for research assistance.

# 5 The use of genetic information outside of the therapeutic health relationship

## An international perspective

*J. Rosel Kim, Shahad Salman and Yann Joly*[1]

## 1. Introduction

Genomic research is progressing rapidly, resulting in the introduction of new increasingly sophisticated genetic tests and assays. With scientific, technical and academic advancements in this discipline, our capacity to predict individuals' future health or to uniquely identify them via their genetic data is improving significantly (Zhen *et al.*, 2004: 183; Homer *et al.*, 2008; Gymrek *et al.*, 2013: 321–324). These privacy concerns have added to the existing concerns that progresses in genomics were giving rise to potential discriminatory practices that could negatively affect human rights and access to important socio-economic goods. According to early surveys, several third parties situated outside of the initial therapeutic or medical research relationship have indeed shown growing interest in human genetic data (Erwin *et al.*, 2010: 1081–1093; Low *et al.*, 1998: 1632–1635; Billings *et al.*, 1992: 476–482).

For example, multiple studies have demonstrated the existence of discriminatory practices affecting individuals tested for, or with a family history of, Huntington's disease in multiple spheres of social interactions (insurance, employment, adoption, etc.) (Bombard *et al.*, 2012: 217–226). However, outside of this well-known highly penetrant monogenic condition and of a small number of similar genetic conditions, the existing evidence is limited and not easy to interpret (Joly *et al.*, 2013: 25). The use of genetic testing for identification purposes (i.e. uniquely identifying individuals through their genetic markers) has a longer history in some fields, such as criminal investigations, where it is now perceived as acceptable and has even become quite routine within certain legally defined boundaries (Rothstein and Talbot, 2006: 153).

1 The authors are particularly grateful for the editorial assistance of M[e] Ida Ngueng Feze. The authors also wish to acknowledge the financial support of Genome Canada and Genome Quebec.

Beyond its impact on human rights, the use of genetic information by third parties may raise other specific social, ethical and legal issues. For example, the use of genetic marker as predictor of a behavioural trait is not particularly reliable and would likely lead to decisions that would not only be discriminatory but also scientifically inaccurate (see, for example, Loos, 2012: 2–226).

This chapter uses a comparative approach to present an international legal and ethical overview on the use of genetic information by third parties outside of the therapeutic or health research relationship. After introducing some basic concepts, this chapter will identify the legal and policy approaches put forward by different countries to govern access to genetic data and prevent abuses. This legal overview will be followed by a closer look at the existing experience of genetic discrimination and at the ethical issues it has generated in developed countries. This section will also discuss key legal cases involving the use of genetic data by third parties.

The comparative approach used throughout the chapter aims to give a broad overview of various incidents involving the use of genetic information outside of the therapeutic and research context and solutions put forward in different jurisdictions to address it. Due to the vast amount of legal and ethical documents on genetic discrimination, this review does not pretend to be exhaustive.

## 2. Context

### *2.1 Definitions and concepts*

Defining genetic information has been proven difficult and even impossible as it results in either a too narrow or too broad definition (Rothstein, 1999: 33–37). Furthermore, genetic information is sometimes defined differently across jurisdictions, creating a lack of coherence at the international level. Genetic information can result from a DNA-based test, family history and genetic test results obtained from research, hospital clinic or direct-to-consumer internet diagnostic services. It can help predict the likelihood of future illness with various degrees of accuracy (Rothstein and Joly, 2009). Genetic information can also uniquely identify an individual if it is sampled and processed without human error (Jobling and Gill, 2004: 735–751).

An important rising concern related to the use of genetic information is genetic discrimination. Genetic discrimination can be defined as differential treatment of an individual based on his genetic characteristics (Pfeffer *et al.*, 2003: 420). It occurs for example when 'genetic data is being used to deny a person equal treatment or equal opportunities' (Hendriks, 2002: 87) to access a social good, such as insurance and employment. Genetic discrimination has also been defined in different ways depending on social, legal, cultural or scholarly contexts (Joly *et al.*, 2013: 25). For instance, lawyers have referred to it as 'legal-illegal (illicit) discrimination' (Otlowski *et al.*, 2007: 367–396), and insurers rather refer to 'rational actuarial discrimination' (Nowlan, 2002: 195–196). In the insurance context, 'actuarial discrimination' is considered a necessary part of the risk assessment process that allows the determination of the insurance premium to be paid by the applicant. In fact, many insurers and insurance associations consider that genetic information should not be treated differently from other types of health data in the insurance underwriting process. Traditionally, the personal insurance industry has always relied on data regarding health status including family history (most of this information being hereditary in nature, hence 'genetic') to underwrite insurance policies (Adjin-Tettey, 2013).

This type of argument from the insurance industry raises a question as to whether genetic information is a unique, more sensitive type of health data that should be treated differently from other types of health data. This belief that genetic information is different and deserves greater protection is known as 'genetic-exceptionalism' (Otlowski *et al.*, 2012: 442). The debate on the relevance of genetic-exceptionalism has been going on for many years without a clear conclusion. Genetic data seems to have some distinguishing features (familial and social in nature, predictive of future health, uniquely identifying, etc.) but upon closer look many of these are actually shared with other types of health or personal information (for example, cholesterol test, HIV status, fingerprints or retina scan, etc.) (Lemmens, 2000: 369; Hoffman, 2010: 38–52).

### 2.2 Genetic discrimination: ethical and social issues

There are different social, ethical and legal issues regarding the use of genetic information by third parties outside of the therapeutic or health research relationship.

First, in a context where human error can occur while administering DNA testing and where genetic tests are predictive models which greatly differ in terms of accuracy and usefulness, the genetic information processed can be inaccurate. For instance, there are many reported cases of technical negligence leading to the production and use of faulty DNA evidence in criminal proceedings (Rothstein and Talbot, 2006: 153). One such case took place in 2012 in the United Kingdom where a man was wrongfully charged with rape after a plastic tray used to collect his DNA sample was not properly disposed of but rather reused in the analysis of a swab taken from the rape victim. In this case, the human error was luckily identified almost two weeks before the man was charged, but he nevertheless had to spend five months in custody before being released (Morris, 2012). Therefore, issues such as the possibility of human or technical error should be taken into consideration when relying on DNA in criminal cases. In the United States, a review of cases has shown erroneous forensic experts' testimony in 63 per cent of wrongful convictions (Saks and Koehler, 2005: 892; Giannelli, 2011: 166).

Interpreting genetic information resulting from genetic testing, apart from well-known highly penetrant monogenic conditions, is another important challenge to the utility of genetic information outside the research context. It should also be recognised that genetic information on complex diseases is, at best, only predictive of a greater probability for a condition or a disease to occur. For instance, some genetic tests use predictive markers such as APOE 4 to identify risks of early onset Alzheimer disease, but only a portion of those carrying the mutations will develop it (Williamson *et al.*, 2009: 80). The use of this information thus becomes problematic when relied upon outside the research context to restrict access to important social goods and opportunities. For example, an individual could be prevented from accessing insurance because an insurer erroneously relied upon the results of a predictive genetic test that has not been sufficiently validated, or has a very weak clinical utility.

The use of genetic information outside of the therapeutic context can, therefore, create important social and ethical concerns. Genetic discrimination can in some instances even prevent individuals from obtaining important socio-economic goods (insurance, financial loan, housing and car) or employment. Theoretically, it can also impact one's familial planning by restricting access to adoption. Incidental cases of healthy individuals being denied a life insurance policy or refused an employment opportunity have made the headlines for the past 20 years (*New York Times*, 1981; Levine, 1995; Kahn, 1998; Borger, 2000; Salleh, 2005). However, a more systematic study of the phenomenon in the field of life insurance has demonstrated that these high-profile cases were limited to rare instances involving a small number of well- known genetic diseases (Joly *et al.*, 2013: 25).

Issues related to genetic information can lead to stigmatisation of an individual and in some cases of his family members as well. For example, in the context of hereditary breast cancer, the social impacts have been numerous and stigmatised the entire Ashkenazi Jewish community. Stigmatisation can also manifest itself if a specific group is over-represented when genetic information is collected for law enforcement purposes such as in the context of a criminal investigation or for immigration purposes. In addition, the use of genetic data by third parties can have a negative psychological impact on the individual subject of the information, leading to anxiety, embarrassment and in more serious cases to depression.

All of these issues suggest that the use of genetic information outside of the therapeutic or research context will likely have an impact on fundamental human rights, such as the right to privacy and the right to equality. To address human rights concerns and mitigate the effect of the ethical and social issues associated with genetic discrimination, countries have responded to the risk of genetic discrimination through different legal and policy approaches.

### *2.3 Legal and policy approaches*

A variety of approaches have been developed internationally and nationally to limit the use of genetic information by third parties or to prohibit genetic discrimination directly. Each approach arises from a particular socio-cultural and historical context. Studying this context provides some explanation on the choices made by the policymakers. Some countries have adopted legal instruments (convention, laws, regulations, etc.); others have preferred not to specifically address the issue of genetic discrimination in their laws.

Policies and regulations developed by various national governments can be grouped under five main approaches: human rights, prohibitive, limitative, moratorium and status quo. A proprietary approach that consists in considering genetic information as the personal property of an individual has also been proposed (Wagner, 2012: 485). However, because it is not very widespread and has been strongly criticised in the literature, we will not discuss it in detail in this section (Dove, 2011: 252–263). Some countries have chosen to combine elements from different approaches to regulate the use of genetic information, as will be further demonstrated for example in the case of Germany.

It should be noted that these approaches have been adopted to address cases where genetic information is used by a third party to predict future health (for example in the context of the risk assessment for an insurance contract). When DNA is collected and genetic information is used for identification purposes, it is generally regulated through context-specific laws (e.g. as immigration acts, criminal codes or laws on biobanks for criminal identification purposes, etc.).

#### *2.3.1 Human rights*

The human rights approach stems from the field of international human rights law (Joly *et al.*, 2010: 355). Different international and European Union human rights norms have included genetics as a ground of illicit discrimination. The United Nations Educational, Scientific and Cultural Organization (UNESCO) issued a Declaration on the Human Genome and Human Rights (1997) where it explicitly forbade genetic discrimination: 'No one shall be subjected to discrimination based on genetic characteristics that is intended to infringe or has the effect of infringing human rights, fundamental freedoms and human dignity' (UNESCO General Conference Resolution 1997: section 6). At the regional level, the UN's Economic and Social Council also issued a Resolution in 2004 called Genetic Privacy and Non-discrimination, where it called on states to take measures against 'the misuse of genetic information leading to discrimination' (UN Economic and Social Council 2004: section 5). The European Union has taken a similar stance by enacting legislation that specifically addresses genetic information. The Council of Europe's Convention on Human Rights and Biomedicine prohibits discrimination on the basis of 'genetic heritage' (Council of Europe Convention on Human Rights and Biomedicine 1997: section 11). It has recently adopted an additional protocol to the Convention on Human Rights and Biomedicine concerning genetic testing for health purposes, where it reaffirms prohibition of discrimination based on genetic heritage and characteristics (Council of Europe Additional Protocol to the Convention on Human Rights and Biomedicine 2009). In 2000, the European Union also went further by adopting its Charter of Fundamental Rights (Charter of Fundamental Rights of the European Union 2000), in which 'genetic features' were included as a ground against illicit discrimination, providing the possibility for contravening national laws to be invalidated (Otlowski *et al.*, 2012: 442).

At the national level, an example of the human rights approach can be found in the French civil code, which restricts the examination of a person's genetic characteristics to medical purposes and scientific research only (C. civ, article 16–10 2004-800). It should be noted that France uses a number of approaches as this disposition of the Civil Code also embodies a prohibitive approach.

### 2.3.2 *Prohibitive*

The prohibitive approach is reflected in laws that specifically prohibit access to, or use of, genetic information in (or outside of) specific circumstances. Austria, Belgium and Norway are some of the first countries in Europe to have prohibited use of genetic testing for insurance purposes (Lemmens, 2000: 369). For instance, the Norwegian legislation not only prohibits the use of genetic information outside the health service but also prohibits asking whether a genetic test has been done (Act of 5 December 2003 No.100). Ireland's Disability Act also prohibits the use of genetic information. It states that 'a person shall not engage in the processing of genetic data in relation to' a policy insurance, employment, etc. (Disability Act 2005 No.14 of 2005).

In the US, in the absence of a universal health care system, genetic discrimination remains an important concern. At the federal level, the Genetic Information Nondiscrimination Act (GINA), adopted in 2008, prohibits health insurers and group health plans from using genetic information as a ground to deny health coverage or charge higher premiums (GINA section 101 (a) (3)), section 101 (b)). However, this law does not apply to life or long-term insurance (GINA section 101 (c) (1)). It also does not apply to members of the US military, federal employees under the Federal Employees Health Benefit Plans and employers of fewer than 15 employees. GINA and its provisions are discussed in greater detail in Section 3. Following the adoption of GINA, the state of California went further by adopting the California Genetic Information Non-discrimination Act (CalGINA), which not only protects against genetic discrimination in employment and health insurance but also applies in other contexts such as mortgage-lending for housing and medical emergency services and care (Wagner, 2011). In addition, the US Health Insurance Portability of the Accountability Act prohibits 'discrimination against individual participants and beneficiaries based on health status' (29 USC: section 1182), including genetic information (Lemmens *et al.*, 2004: 4).

In Germany, the Human Genetic Examination Act (2009) prohibits insurers from requiring applicants to undergo genetic testing. Nonetheless, German insurers are allowed to access insurance applicants' genetic test results previously conducted only when the insurance policy amount is over €300,000. Hence, this is an example of how different approaches (here the prohibitive and the limitative approaches further discussed below) were used in conjunction within the same piece of legislation in order to nuance the use of a broad prohibition on the use of genetic information in the insurance context.

### *2.3.3 Limitative*

This approach has also been referred to as the 'fair limits approach' (Joly *et al.*, 2010: 355) or as a 'two tiered system' (Adjin–Tettey, 2013: 25). It aims to limit the insurer's use of genetic information by permitting access to and use of genetic information only for insurance policies beyond a certain monetary value as determined by legislation (as previously seen with the German legislation).

In Sweden, this approach has been extended beyond genetic testing to also regulate insurers' access to family history (Genetic Integrity Act No.351 of 18 May 2006). The law explicitly prohibits the use of genetic information of an individual for the purpose of contracting a new insurance policy or for its renewal or amendment unless the amount insured is above a certain basic coverage determined by law (Genetic Integrity Act No.351 of 18 May 2006). Such an approach creates two categories of insurance contracts that contribute to guarantee access to basic insurance coverage for all while at the same time preventing potential abuses from applicants who know more about their future health risks than their insurer (Armstrong *et al.*, 2003: 359–364; Bombard and Lemmens, 2010).

### *2.3.4 Moratorium*

The 'moratorium approach' is a flexible approach mostly adopted in common law tradition countries often at the instigation of the insurance industry (Lemmens *et al.*, 2004: 5). This mechanism is an alternative to legislation and enables the insurance industry to self-regulate its members (Adjin–Tettey, 2013: 27). A moratorium will sometimes involve the participation of the government to oversee compliance and effectiveness, adding credibility to the process.

In the UK, there is no legislation directly addressing insurers' use of genetic information, but rather a moratorium (i.e. voluntary agreement) between the industry and the government. The UK has a moratorium (Concordat and Moratorium on Genetics and Insurance) between the government and the Association of British Insurers since 1997 (last renewed in 2012 for five years) (Department of Health UK, 2012), which prevents life and critical-illness insurers from accessing genetic test results if the amount of insurance coverage is under £500,000 for life insurance and £300,000 for critical illness and long-term care insurance (Otlowski *et al.*, 2012: 446).

#### *2.3.5 Status quo*

Some countries chose to maintain the legal status quo and not to specifically regulate the use of genetic information by third parties. A justification for this approach could be that the use of genetic information is already adequately protected in these countries under traditional human rights laws or that their government has adopted a wait-and-see approach towards genetic discrimination while avoiding genetic exceptionalism (Lemmens *et al.*, 2004: 6). The status quo approach has the advantage of leaving sufficient room for industry to self-regulate (Joly *et al.*, 2010: 355). For example, the Canadian Life and Health Insurance Association (CLHIA) issued a position statement, stating that insurers 'would not require an applicant... to undergo genetic testing'. However, according to this position statement, if testing has already taken place and the information is available to the applicant or his physician, this information must be disclosed to the insurer (Canadian Health and Life Insurance Association, 2010). The CLHIA has explicitly stated that its members would seek such information as they do for any other type of health information concerning an applicant (Canadian Health and Life Insurance Association, 2010). In Canada, federal and provincial human rights law (i.e. right to equality and privacy laws) could offer some degree of protection against genetic discrimination. However, the full extent of this protection remains to be determined by Canadian tribunals and courts of justice as very few cases have surfaced so far on this matter (*Quebec (Commission des droits de la personne et des droits de la jeunesse) v. Boisbriand (City)*, 2000).

## 3. Use of genetic information by third parties

### *3.1 Insurance*

Genetic discrimination gained prominence as an issue in the 1980s and the 1990s when reports emerged about insurers accessing potential applicants' genetic information to determine their predisposition to develop a small number of monogenic health conditions (Hudson *et al.*, 1995). A recent review of over 20 years of studies on genetic discrimination has also revealed that 42 per cent of these studies are based on evidence of genetic discrimination considered to be of serious concern (Joly *et al.*, 2013: 11). In Europe, health insurance has not been a major aspect of genetic discrimination concerns, because many European countries provide publicly funded health insurance to their citizens (Otlowski *et al.*, 2012: 442). The lack of evidence of actual genetic discrimination was one of the reasons given by the UK government, in 2008, for not enacting specific legislation on genetic information (Wilkinson, 2009: 2). However, there are a small number of documented cases of genetic discrimination in insurance. Those discussed in the Canadian and US case law will be presented in this section.

As mentioned previously, the US has enacted the Genetic Non-Discrimination Act (GINA) which prohibits a group health plan from demanding or requesting results of a genetic test. Since health insurance in the United States is mainly provided through employers' group insurance contracts, many insurance claims involve employers. GINA also has a specific provision prohibiting genetic discrimination in employment outside of the insurance context, which will be discussed in the following sub-section on employment. The US examples reported in this sub-section occurred prior to or did not involve GINA.

Genetic discrimination insurance cases in the US date back to the 1960s and 1970s, when it became known that some insurers denied coverage or charged a higher premium and employers discriminated against African Americans due to their predisposition to sickle cell disease (Severo, 1981). These early incidents of genetic discrimination were based on an assumption of the existence of a group predisposition, a classification made without any direct confirmation, through individual examination or testing (Grégoire *et al.*, 2009: 1–32). This led Congress to pass the National Sickle Cell Anemia Control Act in 1972, prohibiting states from imposing mandatory sickle cell testing that targeted African Americans (Pub. L. 92–294 1972) Thereafter, in the 1980s and 1990s, largely unverified reports were published documenting additional genetic discrimination cases, where insurers refused health or life insurance underwriting, or claims based on applicants' genetic information obtained through genetic testing or family history (Billings *et al.*, 1992).

In a 1990 Canadian (Quebec) case, a widow unsuccessfully claimed her husband's life insurance benefits after his death following a car accident (*Audet v. L'Industrielle-Alliance*, 1990). The Quebec Superior Court had to determine whether the deceased, being a carrier of the gene for myotonic dystrophy, could be considered to have 'physical or mental abnormalities' within the information requested in the insurance application form. The court considered that these terms included his genetic condition, although he was an asymptomatic carrier, and ruled that the failure to disclose it constituted a legal omission that made the contract void under the civil code of Quebec.

Cases involving discrimination for underwriting purposes are likely to arise more often with the advent of more accessible direct-to-consumer tests. The media of the province of Ontario recently reported the case of a Canadian woman who was refused insurance because of her family history of Huntington's disease (Weeks, 2012; Adjin-Tettey, 2013: 4). She felt compelled to undergo a genetic test because she needed insurance to open her chiropractor clinic. Once informed of her negative test results, the company accepted to insure her. This is an interesting example where an individual can feel pressured to undergo a genetic test to access insurance needed to operate a business although the insurer did not formally ask her to take the test.

### *3.2 Employment*

Employers are interested in a prospective or current employee's genetic information for four main reasons: (1) to know a worker's predisposition to develop certain diseases due to the work environment, (2) to identify employees who could pose a risk to the security of their co-workers, (3) to determine job candidates at higher risk of developing specific diseases or (4) to recruit individuals with specific work-related health qualities or traits. A recent Canadian survey has reported that several tested or untested asymptomatic people at risk for Huntington's disease have experienced genetic discrimination when seeking employment (Bombard *et al.*, 2009: 338). There are several reported cases of genetic discrimination in the context of employment; most of them are found in the US.

Prior to GINA, the first case that confirmed the right of an employee to be free from undergoing a non-consensual genetic test occurred in 1998. In this case, the 9th Circuit Court determined that a research lab at the University of California, Berkeley that collected blood and urine samples from all its employees and screened them for sickle cell anemia, syphilis and pregnancy without their knowledge had violated the Civil Rights Act (*Norman-Bloodsaw v. Lawrence Berkeley Laboratory*, 1998). This is the only appellate-level decision about pre-employment genetic screening in the pre-GINA era. The court determined that this was discriminatory, because testing for sickle cell anemia, syphilis and pregnancy targeted women and African-Americans. Similarly, under the Americans with Disabilities Act, the Burlington Northern Santa Fe Railroad Company had to pay over $2.2 million to its employees in a settlement, because it had required them to undergo genetic testing for predisposition to carpal tunnel syndrome (*Burlington Northern and Santa Fe Railway Company Co v. White*, 2002).

Since 2008, US law, under Title II of GINA, specifically prohibits genetic discrimination in employment. A US case that received some media attention is that of Pamela Fink, who claimed she was dismissed from her job once she had disclosed that she underwent a double mastectomy after testing positive to the BRCA2 gene mutation associated with an increased predisposition to develop breast cancer (Friedman, 2010). She alleged that she received negative reviews from her employer a day before her second surgery and was later dismissed. As a result, she filed the 'first publicly identified case of its kind' (Vorhaus, 2010) alleging breach of GINA against her former employer in 2010. Fink's case is still unresolved and has yet to go to trial (Frisch, 2013).

In 2013, the US Equal Employment Opportunity Commission (EEOC) filed a genetic discrimination lawsuit alleging violation of GINA and the Americans with Disabilities Act, which was settled out of court (US Equal Employment Equality Opportunity Commission, 2013a). In this case, a temporary employee who applied for a permanent position at Fabricut Inc. was given an offer of permanent employment and requested to see a contracted medical examiner for drug and physical tests. She was required to provide information on whether certain diseases were in her family medical history. Thereafter, the medical examiner requested that she sought additional evaluation from her personal physician to determine if she suffered from carpal tunnel syndrome (CTS). Although she provided the test results demonstrating that she did not have CTS, her employer rescinded the job offer.

The EEOC charged Fabricut Inc. with violation of GINA based on their requirements to receive family medical history and for requiring genetic testing for carpal tunnel syndrome. Fabricut settled the case out of court and agreed to a payment of $50,000 to the employee and implementation of new company policies to prevent similar incidents in the future (US Equal Employment Equality Opportunity Commission, 2013b). Even though the outcome of this case was through a settlement, it seems to give employers and their managers important notice to take concrete steps to ensure that any pre-employment medical queries do not violate the anti-discrimination protection now provided by GINA. This case also underlines the challenges that employees may face when requested to undergo medical examination in order to secure employment. They may not be fully aware of their rights (to not undergo genetic testing or provide family history of disease) or may fear a loss of income or of an opportunity to gain employment if they do not comply with such requests.

Another recent case involving GINA has demonstrated some of the limits of the investigative power of the Equal Employment Opportunities Commission. In *Equal Employment Opportunities Commission* [EEOC] *v. Nestlé Prepared Foods* (2012), a worker alleged a violation of GINA because he was required to undergo a 'fitness-for-duty' examination during which the physician was provided access to his family medical history. The EEOC requested information on every examining physician used by Nestlé and employment data (including reasons for non-hire or termination) in order to investigate the allegations of genetic discrimination. However, when Nestléx refused to provide the records, the court concurred and denied EEOC's subpoena request, which it qualified as 'wide-reaching' and lacking relevance (*Equal Employment Opportunities Commission* [EEOC] *v. Nestlé Prepared Foods 2012*; Dreiband and Marchall, 2013: 45).

Although the scope of information requested by EEOC seemed quite broad, the court's decision led some scholars to wonder whether GINA has the potential to fully protect people and underlined its limited reach (Wagner and Vorhaus, 2012). It may be very difficult for the EEOC to effectively conduct an investigation if it cannot have full access to documents related to the allegations or complaints being investigated. However, it could also be viewed in a more positive light as an invitation to EEOC to find a more appropriate balance between the need to protect job applicants against discrimination and the need to respect well recognised privacy law principles.

Another recent case was filed by the EEOC against Abatti Group where there is evidence that at least one applicant for a permanent position was denied hire after the company had requested his family medical history. The employee in question was a temporary worker who had to undergo drug and physical tests and reluctantly disclosed he was once hospitalised for a heart condition. The Abatti Group considered him disabled and dismissed him (US Equal Employment Opportunity Commission 2013c). The case is still at its early filing stage.

Finally, a Maryland court has declared that GINA was not valid against congressional authority under the principle of sovereign immunity (*Culbreth v. Washington Metropolitan Area Transportation Authority*, 2012). These post-GINA cases provide limited contextualisation to fully understand the scope of GINA and its effectiveness at preventing genetic discrimination. This may be due to the fact that the law is still at its early implementation stage, and questions as to what can be considered genetic information, and the extent of the associated liability, are still to be settled (*Poore v. Peterbilt Bristol, LLC, et al.*, 2012, establishing that genetic information under GINA does not include the genetic information of the employee's wife).

There are also important legal cases outside of the US. For instance, in 2003 a German teacher underwent a medical examination to secure permanent government employment (as usually done for all German civil servants). Despite passing her medical examination, she was barred from holding the position due to her familial medical history; her father had Huntington's disease. The German Administrative Court reversed the Hessen region school board's decision and confirmed her permanent employment, underlining that her familial medical history only amounted to a higher probability of developing the disease and not a certainty (Burgermeister, 2003: 827a; Schmitz and Wiesling, 2006: 297). This case received important media coverage in Germany and stirred the genetic discrimination debate (Lemke, 2005: 31). Germany has since then adopted legislation prohibiting employers and insurers from requesting genetic information.

Also, In Australia, in the 2005 case of *Trindall v. NSW Commissioner for Police*, ([2005] FMCA 2 (Australia)) an Australian court found that the police department had discriminated against an officer who was placed on restricted duties because of his status as an asymptomatic sickle cell carrier. Since then, the Australian government modified the Disability Discrimination Act to include 'genetic predisposition' in its definition of disability (Australian Human Rights Commission, 2008). These various decisions demonstrate some of the challenges involved in preventing genetic discrimination in the context of employment.

In Canada, the only available case of genetic discrimination in employment is one in which several employers refused candidates or dismissed employees on the basis of their medical exam (not based on genetic testing) which revealed health conditions such as Crohn's disease (*Quebec Commission des droits de la personne et des droits de la jeunesse v. Montreal (City)*, 2000). Based on the interpretation of human rights law in Canada, the Supreme Court has expanded the term 'handicap' in s 15 of the Quebec Charter of Human Rights and Freedoms to include perceived disabilities (*Quebec (Commission des droits de la personne et des droits de la jeunesse) v. Boisbriand (City)*, 2000). In Canada, where a status quo approach towards genetic discrimination prevails, this decision is interesting as it alludes to the possibility to assert a claim of genetic discrimination on the basis of 'handicap', an established ground of prohibited discrimination. However, the use of this possible defense against genetic discrimination remains to be seen through legal cases that would specifically involve employment discrimination on the basis genetic information.

## 4. Law enforcement

### *4.2 Criminal*

Governments have relied on genetic information in criminal law enforcement since the late 1980s to identify suspects or revive cold cases (Matejik, 2009: 53–90; Jobling and Gill, 2004). In crime control, the gathering of genetic material can be used in identifying suspects, exonerating wrongfully convicted individuals and as a mean of deterrence for criminals who recidivate (Campbell, 2011: 55). Many countries have also begun collecting DNA samples of suspects, arrestees or detainees who have not yet been charged, rapidly expanding the scope of their DNA database (Simoncelli, 2006: 390–397). This subsection will present DNA banks set up for criminal control purposes in different jurisdictions and will then discuss issues related to the destruction of DNA samples and data contained therein.

#### *4.2.1 DNA banks*

Legal and policy approaches for DNA banking differ based on the population from whom genetic material is collected and the length of time it can be stored (Simoncelli, 2006: 390–397). Legislation also varies based on the acceptable methods by which DNA is collected (ex. blood draw or buccal swab) and the legal procedures (with or without judicial approval) to be followed prior to the collection of the DNA sample (Campbell, 2011: 60).

The UK has the largest forensic DNA bank in the world (Rodrigues, 2007), with over 6 million DNA profiles in the National DNA Database (NDNAD) as of 2011, of which over 1 million are from individuals who have not been convicted of a crime (Public Service, 2011). In its original programme, the NDNAD contains DNA profiles from crime scenes, suspected individuals, volunteers and any individual arrested for certain offences whether detained or not (Rodrigues, 2007). On 1 May, 2012, the *Protection of Freedoms Act* was adopted and provided for a statutory time limit beyond which DNA samples from individuals who have been arrested but not convicted (depending on the offence) must be destroyed (Government of United Kingdom, 2013).

The US federal Combined DNA Index System (CODIS) was formalised by the FBI in 1994 and contains DNA profiles from convicted individuals (the Convicted Offender Index) and from crime scenes (the Forensic Index) (Deray, 2011: 757). The National DNA Index System (NDIS) was established in 1998 and contains 'DNA profiles contributed from federal, state, and local participating forensic laboratories' (Federal Bureau of Investigation: Frequently Asked Questions on the CODIS Program and the National DNA Index System, 2013a). These two DNA Banks are managed by the CODIS Unit (Federal Bureau of Investigation: Combined DNA Index System, 2013b). There are also several large DNA databases at the state level (Roman-Santos, 2010: 283). The DNA Fingerprint Act of 2005 (42 USC c 136) allows the federal government to collect DNA samples from an arrestee or a detainee who is not a US citizen (42 USC c 136). After September 11, the Patriot Act extended the scope of DNA collection by including those charged with committing or conspiring to commit terrorist and related acts (Uniting and Strengthening America by Providing Appropriate Tools Required to Intercept and Obstruct Terrorism Act of 2001). Most recently, the US Supreme Court authorised officers to collect and store DNA from suspects arrested and brought to police custody but not yet charged with a crime (*Maryland v. King*, 2013). About 20 states in the United States already allow the collection of genetic material from not-convicted arrestees (Barca, 2013: 212). The courts have addressed the constitutionality of such practice and its associated legislation, which were upheld as seen in the state of California in the case of *Haskell v. Harris* (2012). While an injunction against DNA collection from arrestees was denied, the court ordered a rehearing en banc, meaning that the importance of the matter requires a hearing before a more than three-judge panel (*Haskell v. Harris*, 2012).

As for Canada, its National DNA Data Bank (NDDB) has been in place since 2000 (Campbell, 2011: 55–77). The NDDB maintains the Convicted Offender Index (COI) and the Crime Scene Index (CSI) (Lalonde, 2006:

40). The COI contains biological samples of convicted offenders (designated offences are listed in the DNA Identification Act (1998)) and collection must be authorised by court. The CSI consists of DNA-typing profiles of unsolved crimes (Lalonde, 2006: 40).

### *4.2.2 Issues related to the use of DNA*

The use of DNA for criminal control purposes has been expanded by the use of DNA dragnets. A DNA dragnet involves collecting samples from a large group of individuals (who may not have been charged with a crime) in order to match the DNA sample collected from a crime scene (Rothstein and Talbott, 2006: 153). For instance, in the pursuit that led to the arrest of Craig Harman (Greely *et al.*, 2006: 248–262), a dragnet was used to match a partial DNA sample found on a crime scene. Mr. Harman had thrown a brick from a bridge when he was intoxicated, which hit a truck driver and killed him instantly. When the British DNA database did not yield a match with the DNA sample found on the brick, the police conducted a partial DNA match with samples from individuals living near the crime scene. This investigation provided many matches in the Surrey area, where the crime took place, including that of Harman's brother (Greely *et al.*, 2006: 248–262). Such an example raises the question regarding to what extent the consent to provide a DNA sample can be considered voluntary when it is requested by law enforcement officers conducting an investigation (Rothstein and Talbott, 2006). These ethical questions can be raised in procedures similar to dragnets, such as familial searches where law enforcement officers can request that an individual provides a DNA sample in order to infer whether a member of her/his family has committed a crime (Rothstein and Talbott, 2006: 156).

Policies and legislations governing the collection and use of DNA in the criminal context are well developed and detailed. However, procedures and guidelines on the removal of previously collected genetic information from criminal databases and biobanks are largely underdeveloped. In the US, most states do not have specific legislation or policy on the destruction of DNA samples in such a context – as a result, most states can retain samples indefinitely, unless 'the individual's conviction is overturned or his case is dismissed or the individual is an arrestee who is never convicted or plea bargains.' Wisconsin is the sole exception to this rule and requires the removal of DNA samples once analysis has been completed (Rothstein and Talbott, 2006: 158; Wis Stat Ann, 2007, section 165).

In 2008, the European Court of Human Rights (ECHR) ruled in *S and Marper v. United Kingdom* that article 8 of the European Convention on Human Rights prevented the UK police from indefinitely storing the DNA samples of individuals who had not been convicted of a crime (*S and Marper v. United Kingdom*, 2008). Four years later, in response to the *Marper* case, the UK Parliament enacted the Protection of Freedoms Bill (Protection of Freedoms Act 2012), which is the first UK legislation on this matter.

In Canada, the Commissioner of the Royal Canadian Mounted Police is required to destroy DNA samples within 180 days if a proper authorisation for investigating from the Attorney General of Canada is not provided (DNA Identification Act 1998: c. 37 s 5.2(4)). The Commissioner must also destroy any bodily substance immediately after a person is acquitted of the offence for which the samples were collected (DNA Identification Act 1998: c. 37 s 10 (a) and (b)). This must also be done in the year following the person's discharge or three years after certain conditional discharge (DNA Identification Act 1998: c. 37 s 10 (a) and (b)).

## 5. Immigration

In the process of enforcing immigration laws, officials could be interested in using DNA tests to confirm the identity of applicants, their health status and to prove biological relationships in family reunification cases. This subsection will expose how different jurisdictions have regulated the use of genetic information in immigration and present some key legal cases of genetic discrimination in the context of immigration.

### *5.1 DNA testing in immigration laws*

DNA tests have been used since the early 1990s to assist the decision-making process of immigration authorities in family reunification cases where the information provided is considered incomplete or unsatisfactory (Taitz *et al.*, 2002: 21). At least 20 countries (including 16 European countries) have legislation allowing for this practice, including Australia, Austria, Belgium, Canada, Denmark, Estonia, Finland, France, Germany, Hong Kong Special Administrative Region of China, Hungary, Italy, Lithuania, Malta, the Netherlands, New Zealand, Norway, Switzerland, Sweden, the UK and the US (Heinemann and Lemke, 2012: 811). Each country has a set of different laws, rules and guidelines enabling immigration officers to use DNA testing in the context of family reunification. For instance, Canada and Australia have adopted a last-resort approach. DNA testing is suggested only when documents establishing the biological familial relationship are not considered credible or satisfactory (Department of Immigration and Multicultural Affairs, Australia: Family Section, 1999; Citizenship and Immigration Canada, Social Policy and Programs, 2000; Taitz *et al.*, 2002: 25).

In its 2012 report on the misuse of the right to reunification, the European Migration Network (2012) noted a slightly different approach used by authorities from Italy, Spain, the Netherlands, Luxembourg, Norway and Sweden, who may conduct DNA testing 'if a family is not able to provide any documentation to prove a relationship between the parent(s) and the child' (European Migration Network, 2012: 22). These two approaches denote the need to corroborate declarations made and underline the precedence of biological relationships over psychosocial family relationships in the reunification procedure of the above-mentioned countries.

The use of DNA testing to confirm biological relationships is more frequently done in some countries than others, but statistics are generally not made available or not disclosed (Taitz *et al.*, 2002: 25); however, the overall trend seems to be increasing. For example, Citizenship and Immigration Canada (CIC) Protection Unit estimated that there were 3,500 DNA samples to confirm the existence of a biological relationship taken in 2009 alone (LEXBASE – The International Information Network for Canadian Immigration Practitioners, 2011). In 2007, France tried to expand the use of DNA testing by introducing an immigration bill (Law on Immigration Control, Integration and Asylum 2007) that would have required immigrants to undergo DNA testing in support of their application for a visa to join family members in France. While the bill was adopted, its final version was amended to require DNA testing only for children requesting to join a parent in France. Even in such cases, testing may only be requested where there is serious doubt about the authenticity of the documents in the child's possession, the person to be identified has consented to the DNA test and an administrative tribunal has reviewed the need to use DNA for such identification (Murdock, 2008: 1511).

### *5.2 Issues related to the use of DNA in immigration*

Due to the economic situation and conflicts in some regions, documents may not be available to attest familial relationships. Therefore, in Canada, DNA testing has predominantly been required from people immigrating from Africa, Asia and the Caribbean (Canadian Council for Refugees, 2011). The use of DNA testing can therefore lead to group discrimination in the immigration process due to a more systematic DNA request for applicants or citizens from certain countries. In reunification cases, where the concept of family, as derived in the culture and religion involved, is a sociological and not necessarily biological entity (Taitz *et al.*, 2002: 26), the request for DNA testing can lead to discrimination against certain families. Discrimination against non-biological children can arise where children born through the use of genetic materials from a donation bank (via in vitro fertilisation), adopted children or those born abroad are refused the possibility to reunite with their parents.

A request for DNA testing in the immigration process by an American immigration officer abroad was unsuccessfully challenged in *Parham v. Clinton* (2009). In that case, an American citizen had two children with a non-US citizen in the Philippines (couple married in the Philippines), where he was stationed at the time. When he applied for a 'Consular Report of Birth Abroad' in order for his children to obtain US citizenship, he was required to undergo a DNA test to prove his paternity (on the basis that a consular officer can resolve doubt of paternity by requesting such test (US Department of State, Foreign Affairs Manual: s 1131.5-3(b)(4)). In order to avoid delays and the high cost of DNA tests, the plaintiff obtained an order from a US state court confirming his parental rights in respect of his biological children. When the plaintiff request was also denied by the Bureau of Consular affairs, he brought a lawsuit to the District Court of Southern Texas, alleging that the officer's request for DNA testing was unnecessary and not expressly authorised by statutes. The court dismissed his case on the basis that it did not have the power to review the decision made in his case (lack of subject matter jurisdiction) (*Parham v. Clinton*, 2009: 19). Although this case does not offer a decision on the merits of the case, it provides an interesting illustration of a situation where genetic testing could be required to grant citizenship to children of nationals who are born abroad.

In the case of *MAO v. Canada (Citizenship and Immigration)* (2003), a man was initially prevented from reuniting with one of his sons in a familial sponsorship application. The applicant, a permanent resident of Canada of Somali origin, applied to sponsor his three children born of a previous marriage in Somalia. Despite the extensive documentation provided with his application, including birth and marriage certificates, proof of support and various affidavits, the Canadian immigration officer required him and his children to undergo DNA testing. When the test results revealed that his youngest child was not his biological son, Citizenship and Immigration Canada (CIC) denied his request to sponsor that child, who was separated from his siblings. The applicant argued that, as a Muslim, he was not in a position to adopt the child because, under sharia law, the child ought to be considered his son given that he was born during his marriage and he had been cared for and treated as such since then. When rejecting the applicant's argument, the government asserted that, due to the lack of biological relationship, the child could not be considered a 'dependent child' within the meaning of the applicable legislation.

During the appeal, the Federal Court of Canada sided with the claimant (the applicant for sponsorship) and ordered the DNA test results to be excluded, on the grounds that the claimant had provided sufficient documentation attesting of his family relationship and had been constrained to undergo DNA testing in contravention with CIC's administrative guidelines requiring it to be used as a last resort (Citizenship and Immigration Canada, 2000). Thus, the court determined that CIC intruded into the claimant's privacy and coerced him into taking a DNA test that was not necessary. Although the judgment clearly recognised that the power of the Canadian immigration authority to require genetic testing was very limited, the immigration regulation has since been amended to explicitly define a 'dependent child' as a child who is a biological child or a child legally adopted (Immigration and Refugee Protection Regulations 2002: section 2(1)). This restrictive definition excludes factual, social, cultural or religious filial determinants of paternity, thereby restricting the reunification right and hindering the best interest of children to be reunited with their family, possibly going against the obligation imposed on States Parties to the Convention on the Rights of the Child (United States Assembly, Convention on the Rights of the Child: Treaty Series 1577. 3).

Since this case, other cases in Canada have questioned the discriminatory use of DNA testing in immigration for familial sponsorship. In *Mohamad-Jabir v. Canada* (*Mohamad-Jabir v. Canada (Citizenship and Immigration)*, 2008), (where the applicant refused to undergo DNA testing) and *Canada v. Martinez-Brito* (*Canada (Public Safety and Emergency Preparedness) v. Martinez-Brito*, 2012) (when DNA test results revealed no biological link between family members), applicants were successful in challenging the imposed requirement to undergo genetic testing (in contravention of the last-resort rule) and were able to reunite their family in Canada.

Canadian immigration authorities have also accepted DNA test results after the identity of a Canadian citizen was questioned by embassy representatives when she was returning home. After spending some time abroad, Suaad Hagi Mohamud was prevented from boarding her plane in Kenya because Kenyan authorities and Canadian embassy officers thought she did not resemble her passport photo. To resolve the situation, which had led to her detention in Kenya, her attorney suggested she should undergo a DNA test to prove her identity. When her DNA test results from her son and ex-husband who were in Canada at the time proved to be a match, she was finally allowed to return to Canada where she sought legal relief with the Federal Courts. After almost two years of litigation, the Minister of Foreign Affairs had spent over 1.5 million in legal fees and was criticised by Canadian media. The situation was resolved through an out-of-court undisclosed settlement (Cohen, 2012). Although some of the facts that led to this particular lawsuit suggest caution in extrapolating from the results, it does demonstrate the importance given by Canadian immigration authorities to DNA testing as an identification tool. It also underlined the concern that immigrants from certain countries may still be subject to discriminatory immigration practices, notwithstanding their acquisition of citizenship status.

## 6. Conclusion

The use of genetic information is no longer limited to health care and medical research fields. Third parties have demonstrated a clear interest and ability to use genetic information outside of the therapeutic or health research relationship. This comparative overview has shown that the use of genetic information by insurers, employers and law enforcement agencies has led to cases of genetic discrimination, which raises different ethical, technical, scientific, legal and social issues.

The reliance upon genetic testing for the prediction of one's health or likelihood of illness has shown considerable scientific limitations. The use of DNA testing can also be controversial because of the errors that can occur in its interpretation or administration. For instance, in criminal law enforcement, a familial search can turn up anywhere between a 'zero to a thousand hits' (Barca, 2013: 510) in matches, depending on the size of the DNA database. In immigration cases, decisions based on DNA can be problematic where there are cultural differences, where families can have diverse origins, or where test results are the result of technical or human error (Karlsson *et al.*, 2007: 144). Thus, the use of genetic information by third parties outside of the therapeutic or health research relationship can raise important issues, especially when it can prevent someone from getting access to insurance or employment, deny the right for due process or prevent citizens or permanent residents from reuniting with family members.

Several national jurisdictions have proposed different avenues to limit or mitigate the effect of the use of genetic information by third parties under a human rights, limitative, moratorium or prohibitive approach. Some countries have maintained the status quo in this matter. There is currently little data available on the effectiveness of these various approaches and on the potential negative impact or adverse consequence that they may have. In fact, insurers have not yet legally contested many of these new regulations aimed at preventing them from accessing genetic information. In the UK, Canada and Australia, insurers still have the possibility to access genetic information in some circumstances. With the enactment of GINA, US employers are, for now, the third parties that are most likely to be refused access to genetic information.

In the context of the use of genetic information for law enforcement, the UK was forced to revise its national DNA bank policy and legislation after the European Court of Human Rights' decision that samples of individuals not convicted of a crime could not be kept indefinitely. On the contrary, in the US, courts have confirmed law enforcement's power to collect DNA from suspects and non-convicted arrestees. Finally, at least 20 countries have enacted legislation concerning DNA testing for family reunification purposes in immigration. Regulations have mostly accepted DNA testing in the absence of a conclusive, more traditional proof of filiation or as a last-resort option. However Canadian immigration authorities have in some cases used this option very liberally to require genetic testing in cases where it was not justified by the circumstances. In this matter, Canadian courts have clearly defined the very limited application of the last-resort approach for immigration officials.

In summary, this chapter has demonstrated that the perceived ease of access to and richness of genetic information need to be measured against the background of individual or collective rights found in human rights laws (for example, the right to equality, the right to privacy) and the existing ethical guidelines. Specific social policies for protection of particularly vulnerable individuals (for example, individuals with a family history of Huntington's disease) should also be considered by policymakers rather than the enactment of broad prohibitions which may not always be sufficiently flexible to adequately address the evolving challenges associated with the rapid progress of genetics and genomics.

## References

Adjin-Tettey, E. (2013) 'Potential for genetic discrimination in access to insurance: Is there a dark side to increased availability of genetic information?' *Alberta Law Review* 50: 577–717 at 18 par. 38; 25.

Armstrong, K., Weber, B., FitzGerald, G., Hershey, J. C., Pauly, M. V., Lemaire, J. *et al.* (2003) 'Life insurance and breast cancer risk assessment: Adverse selection, genetic testing decisions, and discrimination' *American Journal of Medical Genetics Part A* 120(3): 359–364.

Australian Human Rights Commission, Changes to the DDA: Disability Discrimination and Other Human Rights Legislation Amendment Act 2008. Available at: www.humanrights.gov.au/changes-dda-disability-discrimination-and-other-human-rights-legislation-amendment-act-2008 [accessed 22 November 2013].

Barca, D. (2013) 'Familial DNA testing, house Bill 3361, and the need for federal oversight' *Hastings Law Journal* 64: 499–527 at 512.

Billings, P., Khon, M., De Cuevas, M., Beckwith, J., Alper, J. and Natowicz, M. (1992) 'Discrimination as a consequence of genetic testing' *American Journal of Human Genetics* 50: 476–482.

Bombard, Y. and Lemmens, T. (2010) Insurance and Genetic Information. Encyclopedia of Life Sciences (ELS). Chichester: John Wiley & Sons.

Bombard, Y., Palin, J., Friedman, J. M., Veenstra, G., Creighton, S., Bottorff, J. L. and Hayden, M. R. (2012) 'Beyond the patient: The broader impact of genetic discrimination among individuals at risk of Huntington disease' *American Journal of Medical Genetics Part B: Neuropsychiatric Genetics* 159(2): 217–226.

Bombard, Y., Veenstra, G., Friedman, J. M., Creighton, S., Currie, L., Paulsen, J. S., *et al.* (2009) 'Perceptions of genetic discrimination among people at risk for Huntington's disease: A cross sectional survey' *British Medical Journal* 338: b2175.

Borger, J. (2000). 'If you'd say I'd get fired for this, I would have laughed' *The Guardian*. 19 September. Available at: www.theguardian.com [accessed 22 November, 2013].

Burgermeister, J. (2003) 'Teacher was refused job because relatives have Huntington's disease' *British Medical Journal* 327(7419): 827a.

Campbell, L. (2011) 'Non-conviction DNA databases and criminal justice: A comparative analysis' Journal of Commonwealth Criminal Law 1: 55–77.

Canadian Council for Refugees (2011) 'DNA tests: A barrier to speedy family reunification'. Available at: http://ccrweb.ca/files/dnatests.pdf [accessed 22 October 2013].

Canadian Health and Life Insurance Association (2010) CLHIA Position Statement on Genetic Testing. Toronto: CLHIA. Available at: www.clhia.ca/domino/html/clhia/clhia_lp4w_lnd_webstation.nsf/resources/Guidelines/$file/Genetic_Testing_CLHIA_Industry_Position_2010.pdf [accessed 3 July 2013].

Citizenship and Immigration Canada, Social Policy and Programs (10 July 2000) 'Revised OP 1, Section 5 – DNA Test for Relationship' CIC OM No. 00–27.

Cohen, T. (7 November 2012) 'Canadian tax payers pay about $1.5 in Suaad Hagi Mohamud case' *The Canadian Immigration Report*. Available at: www.CIReport.ca [accessed 15 May 2014].

Department of Health (UK) (26 June 2012) 'Insurers continue to safeguard cover for those taking predictive genetic tests'. Press release. Available at: www.gov.uk/government/news/insurers-continue-to-safeguard-cover-for-those-taking-predictive-genetic-tests [accessed 22 November 2013].

Department of Immigration and Multicultural Affairs, Family Section (Australia, Author, May 1999).

Deray, E. S. (2011) 'Double-helix double-edged sword: Comparing DNA retention policies of the United States and the United Kingdom' *Vanderbilt Journal of Transnational Law* 44: 745.

Dove, E. (2011) 'The genetic privacy carousel: A discourse on proposed genetic privacy bills and the co-evolution of law and science' *Current Pharmacogenomics and Personalized Medicine* 9(4): 252–263.

Dreiband, E. S. and Marchall, A. B. (2013) Recent Developments at The Equal Employment Opportunity, paper presented, 2013 National Conference on Equal Employment Law of the American Bar Association, 3–6 April, Savannah, Georgia, at 45.

Equal Employment Opportunity Commission [US] (7 May 2013a) 'Fabricut to pay $50,000 to settle EEOC disability and genetic information discrimination lawsuit'. Press Release. Available at: www.eeoc.gov/eeoc/newsroom/release/5-7-13b.cfm [accessed 1 July 2013].

Equal Employment Opportunity Commission [US] (30 September 2013b).

Equal Employment Opportunity Commission [US] (2013c) 'EEOC sues Abatti Group for disability, genetic information discrimination'. Press release. Available at: www.eeoc.gov/eeoc/newsroom/release/9-30-13d.cfm [accessed 22 November 2013].

Erwin, C., Williams, J. K., Juhl, A. R., Mengeling, M., Mills, J. A., Bombard, Y., *et al.* (2010) 'Perception, experience, and response to genetic discrimination in Huntington disease: The international RESPOND-HD study' *American Journal of Medical Genetics Part B: Neuropsychiatric Genetics* 153B(5): 1081–1093.

European Migration Network (2012) *Focused Study: Misuse of the Right to Family Reunification*. European Commission.

Federal Bureau of Investigation (2013a) Frequently Asked Questions (FAQs) on the CODIS Program and the National DNA Index System. Available at: www.fbi.gov/about-us/lab/biometric-analysis/codis/codis-and-ndis-fact-sheet [accessed 17 October 2013].

Federal Bureau of Investigation (2013b) Combined DNA Index System. Available at: www.fbi.gov/about-us/lab/biometric-analysis/codis [accessed 17 October 2013].

Friedman, E. (2010) 'Pamela Fink says she was fired after getting a double mastectomy to prevent breast cancer'. *ABC News*, 30 April. Available at: http://abcnews.go.com/Health/OnCallPlusBreastCancerNews/pamela-fink-fired-testing-positive-breast-cancer-gene/storynew?id=10510163#.UdIX1D7F0gQ [accessed 1 July 2013].

Frisch, J. L. (2013) 'How are employers faring (in court) under GINA?' *The Emplawyerlogist* (blog post). 2 May. Available at: http://theemplawyerologist.com/2013/05/02/how-are-employers-faring-in-court-under-gina/ [accessed 2 July 2013].

Giannelli, P. (2011) 'Wrongful convictions and forensic science: The need to regulate crime labs' *North Carolina Law Review* 86: 163 at 166.

Government of United Kingdom (2013) 'Protection of Freedom Act 2012: How DNA and fingerprint evidence is protected in law'. Policy Paper. Available at: www.gov.uk/government/publications/protection-of-freedoms-act-2012-dna-and-fingerprint-provisions/protection-of-freedoms-act-2012-how-dna-and-finger print-evidence-is-protected-in-law [accessed 22 November 2013].

Greely, H. T., Riordan, D. P., Garrison, N. A. and Mountain, J. L. (2006) 'Family ties: The use of DNA offender databases to catch offenders' kin' *The Journal of Law, Medicine and Ethics* 34(2): 248–262.

Grégoire, G., Alemdjrodo, R. and Chagnon, A. (2009) 'La discrimination génétique et l'assurance-vie: les mesures de protection actuelles suffisent-elles?' *Lex Electronica* 14(1): 1–32.

Gymrek, M., McGuire, A. L., Golan, D., Halperin, E. and Erlich, Y. (2013) 'Identifying personal genomes by surname inference' *Science* 339(6117): 321–324.

Heinemann, T. and Lemke, T. (2012) 'Suspect families: DNA kinship testing in German immigration policy' *Sociology* 811.

Hendriks, A. (2002) 'Genetic discrimination: How to anticipate predictable problems?' *European Journal of Health Law* 9(2): 87–92.

Hoffman, S. (2010) 'Biometrics, retinal scanning, and the right to privacy in the 21st century' *Syracuse Science and Technology Law Reporter* 22(2): 38–52.

Homer, N., Szlinger, S., Redman, M., Duggan, D., Tembe, W., Muehling, J., *et al.* (2008) 'Resolving individuals contributing trace amounts of DNA to highly complex mixtures using high-density SNP genotyping microarrays' *PLoS Genetics* 4(8): e1000167.

Hudson, K. L., Rothenberg, K. H., Andrews, L. B., Kahn, M. J. E. and Collins, F. S. (1995) 'Genetic discrimination and health insurance: An urgent need for reform' *Science* 270(5235): 391.

Jobling, M. A. and Gill, P. (2004) 'Encoded evidence: DNA in forensic analysis' *Nature Reviews Genetics* 5(10): 739–751.

Joly, Y., Braker, M. and Le Huynh, M. (2010) 'Genetic discrimination in private insurance: Global perspectives' *New Genetics and Society* 29(4): 351–368.

Joly, Y., Feze, I. N. and Simard, J. (2013) 'Genetic discrimination and life insurance: A systematic review of the evidence' *BMC Medicine* 11(1): 25.

Kahn, J. P. (1998) 'Genetic testing and insurance'. *CNN*, 26 August. Available at: www.cnn.com/HEALTH/bioethics/9808/genetics.part2/template.html [accessed 22 November 1998].

Karlsson, A. O., Holmlund, G., Egeland, T. and Mostad, P. (2007) 'DNA-testing for immigration cases: The risk of erroneous conclusions' *Forensic Science International* 172(2): 144–149.

Lalonde S. (2006) 'Canada's national DNA data bank: A success story' *Canadian Society of Forensic Science Journal* 39(1): 40.

Lemke, T. (2005) 'Beyond genetic discrimination. Problems and perspectives of a contested notion' *Life Sciences, Society and Policy* 1(3): 22.

Lemmens, T. (2000) Selective justice, genetic discrimination, and insurance: Should we single out genes in our laws? *McGill Law Journal* 45(2): 347–412.

Lemmens, T., Joly, Y. and Knoppers, B. M. (2004) 'Genetics and life insurance: A comparative analysis' *GenEdit* 2: 1–15 .

Levine, J. (1995) 'Scientists isolate cancer gene in Jewish women. *CNN*, 30 September. www.cnn.com/HEALTH/9509/breast_cancer/index.html [accessed 22 November 2013].

LEXBASE – The International Information Network for Canadian Immigration Practitioners (2011) February Report 22(2).

Loos, R. J. F. (2012) 'Genetic determinants of common obesity and their value in prediction' *Best Practice and Research Clinical Endocrinology and Metabolism* 26(2): 211–226.

Low, L., King, S. and Wilkie, T. (1998) 'Genetic discrimination in life insurance: Empirical evidence from a cross sectional survey of genetic support groups in the United Kingdom' *British Medical Journal* 317(7173): 1632–1635.

Matejik, L. A. (2009) 'DNA sampling: Privacy and police investigation in a suspect society' *Arkansas Law Review* 61: 53–90.

Morris, S. (2012) 'Rape accused was victim of forensics error, regulator finds' *The Guardian*, 1 October. Available at: www.theguardian.com/science/2012/oct/01/rape-accused-victim-forensics-error [accessed 22 November 2013].

Murdock, T. R. (2008) 'Whose child is this?: Genetic analysis and family reunification immigration in France' *Vanderbilt Journal of Transnational Law* 41: 1503–1534.

New York Times (1981) 'Air force academy sued over sickle cell policy'. *New York Times*, 4 January. Available at: www.nytimes.com/1981/01/04/us/air-force-academy-sued-over-sickle-cell-policy.html [accessed 22 November 2013].

Nowlan, W. (2002) 'A rational view of insurance and genetic discrimination' *Science* 297(5579): 195–196.

Otlowski, M., Taylor, S. and Bombard, Y. (2012) 'Genetic discrimination: International perspectives' *Annual Review of Genomics and Human Genetics* 13: 433–454.

Otlowski, M. F. A., Stranger, M. J. A., Barlow-Stewart, K., Taylor, S. D. and Treloar, S. (2007) 'Investigating genetic discrimination in the Australian life insurance sector: The use of genetic test results in underwriting 1999–2003' *Journal of Law and Medicine* 14: 367–396.

Pfeffer, N. L., Veach, P. M. and LeRoy, B. S. (2003) 'An investigation of genetic counselors' discussions of genetic discrimination with cancer risk patients' *Journal of Genetic Counseling* 12(5): 419–438.

Public Service (4 March 2011) 'Government store DNA of over 6 million'. Available at: www.publicservice.co.uk/news_story.asp?id=15673 [accessed 28 June 2013].

Rodrigues, R. E. (2007) 'Big bio-brother is here: Wanting, taking and keeping your DNA'. Paper presented at the 2007 Annual Conference of the British and Irish Law, Education and Technology Association in Hertfordshire, 16–17 April. Available at: http://bileta.ac.uk/content/files/conference%20papers/2007/Big%20Bio-Brother%20is%20here%20-%20wanting,%20taking%20and%20keeping%20your%20DNA.pdf [accessed 22 November 2013].

Roman-Santos, C. (2010) 'Concerns associated with expanding DNA databases' *Hastings Science and Technology Law Journal* 2: 267–299.

Rothstein, M. A. (1999) 'Why treating genetic information separately is a bad idea' *Texas Review of Law and Politics* 4(1): 33–37.

Rothstein, M. A. and Talbott, M. K. (2006) 'The expanding use of DNA in law enforcement: What role for privacy? *Journal of Law, Medicine and Ethics* 34: 153.

Rothstein, M. A. and Joly, Y. (2009) 'Genetic information and insurance underwriting: Contemporary issues and approaches in the global economy' in

Atkinson, P., Glasner, P. and Lock, M. (eds), *Handbook of Genetics and Society: Mapping the New Genomic Era*. New York: Routledge, pp. 127–144.

Saks, M. J. and Koehler, J. J. (2005) 'The coming paradigm shift in forensic identification science' *Science* 309(5736): 892–895 at 892 fig.1.

Salleh, A. (2005) 'Genetic discrimination cases investigated'. *ABC Science*, 3 November. Available at: www.abc.net.au/science/articles/2005/11/03/1496914.htm [accessed 22 November 2013].

Schmitz, D. and Wiesing, U. (2006) 'Just a family medical history?' *British medical Journal* 332: 297.

Severo, R. (1981) 'Air academy to drop its ban on applicants with sickle-cell gene' *New York Times*, 4 February. Available at: www.nytimes.com/1981/02/04/us/air-academy-to-drop-its-ban-on-applicants-with-sickle-cell-gene.html [accessed 22 November, 2013] (where the author discusses cases from 1970s).

Simoncelli, T. (2006) 'Dangerous excursions: The case against expanding forensic DNA databases to innocent persons' *The Journal of Law, Medicine and Ethics* 34: 390–397.

Taitz, J., Weekers, J. E. M. and Mosca, D. T. (2002) 'The last resort: Exploring the use of DNA testing for family reunification' *Health and Human Rights* 6(1): 20–32 at 21.

US Department of State, *Foreign Affairs Manual* section 1131.5-3(b)(4).

Vorhaus, D. (2010) 'GINA in action: Woman alleges genetic test led to firing'. *Genomics Law Report*, 28 April. Available at: www.genomicslawreport.com/index.php/2010/04/28/gina-in-action-woman-alleges-genetic-test-led-to-firing/ [accessed 1 July 2013].

Wagner, J. K. (2011) 'A new law to raise GINA's floor in California' *Genomics Law Report*, 7 December. Available at: www.genomicslawreport.com/index.php/2011/12/07/a-new-law-to-raise-ginas-floor-in-california [accessed 22 November 2013].

Wagner, J. K. (2012) 'Cockamamie state laws threaten genetic rights' *Nature Medicine* 18(4): 485. Wagner notes that this property approach may not be very effective, however, because some codes have labelled genetic information as 'real property' – which, in law, means property 'limited to land and anything affixed to land', p. 485.

Wagner, J. K. (2013) 'Ninth circuit orders rehearing of *Haskell v. Harris*' *Genomics Law Report*. Available at: www.genomicslawreport.com/index.php/2013/08/19/ninth-circuit-orders-rehearing-of-haskell-v-harris [accessed 22 November 2013].

Wagner, J. and Vorhaus, D. (2012) 'The burden of enforcing GINA: *EEOC v. Nestlé* illustrates one challenge in pursuing genetic discrimination claims' *Genomics Law Report*, 20 June. Available at: www.genomicslawreport.com/index.php/2012/06/20/the-burden-of-enforcing-gina-eeoc-v-nestle-illustrates-one-challenge-in-pursuing-genetic-discrimination-claims [accessed 3 July 2013].

Weeks, C. (2012) 'Health insurance and "genetic Discrimination": Are rules needed?' *The Globe and Mail*, 1 January. Available at: www.theglobeandmail.com/life/health-and-fitness/health-insurance-and-genetic-discrimination-are-rules-needed/article4197442 [accessed 22 November 2013].

Wilkinson, R. H. (2009) 'The single equality bill: A missed opportunity to legislate on genetic discrimination?' *Studies in Ethics, Law, and Technology* 3(1).

Williamson, J., Goldman, J. and Marder, K. S. (2009) 'Genetic aspects of Alzheimer disease' *The Neurologist* 15(2): 80.

Zhen, L., Owen, A. B. and Altman, R. B. (2004) 'Genomic research and human subject privacy' *Science* 305: 183.

## Cases

*Audet v. L'Industrielle-Alliance* [1990] JQ no. 2532.

*Burlington Northern and Santa Fe Railway Company Co v. White* (2002) 364 F. 3d 789.

*Canada (Public Safety and Emergency Preparedness) v. Martinez-Brito*, 2012 FC 438.

*Culbreth v. Washington Metropolitan Area Transportation Authority*, (No. RWT-10-cv-3321 (D. MD March 20, 2012).

[US] *Equal Employment Opportunities Commission* [EEOC] *v. Nestlé Prepared Foods* No. 5:11-mc-358-JMH-REW, 2012 BL 128495 (E.D. Ky. May 23, 2012).

*Haskell v. Harris*, 669 F 3d 1049 (9th Cir. 2012).

*Maryland v. King*, 569 US___133 S.Ct. 1958, 186 L. Ed. 2d 1_ (2013) [Maryland]. Supreme Court's decision is available at: www.supremecourt.gov/opinions/12pdf/12-207_d18e.pdf.

*MAO v. Canada (Citizenship and Immigration)*, 2003 FC 1406.

*Mohamad-Jabir v. Canada (Citizenship and Immigration)*, 2008 CanLII 35720 (IRB).

*Norman-Bloodsaw v. Lawrence Berkeley Laboratory*, 135 F3d 1260 (U.S. Circuit Court of Appeals for the Ninth Circuit, 1998).

*Parham v. Clinton*, No. H-09-1105, 2009 WL 2870671 (SD Tex), 09-20681 (5th Cir. 2010) (appeal).

*Poore v. Peterbilt Bristol, LLC, et al.*, Case No.1:11CV00088 (Western District, VA April, 2012).

Quebec Commission des droits de la personne et des droits de la jeunesse v. Montreal (City) [2000] 1 S.C.R. 665.

Quebec (Commission des droits de la personne et des droits de la jeunesse) v. Boisbriand (City) [2000] 1 SCR 665.

*S and Marper v. United Kingdom*, 30562/04 [2008] ECHR 1581.

Trindall v.NSW Commissioner for Police [2005] FMCA 2 (Australia).

## Legislation

29 USC §1182 (Section 1182: prohibiting discrimination against individual participants and beneficiaries based on health status).

42 USC c 136, Subchapter III [Violence Against Women Act]; Adam Walsh Child Protection and Safety Act of 2006, PL 109–248; passed as Title X of the Violence Against Women and Department of Justice Reauthorization Act 2005, Public Law 109–162, 119 Stat. 2960.

Act of 5 December 2003 No. 100 relating to the application of biotechnology in human medicine, etc. Cf. earlier Acts of 5 August 1994 No. 56 and 12 June 1987 No. 68 section 5–8.

Additional Protocol to the Convention on Human Rights and Biomedicine concerning genetic testing for health purposes (2008) (entered into force 1 December 2009)

C. civ., art 16-10 (as modified by Loi 2004-800 of 6 August 2004, as modified on 24 March 2012).

Council of Europe, Additional Protocol to the Convention on Human Rights and

Biomedicine, concerning Genetic Testing for Health Purposes, Strasbourg, (2009). Available at: http://conventions.coe.int/Treaty/EN/Treaties/Html/203.htm [accessed 13 November 2013].

Council of Europe, Convention for the Protection of Human Rights and the Dignity of the Human Being with Regard to the Application of Biology and Medicine: Convention on Human Rights and Biomedicine, ETS. No. 164 (1997).

Disability Act 2005, No.14 of 2005, s 42 (Ireland).

DNA Identification Act, SC 1998, c 37.

European Union (2000). Charter of Fundamental Rights. Official Journal of the European Communities, OJ C 364/01 at art. 21. Available at www.europarl.europa.eu/charter/pdf/text_en.pdf [accessed 22 November 2013].

Genetic Information Nondiscrimination Act of 2008, Pub. L. No. 110–233, 122 Stat. 881 (2008).

Human Genetic Examination Act, Germany 2009, 374/09.

Immigration and Refugee Protection Regulations, SOR/2002-227 at s 2(1) (Canada).

Law on Immigration Control, Integration and Asylum. Law No. 2007-1631 of Nov. 20, 2007.

Protection of Freedoms Act 2012 (c 9), s 3 (6) (b) (UK).

Pub. L. 92-294, May 16, 1972, 86 Stat. 136.

The Genetic Integrity Act, No. 351 of 18 May 2006 (Sweden).

UNESCO General Conference Resolution 29 C/17, UNESCO GC, 29th Sess. (1997).

United Nations Economic and Social Council, E.S.C. Res 2004/9 on Genetic Privacy and Non-Discrimination.

United Nations General Assembly. Convention on the Rights of the Child. United Nations, Treaty Series 1577, 3.

Uniting and Strengthening America by Providing Appropriate Tools Required to Intercept and Obstruct Terrorism Act of 2001, Pub L 107-56, Title 5, § 503 [Patriot Act].

Universal Declaration on the Human Genome and Human Rights G.A. Res. 152, UN GAOR, 53rd Sess., UN. Doc A/53/625/Add.2 (1998).

Wis Stat Ann § 165.77 (3).

# Section 3

# The United States legislative experience

Section 3 focuses on the U.S. position and the legislative response and experience in this area. It highlights how the protection of genetic information fits within the civil rights framework of the United States and how the issue gathered momentum over the past twenty years. In examining the U.S. legal and policy response, this section details past and current legal frameworks and offers insight into the effectiveness of the existing legal protections in practice.

This section comprises three chapters, which provide a comprehensive overview of the U.S. framework in this area and draw together the historical background from which GINA was introduced, and the objectives and main provisions of GINA, as well as its effectiveness in practice and the evident gaps in protection. The first chapter, by Peter Blanck and Aisling de Paor, is entitled 'US legislative and policy response: Some historical context to GINA'. The second chapter in this section is entitled 'The Genetic Information Nondiscrimination Act (GINA) 2008' by Michael Waterstone and Anya Prince. The final chapter in this section is entitled 'Genetic discrimination in the workplace after GINA' and is written by Robert Olick.

# 6 US legislative and policy response

## Some historical context to GINA

*Peter Blanck and Aisling de Paor*

### 1. Introduction

This chapter overviews discussion of the US position, in consideration of the US helping to lead the introduction of federal-level legislation in genetic antidiscrimination law and in recognition of the importance of US and EU transatlantic dialogue in the area (Quinn and Flynn, 2012; Quinn and de Paor, 2010; Stein *et al.*, 2010; Hendriks, 1997). Our position is that, when considering law, policy, and regulation of genetic information at the EU level, it is useful to consider transatlantic perspectives, taking into account the relationship between US and EU policy and law, as well as building upon the best practices from this relationship when engaging in law and policy reform (Quinn and Flynn, 2012; Quinn and de Paor, 2010; Stein *et al.*, 2010; Hendriks, 1997). The US and the EU are addressing similar ethical and legal questions stemming from advancing genetic technology, albeit against the backdrop of different historic, cultural and political settings, as will be discussed in this chapter.

This chapter is meant to provide a social, cultural and historical perspective to the contributions in this volume. It briefly chronicles the historical and cultural background to the relevant US federal legislation, the Genetic Information Nondiscrimination Act of 2008 (GINA). It examines historical and legal views on eugenics in the nineteenth- and twentieth-century US and how such early conceptions and policies permeated the legal system, at government levels and in wider US society (Blanck, *et al.*, 2014: 867).

Indeed, as others have documented, throughout the late nineteenth century and early twentieth century, eugenics theories and practices proliferated in US society. In many ways, the historical and social background of genetics in the US set the context for modern-day concerns of genetic discrimination as a civil rights imperative, views that remain entrenched in American society. The history of eugenics has left an indelible imprint on US history, emanating in part from the now infamous US Supreme Court decision in 1927 of *Buck v. Bell* (274 US 200). Justice Oliver Wendell Holmes, Jr. wrote for the court a decision that permanently scarred US consciousness, when he said that the American genetic stable must be protected from the 'feeble-minded' likes of Carrie Buck through compulsory sterilisation. 'Three generations of imbeciles [were] enough', according to Holmes.

This chapter examines how this shameful period of US history has shaped current legislative views. In introducing GINA, this chapter also highlights the journey to passage that GINA endured through Congress and the opposition it met. Recounting is made of the Congressional hearings leading up to GINA, in which the legislation and its preceding bills were debated and contested. Finally, we offer some insights on the US experience and its significance to engaging in transatlantic dialogue with the EU on related law and policy issues going forward.

## 2. Brief historical context

Of course, the present-day conception of genetic discrimination must be considered within the larger political, social and historical context. While Mendel was busy studying inheritance patterns of peas in the late 1860s (as discussed in chapter 2), Darwin was in the Galapagos Islands in 1859, from which he hypothesised about the origin of the species and evolutionary theory (Darwin, 1859; Darwin, 1871). Such views gained popularity around the world, in the US and Europe. In 1883, Francis Galton, the renowned British scientist and cousin of Darwin, coined the phrase 'eugenics'. With this new evolutionary consciousness in the latter part of the nineteenth century, there was a rival growing concern about post-industrialisation social reforms targeted at issues such as prostitution, idleness, alcoholism, mental disease or so-called 'feeblemindedness' (Andrews 1997: 894). The application of Mendel's theories led to popular views that some 'social' conditions, diseases and traits like 'feeblemindedness' were passed on from one generation to the next, in accordance with Mendelian principles (Garver and Garver, 1994: 149). This brew of scientific theory and social reform policy provoked a number of new eugenic laws and policies in the areas of reproduction, immigration and family life. The core Mendelian principles of inheritance and Darwin's evolutionary model came together in a view of 'Social Darwinism', as a justification for eugenic policy in the US.

## 3. Social Darwinism and eugenics in the US

The eugenics movement fitted nicely with the theory of Social Darwinism. With the rise of mass immigration to the US, particularly from what were then held to be the inferior races and ethnicities (Logue and Blanck, 2010), and ongoing racial discrimination, notions thrived for survival of the fittest, advancement of superior human beings and 'rationalisations of inequality' (Kevles, 1999: 435). Social Darwinism was an easy application of evolutionary theory and natural selection, as proposed by Darwin, to the American 'melting pot' (Kevles, 1999: 435). The emerging rationale of social 'improvement' for the worthy, and the enhancement of overall society by way of promotion of desirable biological traits and characteristics and elimination of undesirable traits and characteristics, thrived in this social and historical milieu.

Social Darwinism embodied key theoretical underpinnings of the eugenics movement. Indeed, the principles of Social Darwinism, the history of eugenics in the US, and the resulting misapprehension surrounding genetic science continues to shape current regulatory thought as to genetic information in the US and informs the present ethical debates (GINA: section 2(2) and (3)). The focus on Social Darwinism and eugenics came to be tested in immigration policy and a worthy family life. But, eugenic policies and practices also were evident in daily society and in conceptions of the biologically worthy person.

In the 1920s, for instance, US state fairs known for their livestock breeding competitions came to sponsor 'Fitter Families' contests, which awarded prizes for 'Grade A individuals' in the 'human stock' category (Kevles, 1985: 62). Competition organisers assessed individuals on key indicators, such as education, occupation, race and social position: 'the completed forms were scanned for patterns of presumed inheritance' (Selden, 2005: 212). The human selection contests assessed parents and offspring, deciphering desirable inherited characteristics, physical and intellectual. Such contests presented in the daily consciousness of American life idealised perfect families, focusing on the desirable physical, mental and biological traits (Selden, 2005: 212; Minna Stern, 2002: 742–752).

In early-twentieth-century US, eugenics was accepted by Congress and in local society. In the 1990s thus began the predicable leap towards more regressive programmes of sterilisation, which also took place in Europe (Garver and Garver, 1994: 150). Sterilisation of women on the basis of genetics, typically of poor women who were viewed as less intelligent, came into law. US states introduced sterilisation laws targeting the perceived genetically defective, with justification in early developments in genetic science and patterns of inheritance. From a policy perspective, sterilisation reduced the cost to society of the unworthy (Andrews, 1997: 894). The laws 'rode roughshod over private human rights', with preference for perceived wider societal and public interests (Kevles, 2011: 328). From 1907 to 1937, thirty-two American states introduced compulsory eugenic sterilisation laws, with the objective of controlling the reproductive capacities of genetically undesirable individuals (Larson, 1999; Hyun-Myung Tan, 2009).

As mentioned, in the now infamous US Supreme Court decision, state-sponsored sterilisation in support of eugenics was endorsed in *Buck v. Bell.* Civil War veteran Justice Oliver Wendell Holmes found that

> it is better for all the world if instead of waiting to execute degenerative offspring for crime, or to let them starve for their imbecility, society can prevent those who are manifestly unfit from continuing their

> kind...the principle that sustains compulsory vaccination is broad enough to cover cutting the Fallopian tubes...three generations of imbeciles are enough.
>
> (*Buck v. Bell*, 1927)

Genetic associations of 'imbecility' were accepted at the highest court in the land, as well as the public desire to improve the US genetic pool for generations to come. '[D]espite her appeals to the highest court in the land, Carrie Buck could not be spared from the cruellest corruption of Darwin's theories' (Miller, 2007: 48). The public and high-profile endorsement of state-sponsored sterilisation was complete, and representative of public acceptance of eugenics.

In the US, as also mentioned, the eugenics movement had stark racial associations (Kevles, 2011: 327). With significant immigration – Irish, Germans, Russians and Slovaks – came widespread social prejudice. High nativism arising after the Civil War was part of a social paradigm shift from landed gentry in the south to a new multi-ethnic society of differing nationalities. The desirable ones were perceived to be 'white Protestants of Northern European Stock' and the less desirable population consisted of 'blacks and Jewish and Catholic immigrants', including the Irish, who faced strong discrimination (Kevles, 1985: 75).

The eugenic view was evident in immigration policy of the early twentieth century (Garver and Garver, 1994: 149). In 1924, the US Congress passed the Johnson Immigration Restriction Act (Garver and Garver, 1994: 149). Immigration was based on quotas established in the 1890s' census as this favoured immigration of the so-called Nordic or Anglo-Saxon population, primarily individuals from north-western Europe and Great Britain, and deterred the immigration of those from southern and eastern Europe, particularly Jewish immigrants (Ludmerer, 1972). The objectives were clear and had the aim of controlling the influx of the unwanted.

Even more recently, however, genetic discrimination has been associated with race in the US, beginning in the 1970s with the discovery of the gene associated with sickle cell anaemia, found primarily in African-American individuals. In the 1970s, federal and state governments sponsored screening policies for sickle cell anaemia that were directed towards African Americans, with a view towards identifying those carrying the gene. Even though these policies had a stated public health objective, the results were further stigmatising and discriminatory on the grounds of race, further exacerbating the isolation of African Americans in society (Mitchell and Happe, 2001: 379). To address this discrimination, in 1972 Congress passed the National Sickle Cell Anemia Control Act (Sickle Cell Anaemia 1972).

The predictable pattern of stigmatisation, eugenics and genetic determinism in US history set the table for the introduction of GINA and other civil rights laws. The following section provides an overview of the US civil rights movement and how GINA fitted into these developments.

## 4. US civil rights and disability antidiscrimination law

### *4.1 The evolution of the US civil rights movement*

After the Second World War, with the beginnings of widespread racial integration, the US entered a period of recognition of individual civil liberties, primarily on the basis of race. With widespread societal unrest, there was a growing recognition of individual civil rights. *Brown v. Board of Education* came to symbolise the testing of the prejudicial social boundaries on the basis of race in education (*Brown v. Board of Education of Topeka*, 1954). On the surface the case addressed the constitutionality of racial segregation in education, but more deeply denounced segregation in all its horrific forms (Carson, 2004). *Brown* therefore had wider significance and influence to give birth to the new field of civil rights (Carson, 2004). What followed was the beginning of a policy shift with the passage of the 1954 Civil Rights Act (Schlein, 2008–2009: 329). Of subsequent major significance was the passage of the Civil Rights Act 1964 (now passing its fiftieth anniversary) (Schlein, 2008–2009: 329). The 1964 law forbade 'employers, labor organizations, employment agencies, and other specified entities from failing or refusing to hire or discharging any individual with respect to his compensation, terms, conditions, or privileges of employment, because of such individual's race, color, religion, sex, or national origin' (Civil Rights Act of 1964).

From the Civil Rights for African-Americans came renewed calls for gender equality, which further advanced the equality and non-discrimination framework. US Supreme Court Justice Ruth Ginsburg, then a young lawyer engaged in the women's movement, was instrumental in the march towards US gender equality (Farbstein, 2013). Justice Ginsburg was a driving force behind the Women's Rights Project of the American Civil Liberties Union and litigated landmark cases on gender equality before the Supreme Court, such as *United States v. Virginia* (1996), which struck the Virginia Military Institute's male-only admission policy. The growing conception of individual liberties and rights provided the necessary link to the recognition of civil rights on the basis of disability. Thereafter, the Americans with Disabilities Act of 1990 (ADA) was signed into law, and its amendments passed in 2008 as the Americans with Disabilities Amendment Act (ADAA).

### *4.2 US disability antidiscrimination law*

The ADA is an antidiscrimination law patterned on earlier civil rights acts (Americans with Disabilities Act 1990). Endorsed by a democratic Congress and signed into law by republican President George Bush in 1990, the ADA was the first comprehensive federal disability antidiscrimination (Blanck, 2014b: 4–32; Blanck, 2014a). Also in 1990, the Human Genome Project was born in the US, as is discussed above. At this time, scientists and geneticists were embarking on the new journey to sequence the human genome. There were few genetic tests available, of which the majority were for rare diseases. The Human Genome Project would take thirteen years to complete in 2003. During this period, the US was experiencing a period of national discussion about the proper parameters of the new civil rights movement. By 2008, the ADA had been followed by the ADA Amendment Act, which broadened the rights of persons defined as disabled under the law (Americans with Disabilities Amendment Act 2008). The ADAAA had overturned a series of problematic US Supreme Court decisions (including *Sutton v. United Airlines*, 1999; *Toyota Motor Manufacturing*, 2002) that had restricted interpretation of the ADA.

It is interesting to note that the first ADA case heard by the US Supreme Court involved discrimination on the basis of asymptomatic HIV disease. In *Bragdon v. Abbott* (1998), the Court considered a defence presented by a dentist concerned about treating in his office an HIV-infected, though asymptomatic, patient. The Court found that under the ADA the health care provider must assess the potential risk based on 'the objective, scientific information available to him and others in his profession' (Blanck *et al.*, 2014: 649). Thus, the decision cannot be on the basis of prejudice or subjective beliefs about the underlying nature of the disability.

### *4.3 Note on US health care reform*

Without getting into specifics, we note that the US civil rights paradigm evolved independent of related calls for health care equality. Although genetic discrimination and other misuse of genetic technologies may be covered by the ADA, the general substantive provisions of the much broader health care debate and reform in the US are governed by separate laws and policies. The Patient Protection and Affordable Care Act has survived a constitutional test before the US Supreme Court. This US legislation and its impact on health care more generally is examined in the chapter following by Professors Waterstone and Prince. Needless to say, the development and implementation of health care reform and practice in the US is quite distinct from Europe. In addition, in the US as compared to Europe there is a distinctly different political and social health care overlay involving the issue of abortion, a woman's right to choice and in vitro genetic screening for disability or fertilisation.

Outside the employment context, the Health Insurance Portability and Accountability Act, 1996 (HIPAA) also governs whether and in what manner group health insurers may obtain or consider genetic information in health insurance coverage. HIPAA prohibits group health insurers from using genetic information to vary premiums, limit an individual's eligibility for insurance, or deny insurance coverage. HIPAA is an important piece of the puzzle to tackle genetic discrimination in health insurance. However, despite protections afforded, gaps were evident and HIPAA did not prohibit particular types of genetic discrimination. HIPAA also did not cover individual health insurance plans (Schlein, 2008–2009: 336–337).

## 5. Legislative history preceding GINA and congressional testimony

In consideration of the social and cultural history of eugenics, and the more recent evolution of the US Civil Rights paradigm, this section focuses on GINA and its legislative history. Prior to GINA, there was a patchwork of legislation in place at the state and federal levels.

### *5.1 Patchwork of federal and state protections*

Prior to GINA, different US states approached genetic discrimination differently, resulting in diverging levels of protection as well as undesirable implications for cross-state conformity. In 1991, Wisconsin was the first state to introduce legislation prohibiting health insurers from requesting genetic information and improperly using such information. Since then, many states have introduced state legislation regulating the use of genetic information. At the same time, with new laws like the ADA, there was also no comprehensive federal protection for genetic discrimination.

As mentioned, Title VII of the Civil Rights Act 1964 contains antidiscrimination protections on a number of grounds (including race, religion and sex) and in the employment context (Title VII of the Civil Rights Act 1964). But there was no reference to discrimination on the basis of genetic information (or disability). As also noted, the ADA (1990) and its amendments (2008) provided some protections against disability discrimination, for example in regard to the improper use of medical tests (which could be genetically based). Yet, there was uncertainty as to the scope and application of the existing protections as applied to genetic information. The application of the ADA to genetic antidiscrimination protections was contentious, with diverging opinions, policies and judicial interpretation (Schlein, 2008–2009; Kaplan, 1999–2000).

In 1995, the US Equal Employment Opportunity Commission (EEOC, responsible for administering the employment provisions of the ADA) issued guidance that the ADA prohibits discrimination by employers against employees based on their genetic make-up (EEOC, 1995: 902–945). Whilst the EEOC took a firm stance in favour of the ADA protecting individuals with genetic markers against discrimination on that basis in employment, the interpretation did not have the same force as a focused federal law. This point was not lost on Congress (statement of Miller, 2000). In addition, the EEOC interpretation was further limited in application by a trilogy of opinions by the US Supreme Court on the definition of disability, including *Sutton v. United Air Lines Inc.* (1999); *Murphy v. United Parcel Service Inc.* (1999); *Albertsons Inc. v. Kirkingburg* (1999). These cases limited the ADA definition of disability to those conditions that were not mitigated (decisions later reversed by the ADA Amendments Act) (Blanck *et al.*, 2014).

It turned out that US federal government employees came to have more extensive antidiscrimination protections than did private sector employees pursuant to Executive Order 13145 (2000), which governs the use of genetic information by executive departments and agencies. The Executive Order prohibited discrimination on the basis of protected genetic information in all aspects of employment in executive departments and agencies and limited federal employers' access to, and use of, genetic information. However welcomed, the scope of this Executive Order was limited to federal employees (Josefson, 2000: 468). The legislative position prior to GINA is further discussed by Prince and Waterstone in the following chapter.

Prior to GINA there also were a number of legal challenges to alleged genetic discrimination, for example in the employment context. In *EEOC v. Burlington Northern Santa Fe Railroad* (Roche, 2002: 272), which was referred to during congressional testimony in the GINA passage, the EEOC alleged unlawful genetic discrimination and settled its first court action challenging the use of genetic testing in the workplace under the ADA against the Burlington Northern Santa Fe Railroad (BNSF). The BNSF had tested its employees to identify a genetic marker for carpal tunnel syndrome to address a perceived high incidence of repetitive stress injuries among its employees. At least one employee had been threatened with discipline and possible termination for refusing to take the test. The EEOC found that the alleged genetic discrimination violated the ADA and other disability discrimination laws. As a settlement to the dispute was reached (for the sum of $2.2 million out of court on 18 April 2001), no court precedent was developed as to the applicability of the discrimination theory (EEOC press release, 2001).

In another case, *Norman-Bloodsaw v. Lawrence Berkeley Laboratory* (1998), a Title VII violation was alleged. In this case, the employer subjected its black and female employees to genetic testing for sickle cell trait, syphilis and pregnancy. The court found that the employees' claims under Title VII were valid, as the discriminatory acts of the employer targeted Title VII-protected categories of race and sex. Had there had been genetic information non-discrimination legislation at federal level at the time, it is probable that the actions of the employer in gathering this genetic information would have been forbidden (Miller, 2000).

## *5.2 Congressional hearings and testimony: behind GINA and the opposition*

GINA is the result of more than two dozen proposed bills and underwent a thirteen-year journey through Congress, encountering opposition, as well as a lack of consensus. When the first federal legislation to prevent the misuse of genetic information was introduced in 1995, stakeholders viewed the law as being forward looking, while others called it 'premature' (Hudson *et al.*, 2008: 2662). Indeed, at the time, the legislative initiatives were referred to as 'a remedy in search of a problem' (statement of Fishman, 2007). However, at this time, scientists were still making genetic discoveries and the Human Genome Project had not yet been completed. In addition, there were not many genetic tests readily available. However, science and technology were moving at a rapid pace and the potential for misuse of these new technologies was apparent. Further, in reaction to the skepticism endured in taking a pre-emptive approach, Louise Slaughter (one of the main sponsors of the legislation) referred to the absurdity of waiting for further discrimination to take place before prohibiting it (Slaughter, 2004).

These early legislative developments coincided with new fears surrounding the relatively unknown world of genetics and the fear of discrimination on the basis of genetic information. Prior to introduction of GINA, there was only limited data indicating the extent of the actual discrimination. Yet, on examination of the congressional testimony, it is apparent that passage of GINA was furthered in response to scientific developments that were seen as novel and potentially discriminatory, particularly if left unprotected by the existing legal framework (Roberts, 2010: 442). Congressional testimony referenced the rapid advances in genetic science and technology in light of the Human Genome Project and how such advances were changing understanding and treatment of disease. It also evidenced that these advances produced a myriad of ethical, legal and social implications, which could not be ignored and required appropriate legislative intervention (statement of Collins, 2001a; statement of Collins, 2001b).

During Congressional testimony, reference was made to the reality of genetic discrimination, the fear of genetic discrimination, and surveys and studies that had been carried out (prior to the introduction of GINA) (Miller, 2000). In 1998, the National Center for Genome Resources commissioned a national survey to gauge public attitudes towards genetic issues, which found that 85 per cent of those surveyed believe employers should be prohibited from obtaining genetic information about an individual's genetic conditions and predispositions to disease (The National Center for Genome Resources, 1998). The study highlighted that 36 per cent of those surveyed were not likely to take genetic tests, and 27 per cent would definitely not take such tests if health insurers or employers had a right to access the test results (The National Center for Genome Resources, 1998).

Congressional testimony by Paul Miller (EEOC Commissioner) referenced a 1998 governmental interagency report (issued by the EEOC and the Departments of Labor, Health and Human Services and Justice) (Department of Labor, Department of Health and Human Services, Equal Employment Opportunity Commission, Department of Justice, 1998). The report stated that, '[f]ederal legislation is needed to ensure that knowledge gained from genetic research is fully utilized to improve the health of Americans and not to discriminate against workers' (Department of Labor, Department of Health and Human Services, Equal Employment Opportunity Commission, Department of Justice, 1998). Although the report acknowledges that the ADA provides some level of protection against genetic discrimination, it proposes that these protections were not adequate in consideration of the rapid advances in genetic science. In this report, the Administration proposed that Congress pass legislation to ensure that discoveries generated by the Human Genome Project were used to improve health, and not to discriminate against employees or their families, and to set protections that should be included in such legislation (Department of Labor, Department of Health and Human Services, Equal Employment Opportunity Commission, Department of Justice, 1998). The report recognised gaps in protection and supported the need for a federal-level response.

Others referred to another reason for the general fear of genetic discrimination amongst the public, which was based on a general 'scientific illiteracy' on the topic (Jungreis, 2007: 211). The absence of an informed understanding of genetic science could lead to misconceptions and misinterpretation of genetics and genetic technologies (for example, a common misconception was that only genes determine disease; Rose *et al.*, 2008: 148). Yet, although most diseases have a genetic basis, disease is a complex interaction of genes and environmental elements. It was also observed that, in some cases, in accord with the historical discussion above, 'fear of genetic discrimination [was] tied to the belief that a defective gene is somehow indicative of a defective identity' (Kegley *et al.*, 2000: 200). This fear of genetic inferiority evokes a fear of discrimination on the basis of one's genetic make-up.

## 6. Genetic Information Nondiscrimination Act 2008 – an introduction

GINA was passed in 2008 and heralded as a civil rights law. The late Senator Edward Kennedy referred to it as 'the first civil rights bill of the new century', and it represented a milestone and a stepping-stone in the acknowledgement and protection of a most personal sort of information (press release, Kennedy *et al.*, 2008). GINA was to prevent discrimination in employment and health insurance, thereby facilitating the protection of such personal rights. Yet, it is also pre-emptive legislation, meaning that its objective is to prevent a new form of discrimination before it becomes widespread in the future. This is novel, in that it is a departure from prior antidiscrimination law (Roberts, 2010: 441).

Thus, the 2008 Genetic Information Nondiscrimination Act (GINA) aims to protect against discrimination in the employment context on the basis of one's genetic information (42 USC §§ 2000ff–2000ff-11 et seq. (2006); Blanck *et al.*, 2014: 867–883, from which this summary is derived). Genetic information is defined as information about:

(i) An individual's genetic tests;
(ii) The genetic tests of that individual's family members;
(iii) The manifestation of disease or disorder in family members of the individual (family medical history);
(iv) An individual's request for, or receipt of, genetic services, or the participation in clinical research that includes genetic services by the individual or a family member of the individual; or
(v) The genetic information of a fetus carried by an individual or by a pregnant woman who is a family member of the individual and the genetic information of any embryo legally held by the individual or family member using an assisted reproductive technology.

(42 USC § 2000ff(4) (2006))

Title I of the act applies to insurers and health plans, and prohibits discrimination in determining eligibility or cost of group health insurance premiums based on genetic information, such as increasing premiums for the group based on the results of one enrollee's genetic information or denying enrollment or coverage based on genetic information (29 CFR §§ 1635.4 and 1635.11 (2012)). Similarly, it places restrictions on when insurers may request or collect genetic information.

Title II of the act focuses on employers, employment agencies, labor agencies and training programmes. It prohibits the use of genetic information in the employment context, limits the acquisition of genetic information by the aforementioned entities and expressly restricts the disclosure of such information (42 USC § 2000ff et seq. (2006)).

GINA does not prohibit the collection of genetic information in all circumstances. For instance, GINA provides that it will not be discrimination when: medical enquiries and information collection complies with the family leave or similar state laws, 'the employer conducts DNA analysis for law enforcement purposes' or 'an employer inadvertently requests or requires family medical history of the employee or family member of the employee' among other exceptions (42 USC § 2000ff-1(b)(6) (2006); West, 2012). GINA protections do not apply to employers with fifteen or fewer employees. (42 USC § 2000e(b) (2006)). Further, GINA does not protect against discrimination from life insurance, disability insurance, long-term-care insurance or individual health insurance. (42 USCA. § 300gg-53 (2012)).

The EEOC issued final regulations on November 10, 2010, which clarify the interplay between GINA and other statutes (Final Regulations Under the Genetic Information Nondiscrimination Act of 2008, 75 Fed. Reg.

68,912–68,939 (Nov. 9, 2010)). The regulations note that Congress aimed to extend the protections of Title VII of the Civil Rights Act of 1964 to the area of genetic information (75 Fed. Reg. 68,926 – explaining that the law incorporates by reference the definitions, remedies and procedures of Title VII). To pursue a claim under GINA, the plaintiff first must exhaust administrative remedies. Then, the plaintiff may file a private right of action under any of several different Acts: the Civil Rights Act of 1964, 42 USC §§ 2000e-4 and 2000e-16 (2006), the Age Discrimination in Employment Act, the Rehabilitation Act, or Title I of the ADA (42 USC § 2000ff-6 (2006)).

## 7. Consideration of GINA in the European context? A transatlantic dialogue

The question arises, why consider GINA in the European context? The answer, in part, is because milieu, socio-political history and economic factors all impact the evolution of law and conceptions of disability antidiscrimination policy. GINA arose in a particular US civil rights frame within legal and human rights policy foundations different than that developed in Europe. GINA also evolved from the unique American litigious experience, as part of a history of equal rights struggles in the African-American, women's, gay and disability communities to enforce such rights.

Moreover, there are other important dissimilarities in the health insurance industry and the regulation of insurance in the US and the EU. In the US, for instance, health insurance generally is provided by private health insurers. In addition, the majority of individuals in the US obtain insurance coverage through their employers, although this trend is changing. Employers in the US have varying incentives from employers in other countries to provide health insurance for employees who are, or who may become, ill in the future (Rothstein and Knoppers, 1996: 144). In addition, health insurance obtained through employers often extends coverage to dependents, providing other incentives or disincentives to cover employees who have dependents who are ill and disabled, or who may become so (Rothstein and Knoppers, 1996: 144). Despite fundamental differences between these two jurisdictions, each is grappling with changing demographics and an aging population and workforce. As highlighted in the following section of this book, both the US and EU Member States are concerned about misuse of genetic information in the evolving landscape.

There are, of course, similarities between the US and EU in this area, particularly with reference to the historical experience of eugenics. Concepts of biological determinism were utilised by eugenicists in Europe, as was done in the US, to provide a solution to the perceived social defects of the time. In European history, the Nazi regime provides an obvious illustration of dire effects of eugenics. Others have chronicled how 'the Nazis famously misused genetic information in incredibly discriminatory, invidious, and ultimately genocidal ways' (Annas, 1999: 12). The elimination of those races, ethnicities and persons with disabilities all deemed to be inferior was premised on eugenics (Harper, 1992: 464).

Earlier in the twentieth century, with the rise of Nazism, came state-endorsed mass eugenics (Weindling, 1989; Weindling, 1993: 643). The first involuntary sterilisation law in Germany was passed in 1933, at first to sterilise the mentally and physically infirm (Garver and Garver, 1994: 150). It was a quick step to extend sterilisation policies to 'undesirable' ethnic groups, such as the Jews and Poles (Garver and Garver, 1994: 150). The infamous T4 Euthanasia Programme was initiated in 1939 in Nazi Germany, with the objective of eliminating those with physical or mental disabilities and other vulnerable members of society (Cohen, 2010: 687; Strous, 2006). But, as in the US, eugenic policies were utilised in other countries, such as in the Scandinavian countries, with a view to improving the genetic desirability of the population. In 1934, sterilisation legislation resulting in voluntary as well as compulsory sterilisation was introduced in Denmark, Norway and Sweden (Koch, 2004: 320). With hindsight, it is clear that these eugenic regimes displayed the misuse of science and technology, abridging basic human rights. Historical eugenic stigmatisation evidenced patterns of prejudice and discrimination not known before in human history. They serve as a stark warning of the misapplication of genetic science.

There are notable similarities as regards the structure of the US and the EU, although the EU is not a federal state (unlike the US) and has instead been described as a 'staatenverbund' or an association of sovereign states (Layza, 2010: 399). Both jurisdictions are closely connected states, with common goals and objectives. Accordingly, each jurisdiction has an incentive to ensure consistency and coordination for economic and other purposes, and to facilitate an efficient internal market. As illustrated in Section 4 of this book, however, there is evident a patchwork of protections amongst the EU Member States (as well as a fragmented regulatory framework at EU level).

## 8. Conclusion

The poor, ostracised, unworthy and those perceived as disabled have long been the targets of eugenic policies (Ludmerer, 1972; Kevles, 1985). This stigmatisation and discrimination based on genetic determinism, as discussed in this chapter, is the product of complex historical patterns in society. This background provides a necessary context to understand development of GINA in the US and its evolution in the legislative process.

This historical frame continues to raise questions as to the promised benefits of genetic technology and its realisation in ways that avoid another or new era of social oppression and violation of human and civil rights. This chapter hopefully has provided a brief review of the social, political and historical framework in the US behind GINA to inform similar developments in the EU. GINA is a civil rights antidiscrimination law. Although Europe has a different socio-political and cultural history vis-à-vis the US, there is much to be learned on both sides from a transatlantic dialogue examining legislative and policy frameworks in this area.

## References

Andrews, L. B (1997) 'Past as Prologue: Sobering Thoughts on Genetic Enthusiasm' *Seton Hall Law Review* 27: 893–894.

Annas, G. J. (1999) 'Genetic Privacy: There Ought to be a Law' *Texas Review of Law and Policy* 4: 9.

Blanck, P. (2014a) 'The Struggle for Web Equality by Persons with Cognitive Disabilities' *Behavioral Sciences and the Law* 32(1): 4–32.

Blanck, P. (2014b) *eQuality: The Struggle for Web Accessibility by Persons with Cognitive Disabilities.* Cambridge University Press.

Blanck, P., Waterstone, M., Myhill, W. and Siegal, C. (2014) *Disability Civil Rights Law and Policy: Case and Materials.* 3rd Edition. USA: West Publishers.

Carson, C. (2004) 'Two Cheers for *Brown v. Board of Education*' (2004) *The Journal of American History* 91(1): 26.

Cohen, M. M. (2010) 'Overview of German, Nazi and Holocaust Medicine' (2010) *American Journal of Medical Genetics* 152A(3): 687.

Darwin, C. (1859) *On the Origin of Species.* London: John Murray.

Darwin, C. (1871) *The Descent of Man.* London: D. Appleton & Co.

Farbstein, S. (2013) 'Essays in Honor of Justice Ruth Bader Ginsburg' *Harvard Law Review* 127(1): 423.

Garver, K. L. and Garver, B. (1994) 'The Human Genome Project and Eugenic Concerns' American Journal of Human Genetics 54: 148–150.

Harper, P. (1992) 'Huntington's Disease and the Abuse of Genetics' *American Journal of Human Genetics* 50: 460–464.

Hendriks, A. (1997) 'Genetics, Human Rights and Employment. American and European Perspectives' *Medicine and Law* 16: 557.

Hudson, K. L. *et al.* (2008) 'Keeping Pace with the Times – the Genetic Information Nondiscrimination Act of 2008' *New England Journal of Medicine* 358: 2661–2662.

Hyun-Myung Tan, M. (2009) 'Advancing Civil Rights, the Next Generation: The Genetic Information Nondiscrimination Act of 2008 and Beyond' *Health Matrix* 19: 63.

Josefson, D. (2000) 'Clinton Outlaws Genetic Discrimination in Federal Jobs' *British Medical Journal* 320(723): 468.

Jungreis, R. (2007) 'Fearing Fear Itself: The Proposed Genetic Information Nondiscrimination Act of 2005 and Public Fears about Genetic Information' *Journal of Law and Policy* 15: 211.

Kaplan, D. (1999–2000) 'The Definition of Disability: Perspective of the Disability Community' *Health Law and Policy* 31: 352.

Kegley, J. A. (2000) 'Confused Legal and Medical Policy: The Misconceptions of Genetic Screening' *The Journal of Medicine and Law* 19(2): 197–200.

Kevles, D. (1985) *In the Name of Eugenics: Genetics and the Uses of Human Heredity.* New York: Harvard University Press.

Kevles, D. (1999) 'Eugenics and Human Rights' *British Medical Journal* 319: 435.

Kevles, D. (2011) 'From Eugenics to Patents: Genetics, Law and Human Rights' *Annals of Human Genetics* 75: 326–328.

Koch, L. (2004) 'The Meaning of Eugenics: Reflections on the Government of Genetic Knowledge in the Past and Present' *Science in Context* 17(3): 315–320.

Larson, E. J. (1999) 'Confronting Scientific Authority with Religious Values: Eugenics in American History', in Demy, T. J. and Stewards, G. P. (eds), *Genetic Engineering: A Christian Response – Crucial Considerations in Shaping Life.* USA: Kregal Publications. pp. 105, 106.

Lanza, E. (2010) 'Core of State Sovereign and Boundaries of European Union's Identity in the Lissabon – Urteil' *German Law Journal* 11: 399.

Logue, L. and Blanck, P. (2010) *Race, Ethnicity, and Disability: Veterans and Benefits in Post-Civil War America.* New York: Cambridge University Press.

Ludmerer, K. (1972) *Genetics and American Society: A Historical Appraisal.* USA: Johns Hopkins Press.

Miller, P. S. (2007) 'Genetic Testing and the Future of Disability Insurance: Thinking about Discrimination in the Genetic Age' *Journal of Law, Medicine and Ethics* 35(2): 47.

Mitchell, G. R. and Happe, K. (2001) 'Informed Consent after the Human Genome Project' *Rhetoric and Public Affairs* 4(3): 375–379.

Minna Stern, A. (2002) 'Making Better Babies: Public Health and Race Betterment in Indiana, 1920–1935' *American Journal of Public Health* 92(5): 742–752.

Quinn, G. and de Paor, A. (2010) 'The New Transatlantic Agenda and the United Nations Convention on the Rights of Persons with Disabilities: Taking the US/EU Dialogue to a New Level'. Washington, DC: US International Council on Disability. Available at: www.usicd.org/detail/news.cfm?news_id=463 [accessed 11 May 2014].

Quinn, G. and Flynn, E. (2012) 'Transatlantic Borrowings: The Past and Future of EU Non-Discrimination Law and Policy on the Ground of Disability' *American Journal of Comparative Law* 60: 23.

Roberts, J. L. (2010) 'Preempting Discrimination: Lessons from the Genetic Information Nondiscrimination Act' *Vanderbilt Law Review* 63(2): 439–442.

Roche, P. (2002) 'The Genetic Revolution at Work: Legislative Efforts to Protect Employees' *American Journal of Law and Medicine* 28: 271, 272.

Rose, A. L., Peters, N., Shea, J. A. and Armstrong, K. (2008) 'Attitudes and Misconceptions about Predictive Genetic Testing for Cancer Risk' *Community Genetics* 8: 145–148.

Rothstein, M. A. and Knoppers, B. M. (1996) 'Legal Aspects of Genetics, Work and Insurance in North America and Europe' *European Journal of Health Law* 3: 134–144.

Schlein, D. (2008–2009) 'New Frontiers for Genetic Privacy Law: The Genetic Information Nondiscrimination Act of 2008' *Civil Rights Law Journal* 19(2): 318–337.

Selden, S. (2005) 'Transforming Better Babies into Fitter Families: Archival Resources and the History of the American Eugenics Movement, 1908–1930' Proceedings of the American Philosophical Society 149(2): 212.

Stein, M. A. *et al.* (2010) 'The Law and Politics of US Participation in the UN Convention on the Rights of Persons with Disabilities' in Quinn, G. and Waddington, L. (eds) *2 European Yearbook of Disability Law.* Antwerp: Intersentia.

Strous, R. D. (2006) 'Hitler's Psychiatrists: Healers and Researchers Turned Executioners and Its Relevance Today' *Harvard Review of Psychiatry* 14(1): 30.

Weindling, P. (1989) 'The Sonderweg of German Eugenics: Nationalism and Scientific Internationalism' *British Journal for the History of Science* 22(3): 321.

Weindling, P. (1993) 'The Survival of Eugenics in 20th Century Germany' *American Journal of Human Genetics* 52(3): 643.

## Cases

*Albertsons Inc. v. Kirkingburg* 119 S. Ct. 2162 (1999).

*Bragdon v. Abbott* 524 US 624 (1998).

*Brown v. The Board of Education of Topeka* 347 US 483 (1954).

*Buck v. Bell* 274 US 200 (1927).

*Murphy v. United Parcel Service Inc.* 119 S. Ct 2133 (1999).

*Norman-Bloodsaw v. Lawrence Berkeley Laboratory*, 135 F.3d 1260 (9th Cir. 1998).

*Sutton v. United Air Lines* 527 US 471 (1999).

*Sutton v. United Air Lines Inc.*, 119 S. Ct 2139 (1999)

*Toyota Motor Manufacturing, Kentucky Inc v. Williams* 534 US 184 (2002).

*United States v. Virginia* 518 US 515 (1996).

## Legislation

29 Code of Federal Regulations Part 1635 – Genetic Information Nondiscrimination Act of 2008.

2011 US Code Title 42 – The Public Health and Welfare Chapter 21F – Prohibiting Employment Discrimination on the Basis of Genetic Information (§ 2000ff–2000ff-11).

Age Discrimination in Employment Act of 1967 Pub. L. No. 90–202, 29 U.S.C. § 621.

Americans with Disabilities Act of 1990, Pub. L. No. 101–336 (1991).

Americans with Disabilities Amendment Act of 2008 Pub. L. No. 110–325 (2008).

Executive Order No. 13145, 65 Fed. Reg. 6,877 (2000).

Final Regulations under the Genetic Information Nondiscrimination Act of 2008 75 Fed. Reg. 68,912–68,939.

Genetic Information Nondiscrimination Act of 2008, Pub. L. No. 110–233, 122 Stat. 881 (2008).

Health Insurance Portability and Accountability Act of 1996 Pub. L. No. 104–191 (1996).

Rehabilitation Act of 1973 Pub. L No. 93–112, 87 Stat. 355.

Sickle Cell Anemia Control Act 1972 Pub. L. No. 92–294 (1972).

Title VII of the Civil Rights Act of 1964 Pub. L. No. 88–352 (1964).

## Other

EEOC Press Release, 'EEOC Settles ADA Suit Against BSNF for Genetic Bias (18 April 2001) available at: www.eeoc.gov/press/4-18-01.html [accessed 26 July 2013].

Equal Employment Opportunity Commission (EEOC) *Compliance Manual* (1995) vol. 2, EEOC Order 915.002, 'Definition of the Term "Disability"'.

Interagency report (Department of Labor, Department of Health and Human Services, Equal Employment Opportunity Commission, Department of Justice) (1998) 'Genetic Information and the Workplace,' 20 January, available at: www.dol.gov/dol/aboutdol/history/herman/reports/genetics.htm [accessed 15 May 2014].

Letter from Rep. Slaughter, L. (one of the main sponsors of the legislation) to the Members of the Sec'y Comm. on Genetics, Health and Soc'y (3 September, 2004) in Public Perspectives on Genetic Discrimination. Available at: http://oba.od.nih.gov/oba/sacghs/reports/Public_Perspectives_GenDiscrim.pdf [accessed 16 April 2012].

The National Center for Genome Resources Surrey (1998) 'Attitudes Toward Genetic Testing' (4 March).

Press Release: 'Kennedy, Enzi, Snowe Celebrate Passage of Genetic Information Nondiscrimination Act' (24 April 2008). Available at: www.help.senate.gov/newsroom/press/release/?id=313bfde8-f967-46b4-aa9d-11bc73728813 [accessed 10 June 2014].

Statement of Collins, F. S. (Director, National Human Genome Research Institute, National Institutes of Health), before the Appropriations Subcommittee on Labor, Health and Human Services and Education (11 July 2001a).

Statement of Collins, F. S. before the Health, Education, Labor and Pensions Committee, United States Senate (25 July 2001b).

Statement of Fishman, B. J. (Counsel to GINE Coalition) (2007) 'Protecting Workers from Genetic Discrimination: Hearing before H. Subcomm. on Health, Employment, Labor and Pensions of the H. Comm. on Energy and Commerce', 110th Congress 110-1.

Statement of Paul Steven Miller on Genetic Information in the Workplace, US Equal Employment Equality Commission before the Committee on Health, Education, Labor and Pensions, United States Senate (20 July 2000).

# 7 The Genetic Information Nondiscrimination Act (GINA) 2008

*Anya Prince and Michael Waterstone*

## 1. Introduction

On May 21, 2008, President George W. Bush signed the Genetic Information Nondiscrimination Act (GINA) into law – officially culminating the 13-year journey through Congress. GINA's final form is one of compromise and is simultaneously narrow – encompassing only employment and health insurance – and broad – greatly expanding the definitions of genetic information and discriminatory practices in American law. As discussed in the previous chapter, GINA was passed predominately as a prophylactic law. It was meant to alleviate fears about genetic discrimination more than to address current instances of discriminatory actions. In many ways, this continues to be the law's primary role, as relatively few cases of discrimination have been documented in the United States since its passage. Prior to GINA there were some limited protections within health insurance law and employment law; however, the patchwork of laws did not create comprehensive protections. This chapter will examine the legal framework in place prior to GINA, discuss the major provisions of GINA and comment on the policy reasoning behind many of the law's provisions.

## 2. Legal framework prior to GINA

### *2.1 Health insurance*

The reasoning and motivations of GINA stem from the complex, and often tortured, way that health care is delivered in the United States. In the US, health care is predominantly privatised – while some individuals receive care through government-sponsored programmes such as Medicare and Medicaid, the majority of individuals who are 64 and younger are either uninsured or have private health insurance (National Center for Health Statistics, 2012). At the time that GINA was being debated, private health insurance companies were permitted to take pre-existing conditions into account when determining whether or not to insure an individual. For example, if an applicant for individual health insurance had asthma or had a past history of cancer, the insurance company could deny coverage. The rules regarding pre-existing conditions were different for individual health insurance – plans purchased directly by an individual – versus group health insurance – plans received through an employer, trade association or other group. However, both entities were permitted to look back in an applicant's medical records and impose an exclusion period or, in the case of individual insurance, deny an application for a pre-existing condition. The condition did not have to be officially diagnosed – any symptom for which an individual received medical advice or for which medical care was recommended could constitute a pre-existing condition. These rules were drastically altered by the Patient Protection and Affordable Care Act (ACA), (sometimes known as 'Obamacare'). Under the ACA, beginning January 1, 2014, health insurance companies cannot take into account any medical condition or pre-existing condition when determining enrolment, premiums, or coverage.

The broad, sweeping changes of the ACA were not anticipated in the late 1990s and early 2000s when Congress was debating GINA. Many advocates argued that these changes should be implemented but broad efforts at health care reform had failed in Congress (see, e.g., HR 3600, Health Security Act, November 20, 1993. This bill was championed by President Bill Clinton and First Lady Hillary Clinton, but it failed to pass Congress). Therefore, individuals considering genetic testing or participation in genetic research were understandably concerned that their genetic predispositions would be considered pre-existing conditions in health insurance. The laws in existence in 2008 provided scattered and limited protections to address the concerns. Indeed, only two main laws addressed the use of genetic information in private health insurance for an individual at the time of passage – the Health Insurance Portability and Accountability Act (HIPAA) and the state law if the legislature had passed one.

First, at the federal level, HIPAA prohibits group health insurers from using genetic information in determining eligibility for insurance or in setting individual premiums. Although this law provides some basic protections, there are many gaps. For example, nothing in HIPAA limits group health insurance companies from gathering genetic information. The company is then permitted to turn down whole groups on the basis of the genetic information of one individual – such as declining to contract with a small employer because one of its five employees has a predisposition to Huntington's Disease. Additionally, the company would be permitted to change coverage rules or charge higher premiums for the entire group – such as excluding coverage for prophylactic surgeries or coverage for a particular condition or raising overall group premiums due to one individual's genetic information.

Additionally, HIPAA's protections only apply to group health insurance plans. Therefore, people in the individual market had only state law protections – if any. Finally, HIPAA's genetic discrimination protections were limited because the law does not prohibit employers from discriminating on the basis of genetics. The majority of Americans – 69.7 per cent in 2000 and 59.5 per cent in 2010 – receive insurance through an employer; therefore the ability for employers to discriminate in order to lower group health insurance costs created a substantial gap in the system (SHADAC, 2013: 3). The Americans with Disabilities Act (ADA), discussed further below, arguably created some protection in the employment arena; however, the effectiveness of this law in the genetics arena was questionable.

Second, many states had laws protecting against genetic discrimination in health insurance (NCSL, 2008). These laws varied in protectiveness and effectiveness across state lines. For example, although 47 states had laws regulating the use of genetic information in health insurance, only 42 of the state laws provided protection in the individual markets (NCSL, 2008). Additionally, the majority of these state laws only protected against discrimination based upon genetic test results of the individual being insured. The definition of genetic information at the state law levels generally did not include family medical history (Prince, 2013). GINA's expansion of this definition is discussed further below, but overall the narrow definitions at the state level allowed health insurers to collect information about family medical history, infer genetic predispositions based on family history patterns and discriminate against applicants and insurees based on this information – even in states that had passed anti-discrimination protections in the health insurance arena.

State law effectiveness was also limited because of the federalism system of laws in the US. In areas where both states and the federal government legislate, there are complicated rules about when federal law pre-empts, or trumps, state law. Federal law often pre-empts state law in employer-sponsored plans under the Employee Retirement Income Security Act (ERISA) (Dean and Paris, 2000: 1). For individuals with group health insurance plans, enforcing state law protections was often foreclosed upon due to this pre-emption.

### 2.2 Employment

The employment arena also had potential protections against genetic discrimination at both the state and federal level, but, like the health insurance arena, these protections had many gaps. Overall, most of the evidence of genetic discrimination prior to GINA was anecdotal. There were two publicised cases in the employment context – the *Burlington Northern Santa Fe Railway* case (EEOC, 2001) and *Norman Bloodsaw v. Lawrence Berkeley Lab* (*Norman Bloodsaw 1998*), as discussed in the previous chapter. These cases exemplify the shaky legal footing of employment law based complaints of misuse of genetic information. In 1995, the EEOC issued a guidance indicating that discrimination on the basis of genetic information would constitute discrimination under the ADA's 'regarded as' prong (EEOC

Compliance, 1995: 902–945). Although the EEOC took a broad view of ADA coverage, many scholars believed that courts would not follow this guidance, given the trend during that time to narrowly apply the ADA (Rothstein, 2008: 837). The *Burlington Northern* case was settled out of court and the ADA claims within the *Norman Bloodsaw* case were dismissed; therefore a court precedent was never established for genetic discrimination under the ADA.

In 2008, Congress amended the ADA and in the process rejected many of the narrow court rulings of the past decade (ADAAA, 2008). However, Congress did not specifically address whether the use of genetic information falls under the purview of the ADA (Rothstein, 2008: 837). Therefore, it remains unclear whether an ADA claim for genetic discrimination would be successful. GINA's provisions have arguably mooted this debate in the employment arena.

Thirty-five states also had laws prohibiting genetic discrimination in hiring, firing and setting the terms and conditions of employment. Similar to the health insurance arena, these state laws are limited in scope due to narrow definitions of genetic information at the state level (Prince, 2013).

Scattered federal laws and narrow state laws provided the legal protections against genetic discrimination in the health insurance and employment arena for the general public. Some segments of the population, such as federal employees, had additional protections pre-GINA. The majority of Americans faced uncertainty about their rights after a genetic test due to the patchwork nature of the laws.

### 2.3 Federal employees

In 2000, President Bill Clinton signed Executive Order 13145. The order prohibits federal employers from discriminating against an individual or requesting genetic test results in hiring, benefits and advancement opportunities (EO 13145 2000). The order was one of the first federal actions in the realm of genetic discrimination and set an initial precedent for GINA – including precedent for a more expansive definition of genetic information that included family medical history. Federal employees were limited in the rights under the order because it did not establish a private right of action for individuals harmed by genetic discrimination. Therefore, an employee who expected genetic discrimination had to voice his grievances through administrative channels rather than through court. Although narrow, the Executive Order did illustrate a movement within the federal government to view genetic discrimination as a civil rights and equal employment issue that was essential to address.

Given the complex health insurance system in the United States, the gaps at both the federal and state levels in protecting against genetic discrimination, and the movement in the federal Executive Branch to view genetic discrimination as a civil rights issue, the time was ripe for a comprehensive bill to address the issue at a national level. After a 13-year battle in Congress, highlighted in the previous chapter, this effort was codified in GINA.

## 3. GINA's provisions

GINA is comprised of two major titles – one addressing non-discrimination in health insurance and the other addressing non-discrimination in employment. The definitions used in both titles predominately mirror each other and there are broad trends of limiting the right of entities to gather an individual's genetic information as well as preventing misuse of any information.

### *3.1 Definitions*

The most notable definition in GINA is the broad meaning of genetic information. Genetic information is defined as 'information about [an] individual's genetic tests, the genetic tests of family members of such individual, and the manifestation of a disease or disorder in family members of such individual' (GINA 2008: 29 USC 1191b(d)(6)). The term also includes request for, or receipt of, genetic services – such as genetic counselling or genetic education – and participation in genetic research by either an individual or his or her family member (GINA 2008: 29 USC 1191b(d)(6)). This definition is one of the broadest pieces of GINA and greatly expanded the protections available to individuals. As noted above, most state laws prior to GINA only covered protections for an individual's genetic test result. However, since family history is a primary indicator of the likelihood that an individual has inherited a predisposition, a law protecting genetic tests without protecting family history is essentially moot. With a narrower definition, health insurance companies and employers would be able to use family medical history as a proxy to determine who likely had genetic predispositions.

GINA is not only broad in its inclusion of family medical history, but also in its definition of family member. The definition includes any dependents, as well as any first-, second-, third- or fourth-degree relative of an individual (GINA 2008: 29 USC 1191b(d)(5)). Family members by affinity – such as adoption or marriage – fall under GINA, in addition to blood relatives (GINA Insurance Regulations 2012: 26 CFR 54.9802-3T). Additionally, genetic information refers not only to an individual's information and family member information, but also to any information of a foetus or embryo (GINA 2008: 29 USC 1182(f)).

The definition of genetic information under GINA does not include manifested diseases. For example, an individual's positive HNPCC test showing a predisposition to colon cancer is protected genetic information; however, a polyp discovered during a colonoscopy would not be protected since it is manifested symptom. Therefore, the threshold of protection under GINA is determined by when a disease manifests.

Initially, although 'manifestation' appears several times in the text of GINA, Congress failed to define the concept in the initial bill. GINA's regulations addressed this gap and noted that a disease is manifested when

> an individual has been or could reasonably be diagnosed with the disease, disorder, or pathological condition by a health care professional with appropriate training and expertise in the field of medicine involved. For purposes of this part, a disease, disorder or pathological condition is not manifested if the diagnosis is based principally on genetic information.
>
> (GINA Employment Regulations (2010): 29 CFR 1635.3(g))

The most recent health insurance regulations under GINA have a similar definition of manifestation (GINA Insurance Regulations 2012: 26 CFR 54.9802-3T(a)(6)(i)).

The line between purely genetic information and manifested disease is an ambiguous one and will likely need further development in the courts. In the health insurance arena, due to the ACA, these differences are less of an issue since legal protections banning discrimination based on genetic information and/or medical status have moved together, creating comprehensive legal protections for most people. However, in the employment context, this fuzzy line is more concerning. In employment, GINA's protections end when a disease manifests. Under the ADA – the law that bans certain employers from discriminating against an individual on the basis of a disability – protections only begin when an individual's condition substantially limits a major life activity (ADAAA 2008). Thus, there is a gap in the employment setting because an individual with symptoms that do not substantially limit a major life activity may be discriminated against (Rothstein, 2008).

### *3.2 Title I – health insurance*

Title I of GINA addresses the use of genetic information in health insurance. Due to the complicated US system of insurance coverage, this title of GINA amends a number of different and specific laws. The amendments to each section are similar, creating anti-discrimination protections across a broad spectrum of types of insurance offerings. GINA amends the Employee Retirement Income Security Act of 1974 (ERISA), a law that regulates group health insurance companies, the Public Health Service Act, a law that regulates both the group and individual health insurance markets, the Internal Revenue Code of 1986 and the Social Security Act, a law that regulates Medigap policies. Medigap policies are supplemental plans that individuals purchase in addition to the federal Medicare policies provided to seniors and individuals with disabilities. While each of these differing codes are amended in separate sections, the changes to the codes are essentially the same content.

### *3.2.1 Anti-discrimination provisions*

GINA creates bans over the use of genetic information in health insurance. The law is very broad in what is considered discrimination – generally encompassing two types of banned actions. First, GINA prevents health insurance companies from using genetic information to negatively impact an individual. Therefore, covered insurance companies are not allowed to adjust premium or contribution amounts based on genetic information. Although insurers are not allowed to use genetic information, GINA specifically notes that companies are allowed to adjust premiums based on manifested diseases. Under the ACA, health insurers will no longer be able to take into account manifested diseases when setting premium rates beginning January 1, 2014. However, when GINA was passed, health care reform had not yet been contemplated; therefore this exception had to be made clear in the law.

In the individual market, a health insurance company cannot establish rules for eligibility or continued eligibility based on genetic information, nor impose a pre-existing condition exclusion based on genetic information (GINA 2008: 42 USC 300gg-53(a)(1) and (c)(1)). These specific provisions only appear in the context of individual health insurance. As mentioned above, group health insurance companies were already prohibited from using any medical information, including genetic information, in determining eligibility under HIPAA. Therefore, it was not necessary for Congress to ban group health insurers from using genetic information during eligibility determinations. GINA also amended HIPAA to clarify that genetic information could never be considered a pre-existing condition (GINA 2008: 42 USC 1320d-9). This provision ensures that group health insurance companies, through both HIPAA and GINA, are limited from using genetic information just as individual health insurance companies are.

### *3.2.2 Prohibition on collection of genetic information*

Second, GINA broadly prevents health insurance companies from gathering an individual's genetic information. In most discrimination arenas, such as race, gender and sometimes disability or religion, a person's protected status is apparent to an entity such as an employer or an insurance company from the outset. In genetics however, Congress had the rare opportunity to prevent potentially malicious actors from gathering information about the protected status overall, since a person's genetic status is not apparent. In both insurance and employment, discrimination can be very difficult for a plaintiff to prove. GINA uniquely empowers individuals to control what genetic information is provided to employers and health insurers – preventing these actors from having the tools with which to discriminate from the outset.

GINA prohibits health insurers from accessing genetic information in a number of ways. Insurers are banned from requesting or requiring an individual or the family member of an individual to take a genetic test (GINA 2008: 29 USC 1182(c)(1) and 42 USC 300gg-53(e)(1)). Congress passed GINA in part to encourage positive public health outcomes through increased use of genetic medicine and participation in research. Therefore, GINA clarifies that nothing within the bill prevents health care professionals from requesting an individual undergo a genetic test (GINA 2008: 29 USC 1182(c)(2)).

Under one exception, health insurers are allowed to obtain genetic information, and use such information, to make determinations for whether to pay for a procedure or treatment. Health insurance companies may request only the minimum amount of information necessary to make the determination (GINA 2008: 29 USC 1182(c)(3)). For example, if a woman receives a negative result for a BRCA genetic test, it is common medical practice for genetic counsellors to seek a follow-up test, called BRAC Analysis Large Rearrangement Test (BART). In order to determine whether or not to pay for the BART test, a health insurance company is allowed to ask for the test results of the BRCA test – since it is not medically necessary to seek BART testing unless BRCA testing is negative. However, the insurance company would be prohibited from gathering the results of the BART test, because this is not the 'minimum amount of information necessary' to determine payment for the BART test. The results of the BART test are irrelevant for the determination of payment for that test.

GINA also includes a research exception to the prohibition of requesting genetic testing. This exception follows from the underlying goals of GINA to promote genetic research and public health benefits. Under the research exception, insurers can request, but not require, an individual to go through genetic testing as long as the request is in writing and follows human subjects in research rules, the insurer makes clear that participation is voluntary, no collected genetic information is used in underwriting and the plan notifies the Secretary of the research activities (GINA 2008: 19 USC 1182(c)(4) and 42 USC 300gg-53(d)(4)).

Health insurers are prohibited from obtaining genetic information by requesting, requiring, or purchasing genetic information for underwriting purposes. However, health care professionals often provide complete medical records for a specific time period when an insurance company is going through underwriting. It is not uncommon for these records to include some form of genetic information – indeed it would be a rare occurrence for the records to not include genetic information. If a health insurance company receives genetic information incidentally to other legal medical records requests, this does not violate GINA (GINA 2008: 29 USC 1182(d)(3)). This exception creates a burdensome requirement for health care professionals to redact all genetic information – from test results to family medical history – from a patient's medical records prior to sending them to the insurance company. There is little evidence that this is happening at the ground level. This creates a problematic paradox for patients who wish to stop their health insurance company from accessing genetic information. If it is reasonable for an insurance company to expect that genetic information will be gathered as part of a medical records request, the collection request must explicitly state that genetic information should not be provided (HIPAA Interim Final Rules, 2009). If a health care professional fails to properly redact genetic information, the insurance company has not violated GINA for this incidental collection – leaving the patient with little recourse (Prince, 2012).

Despite this and other gaps in system, GINA vastly altered the insurance landscape by preventing health insurance companies from taking into consideration genetic information. The broad definition of genetic information that includes family medical history creates broad and comprehensive protections within the health insurance arena. This, coupled with the ACA's prohibition of discrimination on the basis of medical status or pre-existing conditions, forms strong patient protections in the health insurance arena.

### *3.2.3 Enforcement*

The penalty for non-compliance for group and individual health insurers is $100 for each day and for each participant whose rights are violated (GINA 2008: 42 USC 300gg-22(b)(3)(B)(i); 29 USC 1132(c)(9); and 26 USC 4980D). The payments last from the date the violation first occurs to the date the failure is corrected. The penalties are heightened to $2,500 if the health insurer was informed of the violation but failed to correct the problem and to $15,000 if the violations are more than de minimis (GINA 2008: 42 USC 300gg-22(b)(3)(C)). Likewise, the penalties are waived if the violations were unknown or were not wilful negligence (GINA 2008: 42 USC 300gg-22(b)(3)(D)). Overall, if the violation was due to a reasonable cause, not wilful neglect, the penalty cannot exceed 'the lesser of 10 per cent of the aggregate amount paid or incurred by the [employer or plan sponsor] during the preceding taxable year for group health plans or $500,000' (GINA 2008: 42 USC 300gg-22(b)(3)(D); 29 USC 1132(c)(9)(D); and 42 USC 300gg-61(b)).

GINA requires states to establish laws and regulations that provide protections against discrimination in health insurance that are equal to, or more protective than, GINA. If a state fails to adequately protect individuals' rights under the state law, the federal government is supposed to step in to enforce the federal rights under GINA. Due to this fragmented enforcement system, it is very difficult to collect evidence of complaints of genetic discrimination in the health insurance arena, since there are essentially more than 50 different enforcement mechanisms – one for each state and territory.

There has been little to no empirical evidence of genetic discrimination in health insurance since 2008 – similar to the debate prior to GINA's passage, any evidence of discrimination has remained anecdotal. It is unclear whether this is due to lack of occurrence of discrimination, lack of reported cases or lack of collected evidence from the fragmented enforcement. Overall, public knowledge of GINA remains as low as 8.8 per cent (Huang *et al.*, 2013), indicating that the general public may not know when violations occur or where to file complaints because they are unaware of the law overall.

### *3.3 Title II – employment*

Title II of GINA regulates the use of genetic information in employment. Like the health insurance title, GINA limits employers in their ability both to discriminate on the basis of genetic information and to gather genetic information from employees and prospective employees. While GINA mirrors many other employment protections in the US, the addition of privacy protections alongside anti-discrimination protections is unique to GINA's employment rights provisions (Roberts, 2014). Title II applies to state and local governments as well as private employers with 15 or more employees. The EEOC, the agency tasked with enforcing other civil rights employment arenas such as race, gender, age, religion and disability, enforces many of the provisions of Title II. Thus, it is likely that, as GINA cases are litigated, courts will turn to existing employment law jurisprudence for guidance in interpretations regarding broader court topics – such as burdens of proof and evidentiary questions.

#### *3.3.1 Anti-discrimination provisions*

As with health insurance companies, GINA prohibits employers from treating employees adversely based on genetic information. This broad prohibition prevents employers from firing, failing to hire or altering the compensation, terms, conditions or privileges of employment (GINA 2008: 42 USC 2000ff-1(a)(1)). Employees cannot be segregated or classified in any manner that would negatively affect their employment based on genetic information (GINA 2008: 42 USC 2000ff-1(a)(2)). For example, an employer could not reassign an employee with a family history of heart disease to a less stressful job (GINA Employment Regulations). Although Congress envisioned individual employment complaints, they were unsure of whether to allow claims of disparate impact under the law. To this end, GINA established a Genetic Nondiscrimination Study Commission to commence in 2014 to make recommendations to Congress on adding a disparate impact cause of action under the law. Employment agencies and labour organisations have similar prohibitions as employers under Section 203 and 204 of GINA (GINA 2008: 42 USC 2000ff-2 and 42 USC 2000ff-3).

### *3.3.2 Prohibition on collection of genetic information*

Employers are not allowed to request, require or purchase an employee's genetic information (GINA 2008: 42 USC 2000ff-1(b)). This provision seemingly makes more sense in the employment arena than in the insurance arena. Health insurers desire to have access to genetic information because it gives them information about a person's medical risk – which equates to the potential cost to the insurance company. While the utility of genetic information to employers is less obvious, it still comes into play. In the US, employers are the primary providers of insurance – and in some cases are the entities that directly cover the cost of care. Therefore, there is a similar potential for employers to seek out information regarding the genetic risk of potential employees in order to save on future health care costs. Additionally, if an employer believes that a prospective employee may develop cancer or another hereditary disease, they may be less likely to want to put in the resources to hire and train the individual.

GINA includes six broad exceptions to the rule against the acquisition of genetic information (GINA 2008: 42 USC 2000ff-1(b)(1)-(6)). First, if an employer inadvertently gathers genetic information, it has not violated GINA for the possession of such information. This exception – often nicknamed the 'water cooler exception' – prevents an employer from violating GINA if they overhear an employee talking about their aunt's diabetes, or other discussion of family medical history. Second, an employer can gather genetic information as part of a wellness programme, but only if the genetic portion of the programme is completely voluntary and the individually identifiable information is not provided to the employer. The employer is allowed to receive aggregate genetic information. For example, a wellness programme can include a health questionnaire that asks employees about family medical history only if that portion of the questionnaire is not tied to the wellness programme incentive. There must be a clear note on the question form that explains this to employees.

Third, certifications for leave under the Family and Medical Leave Act (FMLA) or state law equivalent can gather information about family medical history. Fourth, an employer has not violated GINA by viewing genetic information in commercial or publicly available documents. However, this does not give the employer licence to actively search for genetic information in publicly available media such as newspapers. This exception only applies if the acquisition of genetic information was incidental to viewing the commercial or publicly available sources. Fifth, under very specific sub-rules, an employer can collect genetic information to monitor the biological effects of toxic substances in the workplace. Finally, an employer can conduct genetic analysis of DNA for human remains identification or for law enforcement purposes as a forensic laboratory. This exception is limited to collecting DNA samples for quality control in order to ensure that employee DNA is not mixing with outside forensic samples.

In each of the exceptions, an employer is still prohibited from using the genetic information to discriminate against the employee. All genetic information must be treated as sensitive medical information and kept in a confidential personnel file that is separate from the general HR file of the employee (GINA Employment Regulations (2010): 29 CFR 1635.9(a)). Several exceptions to the requirement of confidentiality do appear in the bill – from disclosing information under a court order to providing information to a governmental public health agency (GINA 2008: 42 USC 2000ff-5(b)).

### *3.3.3 Enforcement*

Congress utilised the existing employment discrimination enforcement framework in GINA. Under the law and regulations, the same rules, fee structure, and damages in place under Title VII of the Civil Rights Act of 1964 are applicable to GINA (GINA 2008: 42 USC 2000ff-6)). The EEOC is thus in charge of enforcing GINA, and individuals who wish to allege genetic discrimination must go through administrative channels before having the right to sue in individual court. Although GINA applies to federal employees, the EEOC only has the jurisdiction to enforce the employment rights of a small segment of federal employees, such as postal workers, employees at the Government Accountability Office or the Smithsonian Institute and certain employees in executive agencies. This authority is granted through the Government Employee Rights Act of 1991 (GERA) (42 USC 2000e-16)). Federal employees who do not fall under the GERA must go through different administrative channels to enforce complaints against their employers. Overall, federal employees are protected through the Executive Order discussed above.

The EEOC has brought several cases under GINA's enforcement provisions to date. Since 2008, the number of complaints filed by individuals under GINA has increased, although the numbers have remained low compared to other employment discrimination claims. Between 2010 and 2013, the EEOC received 1,059 complaints under GINA, with progressively more complaints filed each year. In 2013, 140 complaints were determined by the EEOC to be without cause, but many of the other 333 claims were settled or were resolved through the administrative process in other ways – with total non-litigation benefits paid to plaintiffs of $1 million (EEOC 2013). There has been no publicised private litigation adjudicated after the EEOC process has been exhausted.

The EEOC has filed three cases to enforce GINA's ban on genetic discrimination in employment. Each of these three cases has involved claims regarding employer violations of the ban on collecting genetic information – particularly in cases of post-offer medical examinations. For example, in January 2014, the EEOC settled a case with Founders Pavilion, Inc., a nursing home in New York, based on the company's practice of collecting family medical history during post-offer, pre-employment medical examinations of applicants (EEOC 2014). These cases highlight the EEOC focus on collection of family medical history as a violation of GINA.

## 4. Conclusion

GINA is a broad bill that prohibits both genetic discrimination and the collection of protected genetic information – an expansive term within the legislation. However, GINA is also relatively narrow given that it applies only to health insurers and certain employers. This dichotomy illustrates that GINA was a result of a Congressional compromise after a 13-year legislative battle. While GINA has gone a long way to easing the fears of individuals regarding discrimination – thus encouraging more individuals in society to participate in genetic testing and genetic research – it remains to be seen what the bill's legacy will be. GINA's enforcement and subsequent legislative efforts to fill the gaps left by the bill will shape the ultimate success or failure of the cutting-edge law.

## References

ADA Amendments Act (ADAAA) (2008) Public Law 110-325.

Dean, R. and Paris, L. (2000) *ERISA Basics: Preemption*, American Bar Association. Available at: http://apps.americanbar.org/labor/lel-aba-annual/papers/2000/paris.pdf (accessed 15 September 2013).

Equal Employment Opportunity Commission (EEOC) (1995) *EEOC Compliance Manual* vol. 2, EEOC Order 915.002, 'Definition of the Term "Disability"'. Reprinted in Daily Lab. Rep., Mar. 16, 1995, at E-1, E-23.

Equal Employment Opportunity Commission (EEOC) (2001) 'EEOC Settles ADA Suit Against BNSF for Genetic Bias'. Press release. Available at: www.eeoc.gov/eeoc/newsroom/release/4-18-01.cfm [accessed 15 September 2013].

Equal Employment Opportunity Commission (EEOC) (2013) Genetic Information Non-Discrimination Act Charges (includes concurrent charges with Title VII, ADEA, ADA, and EPA) FY 2010–2013. Available at: www.eeoc.gov/eeoc/statistics/enforcement/genetic.cfm [accessed 26 March 2014].

Equal Employment Opportunity Commission (EEOC) (2014) 'Founders Pavilion Will Pay $370,000 to Settle EEOC Genetic Information Discrimination Lawsuit'. Press release. Available at: www.eeoc.gov/eeoc/newsroom/release/1-13-14.cfm [accessed 26 March 2014].

Executive Order (EO) 13145 (February 8, 2000) *to Prohibit Discrimination in Federal Employment Based on Genetic Information.*

GINA Employment Regulations (2010) *Definitions Specific to GINA*, 29 CFR 1635.3.

Genetic Information Nondiscrimination Act (GINA) (2008) Public Law 110–233.

GINA Insurance Regulations (2012) *Additional Requirements Prohibiting Discrimination Based on Genetic Information*, 26 CFR 54.9802-3T.

Government Employee Rights Act (GERA) (1991).

Health Insurance Portability and Accountability Act (HIPAA) (1996).

HIPAA Interim Final Rules (2009) *Prohibiting Discrimination Based on Genetic Information, Federal Register* 74(193).

HR 3600, Health Security Act (20 November 1993) (103rd Congress, 1993–1994).

Huang, M.Y., Huston, S. A. and Perri, M. (2013) 'Awareness of the US Genetic Information Nondiscrimination Act of 2008: An Online Survey' *Journal of Pharmaceutical Health Services Research* 4(4): 235–238.

National Center for Health Statistics (2012) *FastStats: Health Insurance Coverage*. Available at: www.cdc.gov/nchs/fastats/hinsure.htm [accessed 15 September 2013].

National Conference of State Legislatures (NCSL) (2008) *Genetics and Health Insurance State Anti-Discrimination Laws*. Available at: www.ncsl.org/issues-research/health/genetic-nondiscrimination-in-health-insurance-laws.aspx [accessed 15 September 2013].

*Norman Bloodsaw v. Lawrence Berkeley Lab* (1988) 135 F.3d 1260 (9th Cir.).

Prince, A. (2012) 'Genetic Information and Medical Records – A Cautionary Tale for Patients, Health Care Professionals, and Insurance Companies' *The Health Lawyer* 24(5): The American Bar Association Health Law Section.

Prince, A. (2013) *Comprehensive Protection of Genetic Information: One Size Privacy or Property Models May Not Fit All*. New York: Brooklyn Law Review.

Roberts, J. (2014) *Privacy as a Tool for Antidiscrimination* (forthcoming).

Rothstein, M. (2008) 'GINA, the ADA, and Genetic Discrimination in Employment' Journal of Law, Medicine, and Ethics 38(4): 837.

State Health Access Data Assistance Center (SHADAC) (2013) *State-Level Trends in Employer-Sponsored Health Insurance*, Minneapolis, MN: University of Minnesota. Available at: www.rwjf.org/content/dam/farm/reports/reports/2013/rwjf405434 [accessed 15 September 2013].

# 8 Genetic discrimination in the workplace after GINA

*Robert S. Olick*

## 1. Introduction

If I am denied health insurance or employment because of a positive genetic test that increases my risk of future illness, disease or disability, have I been subjected to genetic discrimination? What if the basis for denying access to these essential goods is a family history of disease or disability, such as colon cancer, diabetes, or muscular dystrophy? Enacted in 2008, the Genetic Information Nondiscrimination Act (GINA) prohibits the discriminatory use of genetic information in both health insurance and employment. As stated by Congresswoman Louise Slaughter, a lead architect of the law, GINA was needed not only to shield against the injustice of genetic discrimination, but also to encourage us to take advantage of and benefit from biomedical advances involving genetic testing and information without fear that this information will be used against us. By removing the threat of genetic discrimination, GINA also encourages us to participate in biomedical research that is essential to promote our health and the public good (Slaughter, 2008). A law 13 years in the making (first introduced in 1995), GINA took effect November 21, 2009. Final implementing regulations for the workplace from the Equal Employment Opportunity Commission (EEOC) were issued on November 9, 2010.

GINA establishes a national and uniform standard of basic required protections, while allowing states to impose even more protective rules. GINA responds to a patchwork of state laws in more than half of states that provide uneven protections against health insurance and employment discrimination based on genetic information (National Conference of State Legislatures, 2008). With respect to health insurance, Title I fills gaps in protections against genetic discrimination under the Health Insurance Portability and Accountability Act (HIPAA), chiefly by extending protections to the individual insurance market, whereas HIPAA applies only to the group insurance market. Since GINA's enactment the Patient Protection and Affordable Care Act of 2010 (ACA) has, among its many signal provisions, proclaimed that we cannot be denied access to health insurance or subjected to discriminatory rate-setting based on pre-existing conditions, and ACA reinforces that genetic information falls under this protective umbrella (Feldman, 2011). With respect to employment, GINA Title II addresses uncertainty regarding the extent to which the Americans With Disabilities Act as amended (ADAA) shields us against genetic discrimination in the workplace; and it complements President Clinton's 2000 Executive Order banning genetic discrimination in the federal workforce (Executive Order 13145, 2000). GINA does not apply to long-term care, life or disability insurance. Failure to shield against adverse coverage decisions in these markets based on genetically based predictions of future disease or disability that may never come to be is a significant shortcoming of GINA that warrants further examination.

This chapter discusses GINA's protections of genetic privacy and against genetic discrimination in the workplace—Title II of GINA. Given the strong and comprehensive federal and state protections against genetic discrimination in health insurance in the aftermath of ACA, the Title II employment provisions are arguably the most significant, and will likely be the most discussed, analyzed, and perhaps litigated provisions of GINA. I begin with GINA's operative definition of genetic information and then summarize the core privacy and nondiscrimination provisions of Title II. The analysis reviews the few cases alleging genetic discrimination brought under GINA as of this writing. Three areas of special importance are discussed: 1) genetic information in employer-based wellness programs; 2) GINA's exclusion from coverage of manifest conditions; and 3) genetic monitoring of the aggregate biological effects of workplace exposure to toxic substances. At various points the discussion draws comparisons to and takes lessons from the ADA, the law that served as a model and foundation for GINA's employment provisions. However, this chapter does not purport to offer comprehensive comparative analysis of the two laws. More comprehensive accounts of GINA, its history, and its core provisions appear elsewhere in this volume.

## 2. Protected genetic information

GINA Title II prohibits employment discrimination on the basis of genetic information. The wide-ranging definition of "genetic information" includes information about the employee's or job applicant's own genetic tests and family history, including genetic tests of family members and "the manifestation of a disease or disorder" in a family member (GINA, 42 U.S.C. §2000ff(4)). For purposes of the law, family includes dependents (including non-genetically-related adopted children) and any other individual who is a first-, second-, third-, or fourth-degree relative of the employee or applicant (GINA, §2000ff(3); EEOC, Federal Register, 68914, 2010). Excluded from the definition is information about the employee's or family member's gender, age, race, or ethnicity not derived from a genetic test (GINA, §2000ff(4)(c)).

The statutory definition of a genetic test is intended to be broad and inclusive. Analysis of a person's DNA, RNA (ribonucleic acid), mutations, chromosomes, and other molecular features indicative of genetic traits are all considered genetic tests, as are any of these types of analyses to determine predisposition to illness or disease or a person's carrier status. Testing at the beginnings of life—amniocentesis, newborn screening, and preimplantation genetic diagnosis—all of which can indicate the genetic traits of one or both genetic contributors—are expressly included by the EEOC, as is pharmacogenetic testing to determine how a person might react to a particular drug or drug dosage (EEOC, Federal Register, 2010, 68933).

Genetic information also encompasses asking for or receiving genetic services concerning the individual or a family member when such services involve a genetic test, genetic counseling to obtain or interpret genetic information, or education about genetics (GINA, 42 U.S.C.§§ 2000ff(B); 2000ff(6)). Participation by the individual or family member in clinical research that includes genetic services (perhaps in connection with a wellness initiative or genetic monitoring) is also covered (GINA, 42 U.S.C.§§ 2000ff(4)(B)). GINA likely will have little impact on the vast amount of genetic research conducted with stored tissue samples at academic medical centers and private companies, much of which involves secondary research with anonymous or anonymized samples (Weir and Olick, 2004). GINA covers both the private and public sectors, employment agencies, labor organizations, and apprenticeship, training, and retraining programs (GINA, 42 U.S.C.§§ 2000ff 1–4). While the law's protections are highly uniform across these domains, the discussion to follow contemplates the private sector workplace of 15 or more employees (smaller businesses are not covered by the law).

## 3. Genetic privacy

Legal and ethical issues involving genetic information are often segmented into rules governing access to information, i.e. genetic privacy, and use of the information, i.e. genetic discrimination. GINA makes it an unlawful employment practice to "request, require or purchase genetic information with respect to an employee or a family member of the employee." Medical examinations to determine ability to perform the job are still permitted as they have been under the ADA, but health care providers who conduct the examination and take the patient's history are to be instructed not to request or record genetic information. This is a significant change from the ADAA that permitted inquiry about genetic information as part of the medical exam both with respect to a conditional offer of employment and subsequently "if job related and consistent with business necessity" (EEOC, Federal Register, 2010; 68934).

GINA's broad privacy protection is qualified by a number of circumstances where acquiring genetic information is permitted, including an inadvertent request or requirement for family medical history of the employee or a family member and compliance with federal and state family and medical leave requirements to certify the reasons and need for leave. Casual and overheard conversations—perhaps the employee is discussing the results of their direct-to-consumer genetic profile testing from 23andMe?—are not protected (the so-called "water cooler" exception), but company managers cannot engage employees in conversation intended to elicit genetic information. Learning of publicly available information in print or electronic media is permitted, however regulations admonish companies not to go in search of genetic information, such as by accessing Facebook or websites for genetic support groups (EEOC, Federal Register, 2010; 68934). Acquisition of genetic information in connection with genetic services is permitted, with the informed consent of the employee. Here the information remains within the confines of the professional relationship with the employee or a family member who is receiving genetic services, consistent with established norms of confidentiality in the health care professional–patient relationship. Further, under GINA's confidentiality provisions, all genetic information whether in print or electronic form is to be kept separate from personnel files and treated as a confidential medical record (GINA, 42 U.S.C.§§ 2000ff 2(b); 5(a)). However, there is cause for concern that genetic information will continue to be routinely obtained and retained in employee health records accessible to employers, at least until such time as electronic or other means for separating genetic and non-genetic information is fully developed and implemented (Rothstein, 2008).

### *3.1 Wellness programs*

GINA permits requesting and obtaining genetic information as part of an employer-sponsored wellness program. Employer wellness programs are borne of the view that a healthy employee is a productive employee. Increasingly common among companies that provide health insurance and want to reduce health care costs, these programs take a number of forms. Some stress overall health awareness, others promote lifestyle changes (such as smoking cessation or weight control), while others target management of specific diseases, such as heart disease. Genetic information, particularly family history, can play a key role in shaping the health and counseling services offered. As one stark example, a health care professional running a cardiac fitness program likely would want to know if the employee's father suffered from Brugada syndrome, a potentially fatal arrhythmia, and if so might ask the employee to take a genetic test (Kapplinger *et al.*, 2010).

Striking a balance between our interests in genetic privacy and nondiscrimination and fostering the benefits of genetic medicine, GINA authorizes obtaining an employee/participant's genetic information with his or her voluntary, written informed consent and requires the information remain confidential within the confines of the professional–employee relationship. Only aggregate, non-identifiable information may be shared with the employer. Underscoring that participation must be voluntary, the EEOC casts a critical eye on incentives to participate and stresses that employees must be told they are not required to answer questions about family history (EEOC, 2010, Federal Register, 68935–68936). Early scholarly analysis suggests that the interface among GINA, ADAA, and ACA raises issues about permissible structuring of participation incentives and whether GINA's limitations undermine the purpose of wellness programs and ACA's efforts to promote greater, more effective use of these programs to improve health and contain costs (Bard, 2011).

## 4. Nondiscrimination in employment

GINA makes it unlawful to fail or refuse to hire, to fire, or otherwise discriminate against any employee with respect to compensation or other terms and conditions of employment because of the employee's genetic information. Companies also may not use genetic information to limit, segregate, or classify employees in a manner that would adversely affect job opportunities or status (GINA, 42 U.S.C.§§ 2000ff(2)(a)(2)). This short section of the law sends a powerful message of protection against genetic discrimination.

GINA's signal achievement is its blanket protection for the many of us who are or may be at increased risk of future disease or disability due to a positive genetic test or family history, but have no symptoms, no impairments, and may never develop the condition. GINA shields us against discriminatory actions based on predictions of future disease or disability, predictions that may often be based on misunderstandings and negative attitudes about genes and disability. In 1995 the EEOC took the position that the "regarded as" prong of the ADA's definition of disability applies to this type of genetic discrimination, a position recently reiterated in one of the few EEOC lawsuits under GINA, discussed below. Legal precedents establishing the ADAA's protections against disability discrimination based on myths, fears, and unfounded negative attitudes arguably should be extended to apply to misunderstandings about genetic traits and related misperceptions about current and future ability to perform the requisite job functions. But commentators generally believe it unlikely that courts will adopt the EEOC's interpretation, noting for example that there is no mention of genetics in the ADA's text and scant evidence in the legislative history that Congress gave serious consideration to the risks of genetic discrimination (Olick, 2000). GINA fills the gap and aims to ensure full protection against genetic discrimination in the workplace based on predicted future disease or disability.

### *4.1 Manifestation of disease or disability*

At the same time, GINA is not intended to supplant ADAA protections against disability discrimination when the employee has manifested a disease or disability. GINA permits acquisition and use of "medical information that is not genetic information about a manifested disease, disorder, or pathological condition of an employee or family member, including a manifested disease, disorder, or pathological condition that has or may have a genetic basis" (GINA, 42 U.S.C.§§ 2000ff-10)). Thus, GINA protects asymptomatic person A whose genetic information increases his risk for future disease or disability, such as diabetes, but likely not person B whose symptomatic diabetic condition has a genetic component. Yet there is no operative definition of manifestation in the law. EEOC regulations define the concept as follows:

> that an individual has been or could reasonably be diagnosed with the disease, disorder or pathological condition by a health care professional with appropriate training and expertise in the field of medicine involved. For purposes of this part, a disease, disorder, or pathological condition is not manifested if the diagnosis is based principally on genetic information or on the results of one or more genetic tests.
>
> (EEOC, 2010, Federal Register, 68917)

This definition leaves some large unanswered questions. Unfelt molecular changes associated with genetic traits do not constitute manifestation, but does manifestation mean that the employee has merely experienced symptoms of the disease? Demonstrates functional impairment? Meets the ADAA test of being substantially limited in a major life activity? Has merely sought medical attention? Been diagnosed or is under the care of a physician? In short, at what stage of a disease process or pathological condition does the employee cease to be protected by GINA? And for purposes of the law, who counts as a health care professional with appropriate training and experience? A family doctor? Oncologist? Cardiologist? Geneticist? Genetic counselor? Who decides whether the diagnosis is based principally on genetic information?

When a disease or disorder has manifested may well be the subject of significant litigation in the years ahead. Law professor Mark Rothstein warns that those in the middle of the spectrum from asymptomatic genetic predisposition (GINA) to fully manifest disabling disease (ADAA)—those with mild, temporary, non-disabling conditions—could find themselves without protection against discrimination under either law (Rothstein, 2008). As Anya Prince, a contributor to this volume, argues, "[i]f the concept of disease manifestation is not carefully drawn, it could undermine the very protections GINA was designed to provide" (Prince and Berkman, 2012). Those whose disease or disability has manifested in some way (or who believe that it has) may find it advisable to seek redress under both the ADAA and GINA, as illustrated by the EEOC actions discussed in the next section.

## 5. Cases alleging discrimination Under GINA

For the period 2010–2013 there were more than 600 charges filed with the EEOC under GINA. Most claims (more than 75 percent) were found to have no reasonable cause or were closed for administrative reasons (for example the complaining party failed to pursue the claim) (EEOC, 2014). As of this writing there have been three lawsuits filed by the EEOC. All allege violations of both the privacy and nondiscrimination provisions of GINA.

In *Fabricut, Inc.*, a temporary memo clerk applied for a permanent job in the same position. She was made a conditional offer of employment and was sent for a pre-employment drug test and physical. The questionnaire she was required to fill out asked a number of questions about specific disorders in her family medical history, including heart disease, cancer, diabetes, arthritis, and "mental disorders." Medical testing revealed a concern about carpal tunnel syndrome. Although the employee's personal physician found that she did not have carpal tunnel, the company denied her the job. The EEOC's lawsuit alleged two violations. First, that Fabricut's actions violated the privacy provisions of GINA that prohibit requesting or requiring genetic information (here, family medical history) and second that refusal to hire on the basis of this information was genetic discrimination. Refusal to hire was also found to violate the ADA because the employee was qualified to hold the position but was wrongly regarded as disabled based on genetic information. Under the consent decree, filed the same day as the lawsuit, Fabricut agreed to take steps to prevent future discrimination and to pay a $50,000 fine (EEOC Press Release, 7 May 2013). This case is of a piece with *Burlington Northern* in which the EEOC prosecuted to settlement an action alleging that the railroad's testing of employees for genetic predisposition to carpal tunnel syndrome without consent constituted genetic discrimination under the ADA (EEOC Press Release, 18 April 2001; Hechler, 2002). *Fabricut* demonstrates the overlap between the two laws with respect to genetic discrimination and the EEOC's continuing commitment to applying the ADA's "regarded as" clause to cases of predicted future disability based on genetic information.

Founders Pavilion, an upstate New York nursing and rehabilitation center, allegedly conducted post-offer, pre-employment medical exams that included requests for information about family medical history—protected genetic information under GINA. The medical exam and inquiry also occurred annually for current employees. When the case could not be settled administratively, the EEOC filed a lawsuit alleging that these practices violated GINA. Founders also allegedly engaged in separate acts of disability discrimination and civil rights violations that included taking adverse actions against female employees because they were pregnant (EEOC Press Release, 16 May 2013). Under the settlement Founders agreed to pay $370,000, a portion of which goes to the 138 persons unlawfully asked for their genetic information, and to change their policies and practices to prevent future instances of genetic, disability, and pregnancy discrimination (EEOC Press Release, 13 January 2014).

In September 2013 the EEOC filed a lawsuit against The Abatti Group and its subsidiaries, alleging that the seed and fertilizer companies had required job applicants to submit to unlawful physical exams, answer questions about their medical conditions, and respond to inquiries about genetic information in the form of family medical histories, in order to get the job. One temporary worker seeking a full-time position as a dispatcher disclosed a prior hospitalization for a heart condition, a condition that also affected his family members. The employee was denied the job, allegedly because the company regarded him as disabled. The EEOC's complaint asserts that the Abatti Group's actions violated both GINA and the ADA and seeks both monetary damages and injunctive relief to prevent future genetic discrimination. The case is unresolved at this time (EEOC Press Release, 30 September 2013).

All three EEOC actions involve unlawful inquiries into family medical history. They appear to also involve misperceptions and ill-founded predictions of future disease or disability. None offers guidance regarding the definition of manifest disease discussed above.

## 6. Genetic monitoring

GINA permits "genetic monitoring of the biological effects of toxic substances in the workplace," provided it is conducted with: 1) written notice; 2) voluntary, written informed consent of the employee; 3) individual results given to the employee; and 4) results known to the health care professional or genetic counselor involved in the monitoring are only shared with the company in the aggregate without identifying individual workers. These requirements do not apply where genetic monitoring is required by law. Genetic monitoring involves periodic evaluations of employees to assess whether genetic changes, such as chromosomal damage or mutations, may have resulted from workplace exposure to toxins (GINA, 42 U.S.C.§§ 2000ff(5); 2000ff-1(b)(5)). The Department of Health and Human Services (DHHS) report *Genetics in the Workplace* identifies numerous genetic factors that play a role in occupational diseases. Genetic monitoring has been an effective tool, for example, in the study of genetic risk factors related to beryllium exposure (DHHS, 2010). GINA's approach balances individual privacy interests with the promotion of occupational safety and health. But whether the law strikes the right balance warrants scrutiny.

GINA represents a significant departure from the ADAA. First, the law does not authorize genetic screening, meaning identifiable testing of individuals for purposes of hiring or job placement. Thus, it prohibits preventive genetic screening for (hyper) susceptibility to workplace conditions that would be permitted under the ADAA in some instances. To illustrate, an employee genetically predisposed to alpha antitrypsin deficiency may have increased susceptibility to chronic obstructive lung disease when exposed to respiratory irritants (American Medical Association, 1991). This employee would only become aware of this risk if the company's genetic monitoring program targeted this condition. The individual with a genetic predisposition to back injury from certain forms of physical exertion (ankylosing spondylitis) seemingly gets no genetic information to protect against on-the-job injury (he could seek private testing). GINA's carefully drawn rules for genetic monitoring rightly favor environmental changes to promote workplace health and safety and shield workers from exclusion or re-assignment based on genetic information (consider the limitation to aggregate data reporting only), but the law also potentially leaves many workers without information pertinent to weighing employment options.

Second, GINA contains no language parallel to the "direct threat" provisions of the ADAA that allow medical screening and unfavorable employment decisions if the employee poses a direct threat to self, others in the workplace, or the public. As interpreted by the EEOC, such employment decisions must be based on an individuated assessment of the person's current ability to do the job. Adverse decisions are permitted only if there is a "significant risk of substantial harm to health and safety" based on medical and other objective evidence (ADAA, 42 U.S.C. §12113(b); EEOC regulations, 29 C.F.R. §1630.2(r)). Courts have upheld medical screening and specific discriminatory actions, for example with respect to law enforcement and emergency personnel, truck drivers, and surgeons, to protect others from harm. Business responsibility to safeguard consumer and public health and safety is deeply engrained in the marketplace and in law, and remains permissible under the ADAA for manifest disabilities and conditions. But anticipatory, preventive examinations and testing may not, under GINA, include genetic information. Consider the airline pilot genetically predisposed to sudden cardiac arrest; or the train conductor at greater risk for macular degeneration due to a genetic trait.

On the current state of genetic knowledge it is doubtful whether predictions of future disability based on genetic information could satisfy the standard of posing a significant risk of substantial harm with respect to the employee's current ability to do the job (DHHS, 2010). But in the years ahead this may well become a thorny question, calling us to balance the likelihood a genetic risk will manifest and when, the imminence and potential magnitude of harm, individual rights, and the allocation of risk, and the reasonable alternatives to denying someone the job (Olick, 2000).

GINA called for the establishment of a commission in 2014, expressly charged to study the developing science of genetics and whether employees should be authorized to allege that employment practices have a disparate adverse impact on groups that share particular genetic traits (GINA, 42 U.S.C.§§ 2000ff 7(b)). At the time of this writing no members have been appointed to this commission. Congress and the commission would be well advised to expand this inquiry to consider whether GINA should permit practices that involve evaluation of genetic information intended to protect individuals, co-workers, and the public from potential harm.

## 7. On genetic forecasts

Here (and in any discussion of genetic discrimination) accurate understanding and critical analysis of the meaning of genetic information is critical. Widespread misunderstanding about the analytical validity (predictive power) of genetic tests and information is common, no less so in the corporate boardroom, often fueled by media portrayals and popular genetalk that overestimate genetic forecasts and mistakenly assume that our genes are our destiny. As suggested throughout this essay, in the vast majority of instances genetic traits identify predispositions to develop certain illnesses, diseases, or conditions. Genetic forecasts are probabilistic, not deterministic (Institute of Medicine, 1994). The predictive force of genetic diagnoses vary not only from one condition to the next, but they can also vary among individuals with the same genetic condition. "[W]ide variation in clinical manifestations of a gene-associated disorder—individuality—is common" (Billings *et al.*, 1992). Moreover, most known genetic conditions are multifactorial, meaning that a combination of factors, such as diet, other health conditions, or environmental exposure influence gene expression and the likelihood of manifestation; some involve multiple gene expression; and still others are late-onset conditions, meaning that gene expression and manifestation may not occur for years or decades from the time of diagnosis, if at all. In other instances a person may be a carrier of a genetic defect, but never become symptomatic. In short, it would be a serious error to paint all genetic conditions, or all persons with the same genetic condition, with the same brush (Institute of Medicine, 1994).

The AMA Council on Ethical and Judicial Affairs concluded in 1991 that genetic tests are "poor predictors of disease and even poorer predictors of disabling disease" and recommended that genetic susceptibility testing not be used as a basis for employment decisions (AMA, 1991). Other recent authorities on genetic monitoring and screening in the workplace reach essentially the same conclusion (DHHS, 2010; ACOEM Task Force, 2010). The developing science of molecular genetics will undoubtedly continue to challenge this assessment.

## 8. Conclusion

GINA has been trumpeted as the first civil rights law of the 21st century, though it should be noted that its narrow focus on health insurance and employment makes it more limited than extant law that proscribes race and gender discrimination (Annas *et al.*, 2008). Some legislative opponents of GINA argued that no law was necessary because genetic discrimination does not happen; that the law is a solution in search of a problem (Slaughter, 2008). Though the prevalence of genetic discrimination is not well established, numerous studies over more than two decades have shown overwhelming concern about genetic privacy and the risks of discrimination in health insurance and employment (Genetics and Public Policy Center, 2007; Geller, *et al.*, 1996).

It bears emphasis that GINA's vision is prospective, to shield us from both risks and fears of genetic discrimination so that we may pursue the benefits of genetic testing and knowledge and the promise of genetic science and research. Whether GINA fulfills its promise in the workplace may well depend on how companies, practitioners, and courts interpret the interplay between GINA, ADAA, and other laws, and in particular the meaning given to the concept of manifest condition. Equally critical, inexorable advances in science and medicine may radically alter the analytical validity of genetic information, at least for some conditions, and may force us to rethink the delicate balance at the nexus of individual privacy, genomic medicine, occupational health and safety, the free market, and the public good.

## References

ACOEM Task Force (2010) "Genetic Screening in the Workplace" *Journal of Occupational and Environmental Medicine* 52(7): 763.

Americans with Disabilities Amendment Act (ADDA) (2008).

American Medical Association Council on Ethical and Judicial Affairs (1991) "Use of Genetic Testing By Employers" *JAMA* 266(13): 1827–1830.

Annas, G. J., Roche, P., and Green, R.C. (2008) "GINA, Genism, and Civil Rights" *Bioethics* 22(7): ii–iv.

Bard, Jennifer S. (2011) "When Public Health and Genetic Privacy Collide: Positive and Normative Theories Explaining How ACA's Expansion of Corporate Wellness Programs Conflicts with GINA's Privacy Rules" *Journal of Law and Medical Ethics* 39: 470–487.

Billings, Paul R. *et al.* (1992) "Discrimination as a Consequence of Genetic Testing" *American Journal of Human Genetics* 50: 476–482.

Department of Health and Human Services, Centers for Disease Control and Prevention, National Institute for Occupational Safety and Health Genetics Working Group (DHHS) (2010) *Genetics in the Workplace: Implications for Occupational Safety and Health.* Washington, DC.

Equal Employment Opportunity Commission (EEOC) (2001) Press release. "EEOC Settles ADA Suit Against BNSF for Genetic Bias." 18 April. Available at www.eeoc.gov/press/4-18-01.html [accessed 14 May, 2014].

Equal Employment Opportunity Commission (EEOC) (2010) "Regulations Under the Genetic Information Nondiscrimination Act of 2008; Final Rule" *Federal Register* 75(216): 68912–68939.

Equal Employment Opportunity Commission (EEOC) (2013) Press release. "Fabricut to Pay $50,000 to Settle EEOC Disability and Genetic Information Discrimination Lawsuit." 7 May. Available at www.eeoc.org [accessed 12 May 2014].

Equal Employment Opportunity Commission (EEOC) (2013) Press release. "EEOC Files Class Genetic Information Discrimination Suit Against Corning Rehab Center." 16 May. Available at www.eeoc.org [accessed 12 May 2014].

Equal Employment Opportunity Commission (EEOC) (2013) Press release. "EEOC Sues Abatti Group for Disability, Genetic Information Discrimination." 30 September. Available at www.eeoc.org [accessed 12 May 2014].

Equal Employment Opportunity Commission (EEOC) (2014) "Genetic Information Non-Discrimination Act Charges." Available at www.eeoc.org [accessed 14 May 2014].

Equal Employment Opportunity Commission (EEOC) (2014) Press release. "Founders Pavilion Will Pay $370,000 to Settle EEOC Genetic Information Discrimination Lawsuit." 13 January. Available at www.eeoc.org [accessed 12 May 2014].

Executive Order 13145 (2000) "To Prohibit Discrimination in Federal Employment Based on Genetic Information" *Federal Register* 65: 6,875.

Feldman, E. (2011) "The Genetic Information Nondiscrimination Act (GINA): Public Policy and Medical Practice in the Age of Personalized Medicine" *Journal of General and Internal Medicine* 27(6): 743–746.

Geller, Lisa N. *et al.* (1996) "Individual, Family, and Societal Dimensions of Genetic Discrimination: A Case Study Analysis" *Science and Engineering Ethics* 2: 71–88.

Genetics and Public Policy Center (2007) White Paper. "U.S. Public Opinion on Uses of Genetic Information and Genetic Discrimination." Available at www.dnapolicy.org/resources/GINAPublic_Opinion_Genetic_Information_Discrimination.pdf [accessed 28 May 2014].

Health Insurance Portability and Accountability Act (HIPAA) (1996).

Hechler, D. (2002) "Railroad to Pay $2.2 Million Over Genetic Testing: Landmark Settlement Under the ADA" *The National Law Journal* 24. 13 May, p. A22.

Institute of Medicine (1994) *Assessing Genetic Risks: Implications for Health and Social Policy*. Washington, DC: National Academy Press.

Kapplinger, J.D., Tester, J.D., Alders, M. *et al.* (2010) "An International Compendium of Mutations in the SCN5-A-encoded Cardiac Sodium Channel in Patients Referred for Brugada Syndrome Genetic Testing" *Heart Rhythm* 7(1): 33–46.

National Conference of State Legislatures (NCSL) (2008) "Genetics and Health Insurance State Anti-Discrimination Laws." Available at: www.ncsl.org/research/health/genetic-nondiscrimination-in-health-insurance-laws.aspx [accessed 7 May 2014].

Olick, R. S. (2000) "Genes in the Workplace: New Frontiers for ADA Law, Policy and Research" in Blanck, P. (ed.), *Employment, Disability, and the Americans With Disabilities Act: Issues in Law, Public Policy and Research*. Northwestern University Press. pp. 285–314.

Patient Protection and Affordable Care Act of 2010 Pub. L. No. 111–148, 124 Stat. 119 (2010).

Prince, A. E. and Berkman, B. E. (2012) "When Does an Illness Begin: Genetic Discrimination and Disease Manifestation" *Journal of Law and Medical Ethics* 40(3): 655–664.

Rothstein, M. A. (2008) "GINA, the ADA, and Genetic Discrimination in Employment" *Journal of Law and Medical Ethics* 36(4): 837–840.

Slaughter, L. M. (2008) "The Genetic Information Nondiscrimination Act: Why Your Personal Genetics are Still Vulnerable to Discrimination" *Surgical Clinics of North America* 88(4): 723–738.

The Genetic Information Nondiscrimination Act of 2008 (GINA). 42 U.S.C. 2000ff et seq, 2012.

Weir, R. F., and Olick, R. S. (2004) *The Stored Tissue Issue: Biomedical Research, Ethics, and Law in the Era of Genomic Medicine.* New York: Oxford University Press.

# Section 4

# Building the case for a European Union regulatory response

Section 4 contains six chapters, the objective of which is to highlight the current position in Europe and build the background to examining the potential need for an EU-level regulatory response. This section provides a comprehensive overview of the relevant perspectives and stakeholders in this area, including employers and insurance companies. This section focuses on existing regulatory frameworks and benchmarks at international level, Council of Europe level and European Union level. It highlights the patchwork of national-level regulation in this area and the differing levels of protection amongst the EU Member States.

The first chapter in this section, by James Davey, is entitled 'Genetic discrimination in insurance: Lessons from *Test Achats*.' The second chapter, 'Employment practices in a new genomic era: Acknowledging competing rights and striking a balance', is written by Aisling de Paor. The third chapter is entitled 'Medical (genetic) examinations for non-health purposes: The relevance of European legal standard setting', by Henriette Roscam Abbing. The fourth chapter, 'National legal and policy responses to genetic discrimination in Europe: The difficulties of regulation', is written by Ine Van Hoyweghen. The fifth chapter, by Mark Taylor', is entitled 'Genetic discrimination and the draft European Union General Data Protection Regulation'. The final chapter in this section, 'Accommodating genes: Disability, discrimination and international human rights law', is written by Janet Lord.

# 9 Genetic discrimination in insurance

## Lessons from *Test Achats*

*James Davey*

> Insurance, therefore, takes from all a contribution; from those who will not need its aid, as well as from those who will; for it is as certain that some will not, as that some will. But as it is uncertain who will, and who will not, it demands this tribute from all to the uncertainty of fate. And it is precisely the moneys thus given away by some, and these only, which supply the fund out of which the misfortune of those whose bad luck it is that their moneys have not been thrown away, are repaired. The afflicted finds his money spent to some purpose; and only the fortunate part with it for nothing. From this point of view the whole beauty of the system of insurance is seen.
>
> D.R. Jaques 'Society on the Basis of Mutual Life Insurance' (1847) 16 *Hunt's Merchant Mag and Com Rev* 152, 158

Insurance has not always been viewed as a corporate behemoth; it was once seen as the basis for a fair and just society. In recent times, the fear is that not all will have equal access to the just results that 'risk pooling' can bring, and the 'genetic underclass' might become the archetypal group not caught by the safety net (McGleenan and Wiesing, 2000: 373). This chapter considers proposals to regulate genetic discrimination in insurance in light of recent litigation in sex discrimination.

### 1. Introduction: A 'GINA' for Europe

The likelihood of pan-European regulation of genetic information by insurers is influenced by two distinct factors: political willingness to act and a sound legal basis for intervention. These issues came together in one place: the recent litigation in sex discrimination in Case C-236/09 *Association belge de Consommateurs Test Achats ASBL v Conseil de Ministres* [2012] 1 WLR 1933 (hereafter, *Test Achats*). The difficulty this dispute caused to European Union legislative bodies (especially the Council of Ministers and the Commission) and the negative reaction of the insurance industry means that legislation to regulate genetic information in insurance at the European level may be further away.

The breadth of the genetic information issue means that it touches upon issues of human rights (such as privacy), areas of commerce (such as insurance) and hybrid realms (such as employment law). Within the United States, some progress has been made towards regulatory intervention (Roberts, 2010) with the adoption of the Genetic Information Nondiscrimination Act 2008 (GINA). GINA added to existing protections in US law by prohibiting the use of genetic information in the pricing of health insurance. Health insurers were prevented from considering any predictive element of genetic data, including family history. However, as Rothstein noted:

> GINA does not apply to life insurance, disability insurance, long-term care insurance, or other potential uses of genetic information. Consequently, it is not clear that its limited protections will be sufficient to allay the fears of individuals currently dissuaded from undergoing genetic testing.
>
> (Rothstein, 2008: 837)

Even this limited intervention may not be replicated in the short term across Europe, as the Treaty capacity to intervene is not yet clearly in place. Art 19 Treaty on the Functioning of the European Union (TFEU) does not mention genetic status as an explicit basis for intervention:

> Without prejudice to the other provisions of the Treaties and within the limits of the powers conferred by them upon the Union, the Council, acting unanimously in accordance with a special legislative procedure and after obtaining the consent of the European Parliament, may take appropriate action to combat discrimination based on sex, racial or ethnic origin, religion or belief, disability, age or sexual orientation.

The focus of this piece is the likely reaction to any proposal to extend the scope of European regulation to the use of genetic information by insurers. The response of the insurance market would be framed by its recent experience in a related area: the regulation of sex as a risk factor in the European Court of Justice (ECJ) ruling in *Test Achats*. This decision considered two areas of considerable importance to the development of legislative protection against genetic discrimination:

1 Is it permissible under European Union law for insurers to discriminate directly on the basis of protected characteristics (such as sex) where there is actuarial evidence of difference between the insured across those groups?
2 Assuming the answer to question 1 is 'No', to what extent is Art 21 of the Charter of Fundamental Rights of the European Union (2000/C

364/01) an effective source of horizontal rights and duties at the EU level?

Before considering these issues in depth, we begin with a review of the current state of anti-discrimination law in insurance at the United Kingdom and European Union levels.

## 2. The regulation of discrimination in insurance: policy considerations in light of the current UK and EU approach

### *2.1 Policy arguments*

The difficulty for policymakers is that insurance and anti-discrimination law each adopt a fundamentally different perspective to risk assessment. Insurance prices an individual's risk status by reference to the past losses of individuals in that group. Viewed experientially (on the basis of past claims records) men and women do drive differently, die differently and make different demands on healthcare services. For the insurance industry, differential pricing based on e.g. gender is not 'discrimination' but the recognition that risk outcomes are gender related, age related and genetically related. The insurance industry has often defended its practices as 'fair discrimination': a modern oxymoron. They assert that they are not discriminating in the legal sense by treating similar cases differently; rather they are treating different cases differently. This clash between the principles of insurance and anti-discrimination law is fundamental (Davey, 2000: 599–609): whether differential treatment based on actuarial experience is 'discrimination' in law or justified differential treatment. This tension is felt at both the national and supranational levels as governments and EU institutions seek to regulate underwriting practices.

The division between the insurance industry and discrimination lawyers can be expressed as two different models of equality: 'fair discrimination' and 'anti-discrimination'. For proponents of 'fair discrimination' (and that encompasses much of the actuarial and insurance professions) differential treatment ought only to be unlawful where there is no statistical evidence of different outcomes. On this view, where there is a statistical correlation it is unjust and/or economically inefficient to force the low risk to subsidise the high risk. An archetypal account of this view is found in Abraham's leading account of insurance regulatory theory: *Distributing Risk: Insurance, Legal Theory and Public Policy* (Abraham, 1986: 20–21). In it, he described a libertarian model of insurance regulation, which permits individuals to benefit from their genetic and social birthright. Put simply, there are winners and losers in society, and the regulation of a commercial sector is not the optimal mechanism for redistribution of wealth or life chances. In his view, that is the role of the welfare state. Moreover, it is unjust to force the low-risk insured to pay disguised subsidies to the high-risk insured when an unfettered use of data would allow a fairer pricing structure.

By contrast, the 'anti-discrimination' approach (see Davey, 2000: 603) restricts insurers' risk classification to variables that are:

a) causally connected to the risk; and
b) controllable; and
c) not associated with historical or invidious discrimination.

This is clearly a much higher level of intervention, and requires justification. One justification stems from the design of risk classification regimes: insurers often select risk factors to minimise cost rather than maximise accuracy of risk assessment. This would mean that factor 'X' may not be included in the risk classification regime for being too (economically) costly to process or verify. An applicant's smoking status is the classic example of this: applicants often state their desired rather than actual status and so insurers frequently ignore this data set even though it would be highly correlated to losses (e.g. for household fires). Equality-minded pressure groups can then respond to insurers by arguing that factor 'Y' might be excluded from risk classification because of its social cost, even if it efficient from the economic perspective. Risk classification is, then, not an attempt to be accurate, but accurate enough to be profitable. Equality law might require it to be only accurate enough to be fair.

The history of insurance regulation in the EU is of a gentle drift from non-regulation of commercial relationships towards 'anti-discrimination', and *Test Achats* is but the most recent point in that trajectory (Wils, 1994).

### *2.2 Substantive regulation: law and 'soft' law controls*

The regulation of discriminatory underwriting practices in the UK derives from a mixture of European Union, national and soft law measures. Unlike many other forms of discrimination that are regulated in the United Kingdom by the Equality Act 2010, genetic discrimination is dealt with by means of a 'soft law' moratorium, agreed by concordat between the Association of British Insurers and government (HM Government and ABI, 2011). This agreement denies insurers use of predictive genetic test results as a factor in risk assessment, within certain financial and regulatory constraints. In the vast majority of cases, as noted by Stirton (Stirton, 2012: 215), genetic test results of any kind will not need to be disclosed:

1. Customers will not be required to disclose the results of predictive genetic tests for policies up to £500,000 of life insurance, or £300,000 for critical illness insurance, or paying annual benefits of £30,000 for income protection insurance ('the financial limits').

More than 97% of policies issued in 2004 were below these limits in each category.

2. When the cumulative value of insurance exceeds the financial limits, insurers may seek information about, and customers must disclose, tests approved by GAIC for use for a particular insurance product, subject to the restrictions in the Concordat.

At present the only test approved by the committee which advised the UK government on genetic testing (the Genetics and Insurance Committee, see (Thomas, 2012)) is that for Huntington's disease (Association of British Insurers, 2013). This is the only genetic test result that would need to be disclosed (under the standard rules of insurance contract law) and then only for policies above the financial limits. This soft law measure therefore goes well beyond any 'fair discrimination' model, to restrict the use of genetic test results information even where the impact on mortality and morbidity is well understood (e.g. Huntington's disease within the moratorium's financial limits). The measure is therefore broad in one sense, although it has significant limitations.

Unlike GINA, the moratorium is restricted to predictive genetic test results and not other forms of genetic information, such as family history. The limited nature of the intervention reflects the solidarity basis of primary healthcare in the United Kingdom. The National Health Service is funded out of general taxation (as a percentage of taxable income), not on an actuarial, risk-assessment basis. The presence of a positive test for any healthcare-related outcome, whether genetic or otherwise, is therefore irrelevant in the provision or pricing of primary healthcare. Where genetic (and other) test results would have significance is in other socially significant insurance products, such as life insurance to back a mortgage application, and it is there that the moratorium has effect. The UK model is therefore both wider and narrower than GINA: the categories of data protected are narrower than in the US, but the types of product regulated are wider.

In order to assess the scope of the moratorium in the United Kingdom, it is useful to place it alongside its statutory brethren: the Equality Act 2010, which regulates other forms of discrimination in insurance. A wide range of factors including sex, age, race, religion, disability, and sexuality may (in relation to some risks) be indicators for high-risk status on the basis of past claims experience. Many of these criteria have a protected status under European Union law and are therefore protected by the 2010 Act. Presently, genetic information is not recognised as a protected characteristic under Art 19 TFEU:

> Without prejudice to the other provisions of the Treaties and within the limits of the powers conferred by them upon the Union, the Council, acting unanimously in accordance with a special legislative procedure

> and after obtaining the consent of the European Parliament, may take appropriate action to combat discrimination based on sex, racial or ethnic origin, religion or belief, disability, age or sexual orientation.

Prior to *Test Achats*, the United Kingdom sought a compromise between protection from discrimination on the basis of protected characteristics and insurers' desire to price products using these criteria. In UK law, the general obligation on service providers to not discriminate is found in section 29 of the Equality Act 2010. Thus section 29(2) provides:

> (2) A service-provider (A) must not, in providing the service, discriminate against a person (B) –
> (a) as to the terms on which A provides the service to B;
> (b) by terminating the provision of the service to B;
> (c) by subjecting B to any other detriment.

Crucially, the notion of discrimination was not equated with differential treatment. Where reasonable, insurers would satisfy section 29 by reliance on reliable actuarial data as to disability or sex. The formula granting this exception was found in Schedule 3, paras 21–22:

It is not a contravention of section 29, so far as relating to relevant discrimination, to do anything in relation to an annuity, life insurance policy, accident insurance policy or similar matter involving the assessment of risk if –

> (a) that thing is done by reference to actuarial or other data from a source on which it is reasonable to rely, and
> (b) it is reasonable to do that thing.

This legitimised *prima facie* direct discrimination on the basis of disability (para 21) or gender reassignment, pregnancy or sex discrimination (para 22). However, it did so by declaring that pricing insurance products differently by reference to actuarial data is not discrimination. The choice of mechanism here is deliberate. In the language of discrimination law: it is not treating similar cases differently; it is treating different cases differently. In this version of 'discrimination', where reliable actuarial data establishes historically different claims patterns between e.g. men and women, it is justifiable to charge each group different prices, 'where it is reasonable to do [so]'. This exception, it should be noted, did not extend to other protected characteristics, which could not be included in insurance risk classification. Race could never be used as a risk factor in underwriting, even where actuarial evidence of difference existed. This schema largely mirrored the atomised position prior to the Equality Act 2010, whereby sex, race and disability discrimination fell under individual statutory regimes (Davey, 2000: 594–599).

It is the 2010 Act, as the national law embodiment of EU anti-discrimination law, and the equivalent legislation in other Member States, that is at issue in the *Test Achats* litigation. In essence, the case tests whether the permission to rely on actuarial data to justify differential treatment is compatible with European Union law.

## 3. *Test Achats*: sex discrimination, motor insurance and EU fundamental rights

### *3.1* Test Achats–*the facts*

It is in light of this regulatory framework that we must assess the decision of the European Court of Justice in *Test Achats* of May 2011. The case was brought by a Belgian consumer rights group, challenging the freedom granted to Belgian insurers to classify drivers applying for motor insurance by gender. The Belgian government (and many others, including the British government) had permitted this behaviour in reliance on Art 5(2), Council Directive 2004/113 EC (the 'Gender Directive'). Art 5(2) provided a derogation from the rule in Art 5(1) which otherwise required that sex should not be used as a risk factor in calculating 'individuals' premiums and benefits' in insurance. The Art 5(2) derogation permitted 'proportionate differences in individuals' premiums and benefits where the use of sex is a determining factor in the assessment of risk based on relevant and accurate actuarial and statistical data' and was subject to review after 5 years. The primary question for reference to the European Court was therefore: 'Is Article 5(2) of Directive 2004/113/EC [the 'Gender Directive'] compatible with Article 6(2) EU, and more specifically with the principle of equality and non-discrimination guaranteed by that provision?'

Following the reference made by the Belgian court for a preliminary ruling, the European Court of Justice found the (potentially) permanent and extensive derogation in Art 5(2) of the Gender Directive to be incompatible with the Treaty provisions requiring non-discrimination on which the Directive was based. Member States were given until the end of 2012 to ensure that insurers complied with the general obligation in Art 5(1) of the Directive and move to a broadly gender-neutral model of insurance. The immediate effect of this was to force a move to a gender-neutral model of insurance pricing within the European Union. However, the long-term effect of the decision is likely to be wider, as the Charter and Treaty provisions of which the Gender Directive fell foul are not restricted to gender discrimination. This may be the starting point of a trend towards gender-, race-, age- and genetic- blind insurance markets.

### *3.2* Test Achats–*the Kokott AG opinion*

The formal decision of the European Court of Justice contained remarkably little discussion of the underlying situation in *Test Achats*. It provides instead a technical decision which can only be properly understood by reading it alongside the opinion given by Advocate General Kokott. For those unfamiliar with European Court of Justice process, the Advocate General (an appointee of the Court) writes a guide to the issues raised for the Court to follow. These opinions are often more explicit in their legal logic than the final decision, as the ECJ judgment is a composite document, agreed by all the members of the Court. The Advocate General's opinion is often a clearer statement of principle, albeit from a single perspective. Whilst the opinion is not legally binding, it often (as here) explains the broader reasons behind the technical decisions adopted by the Court.

The Advocate General in *Test Achats* was the German representative, Juliane Kokott. She is a German qualified legal academic but with additional expertise from studying in the United States as a Fulbright scholar (Kokott, 2013). Her doctorate was in US human rights law, and this is likely to have been influential in her decision. Evidence of her broader understanding of the insurance/equality issue in the United States was evident in her conclusion, suggesting that Art 5(2) was invalid:

> The Court would be keeping good company if it delivered such a judgment: more than 30 years ago the Supreme Court of the United States of America held in connection with pension insurance funds that the Civil Rights Act of 1964 prohibits different treatment of insured persons on the basis of their sex.
>
> ([2012] 1 WLR 1933, 1951)

In her review of the issues, she made clear that the Gender Directive as written must promote the objectives established in the competence-granting provisions. Her analysis of EU equality and anti-discrimination provisions led her to describe an 'anti-discrimination' model of equality law in insurance (as described above). Where this approach is adopted, factors such as race or gender over which the insured has no control, ought not to be the basis for commercial pricing structures, even if actuarial evidence exists.

The limits of these 'uncontrollable' factors are defined, in her view, by the fundamental principles of EU law, and the 'specific prohibitions of discrimination laid down in Article 21(1) of the Charter of Fundamental Rights' ([2012] 1 WLR 1933, 1947). The Charter provision, it will be recalled, includes a freedom from genetic discrimination, and so the precise legal effect of this approach needs careful attention (and is considered in detail below).

For Kokott AG, no logical distinction could be drawn between different risk factors outside the insured's control, such as race and sex. Recall that UK law prohibits race as a risk factor, even if there is empirical evidence of difference. In defining the EU institutions' competence to legislate, she noted:

> The Council may not therefore, for example, permit a person's race and ethnic origin to be used as a ground for differentiation in insurance. In a Union governed by the rule of law, which has declared respect for human dignity, human rights, equality and non-discrimination to be its overriding principles, it would without doubt be extremely inappropriate if for instance, in the context of medical insurance, varying risks of contracting skin cancers were to be linked to the skin colour of the insured person and either a higher or lower premium were thus to be demanded of him.
>
> [2012] 1 WLR 1933, 1947–48)

For Kokott AG, there was an obvious logical step to the issue of direct sexual discrimination:

> It is equally inappropriate to link insurance risks to a person's sex. There is no material reason to assume that the prohibition of discrimination on grounds of sex under European Union law provides less protection than the prohibition of discrimination on the basis of race or ethnic origin under European Union law. Like race and ethnic origin, gender is also a characteristic which is inseparably linked to the insured person as an individual and over which he has no influence. In addition, a person's gender, unlike, for instance, his age, is not subject to any natural changes.
>
> ([2012] 1 WLR 1933, 1948)

The question then arises as to whether differential treatment is always unjustifiable, or whether it was merely impermissible on the facts. In the view of Kokott AG, direct discrimination was only justifiable when necessary, and sex discrimination in motor insurance did not meet this threshold:

> There is then a sweeping assumption that the different life expectancies of male and female insured persons, the difference in their propensity to take risks when driving and the difference in their inclination to utilise medical services – which merely come to light statistically – are essentially due to their sex.
>
> ([2012] 1 WLR 1933, 1949-50)

So, under the analysis of Kokott AG – and this must be correct – sex was merely a proxy variable in motor insurance. It may be that there was a statistically significant difference in the percentage of high-risk drivers who are male rather than female, but they are not high-risk drivers *because* they are male. There is no causal connection, merely a statistical correlation. Moreover, this statistical correlation is subject to change as the behaviour of men and women varies over time:

> In view of social change and the accompanying loss of meaning of traditional role models, the effects of behavioural factors on a person's health and life expectancy can no longer clearly be linked with his sex. To refer once again to a few of the examples just mentioned: both women and men nowadays engage in demanding and sometimes extremely stressful professional activities, members of both sexes consume a not inconsiderable amount of stimulants and even the kind and extent of sporting activities practised by people cannot from the outset be linked to one or other of the sexes.
>
> ([2012] 1 WLR 1933, 1950)

This is a highly persuasive critique of the use of statistical correlation. Despite this, and perhaps because only the headline was read and appreciated – Kokott AG and her opinion were subject to stinging criticism from the insurance industry and media (Johnston, 2011); (Clarke, 2011: 14). Her opinion is open to refutation, but it expertly captured much of EU and US equality law.

### *3.3* Test Achats *– the European Court of Justice decision*

The formal decision of the European Court of Justice contained much less obvious expertise in equality issues than the Kokott AG opinion, which is not surprising. Rather, it provided a technical decision based on EU legislative competence. The difficulty for those promoting the *status quo* was that the power to legislate used by the Council was to achieve anti-discrimination goals, and yet the Art 5(2) exemption worked contrary to that end. As the ECJ stated, the Gender Directive:

> is based on the premise that, for the purposes of applying the principle of equal treatment for men and women, enshrined in articles 21 and 23 of the Charter, the respective situations of men and women with regard to insurance premiums and benefits contracted by them are comparable.
>
> ([2012] 1 WLR 1933, 1961)

However, the inclusion of Art 5(2) created 'a risk that European Union law may permit the derogation from the equal treatment of men and women . . . to persist indefinitely' (*Test Achats*, [2012] 1 WLR 1933, 1961). This then was the difficulty for the EU institutions. Having been persuaded to grant an exemption (and without explaining in the accompanying documentation why they had agreed to such an extension), there was a risk that EU anti-discrimination law would be the basis for a permanent permission to discriminate, and on the basis of weak data. The EU was not under an immediate obligation to regulate in the area (Reich, 2011), but having decided to act, it could not legislate to defeat the purpose of the competence-granting provision.

Having found that Art 5(2) was *ultra vires*, the Court needed to establish the precise legal effect. A retrospective annulment of the provision would require compensation to the many millions of drivers who had been priced according to their gender. To avoid this, the ECJ emphasised that it was the potentially permanent nature of Art 5(2) that was objectionable. By decreeing that the exemption would lapse at the end of its initial 5-year period, it could be transformed into a legally unobjectionable transitional provision.

Within the United Kingdom, the *Test Achats* ruling was implemented by means of the Equality Act 2010 (Amendment) Regulations 2012 (S.I. 2012/2992). It repealed Schedule 3, para 22 for contracts made after 21st Dec 2012. UK insurers may no longer offer differential pricing based on gender even where the actuarial evidence is reasonable and reliable. It should be noted that it did not repeal the equivalent provision (permitting differential treatment on the basis of actuarial data) for disability discrimination.

## 4. Lessons from Test Achats

The potential impact of the *Test Achats* decision goes far beyond the regulation of possible sex discrimination in the motor insurance market. It is a key indicator of the state of social law and policy within the European Union, and of the conflict between Member States and European Union institutions. The future regulation of genetic information in insurance must be considered as now falling within the post-*Test Achats* era. The legal, economic and political ramifications of the move to gender-neutral motor insurance are likely to be considerable. At a legal level it may inspire further challenges. Alternatively, the political backlash may create a substantial 'fire break', impeding the development of rights over genetic information at the EU level.

The legacy of the *Test Achats* decision for genetic discrimination falls into two related categories: one positive, one negative. First, the cloud to accompany the silver lining is the reaction of the insurance industry to *Test Achats* and the backlash in the market and press against anti-discrimination regulation. Second, the positive message for those wanting genetic anti-discrimination law at the EU level: the possible role of the EU Charter of Fundamental Rights.

### *4.1 Lesson 1: the cloud – harmonisation as decontextualised regulation*

The reaction of the insurance industry to the *Test Achats* decision has been almost universally negative. The criticism has been most marked from the actuarial profession. Professor Guillén described the 'European gender nightmare' as anti-competitive:

> I want to emphasize that it is well known by insurance economists that banning costless categorization (like gender) is inefficient. As a consequence, I find it strange that in the current state of economic crisis, our regulatory bodies impose rules that are known to damage performance, rather than promoting solutions, such as partial social insurance, that are known to address categorization efficiently.
>
> (Guillén, 2012: 231–234)

Insurance academics also reacted with alarm (Cameron and Hawke, 2011). In particular, it is the spread of this principle to other types of risk data that has caused most concern. As Cameron and Hawke stated:

> Insurers may well ask whether a prohibition on pricing differently between genders is the final destination in the implementation of European anti-discrimination legislation. Consideration should be given to how European legislation treats age, occupation and other physical and personal attributes, and whether the use of those factors in pricing may also face challenge in future.
>
> (Cameron and Hawke, 2011: 125)

The 'realpolitik' is instructive. Member States negotiated an opt-out from gender-neutral pricing for insurance products. It is likely that the highly effective lobbying machine of the insurance industry helped set the agenda for governments and the European Commission when the Art 5(2) exemption was being considered. Although initially set for a 5-year period, this opt-out was renewable on review. If it had remained unchallenged it is likely that this derogation would have achieved semi-permanent status in due course. When challenged, the opt-out was found to be in breach of EU constitutional principles, as it enshrined a derogation from 'equal treatment', where the establishing powers only mandated action to require equal treatment. Thus, the opt-out fell and Member States were left with an extensive requirement for equal treatment in insurance to which they had not directly consented. This point is crucial: had the negotiating parties known the likely result in *Test Achats* in advance, they might not have legislated for the general clause in such terms. The agreed compromise was for new rights, but with a far-reaching limiting clause. The failure of the limiting clause has extended rights beyond those negotiated and by a substantial margin.

Why does this matter for genetics? At present, the European Union institutions lack direct competence to legislate for anti-discrimination measures in respect of genetic information, unless the Charter of Fundamental Rights is read expansively (Ferri, 2011). *Prima facie*, the EU constitutional settlement left that power with the residual matters that fall within national competence. Regulating genetic information at the EU level would require policymakers to be persuaded to extend the list of characteristics protected under EU law, and thereby further restrict national competence. For those advocating a Europe-wide solution, the judicial unpicking (in *Test Achats*) of the political compromise agreed between Member States in the Gender Directive is unhelpful. Art 19 requires the active co-operation of national government ministers through the Council of Ministers. That body agreed the derogation struck down by the Court. Member States presented with a draft Directive proposing limited regulation of genetic information, with extensive opt-outs and lengthy transitional periods, might be forgiven for thinking: 'Fool me once, shame on you. Fool me twice, shame on me.'

### *4.2 Lesson 2: the silver lining – direct discrimination and EU law*

The interaction between human rights law and private contractual relationships remains a troubled one. Hugh Collins identified the growing invasion of private law space by fundamental rights:

> In Europe, we are currently witnessing in many jurisdictions a transplant of the human rights discourses of constitutional and public law into private law. Surely, it may be asked, the doctrines of private law will reject this transplant of human rights law as an alien species of legal reasoning with incompatible values and legal concepts?
>
> (Collins, 2012: 2)

Collins considered in detail the difficulty in rationalising the use of horizontal direct effect of human rights theories – such as equality and non-discrimination – within a private law framework. This is precisely the battleground in *Test Achats*, and its long-term influence may stem from the extended future use of the EU Charter of Fundamental Rights within private law scenarios. Recall the width of Art 21 of the Charter:

> Any discrimination based on any ground such as sex, race, colour, ethnic or social origin, genetic features, language, religion or belief, political or any other opinion, membership of a national minority, property, birth, disability, age or sexual orientation shall be prohibited.

The fear – expressed so vividly in 'Lesson 1' by the insurance industry – is that nuanced private law considerations will be swept aside by decontextualised harmonisation on public law principles. Commentators (Leczykiewicz, 2013) have suggested that the Charter may have horizontal direct effect despite the self-limiting provision in Art 51:

> 1. The provisions of this Charter are addressed to the institutions and bodies of the Union with due regard for the principle of subsidiarity and to the Member States only when they are implementing Union law. They shall therefore respect the rights, observe the

principles and promote the application thereof in accordance with their respective powers.

2. This Charter does not establish any new power or task for the Community or the Union, or modify powers and tasks defined by the Treaties.

The risk that prior private law assumptions (such as the use of sensitive information in insurance risk classification) will be swept away by the horizontal direct effect enforcement of a Charter of Fundamental Rights (such as equality) is recognised by Collins as one reason why such Charters should be restricted to indirect effect. That would require courts and legislators to recognise and give effect to such rights in their design of private law rights, but would not be immediately enforceable by private parties. The duty would fall on state bodies (such as courts) to reform insurance law to make it compliant. This would allow a nuanced, balanced model to be developed where compromise is achievable. As Collins argues:

> Indirect horizontal effect seems superior in this respect, for it insists that any claims based on rights should be integrated into the existing, carefully considered, settlement between competing rights in private law, which has effectively been tested for generations through litigation in the courts and parliamentary debates.
>
> (Collins, 2012: 22)

This preference for indirect effect assumes that the private law system has a rich and complex prior analysis of the issue (Collins, 2012: 22). The development of insurance contract theory started with the regulation of pre-contractual disclosures and can be traced in English law as far back as *Carter v Boehm* (1766) 97 Eng. Rep. 1162. However, at present it remains an open question whether Article 21(1) of the EU Charter of Fundamental Rights would be directly or indirectly effective in the future. This is of profound significance for those who wish to see European Union-level regulation of genetic discrimination. The prevailing view appears to run contrary to Collins's advice.

At the time of the *Test Achats* decision, the Charter of Fundamental Rights had a somewhat uncertain legal status. Nanopoulos viewed the Charter as a mere codification of existing rights rather than an independent source of rights or duties (Nanopoulos, 2011: 508). Reich (Reich, 2011) also noted that the *Test Achats* decision rested on the 'auto-reference' of the Gender Directive to the Charter as indicative of the political will of the Union. The Council of Ministers could not legitimately promulgate a Directive contrary to the aims of the Charter, and Treaty Provisions, given that it referenced those provisions as the legal basis for intervention.

Moving forwards, we now have the Charter given legislative force. As Leczykiewicz notes 'Article 6(3) TEU ascribes the Charter the same legal value as the Treaties' (Leczykiewicz, 2013: 485). This means that the Charter may have horizontal effect (i.e. between citizens and/or businesses) and not merely vertical effect (between the State and citizens). However, the applicability of horizontal direct effect is not automatic, as Treaty and Charter provisions need to meet certain criteria to be enforceable in this fashion (Craig and De Burca, 2011: 191–211).

Leczykiewicz recently proposed a model of horizontal enforceability for the Charter to reach an appropriate balance between private law and the European Charter of Fundamental Rights. Her initial view is that private autonomy should be respected:

> As for individual contracts where no regulatory effect could be assigned to the employer/trader, we should start from the assumption that the binding nature of a contract is a value which should be respected. The Charter should not be made generally horizontally applicable just because we would like all legal relationships to be compliant with fundamental rights
>
> (Leczykiewicz, 2013: 96)

However, her model recognises that the Charter could be used in a paternalistic fashion where the context demands. Whether interference is justified would depend on the nature of the participants and the dispute:

> certain relationships could be 'generally characterised' by inequality of power, and the Charter could then be applied against the stronger party in those relationships'.
>
> (Leczykiewicz, 2013: 496)

It is likely that consumer insurance contracts would fall within this category. It has long been viewed as the paradigm contract of adhesion. Moreover, under her model, the anti-discrimination provisions in article 21 are exactly the kinds of rights that ought to have horizontal direct effect (Leczykiewicz, 2013: 496).

Ultimately, it is likely that the relationship between the Charter, Treaty provisions and national law will be teased out in future European Court of Justice litigation. There is a clear tension between the Collins and Leczykiewicz models. However, the best hope for a nuanced flexible solution to genetic discrimination law in the European Union may lie outside the legislative process entirely. The UK moratorium has been lauded for its reflexivity and ability to react to shifting social and biotechnological developments (Joly, Knoppers and Godard, 2003). It is much less likely that we would see a nuanced model develop through litigation in which both parties pursue the solution that is optimal to their interests, rather than the best possible solution. A model of pure equality for insurance, with a prohibition on protected characteristics being used in risk assessment would fundamentally alter the insurance industry in an unpredictable fashion. Moreover, 'maximal' protection (e.g. an absolute anti-discrimination model banning the use of age, race, sex and genetic status) would fail to recognise the varying levels of social significance of insurance products across the EU. For Member States with an extensive welfare state, the role of insurance is less than in those jurisdictions where primary healthcare is delivered by insurance. A 'one-size-fits-all' approach to regulation is likely to be insufficiently nuanced to be effective.

## 5. Lessons drawn: towards context through soft law

The potential horizontal effect of the EU Charter of Fundamental Rights provides a pathway for anti-discrimination law to encompass genetic information. However, the breadth of the provision fails to account for the variable situations in which it would be enforced. The lesson from *Test Achats* is that EU anti-discrimination law can be a rather blunt instrument for the protection of the vulnerable. Following *Test Achats*, three different kinds of discriminatory behaviour are now treated as equivalent (and unjustified) under UK law:

1 deliberate discrimination against a group by refusing to supply services at market rate, based purely on prejudice;
2 differential treatment of a group where there is weak statistical evidence of a correlation between membership of that group and high-risk behaviour (e.g. sex and driving risk);
3 following the amendment of the Equality Act 2010, any differential pricing on the basis of sex, even where there is a causal link between the risk factor and increased risk.

What can be done instead? The UK moratorium on genetics represents a better model for intervention because it provides for a flexible, technocratic decision-making process. The use of genetic data could be decided according to the context and the social significance of the product purchased. Under the UK model, insurers have given up their right to information that is not probative, or where the amounts insured are within normal pricing limits. However, this is not an unfettered right to insurance for any amount, and it protects the market against insureds who might over-consume subsidised insurance coverage.

The lesson to be learnt is that, whilst absolute rights are useful in defeating illogical prejudice, they need to be balanced against legitimate commercial interests when the differential treatment is not illogical. To treat all forms of differential treatment as identical is to weaken the case for intervention. The insurance industry has a good memory and an effective team of lobbyists. Those calling for EU regulation on the use of genetic information by insurers should not be surprised if a blanket 'NO!' is given to any call for negotiation and compromise. Insurers have had their fingers burnt, and badly, over a legislative compromise on sex discrimination. They are not likely to come back willingly to the negotiating table any time soon to discuss genetic information: 'once bitten, twice shy'.

## References


Abraham, K. (1986) *Distributing Risk: Insurance, Legal Theory and Public Policy.* 1st edition. New Haven, CT: Yale University Press.

Association of British Insurers (2013) '*Genetics*'. Available at: www.abi.org.uk/Insurance-and-savings/Topics-and-issues/Genetics [accessed 28 October 2013].

Cameron, N. and Hawke, F. (2011) 'Vive La Difference? Non!: ECJ Decides Men and Women Are Equal before the Law, and before the Underwriter' *Insurance Law Journal* 22: 118.

Clarke, M. (2011) 'An Introduction to Insurance Contract Law'. In: J. Burling and K. Lazarus (eds) *Research Handbook on International Insurance Law and Regulation.* Cheltenham: Edward Elgar, pp. 3–18.

Collins, H. (2012) 'On the (In)compatibility of Human Rights Discourse and Private Law'. *LSE Law, Society and Economy Working Papers*, Issue 7.

Craig, P. and De Burca, G. (2011) *EU Law: Text, Cases and Materials.* 5th edition. Oxford: Oxford University Press.

Davey, J. (2000) 'Future Imperfect: Human Genetics and Insurance' *Journal of Business Law* 18: 587.

Ferri, D. (2011) *Legislating at the EU Level: Possibilities and Challenges.* Available at: www.nuigalway.ie/cdlp/documents/delia_ferri.pdf [accessed 28 October 2013].

Guillén, M. (2012) 'Sexless and Beautiful Data: From Quantity to Quality'. *Annals of Actuarial Science* 6: 231–234.

HM Government and ABI, (2011) 'Concordat and Moratorium on Genetics and Insurance'. Available at: www.gov.uk/government/uploads/system/uploads/attachment_data/file/216821/Concordat-and-Moratorium-on-Genetics-and-Insurance-20111.pdf [accessed 28 October 2013].

Johnston, P. (2011) 'We'll all lose in the crazy EU equality drive' *The Telegraph*, 1 March. Available at: www.telegraph.co.uk/comment/columnists/philipjohnston/8353192/Well-all-lose-in-the-crazy-EU-equality-drive.html [accessed 13 May 2014].

Joly, Y., Knoppers, B. and Godard, B. (2003) 'Genetic Information and Life Insurance: A "Real" Risk?' *European Journal of Human Genetics* 11: 561.

Kokott, J. (2013) *J. Kokott Homepage.* Available at: www.julianekokott.de/index.php/en [accessed 28 October 2013].

Leczykiewicz, D. (2013) 'Horizontal Application of the Charter of Fundamental Rights' *European Law Review* 38: 479.

Nanopoulos, E. (2011) 'Insuring the Charter: Who Bears the Cost?' *Cambridge Law Journal* 70 (3): 506.

Reich, N. (2011) 'Non-Discrimination and the Many Faces of Private Law in the Union – Some Thoughts After the 'Test Achats' Judgment' *European Journal of Risk Regulation* 2(2): 283.

Roberts, J. (2010) 'Preempting Discrimination: Lessons from the Genetic Information Nondiscrimination Act' *Vanderbilt Law Review* 63(2): 437.

Rothstein, M. (2008) 'GINA, the ADA, and Genetic Discrimination in Employment' *Journal of Law, Medicine and Ethics* Volume 36(4): 837.

Stirton, R. (2012) 'Insurance, Genetic Information and the Future of Industry Self-Regulation in the UK' *Law, Innovation and Technology* 4(2): 212.

*Test Achats* (2012) Case C-236/09 *Association belge de Consommateurs Test Achats ASBL and others v Conseil de Ministres Weekly Law Reports* 1933.

Thomas, R. (2012) 'Genetics and Insurance in the United Kingdom 1995–2010: The Rise and Fall of "Scientific" Discrimination' *New Genetics and Society* 31: 1–20.

McGleenan, T. and Wiesing, U. (2000) 'Insurance and Genetics: European Policy Options' *European Journal of Health Law* 7(4): 367.

Wils, W. (1994) 'Insurance Risk Classifications in the EC: Regulatory Outlook' *Oxford Journal of Legal Studies* 14(3): 449.

# 10 Employment practices in a new genomic era

## Acknowledging competing rights and striking a balance

*Aisling de Paor*

### 1. Introduction

In consideration of the proliferation of genetic testing technologies, the rapid advances in genomic science and the potential for misuse by third parties, this chapter will examine the impact of advancing genetic technologies and the use of genetic information from the employment perspective. This chapter will build upon the insights offered in Chapter 5 which looks at the use of genetic information outside of the therapeutic relationship. It will highlight an employer's interest in and right to know an employee's genetic information and potential right to use genetic technologies in the workplace. In addition to the obvious financial objectives propelling such an interest, there are also health and safety considerations that may motivate an interest in utilising an employee's genetic information. An employer's interest in genetic information must then be balanced against an employee's fundamental human rights, meaning that an employer must therefore respect, inter alia, an employee's right not to be discriminated against and their right to privacy. An employee's rights in this regard also reflect a wider societal interest of ensuring that there are no unjustified barriers to accessing employment.

This chapter will elucidate the key legal issues arising in the employment context and illustrate the tension created between the employer's rights and the employee's rights (highlighting the inescapable conflict between commercial interests and fundamental human rights), as well as the wider societal perspective. In acknowledging the legitimacy of the competing rights, this chapter will look towards striking a balance of rights and will consider how this balance might be achieved.

The first section will highlight an employer's interest in and right to know genetic information and will detail the motivation behind engaging in genetic testing. The second section will provide an overview of the implications of misusing genetic information, from the viewpoint of the employee and from a societal perspective. This chapter will then highlight the need to consider a balance between the competing rights in the employment context and will offer some tentative conclusions. On examination of the use of genetic information in employment, this chapter will also offer a brief insight into the current legislative framework regarding employment equality and health and safety in the EU. It will also give an insight into some national-level legislative endeavours which have addressed use of genetic information in employment.

## 2. Use of genetic information in employment

Employers may have an interest in genetic information derived from an individual's family medical history, as well as genetic information obtained from the results of genetic tests previously taken. It is also acknowledged that employers may have an interest in requesting that employees undergo genetic testing. As outlined in previous chapters, genetic information and the practice of genetic testing can offer valuable insights into an individual's current health status, as well as predisposition to illness, thereby indicating details of potential future health status, illness and disability. It can also offer insights into an individual's behavioural and personality traits, including the presence of the risk-taking gene, the leadership gene and a range of genetically based characteristics.

Genetic testing in the workplace generally incorporates the practices of genetic screening and genetic monitoring, as described by de Paor and Lowndes in Chapter 2. On considering the basis for an employer's interest in genetic information, it is observed that employers first of all have a financial interest in accessing and using genetic information. It is also acknowledged that they have a concern for protecting the employee and the prospective employee (Otlowski *et al.*, 2009: 640). On the basis of this interest, an employer may wish to use genetic information and engage in genetic testing for health and safety reasons. The following section will elaborate upon the objectives behind an employer's interest in genetic information.

### *2.1 Commercial interests – the preference for healthy and productive workers*

It is observed that employers generally have an interest in maximising employees' fitness and productivity, as well as minimising turnover and employee absenteeism (Rothstein *et al.*, 1998: 401). When employees are in poor health, they are more likely to require sick pay, are more likely to suffer occupational injury or illness, and their illnesses may impact upon the morale of co-workers and other third parties (Rothstein and Knoppers, 1996: 144). Further, when an employee becomes ill or disabled while in employment, productivity may be affected in certain circumstances, and future productivity may be uncertain. The time and expense of training and hiring replacement employees may be considerable, resulting in inefficiency, particularly where there are limited resources. Poor health may also lead to retirement or redundancy, requiring financial payouts to employees. These factors may collectively result in increased costs and overheads for the employer.

When hiring, training or promoting employees, employers therefore have strong economic incentives to select a desirable candidate who will be financially productive and represent a sensible business choice. Hiring or promoting an underqualified and underproductive worker is costly to the employer. In addition, employers who facilitate health insurance for employees have increased economic incentives to be concerned about the productivity, health and wellbeing of workers. Therefore the ill health or potential ill health of employees can have a myriad of adverse financial consequences for employers.

In light of the fact that employers have an interest in minimising employment costs, 'the supposedly predictive nature of genetic information is a very attractive tool in workplace management' (Laurie, 2002: 153). Healthy employees who are perceived to possess desirable genes arguably do not create these financial problems, thereby provoking the incentive to use genetic information. Indeed, obtaining genetic information about employees and potential employees may be viewed as sensible commercial practice (Carr, 2007: 2). Employers may seek to require the use of genetic testing as a prerequisite to employment, or request existing genetic test results or details of family medical history. By selecting genetically attractive employees, employers may seek to employ only those who will remain healthy and productive and those who are least likely to be a liability or costly in the future (Otlowski *et al.*, 2009: 640).

When making decisions regarding promotion or employee benefits, employers have additional incentives to seek access to employees' genetic information. Similarly, genetic information might also be of interest to employers when making termination or redundancy decisions. In economically challenging times, employers may seek to weed out those who are deemed to be genetically inferior and who may be costly and a drain on existing resources. Genetic technologies may therefore be used as a tool for selecting and managing staff.

At a more general level, it may be further argued that an employer has a clear interest in obtaining as much information as possible about a prospective employee in order to choose the most appropriate possible person for the job (Mainsbridge, 2002: 66). Advancing genetic technologies can uncover potentially relevant profiles – for example, the prevalence of the 'risk-taking' gene (Alleyne, 2009; Shane, 2010), which may be appealing to some employers, while others may view this as high risk. As noted in Chapter 2, genetic advances have also detected the genes associated with leadership, which may be appealing to employers in making certain employment decisions. As scientists make further connections between genetics and behavioural and personality traits, employers have additional incentives to take advantage of new technologies to find a candidate who fits the profile of their organisation.

### *2.2 Genetic testing in employment – an extension of medical testing?*

On discussing an employer's interest in genetic technologies, genetic testing could arguably be viewed as an extension of medical testing, which has traditionally been a routine employment practice (Hendriks and Gevers, 1994: 229). An employer is generally concerned with selecting the right physical and psychological profile for a particular job. The employer may wish to ask questions or perform various tests to confirm whether candidates are suitable for employment or whether they would pose a risk to health or safety.

The question then arises as to whether these assessments are 'unnecessary or overly intrusive' (McGreal, 2009: 212). It is noted that, where such medical questions are too personal, 'the focus will inevitably be upon the necessity or justification for such intrusions where they occur' (McGreal, 2009: 212). Indeed, such information has traditionally shaped an employer's decision in assessing the suitability of a candidate. In applying the rationale of this standard employment practice to the practice of genetic testing, there may be scope to argue that, from the employer's perspective, genetic testing is an extension of medical testing in terms of its objective in ascertaining the suitability of the employee. The question then arises as to the necessity or justification for such testing. This falls upon consideration of an employer's right to know and the limits that should be placed on that right, which will be expanded upon throughout this chapter.

It is evident therefore that the employer has clear economic reasons for seeking access to and use of an employee's genetic information. In certain circumstances this interest may be viewed as an extension of the practice of medical testing, depending on the necessity or justification for such testing and bearing in mind the invariably invasive nature of these technologies. The following section will highlight a further reason behind employers' interest in genetic information.

### *2.3 Genetic testing and health and safety considerations*

In highlighting the nature of the employment relationship, it is observed that employers have certain responsibilities and obligations to employees, for example, as regards health and safety. Pursuant to such obligations, employers must broadly ensure a safe place of work and have general regard for an employer's health, safety and welfare. Employers may therefore have an interest in an employee's genetic information for health and safety purposes and to uphold their obligations under health and safety law (Barnard, 2006: 539–573). On the basis of an employer's responsibilities under health and safety law, there may be scope to argue that engaging in genetic monitoring to address occupational illness may facilitate the practice of health surveillance and the monitoring of employees. From a statutory perspective, employers have obligations under a number of European health and safety law instruments (including Directive 89/391/EEC on Safety and Health at Work). Such legislation broadly provides that employers must take steps to ensure the safety, health and welfare of employees. This duty encompasses the requirement to ensure that employees (and others) are not exposed to risks in the workplace.

However, caution must be exercised to ensure the appropriate use of such technology in the workplace, and certain safeguards must be put in place. For example, it is important to have regard to an employee's privacy and data protection rights. Accordingly, best practice would be to ensure that such monitoring is carried out on a voluntary basis and with the employee's informed consent. It is also important to ensure that any such use is not used as a cloak to shield unjust work practices that may be aimed at weeding out certain individuals or groups of individuals.

Employers may also be interested in accessing and using an employee's genetic information with a view to maintaining their duty of care towards the employee and ensuring against any potential liability in tort.

### *2.3.1 Common law duty of care to employees*

On ascertaining the basis of an employer's interest in genetic information, it is noted that an employer has certain responsibilities under common law. In this regard, an employer has an interest in avoiding liability in tort law and breaching the duty of care to an employee. In general terms, it is established that 'the duty of an employer towards a servant is to take reasonable care for the servant's safety in all circumstances of the case' (*Dalton v Frendo* 1997; *Wilsons and Clyde Coal Co. Ltd v English* 1938). In this context, an employer may potentially be found liable for injuries caused to the employee during the course of employment. In relation to the employer's duty of care, the Irish courts, for example, have generally analysed the duty under four categories, including the provision of competent staff, the provision of a safe place of work, the provision of proper equipment and the provision of a safe system of work (McMahon and Binchy, 2000: 500).

As regards the provision of competent staff, it has been established that 'the duty which a master owes to his servant is to use due care to select proper and competent fellow servants' (*Skerrit v Scallan* 1877). In this context, employers will be concerned to select the most appropriate and suitable employees, who are sufficiently competent and have the ability to carry out the job in question, having regard to the requirements of the position and the particular nature of the workplace. This competence may relate to both the qualifications and experience of the employee, as well as physical capacities and fitness to carry out the job from a health perspective. Failure by an employer to fulfil such a duty may potentially result in breach of the duty of care and a finding of negligence. It could be argued that employers should be permitted to engage in genetic testing to facilitate the selection of the most suitable and competent employees and to maintain his or her duty of care under common law.

A further common law duty provides that an employer must ensure that a reasonably safe place of work is provided and maintained for the benefit of the employee (*Gallagher v Mogul of Ireland Ltd* 1975; *Kirwan v National Children's Hospital* 1963). The existence of such a duty towards employees may add weight to the argument that employers should be permitted to use genetic technologies to facilitate such health and safety obligations, albeit under certain conditions. Similar arguments could be made in respect of the duty to provide a safe system of work, which can be construed as an all-encompassing one which gives rise to obligations to ensure that the working environment is safe, secure and free from hazards (*Kinsella v Hammond Land Industries Ltd.* 1962; *Caulfield v George Bell and Co Ltd* 1948).

In light of an employer's obligations under health and safety law, from a statutory and common law perspective, genetic monitoring could therefore potentially be used to screen employees and potential employees, who, because of their genetic make-up, may be at an increased risk of developing certain conditions if exposed to certain occupational chemicals or other hazards (Kaufman, 1999). Individuals with the sickle cell anaemia gene, for example, may be at increased risk for sickle cell anaemia if exposed to carbon monoxide or cyanide. Similarly, carpal tunnel syndrome, a condition affecting the hands and wrists, may also be exacerbated in certain work environments. In the occupational environment carpal tunnel syndrome is associated with tasks including repetitive and awkward hand or wrist motions. Carpal tunnel syndrome may therefore be particularly prevalent in office environments in which employees use computers on a frequent basis, or in environments where an employee is engaged in a significant amount of repetitive work (Palmer *et al.*, 2007: 57–66; Werner, 2006: 201–216; Gell *et al.*, 2005: 47). Surveillance is one way to monitor carpal tunnel syndrome in the workplace. In carrying out surveillance in these circumstances, an employer may wish to genetically test employees or potential employees to ascertain those who might be predisposed to developing these conditions. In this regard, it is observed that such emerging genetic technologies have the potential to modify and transform standard employment practices.

In the context of addressing occupational illness and disease, it is also acknowledged that employees have corresponding duties to take care of their own health and safety in the workplace (*Smith v The Health Service Executive* 2013). In this regard, contributory negligence may be a defence both to an action in negligence and breach of statutory duty. Therefore, the contributory negligence of an employee, for example, in neglecting to have regard for his or her own health and safety, might have an impact on (and potentially mitigate) an employer's negligence in this regard. In the context of this debate, knowledge of one's own genetic make-up, as well as the potential of knowing one's genetic make-up through the use of emerging genetic technologies may arguably trigger action on the part of an employee to take a proactive role in relation to workplace health and safety. Arguably, it may also potentially act as a defence to an employer's liability in certain circumstances. This further highlights the need to be aware of the tension of rights created between employers and employees.

### *2.4 Accuracy of genetic testing*

On examining the legitimacy of an employer's use of genetic technologies, it must be pointed out that, although science is advancing rapidly, the majority of genetic test results are still uncertain and lack accuracy, as highlighted in Chapter 1. Therefore, the scientific validity and effectiveness of genetic technologies must be taken into account in consideration of third-party use. As explained in Chapter 1, most genetic conditions are multifactorial, whereby manifestation of the condition is a result of a complex interaction between genes and environment (for example, heart disease). The existence of genes indicating predisposition to such conditions is therefore only one factor in determining the expression of disease. It is only in the case of monogenic conditions that the expression of a condition can be more accurately predicted (for example, Huntington's disease).

Accordingly, there may be a risk that the information gleaned from genetic technologies may be misunderstood and overestimated. The argument could be made that genetic testing should only be used in the employment context if the scientific validity and accuracy of such technology is reasonably certain and unambiguous. Therefore, arguments in favour of using genetic technologies in employment may be diluted to a certain extent, in consideration of the uncertain predictive value of genetic testing and the potential for misinterpretation (and further misuse) by employers.

As highlighted in this chapter, it is also important that any potential genetic monitoring is used fairly by employers, with legitimate objectives, and not merely as a cloak to shield the elimination of what are deemed to be high-risk or genetically undesirable employees. Indeed historical evidence highlights the potential for such practices, as Blanck and de Paor discuss in Chapter 6. For example, in the United States, monitoring for sickle cell anaemia became prevalent in the 1970s (Mitchell and Happe, 2001: 379). At the time, some job applicants were denied employment, while others were terminated from their jobs because they were found to be carriers of the sickle cell anaemia gene. Although this policy had its roots in a legitimate public health initiative, it translated into a tool to discriminate against and stigmatise African-Americans, who are more likely to carry the sickle cell anaemia gene than any other race (Kaufmann, 1999: 402–403). This concern highlights the challenges and difficulties that arise in trying to reach a balance between the rights of employers and employees (Carr, 2007: 11).

Although there are strong arguments in favour of an employer's use of genetic technologies in certain circumstances, caution must be exercised with a view to maintaining the rights of employees. First, it is important to ensure that an employee's right to privacy and confidentiality as regards personal information is protected, and the right not to be discriminated against is respected. It is also important to ensure that such technologies are not used as a cloak to disguise the weeding out of employees based upon preconceptions. The following section will look more closely at the undesirable consequences of genetic discrimination from the perspective of the employee.

## 3. An employee's perspective – acknowledging fundamental human rights

In consideration of the myriad of personal, sensitive details that genetic technologies can reveal about an individual's current and future health (as well as personality and behavioural tendencies) and the valuable nature of such information, the potential for abuse and violation of fundamental human rights is evident. This section will highlight the potential for abuse of genetic technologies from the employee's perspective and highlight the relevant legislative framework in the EU (and at Member State level). It does not propose to provide a detailed discussion of the application of the relevant legislative framework as this is examined in greater detail in Chapter 15.

### *3.1 Right not to be discriminated against*

Employers arguably have no right to request genetic testing (or use the results of genetic tests previously taken) when an individual shows no indication of a disability or illness that would hamper the current ability to do a job. Making an employment decision on the basis of the probability of an individual developing a certain disability or illness (or indeed the perception of such disease or disability), as opposed to the actual ability to carry out the work, may potentially be unlawful discrimination.

Discrimination based upon actual or perceived genetic characteristics denies an individual equal opportunity on the grounds of a genetic status over which he or she has no control. Discrimination based on genetic information, as described in Chapter 5 by Joly *et al.*, is arguably as unjust as that based on race or gender (or other immutable characteristics). It is noted that 'the right to be treated equally and according to one's abilities in all the diverse aspects of human endeavour is a core social value' (Gostin, 1991: 112). Genetic discrimination and other misuse of genetic information therefore violates basic tenets of justice and is potentially harmful to wider societal values.

Similarly, the potential for indirect discrimination is also recognised in the employment context. In this regard, discrimination may be deemed to arise from employment actions, practices or provisions which are shown to have an adverse effect on an individual or group of individuals. For example, past employment practices, such as genetic screening for sickle cell anaemia in the US in the 1970s, resulted in an adverse impact on African-Americans, as discussed. Other types of genetic tests, such as those indicating susceptibility to breast cancer might also have a more adverse effect on women, than on men. Employers might potentially seek to introduce a genetic screening programme that appears to target all individuals on an equal basis, but produces negative effects for certain individuals, or possibly racial or ethnic groups. Discrimination (both direct and indirect) on the basis of genetic information is a real concern, and one with potentially serious consequences for employees and potential employees.

In the EU, there is strong legislation in favour of equality in the workplace and a prohibition on discrimination on a number of grounds (including disability), encompassing both direct and indirect discrimination (Employment Equality Directive 2000). Although there is no specific provision to protect against discrimination on the grounds of genetic information or genetic features, the ground of disability has been given an increasingly broad definition in recent years by the European Court of Justice (Ring and Werge, 2013; *Commission v Italy 2013*), indicating the potential scope for an expansive interpretation of 'disability' under current EU non-discrimination law. Ferri explores the evolving definition of 'disability' in EU non-discrimination law in further detail in Chapter 15.

The EU Charter of Fundamental Rights has highlighted genetic discrimination as a priority area of reform in the EU. Discrimination on the basis of 'genetic features' is provided for in Article 21 (1), as noted in other chapters in the book (including Chapter 11 and Chapter 15), thereby further illustrating the evolving EU framework in the field of non-discrimination and highlighting an EU-level awareness of the need to protect 'genetic features' in employment (and other contexts). Indeed the specific reference to 'genetic features' in the Charter is a significant development in EU non-discrimination law and may give added weight to the argument that EU-level regulation in this area is perhaps necessary (de Paor, 2013a: 133). However, despite the presence of the EU Charter of Fundamental Rights as a relevant source of guidance, it is pointed out that there is a clear gap in protection for genetic information or genetic features in the current EU non-discrimination framework.

Despite the lack of concrete EU-level protections, there have been a number of notable national-level legislative endeavours which address genetic discrimination in employment, for example, in Germany (Human Genetic Examination Act 2010), Austria (Gene Technology Act 1996 and 2005) and Portugal (Personal Genetic Information and Health Information Act 2005). For example, in Germany, the legislation provides, *inter alia*, that no employer may discriminate against or disadvantage any employees on the basis of the genetic characteristics or on the basis of the genetic characteristics of any persons genetically related to any person (Human Genetic Examination Act 2010: Article 21). The German legislation also recognises the limited right to know for employers. In this regard, Article 20 (3) attempts to strike a balance and relates to genetic testing for occupational safety (setting out a number of conditions necessary in order to conduct genetic testing in these circumstances). In Ireland, genetic testing is provided for under Part 4 of the Disability Act, 2005 (Disability Act 2005: Section 42). Part 4 regulates the use of genetic testing in a number of third-party contexts, including employment, requiring that employers seek the prior consent of the Irish Data Protection Commissioner before the use of genetic testing or genetic information (de Paor, 2013b: 102).

Although there is effectively a patchwork of varying legislation at EU Member State level (as discussed further in Chapter 12 and as also illustrated in Chapter 5), offering differing levels of protection, these national-level legislative endeavours are evidence of a growing awareness to protect genetic information in employment (and other contexts). It is also noted that the US has introduced legislation to deal with genetic discrimination in employment, as detailed in Section 3 of this book.

### *3.2 Right to privacy and other rights at stake*

In addition to discrimination concerns, misuse of genetic information can result in the violation of an employee's privacy (as well as family members' privacy). In consideration of the uniquely private and sensitive nature of genetic information and the potential for misuse of such information, there are compelling reasons to protect genetic privacy. Unauthorised disclosure of genetic information to employers may breach the right to privacy, leaving individuals in a vulnerable position (Taylor, 2012). The right to privacy has a firm position in the EU's human rights framework, for example, as evident from the EU Charter of Fundamental Rights (Article 7 and 8), as well as the European Convention on Human Rights (Article 8). There is also a strong societal interest in ensuring the protection of privacy, as evidenced by the strong data protection laws which are in place in the EU (Data Protection Directive 1995) and the current reform process taking place in the area of EU data protection law (as discussed in Chapter 13). However, although there have been recent proposals to update data protection laws (as discussed by Taylor in Chapter 13), the current EU data protection framework does not yet provide any specific protection for genetic information.

In addition to concerns of discrimination and privacy, there are further ethical issues that arise, such as the right to know one's genetic information and the right not to know (as well as family members' right to know and right not to know) (Takala, 1999: 288). These rights potentially come into conflict with an employer's right to access and use genetic information. From a legal and ethical perspective, misuse of genetic information by employers therefore has undesirable legal and ethical consequences for the employee and that employee's family members. Such information can be used to discriminate against employees and potential employees at the hiring, promotion or termination stages and may impact upon one's privacy. As noted, these fundamental human rights are well embedded in the EU legal framework, (although there are currently limited protections for genetic information). Further, there are additional societal concerns that may arise in the employment context, which merit mentioning.

## 4. Wider societal implications of misusing genetic information in employment

It is acknowledged that individuals who are refused employment on the grounds of genetic status are potentially left without a job. By excluding otherwise suitable individuals from employment, society is drained of skills and innovation. This exclusion 'promotes physical and economic dependency, draining rather than enriching social institutions' (Gostin, 1991: 112–113). Consequently, use of genetic technologies can create employment barriers by effectively classifying individuals by potential future health risk. Society may lose out on the contribution of these individuals, who are in a position to make a productive addition to the community and who are being denied this opportunity, despite their current ability. This may result in the further exclusion and isolation of vulnerable persons, such as persons with putative disabilities, and create further barriers to their integration into the community.

Therefore, access to employment may well act as a gateway to and may impact upon access to other social and economic goods and services. It may impact upon fulfilling civic engagement, including access to political life and active involvement in the community. Access to employment may also potentially affect an individual's social life, friendships and interaction with peers, which has a significant impact on inclusion and active participation in society. Therefore, at a fundamental level, the existence of barriers to employment by way of misusing genetic information may have a profound impact on an individual's private and professional life. In the absence of appropriate controls and regulation, it may ultimately result in the creation of a genetic underclass and the relegation of what are deemed to be genetically undesirable individuals.

## 5. Recognising competing rights and achieving a balance

It has been observed that genetic testing in the employment context is 'a technology both full of promise and fraught with ethical peril' (MacDonald and Williams-Jones, 2002: 238). The use of genetic technologies raises considerations of privacy and discrimination. Just as it is unlawful to refuse to hire someone on the grounds of race or gender, it should be unlawful to refuse to hire an individual on the basis of genetic information (without considering that individual's qualifications and current ability to do the job) (Miller, 1999: 264). Arguably, an otherwise suitable individual should not be prevented from obtaining or maintaining a job based upon having a certain genetic predisposition. Employers also have a responsibility to respect employees' privacy and uphold data protection laws.

In addressing this area, it is important to consider the competing rights and the tension created between commercial interests and fundamental human rights, and assess where the appropriate balance should be struck. From the employer's perspective, genetic technology offers the promise of enhancing employment decisions and facilitating the economic as well as health and safety objectives of the employer. As highlighted, there are strong arguments in favour of an employer's use of genetic technologies, primarily for health and safety reasons, with a view to upholding the duty of care to employees. Indeed, such arguments are strengthened by the presence of an EU health and safety framework that imposes certain obligations on employers to take action to ensure the health, safety and welfare of employees. There are also well established common law duties which employers owe to the employees.

However, controls need to be placed on any right of access, for example, having regard to the accuracy of genetic science. It is important that the limited accuracy of genetic testing be acknowledged, in considering any potential use of such technology. An employee's rights also need to be upheld, as does the potential for abuse of these technologies. As explained, it is important to ensure protection against unfair discrimination in all elements of the employment process and to maintain employee privacy.

It is also necessary to consider society's interest in reaping the benefits of advancing genetic science, as well as society's interest in ensuring unfettered access to employment. These goals may be reached by ensuring that the area is appropriately regulated, taking account of the fundamental rights of employees and the limited right to know of employers in certain workplace scenarios. Although there is strong employment equality legislation in place, there are no specific protections for individuals' genetic information. Upon initial observation, it is therefore questionable whether this balance is achieved in the current EU legislative framework, particularly in consideration of the lack of concrete protections for individuals' genetic information. This may ultimately point to the need for a new, more focused regulatory regime in this area at EU level, as is discussed in Chapter 15. These tentative observations require further investigation and evidence to more critically and accurately ascertain the effectiveness of the current legislative framework in striking a balance between the competing rights and the need for a new regulatory framework.

## 6. Conclusion

It has been observed that 'genetic discrimination foreseeably will be the civil-rights issue of the twenty-first century' (Holmes, 1996: 507). This discrimination (and other misuse) is particularly apparent and foreseeable in the employment context.

As employers become more aware of the potential and the benefits of genetic information (as a useful tool to select and maintain what they perceive to be the most genetically desirable and the most productive employees), there is an increasing possibility that discrimination and breach of privacy will become more widespread and employers will take advantage by misusing sensitive genetic information. It is anticipated that, as genetic science advances and the technology becomes more accessible, employers will have growing incentives to seek access to and use of genetic technologies as a tool for selection and management of employees (Otlowski *et al.*, 2009: 671–672).

Further, as genetic information proliferates, more and more people may be considered genetically inferior. This may potentially signal the creation of a genetic underclass and the relegation of what are perceived to be genetically undesirable individuals. This may lead to the practice of genetic cleansing, not just in employment, but also in other elements of life such as education, political life and society in general (as was highlighted particularly in Chapter 5 by Joly *et al*). The existence of a regulatory vacuum or inadequate regulation may accelerate this genetic underclass and could operate to inhibit the inclusion of persons with disabilities (and older persons) into employment and into society, with undesirable social and economic consequences. As illustrated in this chapter, although there have been a number of national-level legislative endeavours in this area, there is still a legislative vacuum at EU level, with fragmented and inadequate protections available for genetic information.

Addressing genetic discrimination in employment provokes a disconnect between the rights of individuals and the rights of employers and other institutions, leading to an inevitable conflict of rights. This tension or conflict of rights is one of the challenges faced by legislators in considering the appropriate regulation of this area and ascertaining how the balance can be best achieved. Upon initial observation, it is arguable that, in spite of national-level regulatory endeavours and robust employment equality legislation in the EU, this balance is not yet achieved in the EU legal framework. Tackling this issue requires active engagement and discussion with all relevant stakeholders to further decipher the complex contours of this debate, as well as careful consideration of all competing interests at stake.

As we witness the dawn of this new genetic age, such rapidly advancing genetic technology offers enormous potential benefits for medicine, health care and humankind. However, as interest in genetic science escalates, so too does the potential for abuse and violation of fundamental human rights, thereby signalling the importance of appropriate regulation and consideration of the balance of rights, particularly in the employment context, where the incentive to use genetic technologies becomes more enticing.

## References

Alleyne, R. (2009) 'Why Risk Taking Runs in the Family – Scientists Find Gene that Makes You Gamble', *The Telegraph*. 6 May. Available at: www.telegraph.co.uk/news/newstopics/howaboutthat/5279222/Why-risk-taking-runs-in-the-family-scientists-find-gene-that-makes-you-gamble.html [accessed 7 June 2012].

Barnard, C. (2006) *EC Employment Law*. 3rd edition. London: Oxford University Press.

Carr, S. (2007) 'Invisible Actors: Genetic Testing and Genetic Discrimination in the Workplace' *University of Arkansas Little Rock Law Review* 30(1): 11.

de Paor, A. (2013a) 'US and EU Perspectives on Genetic Discrimination in Employment and Insurance: Striking a Balance in a Battlefield of Competing Rights' in Quinn, G. and Waddington, L. (eds) *European Yearbook of Disability Law* 4: 99. Antwerp: Intersentia.

de Paor, A. (2013b) 'The Regulation of Genetic Information in Ireland – Does it Strike an Appropriate Balance of Rights?' *Medico-Legal Journal of Ireland* 19(2): 97.

Gell, N., Werner, R. A., Franzblau, A., Ulin, S. S. and Armstrong, T. J. (2005) 'A Longitudinal Study of Industrial and Clerical Workers: Incidence of Carpal Tunnel Syndrome and Assessment of Risk Factors' *Journal of Occupational Rehabilitation* 15(1): 47.

Gostin, L. O. (1991) 'Genetic Discrimination: The Use of Genetically Based Diagnostic and Prognostic Tests by Employers and Insurers' *American Journal of Law and Medicine* 17: 109, 112–113.

Hendriks, A. and Gevers, S. (1994) '(Pre-)employment Medical Examinations and the Law, with Particular Reference to the European Union' *European Journal of Health Law* 1: 229.

Holmes, E. M. (1996) 'Solving the Insurance/Genetic Fair/Unfair Discrimination Dilemma in Light of the Human Genome Project' *Kentucky Law Journal* 85(3): 505.

Kaufman, M. B. (1999) 'Genetic Discrimination in the Workplace: An Overview of Existing Protections' *Loyola University Chicago Law Journal* 30(3): 393.

Laurie, G. (2002) *Genetic Privacy – A Challenge to Medico-Legal Norms*. London: Cambridge University Press. p. 153.

MacDonald, C. and Williams-Jones, B. (2002) 'Ethics and Genetics: Susceptibility Testing in the Workplace' *Journal of Business Ethics* 35: 235, 238.

Mainsbridge, A. (2002) 'Employers and Genetic Information: A New Frontier in Discrimination' *Macquarie Law Journal* 2: 61, 66.

McGreal, C. (2009) 'Workplace Privacy and Data Protection' in Regan, M. (ed.) *Employment Law*. Dublin: Tottel Publishing.

McMahon, B. and Binchy, W. (2000) The Law of Torts. 3rd edition. Dublin: Butterworths (Ireland) Ltd.

Miller, P. S. (1999) 'Is There a Pink Slip in My Genes? Genetic Discrimination in the Workplace' *Journal of Health Care Law and Policy* 3(2): 225, 264.

Mitchell, G. R. and Happe, K. (2001) 'Informed Consent after the Human Genome Project' *Rhetoric and Public Affairs* 4(3): 375, 379.

Otlowski, M. *et al.* (2009) 'Practices and Attitudes of Australian Employers in Relation to the Use of Genetic Information: Report on a National Study' *Comparative Labor Law and Policy Journal* 31: 637.

Palmer, K. T., Harris, E. C. and Coggon, D. (2007) 'Carpal Tunnel Syndrome and Its Relation to Occupation: A Systemic Literature Review' *Occupational Medicine* 57(1): 57–66.

Rothstein, M. A. and Knoppers, B. (1996) 'Legal Aspects of Genetics, Work and Insurance in North America and Europe' *European Journal of Health Law* 3(2): 143, 144.

Rothstein, M. A. *et al.* (1998) 'Protecting Genetic Privacy by Permitting Employer Access Only to Job-Related Employee Medical Information: Analysis of a Unique Minnesota Law' *American Journal of Law and Medicine* 24(2): 399, 401.

Shane, S. (2010) 'Explaining Innate Risk-Takers', *Bloomberg Businessweek* 12 February. Available at: www.businessweek.com/smallbiz/content/feb2010/sb20100211_567240.htm [accessed 7th June 2012].

Takala, T. (1999) 'The Right to Genetic Ignorance Confirmed' *Bioethics* 13(3–4): 288.

Taylor, M. (2012) *Genetic Data and the Law: A Critical Perspective on Privacy Protection.* London: Cambridge University Press.

Werner, R. A. (2006) 'Evaluation of Work Related Carpal Tunnel Syndrome' *Journal of Occupational Rehabilitation* 16(2): 201–216.

## Cases

Case C-312/11 *European Commission v Italy* [2013] (4 July).

*Caulfield v George Bell and Co Ltd* [1948] IR 326 at 333.

*Dalton v Frendo,* Supreme Court, 15 December 1997, p. 4 of O'Higgins CJ's judgment; cf p. 5 of Griffin J's judgment.

*Gallagher v Mogul of Ireland Ltd* [1975] IR 204 (SC).

Joined cases C-335/11 and C-337/11 HK Danmark, acting on behalf of *Jette Ring v Dansk almennyttigt Boligselskab* (C-335/11) and HK Danmark, acting on behalf of *Lone Skouboe Werge v Dansk Arbejdsgiverforening,* acting on behalf of Pro Display A/S, in liquidation (C-37/11).

*Kinsella v Hammond Land Industries Ltd* (1962) 96 ILTR 1 at 4 (SC).

*Kirwan v National Children's Hospital,* Supreme Court, 10 May 1963.

*Skerrit v Scallan* (1877) IR 11 CL 389 at 401 (Exch.).

*Smith v The Health Service Executive* [2013] IEHC 360.

*Swift v Macken* (1873) IR 8 CL (Exch.).

*Wilsons and Clyde Coal Co. Ltd v English* [1938] AC 57, House of Lords.

## Legislation

Council and Parliament Directive 95/46/EC of 24 October 1995 on the protection of individuals with regard to the processing of personal data and on the free movement of such data [1995] OJ L 281/31.

Council Directive 2000/78/EC of 27 November 2000 establishing a general framework for equal treatment in employment and occupation [2000] OJ L 303/16.

Council Directive 89/391/EEC of 12 June 1989 on the introduction of measures to encourage improvements in the safety and health of workers at work [1989] OJ L 183/1.

# 11 Medical (genetic) examinations for non-health purposes

## The relevance of European legal standard setting

*Henriette Roscam Abbing*

### 1. Introduction

In the absence of treatment options, the use of (genetic) tests for early detection and prediction of (susceptibility for) the development of a serious incurable disease for non-health purposes is problematic for a variety of reasons. These tests are privacy intrusive for the individual and for biological relatives. In the political situation where private insurance serves as an alternative for public provisions, the outcome of these tests can also have consequences for a person's functioning in society. As a result, insurance companies and employers have clear financial interests in selecting candidates at the gate for health (genetic) dispositions. In unstable economic situations, accessibility to employment and socially essential financial services (for example, health, disability, life, critical illness and income protection insurance) can be even more at issue because of the health (genetic) status of the individual.

Generally, private insurers take into account individual risk factors, as discussed in Chapter 9 by Davey. The practice of premium setting is differentiated according to risk-classification. For this purpose, a medical examination (a health assessment, involving a physical intervention and/or asking for health-related information of the individual and biological relatives) is generally required.

In the employment context, a pre-employment medical examination must be justified. If there is no reason why the applicant should undergo special medical fitness requirements, which cannot be overcome by 'reasonable accommodation' of the working environment for those with disabilities or health issues, then such examination should not be carried out. Any such medical examinations should be related to job safety and must be based on occupational duties and potential job hazards (post-offer medical exams).

In this chapter, the use of health (genetic) information as a condition to have access to social goods through private arrangements is discussed from a European human rights perspective. This chapter looks particularly at some of the relevant Council of Europe norms in this area, as well as the

European Union framework and standards applicable. The focus of this discussion is on predictive information concerning a serious disease without prevention or treatment options. Although the issue is relevant for both genetic and non-genetic health information, the emphasis lays on genetic information.

## 2. Medical examinations for non-health purposes – a human rights issue

This section will introduce the issue of medical examinations for non-health purposes as a growing human rights issue in Europe. Within this discussion, it will address the framework surrounding genetic information. Inherent to medical examinations as a condition for obtaining access to basic social goods is an element of compulsion. An obligation to disclose sensitive health (genetic) information in the context of a mandatory health assessment prior to the conclusion of an insurance or employment contract is likely to discourage people from undergoing medical (genetic) examinations necessary for health purposes or to participate in medical research. In relation to the issue at stake, a number of individual and social human rights are relevant: the right to private life (physical and mental integrity, informational privacy), the right to care for health, the right to employment and other relevant socio-economic rights. Related to these rights are the principles of equality and the prohibition of discrimination.

At European level, the Council of Europe plays a significant role in this health and human rights interface, notably with the European Convention on Human Rights, (ECHR, 1950, as amended in 1998), the European Social Charter (ESC, 1961, as amended in 1996) and the health-specific Convention of Human Rights and Dignity of the Human Being with regard to the Application of Biology and Medicine (Convention on Human Rights and Biomedicine, 1997).

Article 12 of the Convention on Human Rights and Biomedicine prohibits tests that are predictive of genetic diseases or which serve either to identify the subject as a carrier of a gene responsible for a disease or to detect a genetic predisposition or sensibility to a disease, unless they are performed for *health purposes* or for *scientific research linked to health purposes*. This prohibition is explained in paragraph 84 of the Explanatory Report, as follows:

> Because there is an apparent risk that use is made of genetic testing possibilities outside health care, for instance in the case of medical examination prior to an employment or insurance contract, it is of importance to clearly distinguish between health purposes for the benefit of the individual on the one hand and third parties' interests, which may be commercial, on the other hand.

However, it is noted that Article 12 is not excluded from the application of Article 26 to place restrictions on the exercise of the rights in the Convention in the interest of public safety, for the prevention of crime, for the protection of public health or for the protection of the rights and freedoms of others (provided it is prescribed law and necessary in a democratic society).

In addition, there is the Additional Protocol to the Convention on Human Rights and Biomedicine concerning Genetic Testing for Health Purposes (2008). This document is a follow-up to the decision of the Committee of Ministers of the Council of Europe, taken in 1996, to draw up a Protocol to the Convention concerning the problems relating to human genetics (Additional Protocol to the Convention on Human Rights and Biomedicine concerning genetic testing for health purposes 2008). The Protocol applies to genetic tests for health reasons. Work on the second pillar of the assignment, 'a legal framework for the protection of human dignity and fundamental rights with regard to the use of genetic testing for purposes other than health and health related research' started in 2008 (Council of Europe Consultation Document on Predictivity, Genetic Testing and Insurance 2012).

The European Union is also committed to the health and human rights interface, especially considering its institutions and bodies are bound by the Charter of Fundamental Rights of the Union (2000). The Charter applies to the Member States when they are implementing European Union law, by virtue of Article 6 of the Lisbon Treaty. The following section will expand upon the European activities in this area, from the perspective of the Council of Europe and the European Union.

## 3. Overview of relevant European activities

### *3.1 Council of Europe*

Discussions in the context of the Council of Europe on medical examinations preceding employment and private insurance started about 25 years ago, in the context of the HIV epidemic. The results of the debate are reflected in Recommendation no R (87) 25 concerning a common European public health policy to fight the acquired immunodeficiency syndrome (AIDS) and in Recommendation no R (89) 14 on the ethical issues of HIV infection in the health care and social settings. The recommendations underline both the importance of avoiding unnecessary interference with the right to private life as well as the interest of social solidarity. Discriminatory measures such as exclusion from employment and health care and social services are not scientifically or ethically justified. In the absence of treatment options, neither HIV testing before or during employment, nor screening for group insurance policies should take place. Health-related data and any other confidential information affecting the privacy of the individual should be protected. In all settings and situations where discrimination and violation of civil and social rights of an individual may arise, there should be an appropriate and confidential system providing speedy redress of violation or discrimination.

Likewise, the Explanatory Memorandum to Council of Europe Recommendation No. R. (1992) 3 on genetic testing and screening for health care purposes emphasises the necessity to extend the protection of a person's private life, in particular in respect of valuable genetic data, to the field of activity of insurance companies (within the limits of insurance law). According to Principle 7 of the Recommendation, insurers should not have the right to require genetic testing or to enquire about results of previously performed tests as a pre-condition for the conclusion or modification of an insurance contract. At the time, there was no scope for derogations 'since neither the protection of health of the person concerned nor that of a third party is at stake, but only the insurance companies own interests'. The legitimate interest of an insurance company to avoid 'adverse selection' (Strohmenger and Wambach, 2000) is not taken into consideration.

The issue of enquiring about the results of tests that were previously performed is dealt with in Recommendation no R (97) 5 on the protection of medical data. According to this Recommendation, genetic data collected for health purposes of the data subject should only be used for those purposes, or to allow the data subject to take a free and informed decision on these matters (Article 4). Article 4.8 contains an exception for judicial use. However, the data may only be used to establish whether there is a genetic link in the framework of adducing evidence, to prevent a real danger or to suppress a specific criminal offence. In no case should the genetic data be used to determine other characteristics which may be linked genetically. For purposes other than those mentioned in Articles 4.7 and 4.8 of the Recommendation, the collection and processing of genetic data should, in principle, only be permitted for health reasons and in particular to avoid any serious prejudice to the health of the data subject or third parties. However, the collection and processing of genetic data in order to predict illness may be allowed for in cases of overriding interest and subject to appropriate safeguards defined by law (Article 4.9).

The Council of Europe guidelines proposed in 2000 in the report on 'Medical examinations preceding employment and/or private insurance' are a response to the concerns raised by medical examinations prior to employment and insurance (Council of Europe 2000). These guidelines take into account the abovementioned European standards.

### *3.2 European Union*

On 16 March, 1989, the European Parliament (EU) adopted a Resolution on the ethical and legal problems of genetic engineering (Official Journal

C 96, 17/04/1989). According to the Resolution, insurers should not have the right to demand information on results of previous genetic analysis or to ask for a genetic analysis before or after the conclusion of an insurance contract. Regarding employment, the European Parliament proposes a statutory ban on the selection of workers on the basis of genetic criteria and on the general use of genomic analysis for mass examinations of employees. It prohibits genetic examinations of workers for the purposes of occupational medicine before taking up the job and, once on the job, they may only be carried out with informed consent. The results of such examinations should only be made available to the person concerned; only that person may pass them on. Genetic data concerning employees must be protected by special measures from abuse by third parties. However, since the adoption of this Resolution, there have been no concrete legislative developments in the European Union in this area.

## 4. A closer look into the principles at stake

In consideration of the fundamental human rights at stake in this area, this section will highlight the core rights provided for in the European human rights framework. It will look particularly at the right to equality and non-discrimination, and the right to privacy, from the perspective of both the Council of Europe and the EU.

### *4.1 Discrimination and equality: access to basic social goods*

#### *4.1.1 European Social Charter*

Part V, Article E of the European Social Charter (ESC) prohibits discrimination on any ground in relation to the generality of the substantive clauses of the Charter (for example, employment, health, social security, and social and medical assistance) (de Shutter, 2011: 40–46). A differential treatment based on an objective and reasonable justification does not amount to discrimination. According to the European Committee of Social Rights, the ESC

> not only prohibits direct discrimination but also forms of indirect discrimination. Such indirect discrimination may arise by failing to take due and positive account of all relevant differences or by failing to take adequate steps to ensure that the rights and collective advantages that are open to all are genuinely accessible by and to all.
>
> (*Autisme-Europe v France* 2002: para 54)

States Parties to the ESC should ensure that the socio-economic rights are accessible to all, even if this necessitates the taking of measures that specifically address the obstacles. In the case of violation, the law must provide for sanctions. It has been held that 'The economic crisis should not have as a consequence the reduction of the protection of the rights recognised by the Charter' (European Committee of Social Rights, Activity report 2009: 17). It has also been stated that 'A differential treatment based on an objective and reasonable justification shall not be deemed discriminatory' (European Social Charter: Part V: Article E).

### *4.1.2 European Convention on Human Rights*

This section will give a brief overview of the European Convention on Human Rights framework in this area. The European Court of Human Rights addresses socio-economic rights whenever they can be considered as an intrinsic part of individual rights. According to the Court:

> There is no water-tight division separating the sphere of social and economic rights from the field covered by the European Convention on Human Rights. While the latter Convention sets forth what are essentially civil and political rights, many of them have implications of a social and economic nature.
>
> (*Airey v Ireland* 1979: para 26)

The interaction between the ESC and the ECHR relates, *inter alia*, to social welfare. It is particularly relevant in the case of alleged discrimination. The Court deals with complaints concerning unequal treatment in social security matters whenever it constitutes 'property' within the meaning of the First Protocol to the ECHR (1952) (Vonk, 2000: 145–155). In that case, article 14 of the ECHR on the prohibition of discrimination taken in conjunction with article 1 of Protocol No. 1 to the ECHR may be invoked. The prohibition of discrimination in article 14 only can be invoked in relation to one of the substantive rights of the ECHR and the Protocols to it. Examples include payment for medical treatment, social welfare and guarantees of a minimum standard of living (European Court of Human Rights, Press Unit, Factsheet – Social Welfare, 2013).

However, it is noted that not every distinction or difference of treatment amounts to discrimination. For example, in the judgment in the case of *Abdulaziz, Cabales and Balkandali v the United Kingdom*, the Court stated that a difference of treatment is discriminatory if it 'has no *objective and reasonable justification*', that is, if it does not pursue a '*legitimate aim*' or if there is not a 'reasonable relationship of *proportionality* between the means employed and the aim sought to be realised' (*Abdulaziz, Cabales and Balkandali v the United Kingdom* 1985).

The margin of appreciation of national authorities can be a wide one in situations which in the interest of social justice and economic well-being might legitimately lead them to adjustments in, for instance, taxation. As indicated in the before-mentioned Gaygusuz judgment, the right to property

> shall not... in any way impair the right of a State to enforce such laws as it deems necessary to control the use of property in accordance with the general interest or to secure the payment of taxes or other contributions or penalties.

However, the changes made to entitlements should not be excessive and disproportionate (*Kjartan Asmundsson v Iceland* 2004; *N.K.M. v Hungary* 2013). In the case of *Koufaki and Adedy v Greece*, which concerned reductions in remuneration benefits, bonuses and retirement pensions of public servants, the subsistence situation was not considered sufficiently put into jeopardy to give rise to discrimination (*Koufaki and Adedy v Greece* 2013). In the case of *N.K.M. v Hungary* on the other hand, the measure in question applied to severance pay in the case of a dismissed civil servant. Although it was intended to protect the public purse against excessive expenditure, it was considered not reasonably proportionate to the legitimate aim pursued (*N.K.M. v Hungary* 2013).

Protocol No. 12 to the ECHR (2000) provides for a general prohibition of discrimination in the context of any right set forth by national law. However, it does not prevent States Parties to it from taking positive measures in order to promote full and effective equality in care, provided there is an objective and reasonable justification for those measures and the proportionality principle is respected.

The list of non-discrimination grounds mentioned in Protocol No. 12 is not exhaustive. The meaning of the term 'discrimination' in Article 1 is intended to be identical to the term used in Article 14 of the ECHR. The prohibition of any form of discrimination against a person on grounds of his or her genetic heritage in Article 11 of the Convention on Human Rights and Biomedicine can be seen as a further specification of the grounds mentioned in Article 1 of the Protocol. In addition, Article 4 provides a general provision on non-discrimination and non-stigmatisation on genetic grounds.

Protocol No. 12 protects against discrimination by public authorities (article 1). It does not impose a general positive obligation on the Parties to take measures to prevent or remedy all instances of discrimination in relations between private persons. But it cannot be totally excluded that the duty to 'secure' in the first paragraph of article 1 might entail positive obligations regarding relations between private persons when they concern relations in the public sphere normally regulated by law, for which the State has a certain responsibility. Judging by the examples mentioned (e.g. arbitrary denial of access to work or to services which private persons may make available to the public such as medical care, or utilities such as water and electricity), there is room for positive obligations in relation to insurance products fulfilling a social protection function (Explanatory Report to Protocol No. 12: para 28).

### *4.1.3 EU non-discrimination law and the EU Charter of Fundamental Rights*

This section will provide a brief overview of relevant EU non-discrimination law and the EU Charter of Fundamental Rights. Article 20 of the EU Charter of Fundamental Rights stipulates everyone's equality before the law. As noted in other chapters of this volume, Article 21 of the Charter prohibits discrimination on any ground, including genetic features. The derogation in insurance services from general unisex premiums and benefits, laid down in Article 5(2) of the Directive 2004/113 EC of 13 December 2004, implementing the principle of equal treatment between men and women in the access to and supply of goods and services, is an example of EU law found incompatible with the Charter (*Association belge de Consommateurs Test Achats ASBL v Conseil de Ministres* 2012).

At present, none of the EU equal treatment Directives prohibit discrimination on the grounds of health or genetic features. Discrimination on the ground of disability is prohibited in employment, occupation and vocational training (as provided in the Employment Equality Directive).

In addition, the proposal for a Council Directive on implementing the principle of equal treatment between persons irrespective of religion or belief, disability, age or sexual orientation (July 2008) does not refer to genetic features (COM (2008) 426 final of 2 July 2008). To stretch the notion of disability to include predictive genetic status would be a bridge too far. Apart from that, clause 2.7 of the draft proposal enables Member States to introduce proportionate differences in treatment in the provision of financial services (insurance and banking services) where for the product the use of age or disability is a key factor in the assessment of risk-based availability of cover for consumers.

The Explanatory Memorandum states

> if insurers are not allowed to take age and disability into account at all, the additional costs will have to be entirely borne by the rest of the 'pool' of those insured, which would result in higher overall costs and lower availability of cover for consumers. The use of age and disability in the assessment of risk must be based on accurate data and statistics.
>
> (Explanatory Memorandum 2008: 8)

EU legislation in the field of insurance (except life insurance) in the context of the European market without frontiers on the other hand allows for measures to protect the general good (complementary cover as an alternative for public/statutory provisions). Such measures must be necessary and proportional to their aim, not unduly restrict the right of establishment or the freedom of service providers and apply in an identical manner to all insurers operating within a Member State (Directive 92/94/EEC: Article 54).

### *4.2 Right to private life*

Everyone has a right to respect for his/her private life (Article 8 of the ECHR). This concerns the right to integrity of the person (physical and mental integrity) and to the protection of personal data (informational privacy). The Convention on Human Rights and Biomedicine guarantees respect for one's integrity and other rights and fundamental freedoms with regard to the application of biology and medicine (Article 1). In the EU Charter of Fundamental Rights, the various aspects of private life are addressed in Article 3 on the integrity of the person, Article 7 on the respect for private and family life and Article 8 on the protection of personal data.

#### *4.2.1 Physical and mental integrity*

Article 3 of the EU Charter of Fundamental Rights recognises everyone's right to respect for physical and mental integrity. In the field of medicine and biology, this is specified in paragraph 2 (for example, the free informed consent of the person concerned).

The Convention on Human Rights and Biomedicine also stipulates informed consent for any intervention in the health field (Article 5). The prohibition (Article 12) to perform predictive genetic tests for non-health purposes does not, per se, exclude genetic testing in other contexts than health care. The criterion is that the test is in the interest of the health of the individual. Relevant in this context is the text in the Explanatory Report (paragraphs 85–86):

> This means that, in particular circumstances, when the working environment could have prejudicial consequences on the health of the individual because of a genetic predisposition, predictive genetic testing may be offered without prejudice to the aim of improving working conditions. The test should be clearly in the interest of the individual's health. The right not to know should also be respected. Insofar as predictive genetic testing, in the case of employment or private insurance contracts, does not have a health purpose, it entails a disproportionate interference in the rights of the individual to privacy. An insurance company will not be entitled to subject the conclusion or modification of an insurance policy to the holding of a predictive test. Nor will it be able to refuse the conclusion or modification of such a policy on the ground that the applicant has not submitted to a test, as the conclusion of a policy cannot reasonably be made conditional of an illegal act.

Also relevant is the interpretation given in the Explanatory Report to the notion of 'intervention' in relation to Article 4 on professional standards and Article 5 on consent, as covering all medical acts next to those performed for the purpose of preventive care, diagnosis, treatment, rehabilitation or research. This interpretation is relevant in the event of an exception to the prohibition of predictive genetic testing for non-health purposes (Article 12) on the basis of Article 26. In that case, Article 11 (on the prohibition of any form of discrimination against a person of his or her genetic heritage) still applies.

### *4.2.2 Informational privacy*

It is observed that confidentiality of health data is crucial for two reasons: first, to respect the privacy of the patient; second, to preserve his/her confidence in the medical profession and in the health system in general. 'Failing appropriate safeguards, a breach of confidentiality may deter the patient from seeking medical assistance and this may be to the detriment of their health' (*Z v Finland* 1997).

EU constitutional law contains a positive obligation to secure the protection of personal data, including health (genetic) data (Treaty on the Functioning of the EU: Article 16 para 2; EU Charter of Fundamental Rights: Article 8). Article 8 of the EU Charter of Fundamental Rights stipulates the fair processing of personal data for a specific purpose and on the basis of consent (or some other legitimate basis laid down by law).

In relation to personal health information, everyone is entitled to medical confidentiality, the right to know and the right not to be informed. Genetic information is a part of the entire spectrum of health information and does not as such represent a separate category (European Commission, 2004). As personal health information belongs to the category of sensitive data, it is subject to special rules, as provided for in the Data Protection Directive, as well as the Convention for the Protection of Individuals with regard to Automated Processing of Personal Data (Council of Europe 1981). Domestic law must provide for appropriate safeguards in this regard.

Incompatible re-use of personal data will be avoided only with a clear definition of the purposes for processing genetic data (finality and proportionality principles). According to the Article 29 Data Protection Working Party, 'The processing of genetic data should be authorised in the employment and insurance fields only in very exceptional cases provided for by law, so as to protect individuals from being discriminated against on the basis of their genetic profile' (Article 29 Working Party Working Document on Genetic Data 2004). It requires an overriding interest on the part of the insurer/employer as well as appropriate safeguards defined by law (Council of Europe, 1997).

## 5. Legitimate interests of employers and insurance companies

Not every distinction or difference of treatment amounts to discrimination. As was stated in the European Court of Human Rights' judgment in the case of *Abdulaziz, Cabales and Balkandali v the United Kingdom*, a difference of treatment is discriminatory if it 'has no *objective and reasonable justification*', that is, if it does not pursue a 'legitimate aim' or if there is not a 'reasonable relationship of *proportionality* between the means employed and the aim sought to be realised' (*Abdulaziz, Cabales and Balkandali v the United Kingdom* 1985: para 72). Considering this stance, this section will highlight the position of employers and insurance companies in this debate. Discussion of the legitimate interests of employers and insurance companies and the tension created between competing rights will be explored in further detail in later chapters of this book.

### *5.1 Employers*

The aims of work-related medical assessments are to protect the candidate against a job-related disease and to eliminate a possible health threat for others because of the health status of the job-candidate (for example, contagious disease, epilepsy for a pilot). Medical assessment should be about job-related health status only, unless the medical examination does not have selective aspects and is only undertaken in order to adapt the working conditions to the employee. Medical examinations are no replacement for the obligation of the employer to take effective preventive measures for healthy working conditions.

Under no circumstances should a pre-employment health assessment be used to reduce the financial risks that the employer may incur for illness or disability of a job-candidate as a consequence of underwriting conditions for employment-related insurances. In this regard, it has been stated that:

> Applicants should not be requested to undergo testing aimed at assessing risks for future illness or disability or to communicate what they already know about those risks, unless the collection of information of this kind is in accordance with national law and necessary with a view to specific health and safety hazards of the job for the candidate or to avoid serious damage to the health of third persons.
>
> (European Commission, 2003)

Medical testing and questions (including family history) (Schmitz and Wiesing, 2006; Gevers and de Wert, 2004: 250–251) in relation to non-job-related future health (genetic) risks are a disproportionate interference with a job candidate's private life and it may result in unjustified exclusion from work.

### *5.2 Insurance companies*

Genetic risks, though unknown until relatively recently, have always been included in insurance coverage whenever the insurance candidate's health plays a role. New and more precise knowledge about their implications have not as a result raised the risk levels for insurance companies, but rather have provoked a financial interest in genetic information. In relation to genetic tests, the prohibition in the Convention on Human Rights and Biomedicine for testing that does not serve the health interest of the individual can be considered as a general norm. Otherwise there would be a disproportional infringement of the private life of the person concerned.

At the same time, any insurance company, in particular life insurance, has a legitimate interest to avoid adverse selection (Strohmenger and Wambach, 2000). This explains the solution in some European countries to legally restrict the possibility to ask for relevant existing predictive (health) genetic information to a financial ceiling of what the insurance candidate normally needs, under appropriate safeguards defined by law. Such an exception is in line with Council of Europe Recommendation no R. (97) 5 on the protection of medical data in the case of an overriding interest of the insurance company. A provision in the law is a more protective solution than a moratorium. For example, the solution of a moratorium is applied by the Association of British Insurers. The position in relation to insurance and the competing interests arising is discussed in greater detail by Davey and Van Hoyweghen in Chapters 9 and 12.

## 6. Conclusion

Under the European Social Charter, States have a due diligence obligation. In the case of *Kiyutin v Russia* the European Court of Human Rights indicated that the existence of a European consensus is a possible additional consideration for determining whether in relation to the prohibition of discrimination a State should be afforded a narrow margin of appreciation or a wide one (*Kiyutin v Russia* 2011). Where there is a common standard which the State has failed to meet, this may constitute a relevant consideration for the Court when it interprets the provisions of the Convention in specific cases.

The use of medical examinations for employment and insurance purposes, in particular if aimed at a latent, serious and incurable disease, is a serious infringement of individual and social human rights. It impacts persons whose social functioning depends on employment and adequate insurance coverage. The human rights involved require equivalent protection at European level. This is particularly important against the background of the EU single market and its objectives of the attainment of a high level of employment, and of social and consumer protection.

It is observed that, in addition to genetic technologies, other medical (health) technology can be misused as a tool for distribution of social goods. To be effective, European standards for pre-employment medical examination and/or private insurance with a social function should not isolate genetic factors from other (predictive) health information (Lemke, 2005: 22–40), taking into account developments in society, medicine and technology. Principally, the standards should be guided by considerations of protection of private life and social policy. Health care and access to employment and other social goods and services ought to be accessible without fear for discrimination.

## References


Article 29 Data Protection Working Party (2004) 'Working document on genetic data', adopted 17 March, 12178/03/EN, WP 91.

Council of Europe (2000) 'Medical examinations preceding employment and/or private insurance, a proposal for European guidelines, Council of Europe', April, p. 35. The report was prepared by a Committee of Experts on the instigation of the European Public Health Committee.

Council of Europe (2009) European Committee of Social Rights, 'Activity report 2009', 25 June, p. 17.

Council of Europe (2013) European Court of Human Rights, Press Unit, Factsheet – 'Social welfare', June.

European Commission (2004) Ethical, legal and social aspects of genetic testing (research development and clinical applications), drawn up by a group of experts, on the request of, and published by the Research Directorate General of the European Commission, Brussels.

European Network of Legal Experts in the Non-discrimination Field (2011) 'The prohibition of discrimination under European Human Rights Law', written by de Schutter, O., European Commission, Directorate General of Justice, pp. 40–46.

Gevers, S. and de Wert, G. (2004) 'Genetic information and access to employment' *The Lancet Neurology* 3(4): 250–251.

Lemke, T. (2005) 'Beyond genetic discrimination. Problems and perspectives of a contested notion' *Genomics, Society and Policy* 1(3): 22.

Schmitz, D. and Wiesing, U. (2006) 'Just a family medical history?' *British Medical Journal* 332(7536): 297–299.

Strohmenger, R. and Wambach, A. (2000) 'Adverse selection and categorical discrimination in the health insurance markets: The effects of genetic tests' *Journal of Health Economics* 19(2): 197–218.

Prof. Dr. Vonk, G. J. (2000) 'Social security and the right to property: Gaygusuz and after'. In: Loof J. P., Ploeger H. and van der Steur A. (eds) *The right to property, the Influence of Article 1 Protocol No. 1 ECHR on several fields of domestic law.* E.M. Meijers Institute, Maastricht. pp. 145–155.


## Legislation

Commission Proposal for a Council Directive of 2 July 2008 on implementing the principle of equal treatment between persons irrespective of religion or belief, disability, age or sexual orientation, COM [2008] 426 final.

Convention for the Protection of Human Rights and Fundamental Freedoms ETS 5; 213 UNTS 221.

Council and Parliament Directive 95/46/EC of 24 October 1995 on the protection of individuals with regard to the processing of personal data and on the free movement of such data [1995] OJ L 281/31.

Council Directive 92/94/EEC of 8 June 1992 on the coordination of laws, regulations and administrative provisions relating to direct insurance other than life assurance (Third Non-Life Insurance Framework Directive).

Council Directive 2000/78/EC of 27 November 2000 establishing a general framework for equal treatment in employment and occupation [2000] OJ L 303/16.

Council of Europe (1981) Convention for the Protection of individuals with regard to Automatic Processing of Personal Data (1981, ETS No. 108).

Council of Europe (1996) European Social Charter (Revised) ETS No. 163.

Council of Europe (1997) Convention for the Protection of Human Rights and the Dignity of the Human Being with Regard to the Application of Biology and Medicine: Convention on Human Rights and Biomedicine (ETS. No. 164).

Council of Europe Recommendation No. R (97) 5 on the Protection of Medical Data (adopted on 13 February 1997).

Council of Europe (2000) Explanatory Report to Protocol No. 12 to the Convention for the Protection of Human Rights and Fundamental Freedoms (ETS No. 177).

Council of Europe (2008) Additional Protocol to the Convention on Human Rights and Biomedicine concerning genetic testing for health purposes.

Council of Europe (2012) Consultation Document on Predictivity, Genetic Testing and Insurance, DH-BIO/INF (2012) 1. Strasbourg: Council of Europe Steering Committee on Bioethics (CDBI).

European Commission (2003). Opinion No. 18 on 'Ethical aspects of genetic testing in the workplace' (July 2003). Brussels: European Commission's Group on Ethics in Science and New Technologies.

Explanatory Memorandum – Recommendation No. R (97) 5 of Committee of Ministers to Member States on the protection of medical data (adopted by the Committee of Ministers on 13 February 1997 at the 584th meeting of the Ministers' Deputies).

Explanatory Memorandum to Proposal for Council Directive on implementing the principle of equal treatment between persons irrespective of religion or belief, disability, age or sexual orientation COM (2008), 426 final.

Parliament Resolution of 17 April 1989 on the ethical and legal problems of genetic engineering [1989] OJ C 96/165–171.

Treaty on the Functioning of the European Union (2008/ C 115/01).

## Cases

*Abdulaziz, Cabales and Balkandali v the United Kingdom* (Appl. no. 9214/80; 9473/81; 9474/81, 28 May 1985).

*Airey v Ireland* (1979–1980) 2 EHRR 305 (9 October 1979).

*Association belge de Consommateurs Test Achats ASBL v Conseil de Ministres* Case C-236/09 [2012].

*Association Internationale Autisme-Europe (AIAE) v France*, Complaint No. 13/2000, decision on the merits of 4 November 2003.
*Kiyutin v Russia* (Appl. No. 2700/10, 10 March 2011, 15 September 2011).
*Kjartan Asmundsson v Iceland* (Appl. No. 60669/00 of 12 October 2004).
*Koufaki and Adedy v Greece* (Appl. No. 57665/12 and 57657/12 of 7 May 2013).
*N.K.M. v Hungary* (Appl. No. 66529/11 of 14 May 2013).
*Z v Finland* (Appl. No. 22009/93, 25 February 1997).

# 12 National legal and policy responses to genetic discrimination in Europe

## The difficulties of regulation

*Ine Van Hoyweghen*

### 1. Introduction

In the 1990s, The Human Genome Project (HGP) garnered significant public debate and attention given its promise to render visible the genome of the human species. While the introduction of this technology has been widely discussed across fields, one of the more contentious debates about genetic testing and its social impact has taken place in the field of private insurance. The promising vision of genomics has cast the shadows of new types of stigmatisation, exclusion and disadvantaging directed at individuals and families regarded as 'genetically ill'. Some of these adverse effects have been debated for about twenty years under the heading of 'genetic discrimination'. The academic literature, the media and the relevant legislation use this term to refer to the unjustified differential treatment of human beings with a (presumed) increased risk of being affected by a genetic disease (Billings *et al.*, 1992).[1] Public fear of genetic discrimination may potentially lead to a decline in genetic tests, refusal to participate in scientific research, discouragement to disclose test results to health care providers/relatives and more interest in direct-to-consumer genetic testing (Allain *et al.*, 2012; Geelen *et al.*, 2012).

To manage these concerns, internationally, policymakers and lawmakers have taken measures to 'prevent' genetic discrimination (Joly *et al.*, 2010; Knoppers *et al.*, 2004; Otlowski *et al.*, 2012). In the United States, the Genetic Nondiscrimination Act (GINA) was the first federal law in 2008 to address the problem of genetic discrimination in employment and health

1 This definition of the concept figured in the first empirical study pertaining to this subject in the early 1990s: '[G]enetic discrimination is defined as discrimination against an individual or against members of that individual's family solely because of real or perceived differences from the "normal" genome of that individual. Genetic discrimination is distinguished from discrimination based on disabilities caused by altered genes by excluding, from the former category, those instances of discrimination against an individual who at the time of the discriminatory act was affected by the genetic disease' (Billings *et al.*, 1992: 477).

insurance. At the European level, explicit bans on discrimination based on genetic characteristics are contained within the European Convention on Human Rights and Biomedicine of the European Council (1997) (Article 11) as well as in the Charter of Fundamental Rights of the EU (2000) (Article 21). As early as the 1990s, a substantial number of European countries enacted genetic non-discrimination regulations (Van Hoyweghen and Horstman, 2008). Although there has been variation in these regulatory approaches within and between specific national contexts – ranging from prohibitive (e.g. France, Belgium), moratorium (e.g. UK, Greece), more general antidiscrimination legislation (e.g. Hungary), to fair limits approaches (e.g. Switzerland, Germany, the Netherlands) – most European countries have reached a consensus that there should be a restriction or even prohibition of the use of genetic testing (results) in private insurance and have installed genetic non-discrimination regulations. These regulations should help alleviate public fear of genetic discrimination, enabling the progress of genetic research and use of genetics in clinical and preventive care.

This chapter provides a unique overview for those unfamiliar with the issues and debates rising from the regulatory efforts to govern genetic discrimination in the European regional context. While it is often stated that the United States has been a pioneer in the field of genetic non-discrimination regulation, it is interesting to have a look at the regulatory developments in this field in European states, which date back to the nineties. For example, in 1992, Belgium explicitly prohibited insurers from using the results of genetic tests when setting premium levels (LVO, 1992). The chapter will focus on the specific policy framings of the debate on genetic discrimination in the European context from its early inception in the 1990s to the realities it currently faces with new genomic technologies, discourses and supranational EU regulatory initiatives. Particular attention is paid to the framing of the issue of genetic discrimination in terms of 'social inclusion', the outline of divergent national genetic non-discrimination regulations, the (un)intended effects of these regulatory framings and how this opens up new possibilities and questions in regard to regulating the issue at the EU supranational level.

## 2. Regulating genetic discrimination through European countries

### *2.1 Legal and policy responses to fears of genetic discrimination*

To understand the origins and rise of genetic non-discrimination regulations in European states, it is necessary to get more insight into the mechanisms that fostered the rise of these state regulations. In the European context, discourses about genetic discrimination have been wed to narratives of genetic determinism, histories of eugenics and an insistence upon social inclusion. To unpack the source of fears of genetic discrimination, each of these narratives is explained briefly. First, underlying this fear has been a deterministic vision of genes as ultimate causal constituents. For example, both advocates and proponents in the debate have used the example of Huntington's disease, a rare monogenetic mutation, to underline their claims and frame the debate in hyperbole. While some monogenetic disorders exhibit a low penetrance, Huntington's disease and other monogenetic disorders with high penetrance guarantee that the individual will develop a disease sometime in the course of his/her life. The location of a fundamental difference between certain humans, seemingly inscribed in the biology of their genes, also evoked shared memories of eugenics (Lemke, 2013) as well as raising important privacy concerns (Godard *et al.*, 2003) that further fuelled fears of genetic discrimination. Last, and most important, European fears of genetic discrimination are attributable to a deep-rooted vision of private insurance as an instrument of solidarity and not one of discrimination.

Generally speaking, twentieth-century European insurance arrangements share a deep-rooted 'culture of solidarity' (Hinrichs, 1995) whereby access to private life insurance is viewed as a social good, a right and not a privilege (Chuffart, 1996). The introduction of genetic testing in insurance was thus viewed as marking a decline in the ethos of solidarity, echoing wider concerns of social inclusion amongst the recent privatisations of European welfare states. This means that already longer-standing fears of privacy and discrimination have thus found expression in the exemplary case of genetic discrimination. This European context has helped shape the issue of genetic discrimination as one that requires *special* treatment in the policy arena. In this way, genetic discrimination has been aligned with a paradigm of 'genetic exceptionalism' (Murray, 1997), used to denote how genetic information is believed to differ from other medical information and subsequently should be treated differently. This mentality has become entrenched through genetics-*specific* policy and legislative efforts in many European countries.

### *2.2 'Genetic discrimination', a national rally for social inclusion*

Having explained the roots of fears of genetic discrimination, it is important to explore how various actors in European states such as patient groups, medical professionals, human rights groups, national policymakers and the wider public have mobilised in the push for genetic non-discrimination regulations. The following paragraph traces how various social groups mobilised around the discourse of 'genetic discrimination', that way translating the issue from a problem originally affecting a small group ('the genetically ill') into a major public issue.

First, genetic patient groups have been active in mobilising the view that genetic discrimination needs particular attention, and therefore requires specific regulatory action. These groups, such as the Genetic Alliance UK, have protested actively against genetic discrimination via various channels such as the media, political campaigns and lobbying. Importantly, genetic patients groups' advocacy has enabled alliances with other – originally non-affected – public and state actors who articulated concern about genetic discrimination as an exemplary case for wider concerns of social inclusion. For instance, policymakers' use of idioms like 'the genetic underclass' strongly appealed to a European welfare state ethos of solidarity. In contrast to the United States, European countries often provide some form of universal access to health care and accord a much more important role to the social dimension of private insurance. In most European countries, politicians and other state actors have been so vigorously committed to the idea of social inclusion that immediate policy action to restrict genetic discrimination has been taken (Van Hoyweghen, 2007).

Genetic discrimination has garnered attention as well from medical professionals and innovation policy actors active in the EU 'knowledge-based bio-economy'.[2] These groups focus their concern on the fact that people may defer genetic testing, given fears of genetic discrimination, which, in turn, thwarts genomic innovation. Furthermore, 'genetic discrimination' has aligned with concerns of supranational European institutions and human rights organisations, having developed in important supranational normative documents on genetic non-discrimination. In Europe, the Council of Europe (CoE)'s Oviedo Convention on Human Rights and Biomedicine (1997) clearly has set the tone by prohibiting any form of discrimination on the grounds of one's genetic heritage and by restricting the use of genetic tests to health purposes or scientific research (Council of Europe, 1997).[3] Also the 2000 Charter of Fundamental Rights of the European Union is of importance here, which includes a broad non-discrimination clause that encompasses genetic features (European Union, 2000). Although these EU documents are not legally binding, they have an important normative function in setting the tone that Europe does not want 'genetic discrimination'.

Moreover, the framing of genetic discrimination has not only stimulated concerns and compassion within the broader public for 'the genetically ill', but has also facilitated the translation of genetic discrimination into an issue that affects 'all of us'. In referring to the fact that 'we all have genes', we are faced with the prospect that genetic discrimination could happen to each and every one of us. As the director of the Genetic Alliance UK stated,

2 See, e.g., 'The economic fruits of frontier life science research'. http://ec.europa.eu/research/biosociety/kbbe/basics_en.htm

3 The Oviedo Convention has been very influential in promoting legislative initiatives in Europe (Otlowski *et al.*, 2012) and, as of June 2013, 28 of the European countries have confirmed it and therefore legally prohibit access to genetic information by insurers (Council of Europe, 2013).

'The fact that we are all susceptible to genetic diseases is a strong factor for solidarity'.[4] The discourse of 'genes affecting all of us' has further mobilised the public in advocating genetic non-discrimination regulations. Here the issue of genetic discrimination expands from linking only with a small affected population to an issue that concerns the entire population.

What this demonstrates is that genes enabled a collective integration in linking people together, giving way to a *hybrid coalition* for political action in the regulatory field and generating a common desirability for genetics-*specific* legislative action. The concerned groups engaging with the issue of genetic discrimination have ranged from the particular group of 'the genetically ill' to the whole collective. The alignment of these different groups and concerns ('genetics + discrimination') as well as the worried press communications about genetic discrimination have pushed national policymakers to take swift action and evoked the need for short-term solutions and political expediency. Over the years, these genetic non-discrimination regulations have become successful in the sense that this policy approach to the issue has spread over Europe, as there started to be 'a trend to legislate' (CEA, 2000: 2). When confronted with public debates on the issue, European national policymakers have been inclined to watch the neighbours and have 'copied and pasted' existing genetic non-discrimination regulations (Van Hoyweghen and Horstman, 2009).[5] With the introduction of these regulations as the gold standard, European national state administrators have thus been aligning with the paradigm of genetic exceptionalism by installing and cementing the new category of 'genetic' into non-discrimination regulations.

### *2.3 Models of genetic discrimination regulation in European countries – a regulatory patchwork*

Today, most European states have introduced regulations to ensure that no individual is discriminated against because of his or her genetic constitution (Joly *et al.*, 2010; Rothstein and Joly 2009; Knoppers *et al.*, 2004). The laws are intended to protect individuals against unfair differential treatment based on genetic knowledge in the fields of employment and

4 'Genes, Medical care: EU regulations against genetic discrimination needed.' http://ec.europa.eu/research/biosociety/news_events/news_genes_medicalcare_en.htm.

5 As this reinsurance manager explained: 'But if you go to the governments, even though the national context is completely different, the first thing policymakers do is to look on the internet and see what other governments are doing. They really do that. And they just pick whatever... they don't care what the insurance system is in that country. They just go and say: 'Oh, that must be a solution then, because we're not going to generate a new solution or something.... Particularly in the number of European countries that in the early 90s have decided to legally ban genetics in insurance. That has generally set some kind of standard' (cited in Van Hoyweghen and Horstman, 2009).

insurance, and to respond to the fears of individuals currently dissuaded from undergoing genetic testing in both clinical and research settings. Some countries have adopted a prohibitive approach banning the use of genetic test results by the insurance industry (e.g., Austria, Belgium, France), whereas others have opted for moratoria requiring the insurance industry neither to request genetic testing nor to use test results for insurance contracts for a certain period of time (United Kingdom, Finland) (Joly *et al.*, 2010; Otlowski *et al.*, 2012).

In addition to the variety of existing regulatory frameworks, there are in principle two legal-political options currently applied to govern the use of genetic information, especially in the employment and insurance sector (see Gerards *et al.*, 2005; Lemke 2013). The first places special emphasis on the protection of genetic data and focuses on the right to genetic privacy. This form of legislation proceeds from the principle that every citizen should be in control of his or her genetic data, which are not to be passed on to non-medical parties without the explicit and informed prior consent of the individual concerned. The legal guarantee of data protection alone, however, is insufficient. If the refusal to reveal genetic information is expected to entail severe social disadvantages (if, for example, insurance policies are denied or career goals threatened), individuals could de facto feel forced to forgo exercising their rights.

In an effort to avoid this, a second regulatory instrument centred on the principle of non-discrimination is often employed. Rather than prohibiting the collection and storage of genetic information by institutional actors, non-discrimination law aims at curbing and preventing the use of such information. Both these legal-political strategies have their advantages and disadvantages and are therefore often combined in legal practice. Although the strategy of data protection limits access to genetic information, the non-discrimination principle prohibits its inappropriate use for organisational decision-making processes.[6]

In the context of insurance underwriting, it is possible to discern different political and legal approaches combining the two strategies to regulate the use of genetic information. The main approaches favoured by policymakers to solve the problem of how to use genetic knowledge in insurance are identified in the literature as the following: (1) a 'fair limits

6 '[T]he nondiscrimination principle requires that the individual must not only show that he has been disadvantaged because of his personal genetic data, but also that other individuals or groups (lacking the relevant genetic defect) have been treated more favorably. This comparative aspect of the nondiscrimination principle seems to make it somewhat less useful and valuable to the individual than the privacy approach, which does not require a comparison to other groups or individuals: to establish a violation of genetic privacy. On the other hand, an advantage of the discrimination approach may be that the individual does not have to show that the insurer or employer has actually invaded his personal privacy by using genetic information' (Gerards *et al.*, 2005: 24).

approach' that permits 'insurers to access and to use genetic information for insurance underwriting only for policies above a legislatively predetermined amount of money'; (2) a 'human rights approach' 'stemming from the field of international human rights law aiming to prevent the discrimination of individuals on the basis of genetic information'; (3) a 'moratorium approach' that is defined as 'a voluntary agreement by a group of insurers (often through an official representative organisation), to neither request genetic testing of insurance applicants nor to use genetic test results for a certain period of time'; (4) a 'prohibitive approach' 'aimed at specifically prohibiting access to or use of genetic information by the insurance industry'; (5) a 'rational discrimination approach' 'permitting the use of genetic information for insurance underwriting only after it has been deemed scientifically valid and clinically significant by an independent expert scientific panel'; and (6) a 'status quo approach' consisting of a 'wait-and-see default approach' to the use of genetic information by insurers. 'This approach allows insurers to develop their own rules pertaining to the use of genetic information in connection with insurance contracts without intervention from the government' (Rothstein and Joly, 2009: 138–139; see also Knoppers *et al.*, 2004; Lemke, 2013).[7]

Table 12.1 shows the approaches that member countries of the Council of Europe have adopted and their instruments to maintain these approaches.

As Table 12.1 illustrates, there has been variation in these regulatory approaches within and between national contexts, reflecting local legal customs and how the boundaries have been set between private and social insurance.[8] For some legal commentators, this has resulted in an emerging 'patchwork of protection' (Gerards *et al.*, 2005: 21) in regard to genetic non-discrimination regulations throughout Europe. In view of the shared nature of the problem of genetic discrimination, and especially in the context of calls for a greater level of harmonisation through EU supranational legislation, this regulatory variety (including its multiple definitions of genetic testing) poses its own challenges and complications, which will be discussed in the next section.

7 For a detailed overview of these national regulatory approaches, see, e.g., Joly *et al.*, 2010.

8 However, a true legal comparative study would be needed to analyse the societal and cultural factors underlying these regulatory responses in different European countries (Soini, 2012). Comparative law is a specific legal academic discipline that studies differences of legal systems, legal orders and laws of different countries. It aspires to go further into the local legal culture and history to be able to understand and explain normative structures and solutions in a given country.

*Table 12.1* Profile of domestic approaches towards protection against genetic discrimination of members of the Council of Europe (only countries where data are available)

| *Country* | *Approach* | *Instrument* |
|---|---|---|
| Albania | Human rights | Convention on Human Rights and Biomedicine (1997) |
| Austria | Prohibitive | Gene Technology Act of 1995 (Section 67) |
| Belgium | Prohibitive | Law of 25 June 1992 on Insurance Contract (Article 95) |
| Bosnia and Herzegovina | Human rights | Convention on Human Rights and Biomedicine (1997) |
| Bulgaria | Human rights | Convention on Human Rights and Biomedicine (1997) |
| Croatia | Human rights | Convention on Human Rights and Biomedicine (1997) |
| Cyprus | Human rights | Convention on Human Rights and Biomedicine (1997) |
| Czech Republic | Human rights | Convention on Human Rights and Biomedicine (1997) |
| Denmark | Prohibitive | Insurance Contract Act of 1997 (Section 3a) |
| | Human rights | Convention on Human Rights and Biomedicine (1997) |
| Estonia | Prohibitive | Human Genes Research Act of 2001 (Chapter 5) |
| | Human rights | Convention on Human Rights and Biomedicine (1997) |
| Finland | Moratorium | Federation of Finnish Insurance Companies, 1999 |
| | Human rights | Convention on Human Rights and Biomedicine (1997) |
| France | Prohibitive | Law No. 2002-303 of 4 March 2002 on Patients' Rights and the Quality of the Health System |
| | | Article 16-13 of the Civil Code |
| | Moratorium | The French Federation of Insurers (1994) |
| | Human rights | Convention on Human Rights and Biomedicine (1997) |
| Georgia | Human rights | Law of Georgia of 5 May 2000 on the Rights of Patients |
| | | Convention on Human Rights and Biomedicine (1997) |
| Germany | Moratorium | German Insurance Association |
| | 'Fair limits' | Formal Commitment (2004) |
| | | Human Genetic Examination Act (2009) |
| Greece | Moratorium | Voluntary Code of Conduct |

*Table 12.1* continued

| *Country* | *Approach* | *Instrument* |
|---|---|---|
| | Other (data protection) | Law 2472/1997 on the Protection of Individuals with regard to the Procession of Personal Data |
| | Human rights | Convention on Human Rights and Biomedicine (1997) |
| Hungary | Human rights | Convention on Human Rights and Biomedicine (1997) |
| Iceland | Human rights | Convention on Human Rights and Biomedicine (1997) |
| Ireland | Prohibitive | The Disability Act (2005) |
| | Moratorium | Voluntary Code of Practice on Genetic Testing |
| | 'Fair limits' | |
| Italy | Other (ethical guidelines) | Bioethical Guidelines for Genetic Testing (1999) |
| | Human rights (signed only) | Convention on Human Rights and Biomedicine (1997) |
| Latvia | Human rights | Human Genome Research Law (2002) |
| | | Convention on Human Rights and Biomedicine (1997) |
| Lithuania | Prohibitive | Law on Insurance 2003 No. IX-1737, article 100 |
| | Human rights | Convention on Human Rights and Biomedicine (1997) |
| Luxembourg | Prohibitive | Law of 27 July 1997 on the Insurance Contract |
| | Human rights (signed only) | Convention on Human Rights and Biomedicine (1997) |
| Moldova | Human rights | Convention on Human Rights and Biomedicine (1997) |
| Montenegro | Human rights | Convention on Human Rights and Biomedicine (1997) |
| Netherlands | Moratorium | Association of Insurers, Moratorium on Genetic |
| | | Investigations – Policy of Disablement and Life Insurers on Genetic Investigations (December 1990) |
| | 'Fair limits' | The Act on Medical Examinations of 1998 (Section 5) |
| | Human rights (signed only) | Convention on Human Rights and Biomedicine (1997) |

*Table 12.1* continued

| *Country* | *Approach* | *Instrument* |
|---|---|---|
| Norway | Prohibitive | Act of 5 December 2003 No. 100 relating to the application of biotechnology in human medicine, etc. |
| | Human rights | Convention on Human Rights and Biomedicine (1997) |
| Poland | Human rights (signed only) | Convention on Human Rights and Biomedicine (1997) |
| Portugal | Prohibitive | Law 12/2005 of 26 January (Section 12) |
| | Human rights | Convention on Human Rights and Biomedicine (1997) |
| Romania | Human rights | Convention on Human Rights and Biomedicine (1997) |
| San Marino | Human rights | Convention on Human Rights and Biomedicine (1997) |
| Serbia | Human rights | Convention on Human Rights and Biomedicine (1997) |
| Slovakia | Human rights | Convention on Human Rights and Biomedicine (1997) |
| Slovenia | Human rights | Convention on Human Rights and Biomedicine (1997) |
| Spain | Prohibitive | Law 14/2007, of 3 July, on Biomedical Research (Article 6) |
| | Human rights | Convention on Human Rights and Biomedicine (1997) |
| | | The Spanish Constitution (1978) |
| Sweden | Prohibitive | Law No. 351 of 18 May 2006 on genetic integrity |
| | Moratorium | Voluntary Code by the Federation of Swedish Insurers |
| | 'Fair limits' | |
| | Human rights (signed only) | Convention on Human Rights and Biomedicine (1997) |
| Switzerland | Prohibitive | Swiss Federal Law on the Genetic Testing of Humans |
| | Moratorium | (2004) |
| | 'Fair limits' | |
| | Human rights | Convention on Human Rights and Biomedicine (1997) |
| Turkey | Moratorium | |
| | Human rights | Convention on Human Rights and Biomedicine (1997) |
| Ukraine | Human rights (signed only) | Convention on Human Rights and Biomedicine (1997) |

*Table 12.1* continued

| *Country* | *Approach* | *Instrument* |
|---|---|---|
| United Kingdom | Moratorium | Concordat and Moratorium on Genetics and Insurance |
| | 'Fair limits' | (2005) |
| | 'Rational discrimination' | |
| Yugoslav Republic of Macedonia | Human rights | Convention on Human Rights and Biomedicine (1997) |

Source: Rothstein and Joly, 2009; Otlowski, Taylor and Bombard, 2012; Council of Europe, 2013; European Commission, 2002; Godard *et al.*, 2003

## 3. The difficulties of regulation – The Babel of genetic non-discrimination regulations

While the former section demonstrates the conventional framing of genetic non-discrimination regulation in European states, it is equally important to analyse the effects these types of regulation have had since implementation. While these regulations have been installed to address the issue of genetic discrimination, it is becoming clear that the workings of these regulations may be more complex than anticipated (Van Hoyweghen, 2007).

One concern is whether genetic non-discrimination regulations in European states have been effective. Although no current evidence exists to suggest increased genetic discrimination after the national laws' enactments, these laws have not prevented genetic information from being used in insurance practices. For instance, in Belgium, despite a legal ban on the use of genetic information in insurance, medical advisors and underwriters in insurance companies still use genetic test results or genetic information derived from physician records or insurance questionnaires. Often this arises from ignorance or misunderstanding of genetic conditions in the context of insurance underwriting. However, it is due as well to the lack of clear definitions of 'genetic data' or 'genetic testing' in the laws (Godard *et al.*, 2003; Soini 2012). Therefore, the boundaries between 'genetic' and 'non-genetic' data are not always distinct in insurance practices. It seems that these laws have not always delivered on their promises. Moreover, some of the laws' definitions seem to be outdated, given the recent progress in genomics knowledge. In genomics medicine, it is increasingly acknowledged that the distinction between genetic and non-genetic information has become artificial. New developments in genomics complicate legal concepts and distinctions. The original scope of protection provided by most European state laws has been rather narrow. For example, some laws exclude chemical tests, blood tests, and routine laboratory tests from the definition of genetic tests. Given that all genetic tests are chemical tests, many are blood tests, and an increasing number are routine, many European states' regulations may only provide the illusion of protection.

Further, European experience demonstrates that these genetic non-discrimination regulations create some unintended effects. While the legislative focus has been on the unacceptability of genetic discrimination, other possible discrimination in insurance practices has arisen (Van Hoyweghen *et al.*, 2007). Smokers, obese individuals and individuals who do not comply with prescribed therapy are confronted with sharply increased prices and possibly with exclusion from insurance coverage. The exclusive legal protection of genetic risks has occurred with an increasing discrimination against lifestyle risks. By providing exclusive legal protection to the group with genetic risks, groups with other non-genetic risks are unintendedly left underprotected. Lifestyle risks are disproportionately disadvantaged by laws that protect against discrimination based exclusively on genetic risks. This may result in inequities between similarly situated individuals. Genetic non-discrimination laws thus raise new issues with respect to responsibility for health risks and stimulate reflection on the question, 'Who deserves our solidarity?'

A further controversy focuses on the question of whether legal protection against genetic discrimination practice requires specific legislation or whether it is already covered by existing regulations. For instance, the question needs to be addressed of whether discrimination against the 'asymptomatic ill' based on genetic characteristics represents a particular case of discrimination against people with disabilities. From this perspective, no specific legislation would be necessary to protect individuals with genetic anomalies as long as regulations exist for protection against ableism (Lemke, 2013).

Finally, these laws may have difficulties in preventing the public fear of genetic discrimination. European experience indicates how, even after these regulatory actions, individuals still fear genetic discrimination, resulting in withdrawal from genetic research and clinical care (Geelen *et al.*, 2012). This fear of genetic discrimination may arise from preceding experiences of discrimination within families living with disease. These 'family histories', encompassing shared experiences of discrimination and of 'being a member of an affected family', seem to affect the way family members decide to undergo or refrain from genetic testing. So, even with legislation, many individuals do not trust insurance companies and other institutions on delicate issues such as their use of genetic information. This latent mistrust makes it even more important for legislation to deliver on its promises.

The former section showed the complexities of the scientific debates and regulatory issues at stake, stretching from issues of regulatory effectiveness and unintended effects such as new discriminations, to persisting fears of genetic discrimination. Concerning the assessment of genetic discrimination and its regulation, there are a number of open questions and controversial debates. In academic discourse, there is still no agreement about how widespread practices of genetic discrimination actually are or about whether genetics-specific regulation is necessary and helpful in this domain (Joly *et al.*, 2013; Henneman and Van Hoyweghen, 2013).[9]

Moreover, the variety in national regulatory responses and their definitions of genetic testing challenges current efforts and/or calls for EU supranational harmonisation in the field. Use of genetic information in different contexts is challenged by the confusing and contradictory terminology in different regulatory instruments, a phenomenon called 'The Babel of genetic data terminology' in a seminal article of Knoppers and Saginur (2005). A systematic review of genetic testing legislation in European states confirmed the extreme variability existing in the concepts and the ambiguous or equivocal use of the term 'genetic testing' (Varga *et al.*, 2012; Sequieros *et al.*, 2012).[10] Many legal documents do not have any definition at all or a clear definition of genetic testing. Thus, the legislator (in different countries) often has not helped to solve the issues for which the law or policy document was intended. If the law is trespassed against, the actual formulation of those instruments may create difficult problems, open to different interpretations. This lack of a generally approved definition of a genetic test makes the analysis of different genetic non-discrimination regulations demanding. In this way, genetic discrimination has become 'a fluctuating regulatory target' (Soini, 2012).

## 4. After regulatory patchwork, poised for European supranational legislation?

Given the difficulty of defining the notion of 'genetic testing' and rapidly accumulating and sometimes also radically changing scientific knowledge, the regulatory task is not easy. Moreover, the idea that the genetic and non-genetic has become a moving target opens up new possibilities and

9 For example, in practice, there is little evidence on actual genetic discrimination by insurance companies. Research that validates the claim that genetic discrimination is occurring has been limited, both in scope and design. Reports of genetic discrimination have been criticized for being anecdotal, subjective experiences of problems, and allegations of discrimination have usually been based on the presence of disease in contrast to genetic predisposition. Most 'incidents' that have been reported seem to relate to life insurance and predictive testing for neurological disorders (e.g. Otlowski *et al.*, 2012). A recent review has shown that, with the notable exception of studies on Huntington's disease, none of the studies has brought irrefutable evidence of a systemic problem of genetic discrimination that would yield a highly negative societal impact (Joly *et al.*, 2013).

10 For example, the authors noticed that definitions of 'genetic testing' may be centred on the material used (e.g. DNA, chromosomes) or the methods applied (e.g. DNA analysis, cytogenetics) or based on the context and purpose of the test or the information derived (Sequeiros *et al.*, 2012).

questions in regard to regulating the issue at the European supranational level. The unfolding of genetic non-discrimination regulations and genomic developments may give way to new controversies and the proliferation of new concerned groups who advocate non-discrimination in private insurance in Europe. These developments actually open up the question of undermining the practice of actuarial risk discrimination and insurers' general 'right to underwrite' (Swiss Re, 2011; General Re, 2009).[11] Given recent genomic developments, genes and genomes have become a moving target in the context of private insurance and have started to challenge some of the distributive mechanisms and principles underlying private insurance risk selection, as will be shortly described hereafter.

First, the successful attention to the specificities of the group of 'the genetically ill' in genetic non-discrimination regulations has produced the emergence of new concerned groups who realise they are excluded from this legal protection. By comparing themselves with the legal category of 'genetic', these groups argue that they are treated unfairly before the law. This kind of logic begins to question the basis of excluding genetic testing, but allowing other forms of predictive testing in life insurance underwriting. This game of comparison between new concerned groups and groups protected by genetic non-discrimination regulations has recently materialised in national and EU supranational policymaking on the topic. The concept of 'predictive testing' first appeared in a report of the German National Ethics Council (NER) on predictive health information in the context of private insurance contracts (German National Ethics Council, 2007). Currently, it is under discussion at the EU policy level in the Council of Europe's (CoE) development of a legal instrument with respect to the use of results from genetic tests in the insurance context (Council of Europe, 2012). Whereas the CoE consultation rounds initially focused on the issue of 'genetic testing' in insurance, discussions are now expanded to consider 'medical examinations providing predictive health information other than genetic testing'.

Whereas genetic non-discrimination regulations single out one form of predictive testing, namely genetic testing, there appears to be a trend to extend regulatory protections to other forms of predictive testing. This transformative power of the issue of genetic testing is also readily acknowledged by those inside the insurance industry. According to the reinsurance company Swiss Re, 'sensitive issues such as genetics have been key catalysts in turning discrimination, privacy and entitlement into key regulatory issues for insurers' (Swiss Re, 2011). The introduction of genetic

11 Insurance underwriting is the long-entrenched practice of selecting who and what the insurance company insures based on risk assessment. Until the issue of genetic discrimination became a reality, this type of risk selection or actuarial discrimination has essentially taken place 'behind the scenes' and beyond public scrutiny.

testing in insurance, by producing affected groups and protection policies, encourages awareness and concern among other groups about general insurance. This may result in claims for more inclusive non-discrimination rights in private insurance.

Second, the conventional framing of genetic non-discrimination has failed to recognise and stay apace with the shift from *genetics* framed in terms of single-gene and complex disorders ('genetic diseases'), towards *genomics*, which is framed according to methods of high-scale analysis, and *postgenomics* (showing the complex interaction between genotype, phenotype, lifestyles and other social environments). Recent research in genetics, genomics and epigenetics has shown that almost every condition or disease is the result of a complex interaction of genetic and non-genetic factors having to do with people's lifestyles, social and natural environments. As a consequence, it has become increasingly difficult to differentiate between 'the genetic' – that which has been 'given' to us – and 'the non-genetic' – that which has been 'made' by us or other humans, e.g. lifestyles, environmental factors, behaviours (Joly *et al.*, 2013). Increasingly, policymakers, patient groups and insurers begin to understand that 'the genetic' has become a problematic category.

Understanding the issue of genetic discrimination from a postgenomic point of view has implications for extending the protection of 'the genetic risk' groups to other insurance risk groups, and perhaps even to 'all of us' (assuming 'we all have flawed genes'). The blurring of the boundaries between genetic and non-genetic information in postgenomic approaches creates a new storyline in the European public policy debate where 'genetic data' is equated with 'medical data'.

Figure 12.1 shows how a reinsurance representative analysed the regulatory trends of the European private life and health insurance market with respect to the issue of genetic discrimination. If all medical disorders are understood as having a genetic component, this may result in claims for *more inclusive* non-discrimination rights in insurance. In this way, the rights-based logic of 'the genetically ill' may be expanded to a rights-based logic for 'all of us', challenging the insurance industry's fundamental 'right to underwrite'. This broadening of the notion of 'genetic data' in public policy discourse involves moving away from the established definition of genetic discrimination, which involves discrimination on the basis of risk status (only), and has important ramifications for legal definitions in genetic non-discrimination regulation in Europe (Van Hoyweghen and Rebert, 2012).

## 5. Conclusion

This chapter has given an overview of the origins, rise and effects of genetic non-discrimination regulation in European states, with a focus on the legislative endeavours in the insurance field. Confronted with the advent of

*Figure 12.1* Medical genetics and regulatory considerations

Source: PowerPoint reinsurance representative, IUC, Geneva, Switzerland, 2005. Reproduced with permission

genetic testing and within a European welfare state tradition of 'social inclusion' reflecting a shared value of solidarity in insurance, most European countries have made an effort to protect the 'genetically at risk' from exclusion from insurance. With the installation of genetic non-discrimination regulations, national policymakers in Europe have articulated political solidarity for the group of the 'genetically ill'. Today, most European states have introduced regulations to ensure that no individual is discriminated against because of his or her genetic constitution. The laws are intended to protect individuals against unfair differential treatment based on genetic knowledge in the fields of employment and insurance, and to respond to the fears of individuals currently dissuaded from undergoing genetic testing in both clinical and research settings.

There has been variation in these regulatory approaches within and between national contexts, resulted in an emerging 'patchwork of protection' in regard to genetic non-discrimination regulation. This regulatory variety, including its multiple definitions of genetic testing, poses its own challenges and complications. The lack of a generally approved definition of a genetic test makes the analysis of different genetic non-discrimination regulations demanding. Use of genetic information in different contexts is challenged by the confusing and contradictory terminology in different regulatory instruments, a phenomenon called 'The Babel of genetic data terminology'. Given the difficulty of defining the notion of 'genetic testing' and rapidly accumulating and sometimes also radically changing scientific knowledge, the regulatory task is not easy. In this way, genetic discrimination has become a moving regulatory target in the European context.

Moreover, the idea that the genetic and non-genetic has become a moving target opens up new possibilities and questions in regard to regulating the issue at European supranational level. Given recent genomic developments, genes and genomes have started to challenge some of the distributive mechanisms and principles underlying private insurance risk selection. Given the rise of postgenomic approaches, the rights-based logic of genetic non-discrimination regulations may, in the future, expand to a rights-based logic for 'all of us'. In this regard, genetic testing has been a key *catalyst* in debates on issues of non-discrimination, risk selection and solidarity.

As we move forward, a series of new ethical and political issues have arisen. The introduction of genetic non-discrimination regulation has given way to a 'fault approach' in insurance, where genetic 'risk carriers' are protected, while lifestyle 'risk takers' are rated accordingly. Moreover, if a genetic mutation is one day traced, can insurers ask policyholders to adjust their lifestyle behaviours and rate their premiums based on the results of regular screenings to monitor such behaviours? The attribution of higher risk based on individually chosen lifestyle is problematic, as it is based on direct causal links that are challenging to prove. For this reason, individual responsibility has been rejected by many as a basis for risk selection and access to private life insurance. It is of little surprise, then, that penetrating socio-political issues arise about who should and who should not carry the burden of health risks. Implicit within these choices are quite formidable reworkings of collective and individual responsibility. Genomics therefore constitutes new ground in the old debates about individual control, responsibility and solidarity in private insurance. This requires public debate on the moral and political ramifications of private insurance. In this sense, genomics forces us to return to first principles: What is the moral mission of private insurance in society and what kind of risk-spreading model (level of solidarity) do we want? The resolution of this issue is a social policy decision that must be based on society's view of what is an ethically defensible basis of risk allocation. Given the recent actions by the CoE's consultation round on 'predictivity, genetic testing and insurance' (Council of Europe, 2012) in the context of the development of a supranational legal instrument, the use of genetic information in private insurance remains a timely and hotly debated topic; certainly one to watch on the EU policy agenda.

Whatever the outcome of these debates, it seems clear that developments in genomics will, in time, transform the insurance business every bit as much as it is transforming the practice of biomedicine. The coming deluge of genomic health information will force European society to openly discuss the trade-offs between risk selection and solidarity that have long been made in the shadows. The use of genetic testing in private insurance thus raises issues at different levels, one in which both EU policymakers and the wider public must engage with in the midst of an economic downturn and added stress on European welfare states. Genetics in insurance not only presents concerns of discrimination and privacy, it also impacts on collective political decision making about the basic structure of Europe as a society.

## References

Allain, D.C., Friedman, S. and Senter, L. (2012) 'Consumer awareness and attitudes about insurance discrimination post enactment of the Genetic Information Nondiscrimination Act' *Familial Cancer* 11(4): 637–644.

Billings, P.R., Kohn, M. A., Decuevas, M., Beckwith, J., Alper, J. S. and Natowicz, M. (1992) 'Discrimination as a consequence of genetic testing' *American Journal of Human Genetics* 50(3): 476–482.

Chuffart, A.A. (1996) 'Genetic testing in Europe' *Journal of Insurance Medicine* 28(2): 125–135.

Comité Européen des Assurances (CEA) (2000) 'Some helpful guidelines for national associations confronted with restrictive legislation regarding insurance and genetics'. Brussels: CEA.

Council of Europe (1997) Convention for the protection of human rights and dignity of the human being with regard to the application of biology and medicine: Convention on human rights and biomedicine. Available at: http://conventions.coe.int/Treaty/en/Treaties/Html/164.htm [accessed 17 May 2013].

Council of Europe (2012) *Consultation Document on Predictivity, Genetic Testing and Insurance* (DH-BIO/INF 1). Strasbourg: Council of Europe Steering Committee on Bioethics (CDBI).

Council of Europe (2013) Convention on human rights and biomedicine: ratifications and signatures. Available at: www.coe.int/t/dg3/healthbioethic/Activities/01_Oviedo%20Convention/ETS164 ap.pdf [accessed 29 May 2013].

European Union (2000) Charter of the fundamental rights of the European Union. *Official Journal of the European Communities* (364/01).

Geelen, E., Horstman, K., Marcelis, C. L. M., Doevendans, P. A. and Van Hoyweghen, I. (2012) 'Unravelling fears of genetic discrimination: An exploratory study of Dutch HCM families in an era of genetic non-discrimination acts' *European Journal of Human Genetics* 20: 1018–1023.

General Re (2009) *The Increasing Value of Basic Risk Selection Principles.* Cologne: General Re Corporation.

Gerards, J.H., Heringa, A.W. and Janssen, H.L. (2005) *Genetic Discrimination and Genetic Privacy in a Comparative Perspective.* Antwerp: Intersentia.

German National Ethics Council (NER) (2007) *Predictive Health Information in the Conclusion of Insurance Contracts.* Berlin: Nationaler Ethikrat.

Godard, B., Raeburn, S., Pembrey, M., Bobrow, M., Farndon, P. and Ayme, S. (2003) 'Genetic information and testing in insurance and employment: technical, social and ethical issues' *European Journal of Human Genetics* 11: S123–S142.

Henneman, L. and Van Hoyweghen, I. (2013) 'Moving beyond public fear of genetic discrimination' *Asia Insurance Review* 1(1): 64–65.

Hinrichs, K. (1995) 'The impact of German health-insurance reforms on redistribution and the culture of solidarity' *Journal of Health Politics Policy and Law* 20(3): 653–687.

Joly, Y., Braker, M. and Le Huynh, M. (2010) 'Genetic discrimination in private insurance: Global perspectives' *New Genetics and Society* 29(4): 351–368.

Joly, Y., Ngueng Feze, I. and Simard, J. (2013) 'Genetic discrimination and life insurance: A systematic review of the evidence' *BMC Medicine* 11(1): 25. Available at: www.ncbi.nlm.nih.gov/pubmed/23369270.

Knoppers, B. M., Saginur, M. (2005) 'The Babel of genetic data terminology' *Nature Biotechnology* 23(8): 925–927.

Knoppers, B. M., Godard, B. and Joly, Y. (2004) 'A comparative international overview'. In: *Genetics and Life Insurance: Medical Underwriting and Social Policy*. Rothstein. M.A. (ed). Cambridge: MIT Press. pp. 173–194.

Landelijke Verzekerinsovereenkomst (LVO) (1992) 'Wet van 25 juni op de landverzekeringsovereenkomst' *Belgisch Staatsblad*, 20 augustus, 18283–18333.

Lemke, T. (2013) *Perspectives on Genetic Discrimination*. London: Routledge.

Murray, T. (1997) 'Genetic exceptionalism and "future diaries": Is genetic information different from other medical information?' In: Rothstein M.A. (ed.) *Genetic Secrets: Protecting Privacy and Confidentiality in the Genetic Era*. New Haven, CT: Yale University Press.

Otlowski, M., Taylor, S. and Bombard, Y. (2012) 'Genetic discrimination: International perspectives' *Annual Review on Human Genetics and Human Genomics* 13: 433–454.

Rothstein, M.A. and Joly, Y. (2009) 'Genetic information and insurance underwriting: Contemporary issues and approaches in the global economy'. In: Atkinson P., Glasner, P. and Lock, M. (eds) *Handbook of Genetics and Society: Mapping the New Genomic Era*. London; New York: Routledge, xxvi, 539.

Sequeiros, J., Paneque, M., Guimarães, B., Rantanen, E., Javaher, P., Nippert, I., Schmidtke, J., Kääriäainen, H., Kristoffersson, U. and Cassiman, J.J. (2012) 'The wide variation of definitions of genetic testing in international recommendations, guidelines and reports' *Community Genetics* 3(2): 113–124.

Soini, S. (2012) 'Genetic testing legislation in Western Europe – A fluctuating regulatory target' Journal of Community Genetics 3(2): 143.

Swiss Re (2011) *Fair Risk Assessment in Life and Health Insurance*. Zurich: Swiss Re Insurance Company.

Van Hoyweghen, I. (2007) Risks in the Making: Travels in Life Insurance and Genetics. Amsterdam: Amsterdam University Press.

Van Hoyweghen, I. and Horstman, K. (2008) 'European practices of genetic information and insurance – Lessons for the Genetic Information Nondiscrimination Act' *Jama – Journal of the American Medical Association* 300(3): 326–327.

Van Hoyweghen, I. and Horstman, K. (2009) 'Evidence-based underwriting in the molecular age. The politics of reinsurance companies towards the genetics issue' *New Genetics and Society* 28(4): 317–337.

Van Hoyweghen, I. and Rebert, L. (2012) 'Your genes in insurance. From genetic discrimination to genomic solidarity' *Personalized Medicine* 9(8): 871–877.

Van Hoyweghen, I., Horstman, K. and Schepers, R. (2007) 'Genetic "risk carriers" and lifestyle "risk takers". Which risks deserve our legal protection in insurance?' *Health Care Analysis* 15(3): 179–193.

Varga, O., Soini, S., Kääriäinen, H., Cassiman, J.J., Nippert, I., Rogowski, W., Nys, H., Kristoffersson, U., Schmidtke, J. and Sequeiros, J. (2012) 'Definitions of genetic testing in European legal documents' *Journal of Community Genetics* 3(2): 125.

# 13 Genetic discrimination and the draft European Union General Data Protection Regulation

*Mark Taylor*

## 1. Introduction

This collection is being put together at a time when it is difficult to say very much that is definitive in relation to the proposed European Union (EU) General Data Protection Regulation ('the Regulation'). A formal draft of the Regulation was published in January 2012, after a draft was leaked in December 2011, and since that time considerable debate has been generated. The Regulation is intended to replace the current EU Data Protection Directive 95/46/EC ('the Directive'). The European Commission intends to take the opportunity to update the rules regarding data protection as it is felt that some changes in information technology, particularly those relating to web 2.0 technologies, have outgrown the original regulatory framework. Since publication by the Commission, very many significant amendments have been proposed to the original draft, including several by the influential Committee on Civil Liberties, Justice and Home Affairs (LIBE Committee) of the European Parliament, and again in what has come to be known as 'the compromise text' in a note authored under the Irish Presidency of the Council of the European Union. Some 3,000 amendments have been suggested in all. Much of the discussion and debate centres on provisions that are not of direct concern to the issue of genetic discrimination. However, some of them are. In what follows I hope to provide a sense of the current direction of travel; to indicate how some of the ambitions of the Regulation intersect with the concern of improved protection from unfair genetic discrimination; to point to a couple of currently contested provisions relevant to the potential scope and nature of such protection; and to indicate why the changes proposed by the Commission, and the amendments subsequently suggested, fall short in an important respect from a comprehensive response to the concerns that people have expressed in relation to genetic discrimination. Unless otherwise indicated, all references are to the Commission text as amended by the proposals of the LIBE committee on 22 November 2013.[1]

A key ambition of the new framework includes assuring consumer trust in the online environment as it continues to develop. It is considered a key purpose of the reform as any lack of trust 'risks slowing down the development of innovative uses of new technologies'.[2] In addition, it is considered an appropriate moment to tackle the lack of harmonisation across the EU on data protection. The nature of the current Directive is that member states must implement its requirements locally through domestic legislation. Although the requirements are themselves common, the fact that they have been implemented differently, has not led to the level of harmonisation that was originally intended. As the Regulation would be directly applicable, and would not require any local implementation, it should successfully achieve a higher degree of harmonisation across the EU.

Tackling the issue of genetic discrimination was not itself a prime motivation. Nevertheless, there are a number of provisions contained within the Regulation with relevance to the issue of genetic discrimination and the potential for regulation. Not least among the relevant changes, which might be introduced by the Regulation, is the fact that for the first time genetic data would be explicitly recognised to fall within a special category of personal data. There is a presumptive prohibition raised in EU data protection law against the processing of data in that special category. The presumption is only to be rebutted if one of a number of specific conditions can be satisfied. This, together with some other proposed changes, does raise the prospect of the Regulation being able to provide some degree of protection from genetic discrimination. Closer examination, however, reveals the limitation of the protection available. Not least amongst the limitations is the persistent focus within the Regulation upon identifiable person-level data. This, it will be suggested, seriously undermines the capacity of the Regulation to effectively address the risk of genetic discrimination and assure the public trust that it is intended to secure.

## 2. The context

The European Commission has proposed a new framework for the protection of personal data in the European Union. This includes a legislative

1 European Parliament (LIBE Committee), Report on the proposal for a Regulation of the European Parliament and of the Council on the protection of individuals with regard to the processing of personal data and on the free movement of such data A7-0402/2013 (21.11.2013) PE501.927V05-00 www.europarl.europa.eu/sides/getDoc.do?type=REPORT&reference=A7-2013-0402&format=XML&language=EN.

2 Proposal for a Regulation of the European Parliament and of the Council on the protection of individuals with regard to the processing of personal data and on the free movement of such data (Brussels, 25.1.2012) p. 1.

proposal for a General Data Protection Regulation. The Regulation would replace the current Data Protection Directive on Personal Data, 95/46/EC. This Directive 'was adopted in 1995 with two objectives in mind: to protect the fundamental right to data protection and to guarantee the free flow of personal data between Member States' (Explanatory Memorandum to the proposed Data Protection Regulation 2012: 1). Since its adoption there have been massive changes in the information-processing environment. Precipitated by significant technical and technological change, the increasingly information-rich and technology-dependent environment has led to considerable social and economic transformation. It is feared that the existing Directive no longer provides an adequate means to address the concerns associated with the changing reality and, in particular, to address 'a widespread public perception that there are significant risks associated notably with online activity' (Explanatory Memorandum to the proposed Data Protection Regulation 2012: 2). In response, the Regulation is intended to

> build a stronger and more coherent data protection framework in the EU, backed by strong enforcement that will allow the digital economy to develop across the internal market, put individuals in charge of their own data and reinforce legal and practical certainty for economic operators and public authorities.
>
> (Explanatory Memorandum to the proposed Data Protection Regulation 2012: 2)

One of the ways that the Regulation is intended to improve the internal dimension of data protection is by improved coherence and predictability and a move away from the existing fragmented picture of data protection across Europe. The current Directive requires local implementation of data protection law within individual states, which are entitled to adopt their own means to achieve the objectives set out in the Directive. The way that they have done so has not resulted in the level of consistency across Europe that was originally intended or anticipated to follow the Directive.

The general concern in relation to consumer confidence, in relation to the transfer of personal data in an online environment, has a specific manifestation in the context of genetic data: if people do not trust that they can engage with the market, for example in relation to direct-to-consumer genetic tests, without exposing themselves to the risk of privacy intrusion, or inappropriate use or disclosure of genetic information, or genetic discrimination, then this will have a chilling effect on economic activity and growth in areas that depend upon the sharing of genetic data. Protection in this area also relates to the broader aim of the Regulation to achieve fuller recognition of fundamental rights. The text of the introduction to the Commission draft summarises the fundamental rights issues relevant to the Regulation, including the right to data protection (Treaty on the

Functioning of the European Union: Article 16) and includes within them Article 21 of the EU Charter of Fundamental Rights and Freedoms: 'the prohibition of any discrimination amongst others on grounds of race, ethnic origin, genetic features, religion or belief, political opinion or any other opinion, disability or sexual orientation.' There is a clear intention that the Regulation should form part of a broader regulatory framework providing protection from unfair discrimination in general and unfair genetic discrimination in particular. This is both to protect economic activity in relation to genetic data but also to protect individual fundamental rights and freedoms, including the right to the protection of personal data. The framework of the Regulation, and the purpose of the EU itself, means that pursuit of the latter objective must be shaped in part by the ambition to achieve the free flow of personal data to the maximum extent compatible with such protection.

## 3. The scope of the draft Regulation

The Regulation applies to all processing of personal data. It is not a sectoral law applying only to one category of personal information e.g. health information. Rather, the omnibus legislative scheme applies to the processing[3] of 'any information relating to an identified or identifiable natural person ("data subject")'[4] whether wholly or partly by computer or in manual form if paper copies are (to be) filed in a structured way and accessible according to specific criteria, unless some specific exemption can be relied upon.[5] Any processing of personal data must satisfy the majority of the requirements of the Regulation. However, some particular provisions are reserved for processing for particular purposes (e.g. for the purposes of research) and for processing data of a type that falls within special categories. Under the existing Directive, data falling within special categories, known more typically as sensitive personal data, is defined to include

3 The term 'processing' is widely defined. In the 'compromise text' '"processing" means any operation or set of operations which is performed upon personal data or sets of personal data, whether or not by automated means, such as collection, recording, organization, structuring, storage, adaptation or alteration, retrieval, consultation, use, disclosure by transmission, dissemination or otherwise making available, alignment or combination or erasure'. This varies from other drafts as it omits the term 'destruction'.

4 Amendment 98, Article 4, see n.1. This text is common to the definition contained in the existing Directive. The text in other drafts is sometimes worded differently although substantively similar.

5 The restrictions to material scope set out in LIBE (22.11.14) text (article 2(2)) include processing '(d) by a natural person in the course of *an* exclusively personal or household activity. *This exemption also shall apply to a publication of personal data where it can be reasonably expected that it will be only accessed by a limited number of persons*' (emphasis in original).

> personal data revealing racial or ethnic origin, political opinions, religious or philosophical beliefs, trade-union membership, and the processing of data concerning health or sex life.
>
> (Article 8(1))

Some genetic data will always have been regarded as falling within this special category because of its concern with health. However, it is now proposed that the list of special categories in the Regulation is extended to expressly include 'genetic data' for the first time. The definition of genetic data has not yet been agreed, but a consensus is emerging.

### *3.1 Definition of genetic data*

In the proposal published by the Commission on 25 January 2012:

> (10) 'genetic data' means all data, of whatever type, concerning the characteristics of an individual which are inherited or acquired during early prenatal development.
>
> (Article 4(10))

After receiving written comments by Member States on the proposals, a note by the Presidency to the Working Party on Data Protection[6] records that

> Several delegations (BE, CH, CY, DE, FR and SE) expressed their surprise regarding the breadth of this definition, which would also cover data about a person's physical appearance.[7]

As a result of the concerns expressed, the (Danish) Presidency suggested narrowing the definition. The suggested redraft was intended 'to make definition dependent on a biological – and therefore presumably technologically neutral (DNA) – indicator.' The definition proposed by the Presidency in June 2012 described 'genetic data' as

> all personal data relating to the genetic characteristics of an individual which have been inherited or acquired during early prenatal development as they result from an analysis of a biological sample from the individual in question, in particular by chromosomal, eoxyribonucleic

6 2012/0011 (COD) 11326/12 Brussels, 22 June 2012.

7 Footnote 64. See also country comments on the definition, e.g. the comment made by Czech Republic (CZ) that 'If it would be stipulated that everyday observations like "black woman" are two genetic data, it would lead to either excessive exceptions from prohibition to process sensitive data or to unforeseen problems in practice' (p. 16) 9897/2/12 REV2.

> acid (DNA) or ribonucleic acid (RNA) analysis or analysis of any other element enabling equivalent information to be obtained.
>
> (Article 4(10))

Since that time several other amendments have been suggested to the Regulation as a whole, not least of all by the lead committee for the European Parliament (the LIBE committee) in a report authored by lead rapporteur Jan Philip Albrecht. Although the draft report (issued on 17 December 2012) suggested no amendment to the original commission definition, in its report (issued on 22 November 2013) the LIBE committee adopted a variation of the text proposed by the Presidency. The only change was that the genetic characteristics would *not* need to be inherited or acquired during early prenatal development.[8] The definition of genetic data to be voted on by the European Parliament is that:

> 'genetic data' means all personal data relating to the genetic characteristics of an individual which have been inherited or acquired as they result from an analysis of a biological sample from the individual in question, in particular by chromosomal, desoxyribonucleic acid (DNA) or ribonucleic acid (RNA) analysis or analysis of any other element enabling equivalent information to be obtained.
>
> (Amendment 98, Article 4 (10))[9]

As the narrower definition is to be found in the most recent text issued by both Parliament and the Council, it seems that it is now most likely that a narrower definition of genetic data will be accepted than was originally proposed. It is also clear that there is a common (although not universal) appetite for express inclusion of genetic data within the scope of sensitive personal data for the first time. Recognising the vagaries that currently abound, what is the significance of genetic data being expressly classified as a sensitive category – as opposed to simply being caught within the general framework of data protection – for the issue of genetic discrimination? Is there much significance to the term being drawn in a broad rather than a narrow way?

### *3.2 Substance*

There is much important detail within the proposed Regulation but, at its heart, it seeks to preserve and further harmonise protection in relation to

8 See Amendment 98 in LIBE Report on the proposal for a Regulation of the European Parliament and of the Council on the protection of individuals with regard to the processing of personal data and on the free movement of such data A7-0402/2013 (21.11.2013) PE501.927V05-00.

9 Amendment 98, Article 4 (10), see n.1.

seven data protection principles. These principles are described in the LIBE committee report[10] as principles relating to (1) Lawfulness, fairness and transparency;[11] (2) Purpose limitation;[12] (3) Data minimization;[13] (4) Accuracy;[14] (5) Storage Minimisation;[15] (6) Effectiveness;[16] (7) Integrity;[17] and (8) Accountability.[18]

The first of these, 'Transparency', requires that data be processed 'lawfully, fairly and in a transparent manner in relation to the data subject'. The conditions of lawful processing are set out in Article 6, and the conditions of transparent information and communication are set out in Article 11, and these apply to the processing of any personal data (not only data falling within special categories). To the extent that genetic data of any description satisfies the definition of 'personal data' it must be processed in a way that is consistent with the principles of data protection and these include the requirements of Article 6 and 11. While these articles provide little in the way of direct protection from unfair genetic discrimination they should, at least, make it more difficult for covert use of genetic data to be lawful.

### *3.2.1 Article 6 – lawfulness of processing*

In order to be lawful, personal data shall be processed in a way that at least

10 See n.1.

11 Processed lawfully, fairly and in a manner transparent in relation to the data subject.

12 Collected for specified, explicit and legitimate purposes and not further processed in a way incompatible with those purposes.

13 Adequate, relevant, and limited to the minimum necessary in relation to the purposes for which they are processed; they shall only be processed if, and as long as, the purposes could not be fulfilled by processing anonymous information that does not involve personal data.

14 Accurate and, where necessary, kept up to date; every reasonable step must be taken to ensure that personal data that are inaccurate, having regard to the purposes for which they are processed, are erased or rectified without delay.

15 Kept in a form which permits direct or indirect identification of data subjects for no longer than is necessary for the purposes for which the personal data are processed; personal data may be stored for longer periods insofar as the data will be processed solely for historical, statistical or scientific research or for archive purposes in accordance with the rules and conditions of Articles 83 and 83a and if a periodic review is carried out to assess the necessity to continue the storage, and if appropriate technical and organisational measures are put in place to limit access to the data only for these purposes.

16 Processed in a way that effectively allows the data subject to exercise his or her rights.

17 Processed in a way that protects against unauthorised or unlawful processing and against accidental loss, destruction or damage, using appropriate technical or organisational measures.

18 Processed under the responsibility and liability of the controller, who shall ensure and be able to demonstrate the compliance with the provisions of this Regulation.

one of the following applies: (1) the data subject has given consent[19] to the processing, or (2) processing is *necessary* for the performance of a contract to which the data subject is party or in order to take steps at the request of the data subject prior to entering into a contract. There are other conditions which might also apply, but these two are the most likely to be relied upon by a party wishing to process genetic data to inform, for example, the terms or possibility of a contractual relationship. While the *necessity* of the processing may provide some kind of a check on any unnecessary use of genetic data, the data subject's consent to the processing will provide a lawful basis for the use of genetic data. This could be a weakness in protection if people consent to data being used to inform contractual decision-making.

There are moves to strengthen any requirement that consent is 'freely given',[20] but this is to avoid coercive practices 'if the data subject has no genuine and free choice and is unable to refuse or withdraw consent without detriment' (Recital 33).[21] While this might provide some limited protection from an employer or insurer 'requiring' an individual to consent to a genetic test, or disclose genetic data, the extent of the protection will depend on just how limited an individual's options must be before consent would be considered to be *not* 'freely given'. The scope of protection that might be offered here is hard to assess prior to any authoritative interpretation by a court.

### *3.2.2 Article 11 – transparent information and communication*

A data controller is responsible for ensuring that steps are taken to provide the individuals to whom the data relates (i.e. data subjects) with information about that processing. This must include information about the purposes of processing and such further information as is necessary to ensure 'fair' processing in respect of the data subject (Article 14). Again, this responsibility upon a data controller will provide limited protection from discriminatory use of genetic data, as it should at least ensure that any (lawful) use is drawn to an individual's attention. Awareness of the reasons for the processing of data are crucial to being able to exercise the rights of

19 Consent is defined in the European Commission proposal to mean any freely given specific, informed and explicit indication of his or her wishes by which the data subject, either by a statement or by a clear affirmative action, signifies agreement to personal data relating to them being processed.

20 See definition of 'consent' above. Also, the Commission proposal contains a provision that states 'consent shall not provide a legal basis for the processing, where there is a significant imbalance between the position of the data subject and the controller' (Article 7(4)). This is removed in the LIBE (22 November 2013) text (see n. 1).

21 Recital 33. Note the LIBE (22 November 2013) text amendments.

a data subject, including being able to challenge the 'relevance'[22] of any data to a particular decision-making process. In the context of unfair discrimination, this does provide some limited scope for redress if an individual considers genetic data to have been taken into irrelevant account. This does, however, rely upon an individual having the wherewithal to bring such a challenge and being in a position to establish the irrelevance of the data to the decision in question.

One of the reasons that the definition of genetic data discussed above is so important in this context is that additional requirements are applied to data that fall within special categories. Some genetic data will fall within the category anyway because it constitutes data concerning health or because the processing of the data reveals racial or ethnic origin (Article 9(1)). Additional genetic data might now fall within the special category because it falls within the definition of 'genetic data' expressly added to the list of special categories. To the extent that genetic data falls within what are defined as special categories, particular rules apply.

### *3.2.3 Article 9 – processing of special categories of data*

Generally, personal data can be processed lawfully where one of a number of conditions is satisfied. However, where the data is also 'sensitive personal data', the processing is prohibited unless one of a number of express conditions for the lifting of the prohibition is satisfied. The first condition under which the general prohibition can be lifted is if the data subject has given his or her explicit consent to the processing. There are a number of other conditions that might also have application in the context of the processing of genetic data to inform differential treatment of individuals on the grounds of genetic data. For example, processing of sensitive (including therefore genetic) data is allowed if '*necessary* for health purposes and subject to the conditions and safeguards referred to in Article 81' (emphasis added). Using genetic data to inform the distinction between persons for the purposes of personalising health care might then, subject to the conditions and safeguards being properly met, be considered permissible. Similarly, data controllers are entitled to process sensitive data if '*necessary* for the purposes of carrying out the obligations and exercising specific rights of the controller in the field of employment law in so far as it is authorised by Union Law or Member State law providing for adequate safeguards' (emphasis added) (Article 9(2)(b)). Thus there are uses of genetic data permitted under Article 9 and some of them may distinguish between persons on the ground of genetics. The extent to which *unfair* discriminatory uses might be curtailed by Article 9 is informed in large part by the challenge that could be

22 Article 5(1)(c) requires that personal data must be 'adequate, relevant, and limited to the minimum necessary in relation to the purposes for which they are processed'.

provided to the 'necessity' of such processing and the restrictions that might be placed upon the conditions of valid explicit consent. As discussed in relation to Article 6, the consent of the data subject would appear to be the condition that might be satisfied in relation to the broadest range of purposes and also the potential weakness if seeking to protect people from discriminatory uses of genetic data. Efforts to strengthen the requirement that consent is 'freely given' have already been noted (Recitals 33 and 34) but, in a contractual market place typified by imbalanced bargaining positions, it is suggested that the courts are likely to take a relatively restrictive reading or upset the certainty of very many contracts.

There are, however, other ways in which the Regulation might move the framework of data protection to improve the rights of data subject and provide better protection from genetic discrimination, especially as the risks relate to individual differentiation on the basis of genetic profile.

### *3.3 Rights of data subjects, prescribed documentation and data protection impact assessments (DPIAs)*

The draft Regulation extends the rights of data subjects from those contained within 95/46/EC. Under 95/46/EC, data subjects have the right of access, rectification (in the case of inaccurate data) and to prevent processing in certain circumstances. Each of these may have some relevance but, for reasons of space, I cannot focus upon them here. Under the Regulation these existing rights are preserved but may also be extended. The original Commission proposal is to prohibit automated profiling without explicit consent (Article 20). This would prohibit activity that has legal *or otherwise significant effects* and is based solely on:

> Automated processing intended to evaluate certain personal aspects relating to this natural person or to analyse or predict in particular the natural person's performance at work, economic situation, location, health, personal preferences, reliability or behavior.
>
> (Article 20(1))

There have been significant amendments to this original proposal. LIBE amendments proposed (22 November 2013) would place conditions upon such profiling and recognise a right to object to profiling, although 'a data subject shall be informed about the right to object to profiling in a highly visible manner' (Article 20(1)). This builds on Article 15(1) of Directive 95/46 on automated individual decisions, and takes account of the Council of Europe's recommendation on profiling CM/Rec (2010) 13. While an additional layer of protection, it can – again – be set aside with the data subject's consent (Article 20(2)(c)).

Other ways in which unfairly discriminatory practices may be discouraged, or prospectively prevented, may be through an increased reliance in the Regulation upon maintaining prescribed documentation and conducting data protection impact assessments (DPIAs). Article 28 requires all data controllers and processors to maintain detailed documentation in relation to the processing of personal data. This will increase the administrative burden but should make clear whether the intention is to use, or disclose, genetic data for purposes that could be described as discriminatory. The original Commission text suggested that DIPAs should be carried out when processing involved 'genetic data' if held in large-scale filing systems (Article 33(2)(d)). The most recent LIBE (22 November 2013) text does not mention genetic data specifically but suggests that DPIAs will have to be carried out under Article 33 prior to processing 'special categories of personal data' in large-scale filing systems (Article 33(1)). The processing of genetic data in such systems would thus continue to require a DPIA, and processing genetic data with discriminatory effects might therefore, on this basis, be typically expected to be subject to a DPIA before the processing takes place. If a DPIA is required, then the LIBE (22 November 2013) text suggests that it should include

> an assessment of the risks to the rights and freedoms of data subjects, including the risk of discrimination being embedded in or reinforced by the operation.
>
> (Article 33(3)(c))

Where a DPIA indicates that processing operations 'present a high degree of specific risks' (Article 33(3)(c)), then the 'controller or processor acting on the controller's behalf shall consult the supervisory authority prior to the processing' (Article 34). This provides perhaps the greatest hope that data processing that might be unfairly discriminatory, and which results from the processing of genetic data in large-scale filing systems or profiling of persons on the basis of genetic data which significantly affects the individual, may be prevented by a supervisory authority *prospectively* following a DPIA.

Another way in which unfairly discriminatory practices may be discouraged is through the use of codes of conduct which are encouraged to be drawn up by associations or other bodies representing categories of controllers or data processors (Recital 76). In briefest summary, one might thus say that the protection that the Regulation might offer does depend upon a number of things that are uncertain in detail at the present time and, even if or when the Regulation passes into law, will depend upon interpretation and implementation in practice, but that there is reason to hope that certain unfair practices would be at least transparent and potentially prospectively proscribed through a combination of DPIA and prior authorisation.

Despite the scope for improved protection in certain respects, it is important to recognise that every indication is that the sole concern of any

Regulation passed will continue to be 'personal data' understood in an individual and atomistic manner. This itself represents a significant limitation on the potential of the Regulation to comprehensively address the risks of genetic discrimination. Genetic research that associates a particular phenotype with genetic characteristics can lead, and has led, to *groups* being discriminated against in particular ways (Billings *et al.*, 1992: 476–482; Geller *et al.*, 1996: 71–88). While action against an individual may require the processing of personal data in relation to *him or her*, which might then engage the data protection framework, the *risks* of discrimination are significantly affected by processing that takes place at the level of the group and outside the proposed scope of the Regulation. For example, if genetic research associates a high risk of cardiac disease with a particular group – and members of that group are then advised to undertake particular clinical tests, then a question about whether a particular clinical test has been recommended may subsequently inform a discriminatory practice. This limitation results from a failure to recognise that the risks of genetic discrimination are raised by the processing of data at a group level *and* from focusing protection upon a particular *type* of data.

## 4. Genetic exceptionalism

Any definition of genetic data is going to be problematic (Taylor, 2004: 365–380). While the original definition was widely recognised to be too broad, a definition that only recognises genetic data that is the result of analysis may be considered to be too narrow. Comments made on behalf of Italy suggested that the definition should be broad enough

> to also cover cases of genetic information which does not result from an analysis, but from elsewhere (e.g. visit to a hospital department dealing with rare genetic disorders).
>
> (Country Comments from General Secretariat to Working Party, 2012: 79)

The definition Italy proposed as an alternative captured genetic data

> as they result *in particular* from an analysis of a biological sample from the individual in question, *such as* by chromosomal, deoxyribonucleic acid (DNA) or ribonucleic acid (RNA) analysis or analysis of any other element enabling equivalent information to be obtained.
>
> (Country Comments from General Secretariat to Working Party, 2012: 79) (emphasis added)

The difficulty with this is that, through recognising analysis of a biological sample to be a sufficient but not a necessary element of any definition, it effectively broadens the scope to that originally proposed by the

Commission: 'all data, of whatever type, concerning the characteristics of an individual which are inherited or acquired during early prenatal development'. In fact, it might extend the scope even further as it would not be limited to genetic variation inherited or acquired during early prenatal development. One response, and it is not one that is likely to be adopted, would be to either recognise that *relevant* genetic data is already captured as health data (Beckwith and Alper, 1998: 205–210) or to move away from a focus upon types of data at all. Note here the opinion of the European Economic and Social Committee on the proposal for a Regulation that '[4.16.1] the best way to proceed would be to create special regimes to match the circumstances, situation and purpose of the processing of data.' The Committee recommended in particular that 'profiling' should also be prohibited in these areas. One advantage of such an approach is that it would allow for measures to target discrimination in particular circumstances – including those where genetic discrimination is of particular concern – but without the problems of the penumbra raised by a definition of genetic data. Whatever happens next it is unlikely that the Regulation will move the European Data Protection Framework from its focus on individual 'personal data' and this will inevitably limit the extent to which it is possible to regulate the processing of genetic data that may give rise to the risk of discriminatory behaviour that undermines people's trust (Taylor, 2012: chapter 5).

## 5. Next steps and conclusion

This is a difficult time to be writing about the draft General Data Protection Regulation. As well as thousands of amendments to the original EC proposal published in January 2012, we had a materially different proposal published by the LIBE committee in January 2013, a different proposal published by the Presidency in May 2013 and a text voted on by the LIBE committee in November 2013. Which parts of these different versions, if any, will eventually comprise an EU Regulation – binding across all member states – is unknown. The aim was originally for the Regulation to be approved by June 2013. This is not now going to happen and the failure to approve it before June 2014 may prove to be a serious setback. The European Parliament and Commission elections took place in May 2014 and a change in personnel may impact upon progress in Parliament toward even an internally unified position. The Council was expected to announce its own amendments in June 2014. No text is now likely to be agreed by both Parliament and Council until 2015 at the earliest.

If the Regulation is approved, then it is expected that there will be a two-year transition period before it is effective. If that point is ever reached, then there will be a more consistent body of data protection law directly applicable across the European Union. That law aims to ensure not only the free flow of personal data across the Union but also to better protect the fundamental rights of individuals, most notably the right to data protection. There is no doubt that the Regulation has the potential to be a relevant means of protecting people from unfair genetic discrimination. If it did not, then it would have no prospect of securing confidence in the disclosure of an increasingly important type of personal data – and securing public confidence is one of its key aims. The nature of the protection offered under the Regulation is similar to that currently provided by the Directive and is similarly limited in a number of ways: it aims to ensure that individuals are given clear information about what is being done with information that relates to them – so that those individuals may challenge the accuracy and relevance of that data to the processing in question. Its Achilles heel may be that people must consent to the disclosure of genetic data to secure the contracts that they freely seek.

The Regulation does also offer scope for further protection through the use of data protection impact assessments and, where relevant, *prior* approval by a supervisory authority. Depending upon how these twin requirements play out in practice, there is genuine scope for improved prospective protection overseen by a supervisory body. While still subject to the limitations of the Directive with respect to a focus upon individual person-level and identifiable data, this nevertheless represents an important opportunity for improved protection from genetic discrimination to be realised through EU data protection law. The draft Regulation and its potential effectiveness in protecting genetic information is further discussed and evaluated in Chapter 15 by Delia Ferri.

## References

Beckwith, J. and Alper, J. S. (1998) 'Reconsidering Genetic Antidiscrimination Legislation' *Journal of Law, Medicine and Ethics* 26: 205–210.

Billings, P. R., Kohn, M. A., de Cuevas, M., Beckwith, J., Alper, J. S. and Natowicz, M. R. (1992) 'Discrimination as a Consequence of Genetic Testing' *American Journal of Human Genetics* 50(3): 476–482.

European Parliament (LIBE Committee) (2013) 'Report on the Proposal for a Regulation of the European Parliament and of the Council on the Protection of Individuals with Regard to the Processing of Personal Data and on the Free Movement of Such Data' A7-0402/2013 (21.11.2013) PE501.927V05-00 www.europarl.europa.eu/sides/getDoc.do?type=REPORT&reference=A7-2013-0402&format=XML&language=EN.

Geller, L. N., Alper, J. S., Billings, P. R., Barash, C. I., Beckwith, J. and Natowicz, M. R. (1996) 'Individual, Family and Societal Dimensions of Genetic Discrimination: A Case Study Analysis' *Science and Engineering Ethics* 2(1): 71–88.

Note by the Presidency to the Working Party on Data Protection and Exchange of Information (2012) 2012/0011 (COD) 11326/12 Brussels, 22 June.

Taylor, M. J. (2004) 'Problems of Practice and Principle if Centring Law Reform on the Concept of Genetic discrimination' *European Journal of Health Law* 11(4): 365–380.

Taylor, M. J. (2012) *Genetic Data and the Law.* London: Cambridge University Press.

## Legislation

Charter of Fundamental Rights of the European Union (7 December 2000) *Official Journal of the European Communities*, 18 December 2000 (2000/C 364/01).

Country Comments from General Secretariat to Working Party, (18 July 2012).

Explanatory Memorandum to the proposed Data Protection Regulation, COM (2012).

Note from the General Secretariat to the Working Group on Information Exchange and Data (2012) 2012/0011 (COD) 9897/2/2012 REV 2.

Proposal for a Regulation of the European Parliament and of the Council on the protection of individuals with regard to the processing of personal data and on the free movement of such data (Brussels, 25.1.2012) p1.

Treaty on the Functioning of the European Union (2008/ C 115/01).

# 14 Accommodating genes

## Disability, discrimination and international human rights law

*Janet E. Lord*

### 1. Introduction

The idea that disabling conditions are a manifestation of deviant abnormality and pathological defect is reflected in the universal experience of disadvantage and exclusion for persons with disabilities. Invidious stereotyping continues to exclude and isolate persons with disabilities and, as a result, disabled people have not generally been accorded the full or equal enjoyment of human rights that human rights law demands. Much of this contemporary animus is rooted in actual or perceived disability linked to genetic heritage. The adoption of the Convention on the Rights of Persons with Disabilities (CRPD or Convention) introduces a disability narrative into the human rights framework. It requires States to undertake reviews to assess, among other things, the socio-contextual conditions within which policies regarding disability are implemented and the resulting impact of such policies (Stein and Lord, 2009). Notably for reflecting on genetic science and its implications for human rights, protection against discrimination and the accommodation of impairment as a natural feature of human diversity animates the CRPD framework. The principles of respect for human difference, along with non-discrimination, inclusion and participation, are likewise salient features of a disability rights analysis rooted in human rights law and the Convention (CRPD, art. 3).

Against these developments, genetic discrimination is attracting the serious attention of disability law scholars and disability advocacy organisations (Stein and Silvers, 2003). The body that monitors CRPD implementation – the Committee on the Rights of Persons with Disabilities – is beginning to turn its attention to the impact of genetic discrimination on persons with disabilities, taking on issues such as disability-related reproductive policies and insurance discrimination, among others.

The adoption of the CRPD accordingly provides a fresh human rights read on the interrelationship of genetic technology and disability rights as reflected in international human rights law. This chapter addresses the implications of the human rights principles in the CRPD in relation to this debate and examines the lively disability advocacy around issues relating to genetic discrimination on the basis of disability in Europe, the United States and elsewhere. It holds that the CRPD is an important lens through which to filter and reflect upon the emerging legal framework to protect against violations of rights in the new context of genetic technology.

## 2. Genetically motivated animus

Genetically motivated animus directed at persons with disabilities has its roots in the eugenics movement that emerged in the United States and Europe during the late nineteenth century (Lord, 2004). As addressed in more detail by Blanck and de Paor, in Section 3, Chapter 6, during that period, eugenicists propagated the idea that birthrates of the so-called 'fit' and 'talented' were on a steep decline, while the birthrate of the 'unfit' and less desirable members of society were rapidly rising (Lord, 2004). Appeals to (bogus) science conferred legitimacy on decidedly racist and otherwise discriminatory ideas.

In the United States, the application of eugenic theories was pursued with vigor, and marginalised groups, particular populations of people with disabilities, were prime targets. An advisory committee of the infamous Eugenics Record Office declared in 1914 that 10 per cent of the American population was 'defective' and should be sterilised and, later, the American Eugenics Society built support for eugenics and forced sterilisation in particular. The United States stood at the forefront of forced sterilisations imposed upon disabled persons, particularly against people with intellectual disabilities, and, between 1907 and 1939, more than 30,000 people in 29 states were sterilised while incarcerated in prisons or institutions for persons with psychiatric disabilities. In 1927, the United States Supreme Court provided its imprimatur on forced sterilisation in *Buck v. Bell*, where an eight to one majority upheld the constitutionality of the 1924 Virginia Eugenical Sterilization Act (*Buck v. Bell*, 1927).

The policies of Nazi Germany targeting persons with disabilities were founded upon an imagined threat to the germ plasm of the German nation. Physical traits – whether real or perceived – were employed as distinguishing features for the application of various Nazi policies. The view, promulgated by esteemed scientists of the time, was that hereditary deafness and blindness, and congenital physical and mental disability threatened the health of the nation and undermined the mythic ideal of a racially pure and strong people. Forced sterilisation and extermination programmes during the Nazi era targeting adults and children with disabilities were thus directly related to the racist Nazi effort to 'purify' and 'cleanse' the nation (Lord, 2004).

Advances in genetic technology provoke a variety concerns, among them ethical and human rights. The prevailing medicalisation of disability within the context of genetic research and experimentation runs afoul of disability rights critique and analysis. Given the impact of the eugenics movement on persons with disabilities and ongoing efforts to control fertility of individuals with disabilities, sometimes through forced interventions such as sterilisation, disability rights scholars and advocates alike are turning their attention to the human rights implications of genetic science in the context of disability, as this volume reveals.

## 3. Medicalising disability

The medicalisation of disability regards disability as a physical or mental impairment of the individual and it also pivots towards the limitations – personal and social – imposed by the impairment (Wassermann *et al.*, 2013). This perspective, according to which disability is inexorably linked to illness requiring medical intervention, takes on numerous forms, from isolation and quarantine, to prenatal testing, rehabilitation, surgical intervention and long-term institutionalisation in medical facilities. The consequences of the medical model are at least threefold.

First, medicalising disability leads to the view that medical and rehabilitative interventions are essential, to the exclusion of other responses. Advances in genetic technology can reinforce this perspective, lending further credence to a perspective that conflates the prevention of disability with purported ideas that seem to conflict with disability rights (i.e. the 'right' not to be born and thereby acquire a disability or the 'right' to genetic enhancement and the amelioration or prevention of impairment).

Second, medicalisation of disability tends to position medical professionals as authoritative while diminishing the voice and participation of persons with disabilities in their own rehabilitation and life choices. This silencing served as the impetus for the emergence of the independent living movement and the disability rights movement in the United States and elsewhere. Third, medicalisation contributes to quality of life assessments by medical professionals in instances where such professionals yield power in respect of medical decision-making. Quality of life assessments are ubiquitous in medical decision-making and many other evaluative processes linked to human health (Groce *et al.*, 2000). Genetic science broadens the aperture for such assessments and thus reinforces pre-existing concerns regarding quality of life assessments for persons with disabilities. Assumptions about quality of life and the devaluation that negative assessments evoke have been criticised by the Committee on the Rights of the Child, the treaty body that monitors implementation of the Convention on the Rights of the Child, as follows:

> All children were equal members of the human race, discriminatory laws which denied their right to life should be repealed. Public debate should take place on the unspoken assumption, underlying much medical and scientific research, that we should be striving towards the goal of perfection in human beings. It was one thing to work to eliminate impairment

> but quite another to eliminate the person with the impairment. We must be clear what we mean when we talk about prevention. It was of course vitally important to work towards the creation of a safer world for children in which the risks of impairment and harm were minimized, but the solution was not through the denial of life itself as a preventive strategy. Rather, we must celebrate diversity and learn to celebrate the birth of every child, with or without disability.
>
> (CRC Committee, 2000)

Disability studies scholars similarly emphasise that policies grounded in quality of life assessments too often have the effect of reinforcing the historical stigmatisation of a person with disabilities (Groce *et al.*, 2000; Silvers, 1998; Stein *et al.*, 2012). These insights have spurred changes in conceptualisations of quality of life assessments, resulting in person-centered quality of life approaches informed by self-determination and social inclusion, among other concepts. As Asch and others have emphasised, traditional quality of life assessments can have the effect of offending human rights principles, including human dignity and respect for difference, among others (Asch, 2003). The shift away from medicalisation of disability toward a nuanced, socio-contextual understanding is reflected in international disability rights and should form the point of departure for any consideration of genetic science and its implications for human rights and disability.

## 4. The reframing of disability in the CRPD

The United Nations adopted the CRPD together with its Optional Protocol, by consensus on December 13, 2006. The Convention provides, in the form of a legally binding core human rights convention, a disability-specific framework for the civil, political, economic, social and cultural rights of persons with disabilities. It has been ratified by more than 130 States and by the European Union. It is one of the most widely ratified human rights conventions. As such, the CRPD is the benchmark against which to assess the human rights of persons with disabilities in the context of genetic science.

The preamble of the CRPD, together with Article 1, captures the idea associated with the social model of disability in describing disability as a condition arising from 'interaction with various barriers [that] may hinder [disabled peoples'] full and effective participation in society on an equal basis with others' (CRPD, art. 1). A social model perspective, properly understood, does not deny the reality of impairment or its impact on an individual (Asch, 2003). It does, however, challenge physical and social environments – and legal frameworks – to accommodate impairment as an anticipated incident of human diversity (Kayess and French, 2008). Barriers experienced by persons with disabilities according to this perspective are derivative of bias and not inherently biological. The adoption of a social model of disability, together with the rights framework offered in the CRPD, positions the limitations experienced by individuals with disability in functioning in a neutral frame, and does not demand enhancements or improvements to a body or mind presumed to be deficient. Many health policies (and indeed other types of policies) operate on the assumption that disabling conditions are pathological and defective and not on the assumption of disabling conditions as a social model, rights-based understanding of disability, in other words a *socially ascribed* deficit (Pillay, 2010).

A human rights-based perspective of disability, then, focuses on recognising and then creating the conditions necessary for individual self-determined living in community with others, together with providing protection against State interference with individual choice and autonomy. Societal responses to disability must comport with, qua the CRPD, accommodation, inclusion and support. Health policies, as such, are required to pitch toward these principles and not, for example, policies and practices that are autonomy-diminishing (e.g. genetic research on human subjects, absent informed consent), discriminatory on the basis of disability (e.g. disability-based insurance exclusions) or offensive to human dignity (e.g. directive genetic counselling regarding disabling traits or genetic screening protocols premised on speculative quality of life assessments).

### *4.1 CRPD purpose and principles*

Policies motivated by the emergence of genetic technologies, as with all health policies, must not offend the object and purpose of the CRPD and must be consistent with its principles (Vienna Convention, 1969).[1] Thus, States Parties are obliged to review laws, policies and programmes in the light of the CRPD and to assess conformity with its purpose 'to promote, protect and ensure the full and equal enjoyment of all human rights and fundamental freedoms by all persons with disabilities, and to promote respect for their inherent dignity' (CRPD, 2006, art. 1).

The principles in Article 3 of the CRPD are to be applied to enable the rights of persons with disabilities and, thus, must be disability-specific in their application (CRPD Committee, 2009). Reflected in human rights law generally, States are obligated to apply the principles systematically and with discipline and analytical rigor across the CRPD, including in relation to genetic technology. Policies that potentially offend one or more of the general principles of human rights law must be treated with extreme caution and heightened scrutiny and are subject to immediate review. Of particular relevance in the context of guarding against genetic discrimination in the context of disability are (in addition to the principle of

1 Article 26 of the Vienna Convention on the Law of Treaties expresses the principle of *pacta sunt servanda* and states that '[e]very treaty in force is binding upon the parties to it and must be performed by them in good faith'.

non-discrimination) the following principles: (1) respect for inherent dignity; (2) full and effective participation and inclusion in society; and (3) respect for difference and acceptance of persons with disabilities as part of human diversity and humanity.

The reference to 'respect for inherent dignity' in Article 3 of the CRPD echoes the preamble to the Universal Declaration of Human Rights which emphasises that 'recognition of the inherent dignity and of the equal and inalienable rights of all members of the human family is the foundation of freedom, justice, and peace in the world' (UDHR, 1948). International human rights tribunals have repeatedly stressed the importance of interpreting human rights conventions in keeping with human dignity (ECHR, 2001; ECHR, 2002). Respect for dignity is denied when persons with disabilities are devalued and discounted, including when they are barred from meaningful consultation in decision-making that affects their interests. Dignitarian interests are also at stake when health policies – such as disability-selective antenatal screening policies – characterise, whether explicitly or implicitly, disabling conditions, such as Down syndrome, as burdensome, lacking in quality and the like.

The principle of participation and inclusion – an expression of due process wherein persons whose interests are most affected are entitled to a voice in decision-making processes concerning those interests – is a fundamental principle of human rights law and is articulated in the CRPD as a general principle and obligation in Article 4(3) (CRPD, 2006, arts 3 and 4(3)). Beyond the better outcomes associated with meaningful participation, protecting the due process rights of persons most affected reflects and works to ensure dignity.

The implications of the right to participate in decision-making along with recognition of legal capacity to guard against abuses in the context of genetic science is clear – persons with disabilities are to be accorded recognition as persons with legal capacity and, hence, the attendant right to participate in decision-making. Where support is needed to facilitate the exercise of legal capacity, including participating in decision-making processes, it must be provided. Thus, for example, a group of advocates in New Zealand have protested against the process associated with government-funded antenatal screening (Saving Downs, 2012). Holding that such programmes ultimately impact on the number of children born with Down syndrome, as well as other disabling conditions such as Spina Bifida, such programmes must, they argue with persuasion, involve the participation of those persons whose interests are acutely impacted by the adoption of such policies (Saving Downs, Action So Far; Harmon, 2007).

The principle of 'respect for difference and acceptance of persons with disabilities as part of human diversity and humanity' expresses the values that underpin human rights law more generally (CRPD, 2006, art. 3). This principle acknowledges, for example, a basic idea of human rights law that individuals are active subjects of human rights, as opposed to objects to be acted upon. Moreover, in recognising disability as a natural part of human diversity and in underscoring respect and indeed acceptance – as opposed to a lower threshold of tolerance – of difference, the provision serves as an affront to conceptualisations of disability that are grounded in outmoded models conveying paternalism, pity, charity and the like.

Of particular consequence in this context is assessing whether a particular policy aligns with the principle of respect for difference. Is the development of a genetic screening protocol for Down Syndrome or other condition developed in consultation with people with Down Syndrome? Do genetic screening protocols pitch towards the promotion of safe birth outcomes? Do appeals for genetic testing convey pejorative messaging in their content? Do Deaf parents enjoy equal access to IVF? Are insurance policies discriminatory on the basis of (prospective) health status derived from genetic testing results? These and other queries are relevant in applying a rights-based perspective to medical decision-making as well as law and policy connected with genetic technology and its use.

### *4.2 Right to life*

The CRPD reaffirms the right to life, widely recognised as a core principle of human rights law (CRC Committee, General Comment 5, 2003). The provision is a particularly spare one, and, as such, is essentially stripped of any contextual elements that would link the right to the particular situation of persons with disabilities in the context of genetic discrimination. It thus gives little guidance as to the application of the right to life in connection with genetically based actions. Other provisions, however, are more directly relevant to sorting through the human rights issues that genetic discrimination in the context of persons with disabilities raises.

### *4.3 Disability and genetic discrimination*

Silvers, applying concerns regarding the widespread usage of genetic testing resulting from the Human Genome Project to the particular situation of persons with disabilities, observes that 'individuals with genetic vulnerabilities that put them at more than species-typical risk for illness are also at risk of such stigmatization' and, further, that 'people who test positive for alleles associated with disease may encounter discrimination in employment and others areas of civic and commercial life, even though they never become symptomatic' (Silvers, 1998; Silvers and Stein, 2003). These are concerns that genetic testing will inevitably lead to the use of genetic information for discriminatory purposes and impact on individuals with disabilities who are or are thought to have genetic differences associated with their impairment. Such concerns regarding genetic discrimination in the context of disability include insurance and employment discrimination, but also extend to discrimination by many other actors, among them, health professionals who provide access to a range of services, financial institutions, immigration officials, housing and licensing agencies (e.g. professional agencies, motor vehicle administrations, recreational licensing agencies) and bodies relating to families such as foster parent and adoption agencies (Nelkin, 1992; Nelkin and Tancredi, 1989).

CRPD non-discrimination and equality provisions are elaborated in Article 5, which requires States Parties to ensure the equality of individuals with disabilities, and prohibits any discrimination on the basis of disability (CRPD, 2006, arts. 5 and 2). The CRPD defines disability discrimination as 'any distinction, exclusion or restriction on the basis of disability' that 'has the purpose or effect of impairing or nullifying the recognition, enjoyment or exercise, on an equal basis with others, of all human rights and fundamental freedoms' and it extends to 'all forms of discrimination, including denial of reasonable accommodation' (CRPD, 2006, art. 2). Disability discrimination applies not only to persons with disabilities, but also to people associated with disabled persons, such as family members, friends or caregivers.

The Committee on the Rights of Persons with Disabilities, in one of its first concluding observations on a state report, signalled its understanding of disability discrimination in a context directly related to genetic testing for disabling traits. It observed that Spanish legislation, Act2/2010 of 3 March 2010, on sexual and reproductive health decriminalising voluntary termination of pregnancy included a problematic distinction according to which pregnancy could be terminated beyond the regular 14 week threshold to 22 weeks provided there is a 'risk of serious anomalies in the foetus', 'if the foetus has a disability' and, beyond week 22 in case of 'an extremely serious and incurable illness' detected in the foetus (CRPD Committee, 2011). In its concluding observations, the CRPD Committee recommended that Spain 'abolish the distinction made in the Act 2/2010 in the period allowed under law within which a pregnancy can be terminated based solely on disability' (CRPD Committee, 2011). In this regard the Committee signalled its implicit linkage between disability discrimination and the termination policy in Spain with direct implications for genetic testing in the context of disability.

### *4.4 Informed consent and supported decision-making*

The historical context for understanding informed consent and decision-making for persons with disabilities is grim, especially, but not exclusively, in the context of institutional settings such as hospitals, orphanages, social care homes, rehabilitation clinics and the like. Too often decision-making in such contexts lies in favour of institutional and substituted decision-making, a deeply flawed perspective when set against the aim of the CRPD, which is to preserve the autonomy and participation of persons with disabilities, including medical decision-making (CRPD, 2006, arts. 2, 4(3), 15, and 25).

The primary right that aims to ensure autonomy, personal choice and decisional capacity is the right to equal recognition before the law, reflected in Article 12 of the CRPD. The abridgement of legal capacity in the health care setting is particularly deleterious for persons with disabilities. Legal capacity is variously undermined in such settings through coercive regimes facilitating substituted decisions, such as forced institutionalisation and compelled 'medical' treatments that include restraints, abortion and sterilisation. Legal capacity is similarly diminished through prohibitions on entering into contracts, disposal of property, control of finances and participation in judicial and administrative proceedings. They manifest in sweeping denials of individual liberty exemplified in plenary guardianship regimes, segregated congregate living arrangements, explicit proscriptions on voting, marrying and parenting, as well as rampant exclusions from education, work and recreational pursuits.

A holistic reading of the CRPD calls for a robust interpretation of the prohibition against taking medical decisions in the absence of informed consent or substituted decision-making. Notably, the CRPD Committee and related practice recognises forced and non-consensual administration of medical treatment as a form of torture or inhuman treatment (Special Rapporteur, 2008). Moreover, Article 15 of the CRPD, read together with Article 17 (respect for mental and physical integrity), Article 19 (right to independent living in the community) and Article 12 (legal capacity), in particular, require the application of a highly robust informed consent regime which is clearly pertinent to protection against genetic discrimination and misuses of genetic technology.

Advances in genetic research, while holding promise in advancing health care through earlier diagnosis and more effective prevention and treatment of disease, trigger concerns regarding informed consent, not only with respect to prospective diagnosis of disability, but also in respect of persons with disabilities in institutions. Highly marginalised groups have long been the targets of medical research when institutionalised in hospitals, social care homes and residential schools of children with disabilities, as illustrative cases in both Europe and the United States disclose (Stein and Lord, 2009). Protections must be directed at protecting individuals with disabilities from research abuse by government or third-party researchers. Practices such as housing a genetic research center within the same building as a school for children with disabilities, for instance, raises serious ethical and human rights concerns.[2]

2 The Shafallah Center for Children with Special Needs in Doha, Qatar, for instance, houses a genetic research laboratory within the same building as its school for children with intellectual disabilities. Moreover, many of the staff at Shafallah don white coats which further evokes the sense of a medically oriented institution as opposed to a school within the community. While undertaking genetic research may be advantageous for persons with disabilities as for all, housing a research lab within a school for children with disabilities clearly gives the appearance of something other than a social, rights-based approach to inclusive education.

### *4.5 Physical and mental integrity*

Disability discrimination, including the failure to reasonably accommodate persons with disabilities, frequently manifests in violations of physical and mental integrity, making disability a risk factor when considering vulnerability to torture and other forms of inhuman or degrading treatment (Special Rapporteur, 2008; OHCHR, 2007). Genetic factors can be the motivation for violations of physical and mental integrity and are not relegated to the annals of history, as disability-based persecution in North Korea rooted at least in part on genetic heritage, discloses (Lord, 2013). The long-term and even permanent institutionalisation of persons with disabilities in psychiatric facilities and social care homes, frequently in isolated environs within rural areas or locations set apart from established communities, exposes such individuals to a variety of risks, some based on genetic discrimination (Benko, 2001). Regulating genetic science ought to arouse serious attention when set against a long background of egregious human rights violations against persons with disabilities including forced sterilisation, bogus remedies said to 'cure' disabling conditions, psycho-surgery such as lobotomies, and torturous medical experimentation (Lord, 2013).

### *4.6 Access to health care*

Access to health care in the context of disability raises two principal concerns. The first is the imposition of health services thought, or presumed, to be beneficial for persons with disabilities that are coercive or altogether involuntary and that may be premised in whole or in part on perceived genetic dysfunction. The second is the equal access of persons with disabilities to the same level of medical care within the same systems as others. Article 25 of the CRPD requires that individuals with disabilities have access to 'the highest attainable standard of health without discrimination on the basis of disability' by ensuring their equal right to 'the same range, quality and standard of free or affordable health care' and related services provided to the non-disabled general population (CRPD, 2006, art. 25).

Non-discrimination requires that mental and physical health care services must be available without discrimination on the basis of disability or any other prohibited ground. States must take positive measures to ensure equality of access to persons with disabilities. These services include sexual and reproductive health, prevention of additional disabilities, and health-related rehabilitation. A further component of the obligation is to adopt measures that raise awareness about 'human rights, dignity, autonomy and needs of persons with disabilities through training and the promulgation of ethical standards for public and private health care' (CRPD, 2006, art. 25). This dovetails with the obligation in Article 8 requiring States Parties to conduct effective awareness-raising to promote a positive image of persons with disabilities (CRPD, art. 8). States are specifically required to 'adopt immediate, effective and appropriate measures' in order (1) to raise awareness throughout society, including at the family level, of the rights of persons with disabilities, and to foster respect for the rights and dignity of persons with disability; (2) to combat stereotypes, prejudices and harmful practices relating to persons with disability in all areas of life; and (3) to promote awareness of the capabilities and contributions of persons with disabilities (CRPD, art. 8). Advances in genetic science accordingly raise a number of questions related to the right to health for persons with disabilities, among them, access and use of genetic information, genetic privacy, access to health insurance and family-related reproductive rights connected to health.

### *4.7 Access to genetic information*

All persons, including persons with disabilities – and indeed those with whom they are associated – have the equal rights to find, receive and impart information (CRPD, 2006, art. 21). The right to information in the health care context requires that such information be available, accessible, acceptable and of good quality and that such information must also align with general principles of human rights, and, in the case of the CRPD, with Article 3. This right must be implemented consistent with human rights principles, including the respect for difference and diversity, and in keeping with the social model understanding of disability.

Under the foregoing framework for analysis, genetic information, such as results of screening tests, must, insofar as they impart information to prospective parents, conform to the general principles of human rights, including respect for dignity. Studies of information currently provided to prospective parents within the context of disability-selective antenatal screening policy raise concerns and suggest that the standard required of health information is not always satisfied (Lord, 2012). A component of ensuring access to information consistent within human rights principles and in keeping with medical ethics is neutral, or non-directive imparting of information (Asch, 2003). Part of ensuring that information is of good quality in the context of genetic counselling and screening protocols is providing information in a way that does not favor one decision over another. Adrienne Asch, one of the most articulate voices in this context, in discussing research findings, observed:

> In situations where parents were raising infants and children with Down syndrome and cystic fibrosis, counsellors stressed ways in which lives of the affected children would resemble those of non-disabled peers, focusing on capacities for education, stimulation, play and relationships. By contrast, the stories given to prospective parents if the diagnosis was made prenatally concentrated on medical complications and differences from the lives of non-disabled children.
>
> (Asch, 2003: 334)

Significantly, studies of families with children with Down syndrome have found that most cope well and report benefits as well as challenges associated with having a child with Down syndrome (Skotko and Levine, 2006). Studies also find positive effects for many brothers and sisters growing up with a sibling with Down syndrome (Skotko and Levine, 2006). This context, as others where genetic science is brought to bear on decision-making, raises challenging questions regarding information provision and use.

### *4.8 Right to genetic privacy*

Central to the issue of ensuring that genetic information is not used to disadvantage individuals perceived or possessing a particular genetic identity is the protection of genetic information, not only in terms of its collection within a consensual framework, but also in terms of its use. The protection of medical privacy is well established in human rights law and States must ensure that public and private actors protect medical privacy, as guaranteed in the CRPD. Implementation should entail measures that place strict limits on access to health information and ensure respect for health-related decisions, self-determination, and physical and mental integrity. Complementing human rights protections are standards of professional ethics, which are likewise safeguards applicable to various medical professionals, hospitals, insurers and other entities with access to health information to maintain the confidentiality of medical communications and the security of medical records, including, of course, mental health records and pharmacy records, and records within institutions such as social care homes, segregated schools and psychiatric facilities.

The CRPD, read holistically, imposes a range of obligations on States pertinent to the protection of genetic privacy, among other aspects of privacy. This broad range of protections includes: (1) respect for informational privacy (e.g. confidentiality, anonymity, secrecy and data security); (2) physical privacy (e.g. modesty and bodily integrity) (CRPD, art. 17); associational privacy (e.g. relational sharing of information); proprietary privacy (e.g. self-ownership and control over genetic data and body tissues); and decisional privacy (e.g. autonomy and choice in medical and rehabilitation decision-making) (CRPD, arts. 3, 12, 25). Also of potential relevance in this context is Article 31 of the CRPD on disability data and statistics. The initial drafting of the CRPD from the outset focused on the misuse of such data. Drawing from the recognition of the need for statistical information as a means of effective disability rights implementation and monitoring, Article 31 effectively incorporates the following principles in relation to individual subjects of statistical inquiry: (1) avoidance of undue intrusion; (2) obtaining informed consent; (3) protecting the interests of subjects; (4) maintaining confidentiality of records; and (5) inhibiting the disclosure of identities.

Whether and how individuals are able to exercise their right to privacy in health contexts depends largely on their status in society; poverty, disability and other marginal status undermine privacy protections in health contexts (Marx, 2007). Accordingly, persons with disabilities who are dependent on caregivers, or who live in institutions, are particularly at risk of having their right to privacy undermined. Children with disabilities, along with adults who are under guardianship and thus stripped of their legal capacity, are dependent on government entitlement programmes or detained, for instance in a psychiatric ward, lack substantial control over medical privacy. This raises the question of how to ensure protection for individuals particularly at risk of privacy invasions, whether in the context of genetic research or treatment, or otherwise.

### *4.9 Genetic information as property*

International human rights law prohibits discrimination in the context of property rights (UDHR, art. 17) and the CRPD clarifies that persons with disabilities may need specific protection in ensuring their property rights. Accordingly, it requires States to ensure that persons with disabilities are not arbitrarily deprived of their property and protects against discrimination in, among other things, owning or inheriting property (CRPD, 2006, art. 12(5). The use of one's genetic material and proprietary interests are at issue given the possibility of putting genes, genomes and bio-banked tissue to use in health care and health research undertakings. While scholars continue to argue that individuals have privacy interests in their genes, genomes and bio-banked tissue, instances of taking tissue to develop cell lines, as in the case of Henrietta Lacks whose cell line – created without her knowledge or consent – was used to treat and eradicate polio and other conditions suggest otherwise (Skloot, 2011). Neither Lacks nor her relatives ever received any compensation and, in a California case involving a similar unauthorised taking, the court was unwilling to designate DNA or tissue as property (Radin, 1987). Given the serious abridgments of privacy (and property) rights against persons with disabilities, including in the context of medical research, these are interests that should be a primary concern of disability rights.

### *4.10 Access to insurance*

The spectre of genetically based discrimination gives rise to concerns that already significant barriers in equal access to public and private insurance for persons with disabilities will be increased. As discussed in detail in the chapter on insurance discrimination (Chapter 9), health insurance policies frequently discriminate against persons with disabilities, as in the case where persons with disabilities are refused health insurance coverage due to the existence of a disability or where health insurance is made contingent on the exclusion of a particular health condition or disability-related health issue from coverage under the policy. Here, the CRPD is unequivocal that persons with disabilities must have equal access to public and private health insurance. Thus laws related to health insurance – whether private or public – should ensure that persons with disabilities have a right to access health care, including through health insurance, and that conditions for accessing insurance do not discriminate against persons with disabilities.

## 5. Family and reproductive rights and genetic diagnosis

Access to assistive reproductive technology (ART) is supported on human rights grounds as an element of the right to privacy and autonomy in medical decision-making. It also connects to the right, reflected in the CRPD, for persons with disabilities to be free from discrimination in all matters relating to marriage, family, parenthood and relationships (CRPD, 2006, art. 21). Rights to procreative privacy, together with the right to use and benefit from technology to bear children, raise questions regarding equal access to ART for persons with disabilities. Barriers rooted in disability stereotyping include, for instance, the question of equal access to ART for a Deaf parent(s) and selection for deafness; access to fertility treatment for a cognitively disabled parent(s). Conversely, disability-based testing for conditions such as Down syndrome or cystic fibrosis impart, according to some commentators, the harmful the message that persons with disabling conditions are unwelcome in society (Asch, 2003; Parens and Asch, 2000; Asch, 1989). Moreover, screening for immutable disability characteristics such as Down Syndrome – where there is no potential therapeutic value – reinforces internalised oppression according to which disabled persons are devalued, tagged with their impairments and branded as a burden (Houghton, 2004; Newell, 1999; Davis, 1987).

## 6. Equal access to grievance mechanisms

In recognising that rights are to be accorded to persons with disabilities across the wide range of obligations pertinent to the use (and misuse) of genetic technology, it is also clear that States are accountable in situations where rights are abridged. This includes, for example, the provision of safeguards against abuse of supported decision-making in the health context or against genetic discrimination (CRPD, arts. 5 and 12). Likewise States must undertake measures to ensure that persons with disabilities have effective access to justice on an equal basis with others in order to assert their right to access health facilities, goods and services (CRPD, art. 13). Equal access might include a range of judicial, administrative and other grievance mechanisms that can be relevant in the health sphere, for example, courts and tribunals, including anti-discrimination or health care complaints, health ombudsmen, health arbitration procedures, institutional review boards, medical profession boards and other complaints mechanisms.

## 7. Conclusion

The conceptualisation of disability in human rights law has evolved over the past 60 years. The received narrative according to which disability rights were, at best, a limited basket of medical and social welfare benefits has given way to an acknowledgement that disability rights connect to all rights in the human rights framework and thus protect 1 billion persons worldwide. Moreover, the human rights of persons with disabilities are not subject to contingent enjoyment, to be accorded, but then clawed back via 'to the extent feasible' or 'subject to available resources' as in prior, conditional articulations of disability rights (Declaration of Disabled Persons, 1975; Convention on the Rights of the Child, 1989).

Correspondingly, disability is no longer viewed as medical pathology or genetic dysfunction, but as a complex, multifaceted and evolving concept. One of the points of analysis contemplated by the CRPD is a review of health-related policies arising from advances in genetic science, the socio-contextual conditions within which they are applied and the resulting impact of such policies. The CRPD thus compels an analysis of laws and policies, and the extent to which they accommodate impairment as an accepted incident of human diversity and evoke respect for human difference. European regulatory responses to human rights in the context of genetic technology must accordingly align with the CRPD and cast a sceptical eye over policies that offend disability rights principles. There is bound to be continued disagreement about the limits of individual autonomy and individual choice as conceived in the CRPD in the context of genetic science, some of which will inevitably place disability rights principles in a difficult tension with mainstream human rights standards such as non-discrimination, privacy and informed consent among others.

## References

Asch, A. (2003) 'Disability Equality and Prenatal Testing: Contradictory or Compatible?' *Florida State University Law Review* 30 (2): 315–342.

Asch, A. (1989) 'Reproductive Technology and Disability' in Cohen, Sherrill and Taub, Nadine (eds) *Reproductive Laws For the 1990s*. Clifton, NJ: Humana Press, pp. 69–78.

Benko, D. and Benowitz, B. (2001) 'The Application of Universal Human Rights Law to People with Mental Disabilities' *Human Rights Brief* 9: 11.

*Buck v. Bell* (1927) 274 U.S. 200.

Committee on the Rights of the Child (2000) CRC/C/15/Add.115 23 Feb. (para. 329).

Committee on the Rights of the Child (2003) General Comment No. 5.

Committee on the Rights of Persons with Disabilities (2009) *Guidelines on Treaty-specific Document To Be Submitted by States Parties under Article 35, Paragraph 1, of the*

*Convention on the Rights of Persons with Disabilities*, Annex 1, Part B, at p. 7.

Committee on the Rights of Persons with Disabilities (2011) 'Consideration of Reports submitted by States under Article 35, Concluding Observations – Spain' (19 May): www.ohchr.org/EN/HRBodies/CRPD/Pages/Session6.aspx [accessed 15 June 2014].

Convention on the Rights of Persons with Disabilities (2007) G.A. Res. 61/106, 2006, opened for signature Mar. 30, 46 I.L.M. 433.

Convention on the Rights of the Child (1989) G.A. Res. 44/25, U.N. GAOR, 44th Sess., Supp. No. 49, at 161, U.N. Doc. A/44/49 [hereinafter CRC].

Davis, A. (1987) 'Women with Disabilities: Abortion and Liberation' *Disability, Handicap and Society* 2: 276.

European Court of Human Rights (ECHR) (2001) *Refah Partisi and others v. Turkey* of 31 July, Application no. 41340/98, para. 43.

European Court of Human Rights (ECHR) (2002) *Pretty v. United Kingdom* of 29 April, Application no. 2346/02, para. 65.

Groce, N. E., Chamie, M. and Me, A. (2000) 'Measuring the Quality of Life: Rethinking the World Bank's Disability Adjusted Life Years', *Disability World* 3.

Harmon, A. (2007) 'Prenatal Tests Put Down Syndrome in Hard Focus', *New York Times*. Available at: www.nytimes.com/2007/05/09/us/09down.html?_r=1 [accessed 15 June 2014].

Hougton, H. (1994) 'Does Prenatal Diagnosis Discriminate against the Disabled?' in McKie, J. (ed.) *Ethical Issues in Prenatal Diagnosis and Termination of Pregnancy*, pp. 97–102.

Kayess, R. and French, P. (2008) 'Out of Darkness into Light? Introducing the Convention on the Rights of Persons with Disabilities' *Human Rights Law Review* 8(1).

Lord, J. E. (2004) 'People with Disabilities' in Shelton, D. L. (ed.) *Encyclopedia of Genocide and Crimes Against Humanity* Vol. 1. New York: Macmillan Reference USA, p. 257.

Lord, J. E. (2012) 'Screened Out of Existence: The Convention on the Rights of Persons with Disabilities and Selective Screening Policies' *International Journal Disability, Community and Rehabilitation* 12(2).

Lord, J. E. (2013) 'Nothing to Celebrate: North Koreans with Disabilities' *Foreign Policy in Focus* (3 December).

Marx, G. T. (2007) 'Privacy and Social Stratification' *Knowledge, Technology and Policy* 20(2): 91–95.

Nelkin, D. (1992) 'The Social Power of Genetic Information' in Kevles, D. and Hood, L. *Code of Codes: Scientific and Social Issues in the Human Genome Project*. USA: Harvard University Press, pp. 177–190.

Nelkin, D., and Tancredi, L. (1989) *Dangerous Diagnostics: The Social Power of Biological Information*. New York: Basic Books.

Newell, C. (1999) 'Critical Reflections on Disability, Difference and Genetic Testing' in O'Sullivan, G., Sharman, E. and Short, S. (eds) *Goodbye Normal Gene: Confronting the Genetic Revolution*. Pluto Press, pp. 58–71.

Office of the High Commissioner for Human Rights (OHCHR) (2007), Expert Seminar on Freedom from Torture and Ill-Treatment and Persons with Disabilities (11 December). Available at: www2.ohchr.org/english/issues/disability/docs/torture/seminartorturereportfinal.doc [hereinafter OCHR Report] [accessed 15 June 2014].

Optional Protocol to the Convention on the Rights of Persons with Disabilities, opened for signature Mar. 30, 2007, 46 I.L.M. 433 [hereinafter Optional Protocol].

Parens, E. and Asch, A. (2000) 'The Disability Rights Critique of Prenatal Genetic Testing: Reflections and Recommendations' in Parens E. and Asch, A. (eds) *Prenatal Testing and Disability*. Georgetown University Press, p. 2.

Pillay, N. (2010) UN High Commissioner for Human Rights, Foreword, 'Monitoring the Convention on the Rights of Persons with Disabilities: Guidance for Human Rights Monitors' 5.

Radin, M. (1987) 'Market-Inalienability' *Harvard Law Review* 100(8): 1849–1937.

Saving Downs, Submission to the Human Rights Commission, 'Action so Far'. Available at: www.savingdowns.com/action-so-far [accessed 15 June 2014].

Saving Downs, *Mothers Being Encouraged to Have Late Term Abortions for Down Syndrome and Spina Bifida*. Available at: www.savingdowns.com/mothers-being-encouraged-to-have-late-term-abortions-for-down-syndrome-and-spina-bifida [accessed 15 June 2014].

Saving Downs (2012) Comments from Saving Downs, Antenatal Screening for Down Syndrome and Other Conditions – Draft Guidelines for Health Practitioners (on file with the author).

Silvers, A. (1998) 'Formal Justice' in Silvers, A., Wasserman, D. T. and Mahowald, M. (eds) *Disability, Difference, Discrimination: Perspectives on Justice in Bioethics and Public Policy*. Lanham, MD: Rowman and Littlefield Publishers, Inc., pp. 13–146.

Skloot, R. (2011) *The Immortal Life of Henrietta Lacks*, Broadway Books.

Silvers, A. and Stein, M. A. (2003) 'Essentially Empirical: The Role of Biological and Legal Classification in Effectively Prohibiting Genetic Discrimination' in Figueroa, Robert and Harding, Sandra (eds) *Science and Other Cultures: Issues in Philosophies of Science and Technology*. Routledge, p. 129.

Skotko, B.G. and Levine, S.P. (2006) 'What the Other Children Are Thinking: Brothers and Sisters of Persons with Down Syndrome' *American Journal of Medical Genetics* 142C: Part C: Seminars in Medical Genetics, pp. 180–186.

Special Rapporteur on Torture and Other Cruel, Inhuman or Degrading Treatment or Punishment (2008) *Interim Report*, §§ 37–76, UN Doc. A/63/175 (July 28) (by Manfred Nowak).

Stein, M. A. and Lord, J. E. (2009) in Quinn, G. and Arnardóttir, O. M. (eds) *The UN Convention on the Rights of Persons with Disabilities: European and Scandinavian Perspectives*. Leiden: Martinus Nijhof, pp. 17–39.

Stein, M. A., Lord, J. E. and Weiss, D. (2012) in Rhodes, R., Battin, M. and Silvers, A. (eds) *Medicine and Social Justice: Essays on the Distribution of Health Care*. New York: Oxford University Press, pp. 245–265.

Universal Declaration of Human Rights (UDHR) (1948), G.A. Res. 217 (III) A, preamble, U.N. Doc. A/RES/217(III) (10 December) [hereinafter UDHR].

Vienna Convention on the Law of Treaties (23 May 1969) 1155 UNTS, p. 331 at art. 26 [hereinafter Vienna Convention].

Wasserman, D., Asch, A., Blustein, J. and Putnam, D. (2013) 'Disability: Definitions, Models, Experience,' in Zalta, E. N. (ed.) *The Stanford Encyclopedia of Philosophy* (fall). Available at: http://plato.stanford.edu/archives/fall2013/entries/disability [accessed 15 June 2014].

# Section 5

# Considering the way forward for the EU

Section 5 provides further evaluation of the scope of current EU legislation in regulating genetic information. In evaluating the current position in the EU, this section focuses on the reach of current non-discrimination and data protection law and highlights the evident gaps in protection. This section addresses the theory that, in light of the significant developments in genetic technology and the corresponding potential for misuse of genetic information, comprehensive and uniform legislation is preferable at EU level. It presents proposals for reform in the shape of a new genetic information non-discrimination directive.

This section comprises one chapter entitled 'Genetic discrimination: Is it time for the EU to take on a new challenge?', by Delia Ferri, and the Conclusion.

# 15 Genetic discrimination

## Is it time for the EU to take on a new challenge?

*Delia Ferri*

### 1. Introduction

It is fifteen years since Andrew Niccol directed the movie *Gattaca*. This film described a future society driven by liberal eugenics, where the classification of genetic inferiority was used as a rallying point and where genetic discrimination was the rule. At the time when *Gattaca* was released, nobody considered that disturbing scenario to be a likely image of the future.

However, nowadays, genetic testing has become widespread and less expensive. Although public attitudes towards genetic testing itself are generally positive (Henneman and Van Hoyweghen, 2013) and people acknowledge that genetic therapy has been displaying a great potential to prevent and treat diseases, the anxiety that genetic data can be misused to discriminate against a person is rapidly growing (Geelen *et al.*, 2012). *Gattaca* seems no longer a worrying fiction and there is the fear that the worst-case scenario evoked by Niccol could turn into reality.

Genetic discrimination, conceived as unjustified unequal treatment of persons owing to their genetic characteristics (Gerards, 2005: 24), is likely to take the form of disadvantages in work life (Lemke, 2005; Stefanini, 2008: 69–71; Trojsi, 2009; Lemke, 2013) and of denial, or increase in price, of insurance (Lemke, 2005; Viola de Azevedo Cunha, 2013: 65–78; Adjin-Tettey, 2013). Other fields in which the use of genetic data is relevant are forensic science and criminal procedure, but they are out of the scope of this paper (Scaffardi, 2008; Belfiore, 2011; Barbujani and Tassi, 2012). In the US, according to the Coalition for Genetic Fairness (2004), employers have considered a genetic test as a predictor of the future health of an employee, and of his/her level of future absenteeism or low work rate. The Coalition reported several cases of exclusion of job applicants on the basis of predicted future health conditions, and, more generally, of genetic testing used to discriminate in the workplace. In the UK, the NGO GeneWatch has largely advocated that insurance companies would like to (mis)use predictive genetic test results in decisions about insurance.

Legal scholarship has highlighted that there is still little evidence on actual genetic discrimination (Joly *et al.*, 2013). Nevertheless, to manage the increasing concerns about potential misuses of genetic information, a body of international soft and hard law documents on the use of genetic testing and new biotechnology techniques has been developed (Lemke, 2013). The most relevant example of international binding law is the European Convention for the Protection of Human Rights and Dignity of the Human Being with Regard to the Application of Biology and Medicine (Oviedo Convention), approved by the Council of Europe in 1997. This Convention bans all forms of discrimination based on a person's genetic features and allows predictive genetic tests only for health or scientific research purposes (Campiglio, 2008; Motoc, 2009; Beqiraj, 2011).

In addition, national legislation to inhibit the misuse of genetic data and to protect people discriminated against on the ground of genetic information has been approved in many states. The most significant case is the US Genetic Information Nondiscrimination Act (GINA), passed in 2008 (discussed in Section 3 of this book), but also a few European countries have approved laws to protect genetic data and, in some cases, to ban their discriminatory use (Stefanini, 2008; Rothstein and Joly, 2009; Annecca, 2011; Lemke 2013: 27; de Paor, 2013b). De Paor observes that an ongoing engagement with questions of genetic privacy and genetic discrimination has determined a 'patchwork' of different legislative acts with no common ground, and the Oviedo Convention has brought very little results in terms of harmonisation of legislation in Europe (de Paor, 2013a; de Paor, 2013b). Different legislative approaches, focusing on the protection of access to and disclosure of an individual's genetic information, or on the prevention of a discriminatory use of genetic data, still reflect constitutional and cultural differences with regard to genetics, but also diverse social welfare systems.

However, this 'patchwork' of legislation is regrettable in the context of the European Union (EU): it is highly detrimental to the right to non-discrimination provided for in the Treaties (i.e. the Treaty on the European Union – TEU and the Treaty on the Functioning of the European Union – TEFU) and in the EU Charter of Fundamental Rights (EU CFR). It is also harmful to the high level of consumer and health protection that the EU is committed to ensure for its citizens (Roscam Abbing, 2012). Although it could be argued that public health systems, in place in most part of continental Europe, slightly reduce the probability that insurance companies mistreat sensitive genetic information, different legislation may threaten the 'four freedoms', in particular the freedom of movement granted to all EU citizens,[1] and endanger the 'sacred' Internal

1 Article 18 TFEU prohibits discrimination on the ground of nationality, and Article 20 TFEU establishes the 'Citizenship of the Union'. It stipulates that '[e]very person holding the nationality of a Member State shall be a citizen of the Union', and that the EU citizenship complements and does not replace national citizenship. Article 20(2) TFEU states that citizens of the EU enjoy *inter alia* the right to move and reside freely within the territory of the Member States. Article 45 TFEU provides for the freedom of movement for workers and states that 'such freedom of movement shall entail the abolition of any discrimination based on nationality between workers of the Member States as regards employment, remuneration and other conditions of work and employment'.

Market (Article 26 Treaty on the Functioning of the European Union).[2] On one hand, insurance companies might try to misuse genetic data in those countries in which no efficient legislation has been passed. On the other hand, insurance companies themselves might be prevented from operating freely within the Internal Market if there is no level playing field on the use of genetic information. In addition, European employees with a certain genetic make-up could be prevented from moving across the EU so as not to incur discrimination in those places where genetic testing can be required and there is no effective anti-discrimination legislation.

In 1989, the European Parliament had already called for an EU ban of the use of genetic testing in insurance matters to eliminate the risks of discrimination (European Parliament's Resolution on the ethical and legal problems concerning genetic manipulation, 1989) and, in 2003, the Group on Ethics in Science and New Technologies (EGE) had called for urgent EU action on genetic discrimination (EGE, 2003). However, at the time of writing this chapter, the EU has not legislated yet on genetic discrimination. The proposal for a new non-discrimination directive, which is currently under discussion, does not mention genetic data, or genetic discrimination. The EU is engaged in a reform of legislation on data protection, which would introduce 'genetic data' among the categories of sensitive data, but the entry into force of this reformed legal framework should not be expected too soon.

Against this background, this chapter aims to examine the efforts to protect the privacy and non-discrimination of genetic information in the EU, and to critically discuss the extent of EU competence to legislate on genetic discrimination.

This chapter does not examine ethical issues related to genetic testing, nor the complex regulatory issues linked to genetic testing in the clinical setting, as these issues are discussed in previous chapters of this book. It neither addresses, from a theoretical standpoint, the merits and drawbacks of adopting a stand-alone approach to protect genetic information and ban genetic discrimination through *ad hoc* legislation. Further, it does not discuss the challenges of 'genetic exceptionalism' theories (Murray, 1997; *contra*, among others, Rothstein and Joly, 2009). Rather, this chapter focuses on the EU's role in protecting genetic data and in banning genetic discrimination. It relies on the assumption that genetic data are different from health data, as underlined by the EU's Article 29 Data Protection Working Party (Article 29 DPWP) in a Working Document on Genetic Data (Article 29 DPWP, 2004), and on the conviction that a pure privacy approach is not sufficient to protect European citizens from genetic discrimination (de Paor, 2013a).

2 Article 26 TFEU. According to this provision: 'The internal market shall comprise an area without internal frontiers in which the free movement of goods, persons, services and capital is ensured in accordance with the provisions of the Treaties'.

This chapter is structured as follows. After these introductory remarks, section 2 briefly examines the right to privacy of genetic information in the EU and the legal framework on data protection currently in force. Section 3 focuses on the proposal for a new data protection regulation and outlines its drawbacks. Section 4 discusses in a general fashion the extent to which genetic discrimination is addressed in the EU legal framework. Section 5 examines the proposal for a new directive on non-discrimination. Section 6 examines the extent of EU competence to pass a new *ad hoc* non-discrimination genetic information directive. Section 7 offers a few tentative conclusions.

## 2. The right to privacy of genetic information in the EU: a brief overview

The EU legal framework provides for the right to privacy at the constitutional level and protects personal data through a comprehensive set of legislative acts.

Article 16 TFEU states that '[e]veryone has the right to the protection of personal data concerning them'. It also provides a specific legal basis for the adoption of rules on the protection of personal data processed by EU institutions, bodies, offices and agencies, and by the Member States when carrying out activities which fall within the scope of Union law, and of rules relating to the free movement of such data. Article 7 of the Charter of Fundamental Rights of the European Union (EU CFR) provides that '[e]veryone has the right to respect for his or her private and family life, home and communications'. Article 8 EU CFR enshrines protection of personal data as a fundamental right. According to this provision, data

> must be processed fairly for specified purposes and on the basis of the consent of the person concerned or some other legitimate basis laid down by law. Everyone has the right of access to data which has been collected concerning him or her, and the right to have it rectified.

Nevertheless, the right to the protection of personal data is not absolute, but must be considered in relation to its function in society (*inter alia Institut professionnel des agents immobiliers (IPI) v. Geoffrey Englebert* (unpublished); Joined Cases *Volker und Markus Schecke and Eifert* 2010).

The right to respect for private life with regard to the processing of personal data concerns any information relating to an identified or identifiable individual (Joined Cases *Volker und Markus Schecke and Eifert* 2010: paragraph 52, and Joined Cases *ASNEF and FECEMD* 2011: paragraph 42) and this broad definition is likely to include genetic data. This leads us to affirm that the right to the protection of genetic data is firmly embedded in the EU constitutional framework.

At present, the most relevant legislative acts in the field of data protection are Directive 95/46/EC and Regulation 45/2001/EC. Another important EU legislative measure is Directive 2002/58/EC concerning the processing of personal data and the protection of privacy in electronic communications.[3] The latter regulation concerns the processing of personal data by all EU institutions and bodies, insofar as such processing is carried out in the exercise of activities that fall entirely or partially within the scope of EU law. Since the definitions and the substance of the regulation closely follow the approach of Directive 95/46/EC, we limit ourselves to discussing the most relevant aspects of Directive 95/46/EC (hereinafter 'the directive') for the purpose of this analysis.

Directive 95/46/EC sets out a regulatory framework for the protection of personal data and covers all information relating to an identified or identifiable person, either directly or indirectly. The directive seeks to strike a balance between a high level of protection for the privacy of individuals and the free movement of personal data within the European Union (EU). To do so, it provides for strict limits on the collection and use of personal data and demands that each Member State set up an independent national body responsible for the protection of these data.

According to the directive, processing of personal data must be lawful and fair to the individuals concerned; the purposes of the processing should be explicit and legitimate and must be determined at the time of the collection of the data; data must be relevant and not excessive in relation to the purpose for which they are processed. Data must be accurate and, where necessary, kept up to date. Significantly, according to Article 8 para. 1, Member States must prohibit the processing of personal data revealing racial or ethnic origin, political opinions, religious or philosophical beliefs or trade union membership, and of data concerning health or sex life. However, this prohibition does not apply, *inter alia*, when: the data subject has given his explicit consent to the processing of those data; or processing is necessary for the purposes of carrying out the obligations and specific rights of the controller in the field of employment law. In addition, the prohibition laid down in Article 8 para. 1 does not apply where

3 [2001] OJ L 8/1. Another important EU legislative measure is Directive 2002/58/EC concerning the processing of personal data and the protection of privacy in electronic communications. This act complements Directive 95/46/EC with respect to the processing of personal data of natural persons in the electronic communications sector ([2002] OJ L 201/37). The E-Privacy Directive covers the 'protection of fundamental rights and freedoms, and in particular the right of privacy and confidentiality' in the e-communication sector (Article 1). Only the provision of publicly available e-communication services provided through a public network is concerned (Article 2). This Directive specifies how e-communication service providers should deal with the private data of their clients and remedy any breaches that might occur, as well as ensuring the free movement of such data and linked services in the EU. There are no specific provisions concerning persons with disabilities in the directive.

processing of the data is required for the purposes of preventive medicine, medical diagnosis, the provision of care or treatment or the management of health care services (Hervey and McHale, 2004: 165–85). These data protection rules set by the EU apply in cross-border health care, as stated in paragraph 25 of the preamble of Directive 2011/24/EU on the application of patients' rights in cross-border health care.[4]

Although we consider genetic data different, and 'more sensitive', than health information (Murray, 1997), it could be argued that genetic data falls within the scope of the directive because they are encompassed by the broad definition of personal data. In the absence of any specific provision, it is possible that genetic data can be included among health data: genetic data describe not only physical characteristics, but also a set of indications of current and future state of health of an individual, although these may not be absolutely certain, and might enjoy the legal protection granted by Article 8 of the directive (Scaffardi, 2008).

However, the lack of any specific definition of health data as inclusive of genetic and non-genetic information is a clear drawback: the task to effectively protect genetic data, without any legal certainty, is left to the interpreter. In addition, even considering that genetic information is encompassed within the bulk of health data, the legal protection provided by the directive is clearly insufficient. Article 8 provides for vague and wide exceptions to the general prohibition of use. Third parties can access genetic information by way of obtaining consent from the individual in question, and in a relationship in which there is a clear imbalance, such as the one between insurance companies and clients or between the employer and the employee, the consent of the employee to release genetic data can hardly be considered free (de Paor, 2013b). The exception which allows processing of data when this is necessary for the purposes of carrying out the obligations and specific rights of the controller in the field of employment law (at least potentially) opens the door to the use of genetic data by employers.

## 3. A small step towards the better protection of genetic data: the proposal for a new data protection regulation

The inadequacy of EU data protection legislation in protecting genetic data was first highlighted by Article 29 DPWP in 2004. In 2010, in its Communication on 'A comprehensive approach on personal data protection in the European Union',[5] the Commission stated that the EU needs a more comprehensive and coherent policy on data protection and expressly underlined the necessity to examine whether genetic information should

4 [2011] L88/45.

5 COM (2010) 609 final. See also at http://europa.eu/rapid/press-release_IP-12-46_en.htm?locale=en.

be added as a sensitive category of data. On 25 January 2012, the Commission adopted a package for reforming the European data protection framework, in order to modernise the EU legal system for the protection of personal data, to strengthen individuals' rights and ensure a free flow of personal data within the EU, and to improve the clarity and coherence of the EU rules. The package includes a 'Proposal for a Regulation on the protection of individuals with regard to the processing of personal data and on the free movement of such data', (COM (2012) 11 final)[6] and 'Proposal for a Directive on the protection of individuals with regard to the processing of personal data by competent authorities for the purposes of prevention, investigation, detection or prosecution of criminal offences or the execution of criminal penalties, and the free movement of such data' (COM (2012)10 final).[7] The package is currently under discussion, and the European Parliament and the Council had aimed to reach an agreement before the European elections in May 2014.

For the purpose of this analysis, the proposed regulation, which is supposed to replace Directive 95/46/EC, is particularly relevant. Without exploring the text in its complexity, we focus on few general aspects and on the provision related to the protection of genetic data.

First, the proposed regulation, once approved, will provide for a harmonised set of rules in the EU. Although Directive 95/46/EC amounts to harmonisation which is generally complete, the Court of Justice of the European Union (CJEU) found that its provisions are relatively general, given that it has to be applied to a large number of very different situations, and that, in many instances, it is left to the Member States to decide the details or choose between options (Lindqvist 2003).[8] The choice to pass a regulation, instead of another directive, is aimed at reducing the leeway left to Member States so as to reduce legal fragmentation and ensure greater legal certainty on data protection.

Once approved, the regulation will apply to the processing of personal data wholly or partly by automated means and to the processing other than by automated means of personal data which form part of a filing system or are intended to form part of a filing system (Article 2 of the proposed regulation).

Through the regulation, consumers are granted clear entitlements to their own data and are protected through remedies grounded in 'property rules' (Victor, 2013). Article 6 outlines a limited set of circumstances in which the collection and processing of data is lawful, the strongest of which is explicit consent by the data subject. Article 6 also lists specific circumstances where no explicit consent has been proffered, but the data user has some obligation that requires the data processing. For example, if

6 COM (2012)11 final.
7 COM (2012)10 final.
8 Case C-101/01 *Lindqvist* [2003] ECR I-2971.

'processing is necessary for the performance of a contract to which the data subject is party', it is lawful even without the explicit consent of the data subject. However, even in these special situations where the data subject has not explicitly consented to processing, the consumer must still be explicitly informed that data has been collected. Unless the data user can demonstrate 'compelling legitimate grounds for the processing', the data user must also erase this data.

Significantly, 'genetic data' are defined by Article 4 as 'all data, of whatever type, concerning the characteristics of an individual which are inherited or acquired during early prenatal development'. Article 9 of the proposed regulation, building on Article 8 of Directive 95/46/EC, specifically prohibits the processing of *inter alia* genetic data, although it allows for exceptions. In particular, the proposal of the Commission includes among exceptions the case in which 'the data subject has given consent to the processing of those personal data'. Article 7 of the proposed regulation specifies that, where processing is based on consent, a company could process personal data only after obtaining clear permission from the data subject, who could withdraw his/her consent at any time. A person's consent means 'any freely given, specific, informed and explicit indication of his/her wishes, either by a statement or by a clear affirmative action'.

Among the exceptions Article 9 also lists the case in which

> processing is necessary for the purposes of carrying out the obligations and exercising specific rights of the controller in the field of employment law in so far as it is authorised by Union law or Member State law providing for adequate safeguards.

Article 33 of the proposed regulation introduces the obligation of controllers and processors to carry out a data protection impact assessment prior to risky processing operations and include among them genetic data.

As highlighted by de Paor, the proposed regulation has the merit of introducing genetic data as a specific category of sensitive data (de Paor, 2013a). However, it is submitted here that, as it stands, the text has clear drawbacks. Apparently the new text adopts a 'genetic exceptionalism' approach, but, by contrast, genetic data are not given any special statute. They are governed as other sensitive data and enjoy the same level of protection. The exceptions provided for in Article 9, not too differently from those provided in Article 8 of Directive 96/45/EC, leave the door open to the misuse of genetic data. More generally, despite an intention to ensure uniformity, the proposed regulation contains numerous provisions that grant the Member States or their data-protection agencies the power to make decisions independently. In particular, Article 21 of the proposed regulation grants to Member States the power to restrict through legislative measures certain rights and obligations provided for to safeguard, as necessary: public security; the prevention, investigation, detection and prosecution of criminal offences; important economic or financial interests of the Member States and the EU. While this provision is substantially similar to Article 13 of Directive 95/46/EC, Member States might use their discretion to introduce exceptions that threaten the privacy of genetic data in fields such as insurance, if they have substantial economic interests in doing so.

The Civil Liberties Committee of the European Parliament, in examining the proposed regulation, stipulated that the text should make clear that the execution of a contract or the provision of a service (for example, an insurance service) cannot be made conditional upon consent to processing personal data that is not strictly needed for the completion of that contract or service. This position, if adopted, could minimise possible misuse of genetic data by insurance companies. Other improvements and amendments, designed to strengthen the protection of genetic data, could also be adopted in the final text, although, at this stage, this seems improbable.

Even though improved, the EU privacy regime would not protect against the discriminatory use of genetic information. Without discussing in great detail the pros and cons of different regulatory frameworks (i.e. privacy and non-discrimination frameworks), we limit ourselves to a few pragmatic remarks. As genetic testing is now a reality and can be performed for different purposes within and outside the medical field, genetic information becomes more and more appealing to employers and other third parties: thus genetic information is likely to become requested in application forms. Although aware of their right to privacy, job applicants or insurance seekers may feel compelled to disclose such information. Individuals may feel that, for professional reasons, it is necessary to agree to disclosure. In addition, if individuals refuse to disclose such information, an employer or other third party may nevertheless mistreat the individual, or raise assumptions as to the individual's perceived genetic profile (de Paor, 2013a; de Paor, 2013b). For these reasons, uniform EU data protection legislation is necessary but not sufficient. Non-discrimination provisions are the sole tool to successfully prevent EU citizens being treated in a more disadvantageous way than other comparable individuals on the ground of genetic data (de Paor, 2013a) and to prohibit discriminatory practices that, as mentioned above, although not yet widespread in Europe, are already taking place *de facto* in some Member States.

## 4. EU equality law: Are EU citizens protected from genetic discrimination?

In the current constitutional framework the principle of non-discrimination and equality is firmly embedded in the Treaties. Article 2 TEU on the values of the EU states that the Union is founded *inter alia* on equality and that '[t]hese values are common to the Member States in a society in which pluralism, non-discrimination, tolerance, justice, solidarity and equality between women and men prevail'. Article 3 TEU states that the EU 'shall combat social exclusion and discrimination'. Article 9 TEU mentions the equality of citizens in front of the European institutions, and Article 21 TEU sets forth the respect of the principle of equality in EU external action. Although these articles do not create any legal rights, their prominent position in the TEU shows that the EU is committed to ensuring equality (Howard, 2011; Ellis and Watson, 2012).

The TFEU contains a horizontal clause on non-discrimination in Article 10 TFEU,[9] and provides the EU with a legal basis for the EU non-discrimination legislation. Article 19 TFEU (former Article 13 EC) allows the EU to take action to combat discrimination on the named grounds of sex, racial or ethnic origin, religion or belief, disability, age or sexual orientation.

As will be further discussed below, none of the Treaty provisions mentions genetic data or health as grounds of discrimination. By contrast, genetic features are included as a ground of discrimination in Article 21 EU CFR. The EU CFR establishes a right to equality before the law and a prohibition of discrimination on a wider list of grounds than Article 19 TFEU, and this list is extensive, and open-ended, as will be clear from the words 'any grounds such as' (Howard, 2011: 787). Nevertheless, as clarified in the Explanation of the Charter, Article 21 EU CFR does not create any power to enact anti-discrimination laws in the areas of competence of Member States, nor does it lay down a sweeping ban of discrimination in wide-ranging areas.

Having regard to secondary legislation, former Article 13 EC (i.e. Article 19 TFEU) has been the legal base for several equality directives (so-called Article 13 Directives), which build upon the experience gained in the legislation to combat gender discrimination at the EU level.[10] Among the non-discrimination instruments, the most relevant in this context and for the purpose of the subsequent analysis, is Directive 2000/78/EC of 27 November 2000 establishing a general framework for equal treatment in employment and occupation (Employment Equality Directive). As provided for in Article 1 of this Employment Equality Directive, its purpose is

9 Article 10 TFEU reads as follows: '[i]n defining and implementing its policies and activities, the Union shall aim to combat discrimination based on sex, racial or ethnic origin, religion or belief, disability, age or sexual orientation'.

10 These Directives include: Directive 2000/78/EC of 27 November 2000 establishing a general framework for equal treatment in employment and occupation [2000] OJ L 303/16; Directive 2000/43/EC of 29 June 2000 implementing the principle of equal treatment between persons irrespective of racial or ethnic origin [2000] OJ L 180/22; Council Directive 2004/113/EC implementing the principle of equal treatment between men and women in the access to and supply of goods and services of 13 December 2004 [2004] OJ L ; Directive 2006/54/EC of the EP and of the Council of 5 July 2006 on the implementation of the principle of equal opportunities and equal treatment of men and women in matters of employment and occupation (recast) [2006] OJ L 204/23.

> to lay down a general framework for combating discrimination on the grounds of religion or belief, disability, age or sexual orientation as regards employment and occupation, with a view to putting into effect in the Member States the principle of equal treatment.

There is a significant amount of literature on the Employment Equality Directive and several of the CJEU's decisions have shaped the meaning and the scope of each of its provisions (Ellis and Watson, 2012; Waddington, 2013). For the purpose of this analysis, it suffices to point out that this directive bans both direct discrimination (differential treatment based on a specific characteristic) and indirect discrimination (any provision, criterion or practice which is neutral on its face but is liable to adversely affect one or more specific individuals or incite discrimination). Settled CJEU case law states that the principle of non-discrimination requires that comparable situations must not be treated differently and that different situations must not be treated in the same way, and a different treatment may be justified only if it is based on objective considerations and only if it is proportionate to the legitimate objective being pursued (*Carlos Garcia Avello v. Etat Belge* 2003). Harassment, which creates a hostile environment, is also deemed to be discrimination. The Employment Equality Directive requires Member States to provide for effective judicial remedies, bestow representative associations with *locus standi* to bring actions on behalf of individuals and provide for sanctions. Notably, the Employment Equality Directive imposes only minimum requirements and allows Member States to apply provisions which are more favorable to the protection of equal treatment than those laid down in the directive.

As it appears from Article 1, the Employment Equality Directive covers six grounds of discrimination and does not include genetic features among them. Is this missing ground an obstacle to ensuring protection from discrimination based solely on the nature of an individual's genotype?

It might be argued that a broad understanding of the concept of disability discrimination could also cover genetic discrimination. It is outside the scope of this chapter to explore the link between disability and genetic features in depth: we limit ourselves to recalling that genetic testing can predict a low or high probability of future disability, or can predict that certain genotypes will indicate disability in the future. The Employment Equality Directive could accordingly cover, under 'disability discrimination', any other discrimination on the ground of the prediction of future illness, or future loss of functions in a currently asymptomatic individual, or on the ground of a genetic vulnerability to future health problems.

At present, there is no definition of disability in the Employment Equality Directive, nor in other pieces of legislation. Thus, there are no textual arguments against a wide interpretation. It is noted that this wide interpretation would be in line with Article 21 EU CFR, which by virtue of Article 6(1) TEU, has a constitutional value. In addition, such an extensive interpretation could be considered to be in compliance with the UN Convention on the Rights of Persons with Disabilities (hereinafter 'the Convention' and the 'CRPD'), ratified by the the European Community (now, of course, the EU) by means of the Council decision of 26 November 2009 (Council Decision 2010/48/EC).[11]

In this respect, it must be recalled that Article 1 CRPD states that

> Persons with disabilities include those who have long-term physical, mental, intellectual or sensory impairments which in interaction with various barriers may hinder their full and effective participation in society on an equal basis with others.

This is not a strict definition (it is placed in the article on 'Purpose' rather than under Article 2 on 'Definitions') and it is non-exhaustive (Marchisio et *al.*, 2010). This means that implementing legislation should treat disability as a socially constructed phenomenon and could include disabled people with short-term conditions and also genetic differences. Article 2 defines 'Discrimination on the basis of disability' as follows:

> any distinction, exclusion or restriction on the basis of disability which has the purpose or effect of impairing or nullifying the recognition, enjoyment or exercise, on an equal basis with others, of all human rights and fundamental freedoms in the political, economic, social, cultural, civil or any other field. It includes all forms of discrimination, including denial of reasonable accommodation.

The quoted wide-ranging notion of discrimination covers not only persons with actual disabilities, but also persons with 'putative' disabilities, or persons who, while not having a disability presently, might acquire a disability in the future, or persons who simply are perceived as having a disability.

The CRPD currently enjoys a quasi-constitutional status in the EU legal system, beneath the Treaties but above secondary law. As a consequence, to put it simply, EU secondary law must, so far as is possible, be interpreted in a manner that is consistent with the CRPD: if the wording of secondary EU legislation is open to more than one interpretation, preference should be given, as far as possible, to the interpretation which renders the European provision consistent with the Convention (Casolari, 2011; *Commission v. Germany* 1996). The CJEU has recognised the existence of this duty of consistent interpretation, by virtue of the 'sub-constitutional' ranking of international agreements in the EU, independently of the direct effect of the international law provisions concerned (Ferri, 2010; Ferri, 2013; *Řízení*

11 Council Decision 2010/48/EC, [2010] OJ L 23/35.

*Letového Provozu ČR, s. p. v. Bundesamt für Finanzen*: para 52; *Interfood GmbH v. Hauptzollamt Hamburg*: para 6).

Up to now, the CJEU has not been confronted with any question regarding the potential of the directive to be extended to genetic discrimination. However, the Court has released a few decisions on disability discrimination. In the absence of a legislative definition, the CJEU, in *Chacon Navas* (2006), had adopted a narrow concept of disability, based on the antiquated medical model of disability,[12] and had clearly distinguished sickness from disability (Waddington, 2007). In *Chacon Navas*, the Court clarified that fundamental rights which form an integral part of the general principles of EU law include the general principle of non-discrimination, but

> it does not follow from this that the scope of Directive 2000/78 should be extended by analogy beyond the discrimination based on the grounds listed exhaustively in Article 1 thereof.

In the *Coleman* case (2008), the CJEU admitted discrimination by association, accepting that discrimination and harassment because of association with a person with a disability was also covered by the Employment Equality Directive (Waddington, 2009). However, in this decision the Court again highlighted that

> the scope of Directive 2000/78 cannot be extended beyond the discrimination based on the grounds listed exhaustively in Article 1 of the directive, with the result that a person who has been dismissed by his employer solely on account of sickness cannot fall within the scope of the general framework established by Directive 2000/78.

This case law has been recently overcome: the CJEU has embraced a more wide-ranging definition of disability openly in line with Article 1 CRPD, and reflective of the social model of disability.

In Joined Cases *Ring and Werge* (2013) the CJEU distanced itself from the position it took in *Chacon Navas* and interpreted the definition of disability in light of the CRPD. The most recent case, in line with *Ring and Werge*, is

12 The medical model tends to view persons with disabilities as objects who are to be managed or cared for, while the social emphasises respect for the equal human rights of persons with disabilities (Barnes and Mercer, 2010). As noted by Waddington, according to the CJEU the cause of the disadvantage is the 'impairment' which an individual has. Therefore, the problem lies in the impaired individual, and not in the reaction of society to the impairment or the organisation of society. This model can be contrasted with a social model of disability, which is reflected in the CRPD. The social model is based on a socio-political approach which argues that disability stems primarily from the failure of the social environment to adjust to the needs and aspirations of people with impairments (Waddington, 2013).

*Commission v. Italy* (2013). The case originated from action for failure to fulfil EU obligations brought by the Commission against Italy. The Commission affirmed that Italy did not correctly transpose Directive 2000/78 into its national law and, in particular, it did not ensure, that reasonable accommodation in the workplace is to apply to all persons with disabilities, all employers and all aspects of the employment relationship (in breach of the directive). In its decision the CJEU confirmed that, while it is true that the concept of a 'disability' is not directly defined in the Employment Equality Directive, it should be interpreted, on the basis of the CRPD.

We can conclude that 'genetic features' is a missing ground in the Employment Equality Directive, as well as in Article 19 TFEU. However, *Ring and Werge* and *Commission v. Italy* leave the door open to the wide interpretation of the Employment Equality Directive in light of the CRPD to cover under disability discrimination also genetic discrimination.

## 5. The European Commission's 2008 proposal for a new Equality Directive

It is noted that there is no actual, concrete protection against genetic discrimination in the EU. Even though the Court of Justice enhanced the protection provided by the directive through its interpretation, as envisaged above, genetic discrimination would be banned only in the employment context, excluding the insurance field.

In 2008, the Commission proposed a new directive (COM (2008) 426) extending the material scope of the provisions against discrimination on the ground of religion and belief, disability, age and sexual orientation beyond the area of employment, into the fields of social protection, including social security and health care; social advantages; education; and access to and supply of goods and other services which are available to the public, including housing (Bell, 2009; Howard, 2011; Waddington, 2011; Ellis and Watson, 2012: 372). The proposed directive replicates those parts of the material scope of the Racial Equality Directive which were not included in the Employment Equality Directive. However, as noted by Howard (2011), the scope is still not as broad that of the Race Directive, as Article 3 of the proposal contains more exceptions (Howard, 2011: 789). Waddington, in her analysis of the proposal, underlines that many Member States are still querying the extent of the EU power to legislate in areas such as health and social protection, and this makes the scope of the proposal blurred and still vague.

The original text of the proposal follows the pattern of the existing directives, with few notable exceptions. For instance, as underlined by Bell, the most striking novelty lies in the definition of discrimination: the proposal conceptualises 'denial of reasonable accommodation' as a form of discrimination, in compliance with the CRPD (Bell, 2009: 10).

For the purpose of this investigation, it is noted that the proposal as it stands does not mention genetic features and replicates the choice of the existing directives in not providing any definition of the discrimination grounds.

The European Parliament released a 'Legislative Resolution to the Proposal' in which it proposes a number of amendments (2009).[13] These include adding the reference to the fact that the directive complies with the CRPD (Recital 2b of the Preamble) and a provision that would make clear that assumptive discrimination (i.e. discrimination against someone because the discriminator thinks they have a particular religion or belief, disability, age or sexual orientation) is included (Article 4 para 4a). Another interesting amendment suggested by the European Parliament is to add to Article 4(1) of the directive a sentence that makes it clear that 'disability' is understood in the light of the CRPD, which includes persons with chronic diseases. However, no attempts to include genetic features as a ground of discrimination or to mention genetic discrimination have been made.

If approved as it stands, it is highly doubtful that the text will advance the protection of EU citizens from genetic discrimination. Nevertheless, genetic discrimination should be again covered under the umbrella concept of disability.

Analogously, in the event that the amendments proposed by the Parliament are approved, no clear protection against a more disadvantageous treatment on the sole ground of genetic data is given. Nevertheless, the direct reference to the CRPD could favour the extensive interpretation of the ground of disability. The inclusion of a provision on assumptive discrimination could also facilitate the protection against genetic discrimination, given that the discriminatory treatment is based on perceived – not actual – disability. But, again, in any event, a key role will be left to the CJEU.

Even if the Court ruled that genetic discrimination would be covered by the directive, the text (as it stands now) contains an exception which is likely to hamper protection in the insurance context. Article 2(7) authorises 'proportionate differences in treatment' in financial services, provided that 'age or disability is a key factor in the assessment of risk based on relevant and accurate actuarial or statistical data'. In the Explanatory Memorandum, the Commission argues that 'the use of age or disability by insurers and banks to assess the risk profile of customers does not necessarily represent discrimination: it depends on the product'. This wording, at least potentially, could be used to allow insurance companies to charge

13 P6_TA(2009)0211 European Parliament Legislative Resolution of 2 April 2009 on the Proposal for a Council Directive Implementing the Principle of Equal Treatment between Persons Irrespective of Religion or Belief, Disability, Age or Sexual Orientation (COM (2008)0426-C6-291/2008-2008/0140(CNS)).

individuals different rates or vary coverage based on genetic predisposition, or even to discourage some at-risk individuals from getting an insurance contract.

It is too soon to make any concluding remarks on this proposal. At this stage, it is fairly unclear whether and when the text will be adopted. Even less clear is whether the text will be modified again by the Council, whether any of the amendments proposed by the Parliament will be approved and included in the final text. The proposed directive has been examined in the Council for more than four years now, and still discussions seem needed on a number of issues, such as the division of competences, the overall scope and subsidiarity and the disability provisions. At the time of the May 2014 Parliament elections, it seemed likely that the text would not be adopted within a short space of time.

Future debates could hopefully bring some developments in the text. Although the inclusion of genetic features as a ground of discrimination seems quite challenging, the provision on assumptive discrimination proposed by the Parliament could be made clearer and more explicit. Even in the best-case scenario, though, the proposed directive is only confined to addressing some of the perceived shortcomings of the Employment Equality Directive. As underlined by several scholars, it does not attempt to make a wider reform of EU anti-discrimination legislation. For this reason, it appears inadequate to address and prevent the misuse of genetic data outside the employment context.

## 6. The way forward: a new 'Genetic-Discrimination Directive'?

Currently the EU does not provide any satisfactory protection against the misuse of genetic information. As discussed in the preceding section, the proposal for a new directive extending the material scope of the provisions against discrimination on the ground of religion and belief, disability, age and sexual orientation beyond the area of employment does not contemplate the prohibition of unjustified disadvantage based on unalterable personal characteristics. Regardless of any interpretative efforts on the existing text of the Employment Equality Directive, and any possible improvement of the text of the proposal, the best solution would probably involve passing a new 'stand-alone' directive, aimed at preventing the discriminatory use of genetic information in employment and in access to goods and services. Although adopting a horizontal approach would strengthen the idea that all forms of discrimination are equally abhorrent and would discourage the creation of any hierarchy among the grounds, a stand-alone piece of legislation would potentially capture the specific characteristic of genetic information and the challenges linked to the stigma of genetic conditions.

The most relevant question in this respect is whether the EU actually has the competence to adopt such a piece of legislation. From 1997 (when former Article 13 EC was added), the EU has acquired a solid cross-cutting competence on non-discrimination on different grounds, beside the nationality and sex one which was affirmed first (Bell 2002; Ellis 2005; Martin, 2006). As mentioned above, the TFEU contains a horizontal clause on non-discrimination in Article 10 TFEU and provides the EU with a legal basis for EU non-discrimination legislation. However, EU action can only been taken in those areas which fall within the limits of the powers conferred by the Treaty. Even though 'what falls within the scope of EU law differs depending on the context and on what idea the scope of EU law is based' (Derlén and Lindholm, 2012: 97), in general terms, it can be stated that employment and insurance fall within the scope of EU powers.[14]

Article 19 TFEU, which is the legal basis for non-discrimination acts, does not mention 'genetic information' or 'health' as a prohibited ground. Excluding the modification of Article 19 TFEU to include a new ground of discrimination (procedure set forth in Article 48 TEU would be long and complex), as underlined in section 5 with regard to the Employment Equality Directive, and as emphasised by Gerards and Janssen, there would be the possibility that discrimination on the ground of genetic make-up is covered by the wider ground of (future) disability (Gerards and Janssen, 2006). Whilst such a wide interpretation might be almost clear with regard to the directive, having regard to the latest CJEU's decision, it should not be expected too easily in regard to Article 19 TFEU. There is no obligation to interpret the Treaties in light of the CRPD. This is evident in *Microsoft Corp. v. Commission* (2007), when the Court of First Instance rejected the argument of the applicant, according to which former Article 82 EC (now Article 102 TFEU) had to be interpreted in the light of the TRIPS Agreement (Agreement on Trade Related Aspects of Intellectual Property Rights). The Court held

> that the principle of consistent interpretation... invoked by the Court of Justice applies only where the international agreement at issue prevails over the provision of Community law concerned. Since an international agreement... does not prevail over primary Community

14 The EU has a shared competence in the field of employment (covering freedom of movement, equal treatment, working conditions, including working time, part-time and fixed-term work, and posting of workers, information and consultation of workers, including in the event of collective redundancies and transfers of undertakings) and has also a solid competence in the field of insurance within the realisation of the internal market (freedom of movement of services and capitals). Currently, the TFEU considers insurance in Article 58 para. 2 (liberalisation of banking and insurance). Article 58 para 2 reads as follows: 'The liberalisation of banking and insurance services connected with movements of capital shall be effected in step with the liberalisation of movement of capital'.

> law, that principle does not apply where, as here, the provision which falls to be interpreted is Article 82 EC.

However, even though the principle of consistent interpretation does not apply to EU primary law, as underlined by de Paor:

> the conclusion of the UN CRPD by the EU provides an added dimension to the debate of regulating genetic information . . . [and] acts as an impetus to action in this area.
>
> (de Paor, 2013b)

In addition, Article 19 TFEU might be a suitable legal basis for a directive on genetic discrimination if its content is interpreted in light of Article 21 EU CFR. Although the Charter does not alter the extent of powers granted under Article 19 TFEU, it has, by virtue of Article 6(1) TEU, the same legal value as the Treaties. As a consequence, respect for fundamental rights is a legal requirement, subject to the scrutiny of the CJEU, and a condition of the lawfulness of EU acts (Joined Cases *Volker und Markus Schecke and Eifert* 2010). In addition, the Commission in its Strategy on Smart Regulation (COM (2010) 543 final) and in the Communication on Strategy for the effective implementation of the Charter of Fundamental Rights (COM (2010) 573 final) affirmed that the Charter should be taken into account throughout the policy cycle.

Again, the CJEU could play a vital role in enforcing the potential of the Charter in the protection of EU citizens from genetic discrimination. As underlined by Howard, in line with other scholars,

> although the Charter does not create new rights, both the way the Charter itself is interpreted by the Court of Justice and the way this Court could use it to interpret other provisions of EU law could extend the existing rights and the protection against discrimination in new directions.

A new directive on non-discrimination on ground of genetic data based on Article 19 TFEU read in conjunction with Article 21 EU CFR and the CRPD appears feasible. As regards a directive on non-discrimination on the ground of genetic data, a double legal basis could also offer a viable solution.

It is worth recalling that the choice of the legal base for a measure may not depend simply on an institution's conviction as to the objective pursued but must be based on objective factors which are amenable to judicial review (*Commission of the European Communities v. Council of the European Communities* 1989). In general, if an EU measure has more than one purpose and one of the purposes can be identified as the main or predominant purpose, that measure must be adopted on the legal base corresponding with that main purpose. Only in exceptional circumstances, when a measure has more than one purpose without one being secondary, can it be based on more than one legal base ('dual legal base').

A well tailored piece of legislation banning genetic discrimination in the fields of employment and access to goods and services would create a level playing field on the use of genetic information by business operators. It would enhance the functioning of the Internal Market. Hence, together with Article 19 TFEU, an additional legal basis could be found in Article 114 TFEU (which aims to ensure the effective functioning of the internal market in the EU). Article 114 previously acted as the legal basis for various pieces of legislation which include a disability dimension (Waddington, 2009), and also the concluding decision of the CRPD was based on both Article 19 and 114 TFEU (former Article 13 and 95 EC). The latter example, in particular, might offer an influential precedent and inspire a double-based proposal.

## 7. Conclusion

Having conducted the above analysis, it is quite challenging to draw definite conclusions from this blurred and changing legislative scenario.

Up to now, the EU proposes to adopt a privacy approach to protect access to and disclosure of an individual's genetic information. Even if the current text of the 'Proposal for a Regulation on the protection of individuals with regard to the processing of personal data and on the free movement of such data' presents some drawbacks, it definitely represents a welcome step forward in the protection of genetic information. But even if employers and insurers or other actors are prohibited from having access to genetic information, EU citizens will also have to be protected from the misuse of such information.

In the early 1990s, legal scholarship (in particular in the US) had already underlined that the use of genetic tests could lead to discrimination based solely on the nature of an individual's genotype (*inter alia* Gostin, 1991). But in addition to the academic discourse, there has been a growing understanding that the spread of genetic testing brings with it the risk of discrimination (Rothstein and Knoppers, 1996). Notwithstanding these developments, as Lemke recognises in his latest book, as genetic discrimination is a multifaceted and complex phenomenon (Lemke, 2013), there is the need for the law to address it. Such a need is particularly strong in the EU which is committed to equality, but is also founded on an Internal Market without any barriers.

Even by exploiting the potential of interpretation by including discrimination on grounds of genetic make-up under the wider ground of (future) disability, due to its limited scope, the Employment Equality Directive offers a low degree of protection. The 2008 Proposal for a New Equality Directive ignores genetic discrimination and provides very little innovation in this regard. Even if approved (and this outcome cannot be taken for granted), the text hypothetically offers little safeguard.

The preferable way forward, although a lengthy procedure due to the complexity of the EU legislative process, appears a new single-ground directive to ban any disadvantageous treatment of an individual based solely or primarily on his or her genotype or because of a specific genetic defect. The EU has competence to legislate, and although there is also the possibility that some Member States may question this competence or do not support the adoption of specific legislation, this seems to be the preferable avenue to pursue in order for the EU to usher in the new era of genetic evolution.

## References


Adjin-Tettey, Elizabeth, A. (2013) 'Potential for Genetic Discrimination in Access to Insurance: Is There a Dark Side to Increased Availability of Genetic Information?' *Alberta Law Review* 50(3): 577.

Annecca, M.T. (2011) 'Test Genetici e Diritti della Persona', in Canestrari S. *et al.* (eds) *Trattato di Biodiritto. Il Governo del Corpo.* Milano: Giuffrè, pp. 391–422.

Article 29 Data Protection Working Party (Article 29 DPWP) (2004) *Working Document on Genetic Data.* Available at: http://ec.europa.eu/justice/policies/privacy/docs/wpdocs/2004/wp91_en.pdf [accessed 30 November 2013].

Barbujani, G. and Tassi, F. (2012) 'Genetic Data in Forensic Science: Use, Misuse and Abuse', in Bin, R. and Lucchi, N. (eds) *Biotech Innovations and Fundamental Rights.* Milan-Dordrecht: Springer, pp. 243–60.

Barnes, C. and Mercer, G. (2010) *Exploring Disability.* Cambridge: Polity Press.

Belfiore, R. (2011) 'Raccolta e scambio dei dati genetici nell'Unione europea? Available at: www.biodiritto.org/images/progetto/Belfiore.pdf [accessed 30 November 2013].

Bell, M. (2009) 'Advancing EU Anti-discrimination Law: The European Commission's 2008 Proposal for a New Directive' *Equal Rights Review* 3: 7–18.

Bell, M. (2002) *Anti-discrimination Law and the European Union.* Oxford; New York: Oxford University Press.

Beqiraj, J. (2011) 'Prohibition of Genetic Discrimination: Applicative Perspectives under the Lens of Human Rights Protection' *La Comunità internazionale*, pp. 91–112.

Campiglio, C. (2008) 'Il principio di non discriminazione genetica nella recente prassi internazionale' *Diritti umani e diritto internazionale*, pp. 513–534.

Casolari, F. (2011) 'Giving Indirect Effect to International Law within the EU Legal Order: The Doctrine of Consistent Interpretation', in Cannizzaro, E., Palchetti, P. and Wessel, R. A. (eds) *International Law as Law of the European Union.* Leiden/Boston: Martinus Nijhoff Publishers, pp. 394–422.

Coalition for Genetic Fairness (2004) *Faces of Genetic Discrimination.* Available at: www.nationalpartnership.org/site/DocServer/FacesofGeneticDiscrimination.pdf?docID=971 [accessed 30 November 2013].

de Paor, A. (2013a) 'US and EU Perspectives On Genetic Discrimination in Employment and Insurance: Striking A Balance in a Battlefield of Competing Rights? in Waddington, L., Quinn, G. and Flynn, E. (eds) *European Yearbook of Disability Law* 4: 99–144. Antwerp: Intersentia.

de Paor, A. (2013b) 'Advancing Science and Controlling the Misuse of Genetic

Information in Employment and Insurance – Towards an Effective European Union Level Regulatory Framework' (unpublished).

Derlén, M. and Lindholm, J. (2012) 'Three Ideas: The Scope of EU Law Protecting Against Discrimination' in: Derlén, M. and Lindholm, J. (eds) *Volume in Honor of Pär Hallström.* Uppsala: Iustus, pp. 77–100. Available at: http://ssrn.com/abstract=2114247 [accessed 30 November 2013].

Ellis, E. (2005) *EU Anti-Discrimination Law.* Oxford; New York: Oxford University Press.

Ellis, E. and Watson, P. (2012) *EU Anti-Discrimination Law.* Oxford; New York: Oxford University Press.

European Group on Ethics in Science and New Technologies – EGE (2003) Opinion No.18 – 'Ethical Aspects of Genetic Testing in the Workplace'. Available at: http://ec.europa.eu/bepa/european-group-ethics/docs/avis18_compl_en.pdf [accessed 30 November 2013].

Ferri, D. (2013) *The UN Convention on the Rights of Persons with Disabilities as an 'Integral Part' of EU Law,* EUI Working Papers, AEL 2013/10 (forthcoming).

Ferri, D. (2010) 'The Conclusion of the UN Convention on the Rights of Persons with Disabilities by the EC/EU: A Constitutional Perspective' in Waddington, L. and Quinn, G. (eds) *European Yearbook of Disability Law* 2: 47. Antwerp: Intersentia.

Geelen, E., Horstman, K., Marcelis, C. L. M., Doevendans, P. A. and Van Hoyweghen, I. (2012) 'Unravelling Fears of Genetic Discrimination: An Exploratory Study of Dutch HCM Families in an Era of Genetic Non-discrimination Acts' *European Journal of Human Genetics* 20: 1018–1023.

GeneWatch, *Genetic Discrimination by Insurers and Employers: Still Looming on the Horizon* Available at: www.genewatch.org/uploads/f03c6d66a9b354535738483c1c3d49e4/GeneticTestingUpdate2006.pdf [accessed 30 November 2013].

Gerards, J. (2005) 'General Issues Concerning Genetic Information' in Gerards, J. H., Heringa, W. A. and Janssen, H. L. (eds) *Genetic Discrimination and Genetic Privacy in a Comparative Perspective.* Antwep: Intersentia, p. 24.

Gerards, J. and Janssen, H. L. (2006) 'Regulation of Genetic and Other Health Information in a Comparative Perspective' *European Journal of Health Law* 13: 372–374.

Gostin, L. (1991) 'Genetic Discrimination: The Use of Genetically Based Diagnostic and Prognostic Tests by Employers and Insurers' *American Journal of Law and Medicine* 17: 109–114.

Henneman, L. and Van Hoyweghen, I. (2013) 'Moving Beyond Public Fear of Genetic Discrimination' *Health and Ageing Newsletter* 28, April. Available at: www.genevaassociation.org/media/77290/ga2013-health28-henneman-van_hoyweghen.pdf [accessed 30 November 2013].

Hervey, T. and McHale, J. V. (2004) *Health Law and the European Union.* Cambridge; New York: Cambridge University Press.

Howard, E. (2011) 'EU Equality Law: Three Recent Developments' *European Law Journal* 17: 785–803.

Joly, Y., Ngueng Feze, I. and Simard, J. (2013) 'Genetic Discrimination and Life Insurance: A Systematic Review of the Evidence' *BMC Medicine* 11(1): 25. Available at: www.ncbi.nlm.nih.gov/pubmed/23369270 [accessed 30 November 2013].

Lemke, T. (2013) *Perspectives on Genetic Discrimination.* New York: Routledge.

Lemke, T. (2005) 'Beyond Genetic Discrimination. Problems and Perspectives of a Contested Notion' *Genomics, Society and Policy* 1: 22–40.

Marchisio, S., Cera, R. and Della Fina, V. (2010) *La Convenzione delle Nazioni Unite sui diritti delle persone con disabilità. Commentario.* Roma: Aracne.

Martin, D. (2006) *Égalité et non-discrimination dans la jurisprudence communotaire.* Bruxelles: Buylant.

Motoc, I. V. (2009) 'The International Law of Genetic Discrimination: The Power of Never Again' in Murphy, T. (ed.) *New Technologies and Human Rights.* Oxford: Oxford University Press.

Murray, T. H. (1997) 'Genetic Exceptionalism and 'Future Diaries': Is Genetic Information Different from Other Medical Information?' in Rothstein, M. A. (ed.) *Genetic Secrets: Protecting Privacy and Confidentiality in the Genetic Era.* New Haven, CT: Yale University Press.

Roscam Abbing, H. (2012) 'Medical Examinations, Insurance and Employment: Where Are the European Standards?' *European Journal of Health Law* 19: 115–120.

Rothstein, M. A. and Knoppers, B. (1996) 'Legal Aspects of Genetics, Work and Insurance in North America and Europe' *European Journal of Health Law* 3: 143–161.

Rothstein, M. A. and Joly, Y. (2009) 'Genetic Information and Insurance Underwriting: Contemporary Issues and Approaches in the Global Economy' in Atkinson, P., Glaser, P. and Lock, M. (eds) *Handbook of Genetics and Society: Mapping the New Genomic Era.* London: Routledge.

Scaffardi, L. (2008) 'Legal Protection and Ethical Management of Genetic Databases: Challenges of the European Process of Harmonization', *Jean Monnet Working Papers.* Available at: www.jeanmonnetprogram.org/archive/papers/08/081901.pdf [accessed 15 May 2014].

Stefanini, E. (2008) *Dati genetici e diritti fondamentali. Profili di diritto comparato ed europeo.* Padova: Cedam.

Trojsi, A. (2009) '"Biodiritto del lavoro" e tutela antidiscriminatoria: i Dati genetici del lavoratore'. Available at: www.biodiritto.org/images/progetto/TROJSI.pdf [accessed 30 November 2013].

Victor, J. M. (2013) 'The EU General Data Protection Regulation: Toward a Property Regime for Protecting Data Privacy' *Yale Law Journal* 513. Available at: http://ssrn.com/abstract=2317903 [accessed 30 November 2013].

Viola de Azevedo Cunha, M. (2013) *Market Integration Through Data Protection: An Analysis of the Insurance and Financial Industries in the EU.* Milan; Dordrecht: Springer.

Waddington, L. (2013) 'Equal to the Task? Re-Examining EU Equality Law in Light of the United Nations Convention on the Rights of Persons with Disabilities' in Waddington, L., Quinn, G. and Flynn, E. (eds) *European Yearbook of Disability Law* 4: 169–200. Antwerp: Intersentia.

Waddington, L. (2011) 'Future Prospects for EU Equality Law. Lessons to be Learnt from the Proposed Equal Treatment Directive' *European Law Review* 2: 163–184.

Waddington, L. (2009) 'Case C-303/06, *S. Coleman v. Attridge Law and Steve Law,* Judgment of the Grand Chamber of the Court of Justice of 17 July 2008' *Common Market Law Review* 46(2): 665–681.

Waddington, L. (2007) Case C-13/05, *Chacón Navas v. Eurest Colectividades SA,* Judgment of the Grand Chamber of 11 July 2006 *Common Market Law Review* 44(2): 487–499.

## Cases

Joined Cases C-468/10 and C-469/10 *ASNEF and FECEMD* [2011] ECR I-12181.
Case C-148/02 *Carlos Garcia Avello v. Etat Belge* [2003] ECR I-11613.
Case C-61/94 *Commission v. Germany* [1996] ECR I-3989.
Case C-312/11 *Commission v. Italy* 4 July 2013 (not yet published).
Case C-11/88 *Commission of the European Communities v. Council of the European Communities* [1989] ECR *3799.*
Joined Cases C- 335/11 and C- 337/11 *HK Danmark, acting on behalf of Jette Ring v. Dansk almennyttigt Boligselskab* (C-335/11) and *HK Danmark, acting on behalf of Lone Skouboe Werge v. Dansk Arbejdsgiverforening, acting on behalf of Pro Display A/S, in liquidation* (C-337/11), 11 April 2013 (not yet published).
Case C-473/12 *Institut professionnel des agents immobiliers (IPI) v. Geoffrey Englebert* (not yet published).
Case 92/71 *Interfood GmbH v. Hauptzollamt Hamburg* [1972] ECR 231.
Case C-101/01 *Lindqvist* [2003] ECR I-2971.
Case T-201/04 *Microsoft Corp. v. Commission* [2007] ECR II-3601 [798].
Case C-335/05 *Řízení Letového Provozu ČR, s. p. v. Bundesamt für Finanzen* [2007] ECR I-4307.
Case C- 303/06 *S. Coleman v. Attridge Law and Steve Law* [2008] ECR I-5603.
Case C-13/05 *Sonia Chacón Navas v. Eurest Colectividades SA* [2006] ECR I-6467.
Joined Cases C-92/09 and C-93/09 *Volker und Markus Schecke and Eifert* [2010] ECR I-11063.

## Legislation

Charter of Fundamental Rights of the European Union, 7 December 2000, *Official Journal of the European Communities*, 18 December 2000 (2000/C 364/01).
Charter of Fundamental Rights COM (2010) 543 final.
Commission in its Strategy on Smart Regulation (COM (2010) 543 final.
Council and Parliament Directive 95/46/EC of 24 October 1995 on the protection of individuals with regard to the processing of personal data and on the free movement of such data [1995] OJ L 281/31.
Council Decision 2010/48/EC [2010] OJ L 23/35.
Council Directive 2000/78/EC of 27 November 2000 establishing a general framework for equal treatment in employment and occupation [2000] OJ L 303/16.
Council of Europe, Convention for the Protection of Human Rights and the Dignity of the Human Being with regard to the application of biology and msedicine: Convention on Human Rights and Biomedicine, ETS. No. 164 (1997).
European Parliament's Resolution on the ethical and legal problems concerning genetic manipulation, 16 March 1989.
Proposal for a Council Directive on implementing the principle of equal treatment between persons irrespective of religion or belief, disability, age or sexual orientation, COM (2008) 426 final.
Proposal for a Directive on the protection of individuals with regard to the processing of personal data by competent authorities for the purposes of prevention, investigation, detection or prosecution of criminal offences or the execution of criminal penalties, and the free movement of such data (COM (2012) 10 final).

Proposal for a Regulation of the European Parliament and of the Council on the protection of individuals with regard to the processing of personal data and on the free movement of such data (General Data Protection Regulation) COM (2012) 11 final.
Treaty on the European Union (2007/ C 306/01).
Treaty on the Functioning of the European Union (2008/ C 115/01).

# 16 Conclusion

*Aisling de Paor, Gerard Quinn and Peter Blanck*

Against the backdrop of ground-breaking scientific and technological developments in the field of genetics, this book provides insights into the myriad of ethical and legal dilemmas arising as science and technology continue to advance. It illustrated the multifaceted nature of this field and explored ways of addressing these issues. It examined US and EU perspectives on this issue, drawing upon the US experience in considering the way forward and the future orientation of EU law and policy in this area.

This book considers the need for an EU-level regulatory response to address and control the use of genetic information by third parties, such as employers and insurance companies, through the examination of transatlantic perspectives, assessing the current fragmented patchwork of protections in the EU and considering the relevant regulatory benchmarks, such as the EU Charter of Fundamental Rights and the United Nations Convention on the Rights of Persons with Disabilities.

On drawing these objectives together, the following section presents the conclusions, which are divided into five parts and offer evaluations based on the chapters contributed. This chapter then presents the final conclusions found, including the suggestions for a legislative framework at EU level.

## 1. Section 1

By highlighting the scientific and technological framework, Chapter 2 explains that genetic science and technology is advancing rapidly, with the result that genetic testing technologies are becoming more sophisticated and refined. Genetic information is more available and accessible to individuals and to interested third parties, for health purposes and also for non-health purposes. This chapter provides insights into potential as well as limitations of genetic science and technology. Scientific and technological advances are revealing the genetic basis of a wide range of disease and disability, as well as behaviour and personality traits. It offers the potential for predicting the onset and potential severity of future disability and disease. With these genetic advances come economic opportunities, as well as challenging ethical, social and legal considerations. This chapter provides the necessary scientific context for examination of these issues.

## 2. Section 2

Against this scientific backdrop, Section 2 extrapolates the ethical and legal issues as well as some of the public policy concerns arising as a result of scientific and technological advances. Although there are no definitive answers to these ethical and legal issues, these chapters provide an ethical perspective to this discussion, introduce legal issues and highlight use and application of genetic information in clinical and third-party settings.

The first chapter in this section provides a theoretical framework and introduces the concept of diversity ethics as a means of addressing the impact of emerging genetic technologies. This chapter advocates the notion of genetic diversity in society and recognising individuals' inherent differences. By highlighting historical abuses of science and genetics, this chapter offers insights into the potential for a new type of eugenics movement to advance in Europe and the undesirable implications of such a regime. Indeed, such a new form of subtle eugenics is a possibility if the appropriate regulatory and policy safeguards are not in place.

Stein *et al.* explore the use of genetic technologies in the clinical context and highlight the bioethical challenges presented when genetic information is used and misused in medicine, with particular focus on concerns arising as regards informed consent. This chapter examines ethical issues raised in the reproductive context, detailing the complex choices presented for patients, as well as the clinical responsibility necessary. On highlighting the practical challenges presented in clinical practice, this chapter advocates greater awareness, education and training amongst the medical community, at all levels, with a view to enhancing the application and effectiveness of genomics for patients.

Joly *et al.* provide an overview of the use and application of genetic technologies outside of the therapeutic relationship. This chapter offers insights into the misuse of genetic information in a range of third-party contexts from an ethical, social and legal perspective. In providing an overview of the regulatory regimes at national and international level, this chapter illustrates approaches taken, as well as the regulatory concerns arising in the field. It looks at the case law that has been generated in this area, illustrating the complexity of the issues arising.

Sections 1 and 2 of this book provide a background framework from which to consider the issue of regulation. By highlighting the concerns arising at the intersection of advancing science, technology and ethics, it facilitates a focused discussion of this topic and presents a picture indicating the need for regulation in this area.

## 3. Section 3

Section 3 focuses on the US legislative response. The US is arguably a pioneer in this area and has introduced federal-level legislation tailored to the regulation of genetic information in the fields of employment and health insurance. There is much to be learned from the US approach as illustrated in these three chapters. GINA is a pre-emptive law, introduced with a view to enhancing public confidence, anticipating a type of discrimination that is likely to accelerate in the future, as science and technology continue to advance.

This section highlights the historical background and civil rights framework within which GINA was introduced. The legislation was needed in consideration of the history of eugenics and misuse of science in the US, as depicted by Blanck and de Paor. Such history of eugenics is also evident in Europe, which may provide the historical context to compel legislation in this area in the EU. Similarly, there is an absence of evidence of genetic discrimination and misuse of genetic information in the EU in this area (as was the case in the US). This section looks at the legislative framework in place prior to GINA. GINA was introduced to address the unsatisfactory patchwork of laws at state level, as well as the incomplete protections at federal level. This is comparable to the current patchwork of laws that exists amongst the EU Member States and the fragmented protections at EU level.

This section analyses GINA in detail, with a focus on the objective and rationale of the legislation, as well as its definitions, provisions and exceptions. It looks at enforcement and penalty provisions contained in the legislation and how this is operating in practice, highlighting the challenges encountered in regulating this area. The decision to adopt a non-discrimination approach is noted, and such an approach similarly merits consideration in the European context, and indeed may support an argument that a more uniform EU-level approach is preferable.

Section 3 also examines the effectiveness of GINA as a non-discrimination law and looks at its impact in practice, in addressing the misuse of genetic information in the employment and health insurance fields. It highlights shortcomings with the legislation and practical challenges arising, particularly in the employment context. Although not a perfect piece of legislation, and although there are evident gaps in protection, GINA has had a positive impact upon the protection of genetic information in certain scenarios, and in terms of recognising this issue within the civil rights framework. The US did well to reconcile the competing interests at stake including the concerns of genetic discrimination, genetic privacy and the legitimate interests of employers and insurers. The EU can look to the US and reflect upon how it has achieved this balance in light of its social, cultural and historical background.

## 4. Section 4

In light of the scientific and technological background, and in consideration of the comparative benchmark in the US, Section 4 focuses on the EU perspectives and builds the case for an EU-level regulatory response. It looks at the current legislative framework, at Member State level and EU level, with focus on non-discrimination and privacy, as well as the emerging legislative benchmarks which are of relevance in this area. This section identifies the gaps in protection and the relevant legislative reforms taking place.

This section also focuses particularly on the perspectives of relevant stakeholders, particularly in the contexts of employment and insurance, as reflected in Davey's and de Paor's chapters. These chapters extrapolate the ethical and legal issues arising in these contexts and the relevant legislative position in the EU. They refer to the conflict of competing rights that arises between commercial interests and fundamental human rights, and highlight the need to recognise a balance and acknowledge the position of all stakeholders.

This section highlights the moral framework of the Council of Europe in this area, as illustrated particularly in Roscam Abbing's chapter. There is a growing awareness in the Council of Europe of scientific and technological developments, and the challenges presented from an ethical and legal perspective. The European Convention of Human Rights provides a human rights framework, and the case law of the European Court of Human Rights has recognised the privacy of genetic information, as well as discrimination on the basis of genetic predisposition to disability. Although it has limited application and effectiveness, the Biomedicine Convention (and its Protocol) provides guidance on these issues, from a moral perspective. This chapter found that soft law instruments of the Council of Europe have addressed this area and offer guidance. The Council of Europe has acknowledged the need to respond to scientific and technological advances and formulate a regulatory response based on a human rights framework.

Section 4 documents the significant diversity in the EU Member State responses, thereby indicating a patchwork of diverging protections. It also highlights the challenges of regulating this area, as well as the current lack of empirical evidence in the EU (as to the effectiveness of national laws and the incidence of genetic discrimination). This points to the need for empirical evidence in this area, in advance of legislative endeavours at EU level. There is accordingly a need to engage in such empirical research to provide further details, insight and evidence of the incidence of genetic discrimination, breach of privacy and other misuse of genetic information. There is a need for research indicating how existing legislative endeavours (for example, at Member State level) are operating in practice, with a view to ascertaining modes of regulation as well as legislative challenges in this field.

Section 4 examines the position of EU data protection law, and the protection of genetic information under this framework. It focuses on the reform process that is taking place in this area, and evaluates the extent to which this new legislative framework will protect an individual's genetic data. Although offering additional protections for the privacy of genetic data, the introduction of the enhanced data protection framework has been delayed. In addition, it is unlikely that such an enhanced data protection framework will fully protect individuals' genetic information, particularly considering the potential for discrimination and other misuse of genetic information.

Section 4 also highlights the relevance of the United Nations Convention on the Rights of Persons with Disabilities in this field, and offers insights into the disability perspectives, for example, regarding the sensitive issue of genetic screening in reproduction. It highlights the United Nations Convention on the Rights of Persons with Disabilities as an international platform to discuss these issues and offer guidance on best practice from an international human rights perspective.

## 5. Section 5

Section 5 examines the EU framework in detail. It looks at the reach of current protections, from a data protection and non-discrimination framework. In the field of non-discrimination it focuses on the disability ground and the evolving definition of disability in the EU, with particular reference to the developing case law of the European Court of Justice. On identification of the gaps in protection at EU level, this section explores the legal bases for action in the field of genetic discrimination, from a non-discrimination and Internal Market perspective.

The proposal made in Section 5 is the need for an EU-level response to address the discriminatory use of genetic information. In support of such a proposal, arguments are made in support of the EU's competence to act, and reference is made to the United Nations Convention on the Rights of Persons with Disabilities and the EU Charter of Fundamental Rights, both of which act as an impetus to action in this area and add weight to these proposals.

## 6. Final conclusion

Genetic science and technology is advancing at a rapid pace, creating new opportunities and opening new vistas in the field of medicine, and indeed in society in general. As highlighted throughout this book, there is an emerging consensus that technological innovation in the field of genetics is giving rise to economic opportunities, together with complex ethical, social and legal considerations. Accordingly, there is a wide range of human rights as well as commercial interests at stake. As interest in genetic science and technology is growing, appropriate and well balanced regulation is therefore necessary. If left unregulated, there is a real possibility that discrimination and other abuse will become more widespread, and employers, insurance companies (and other interested third parties such as banks, educational institutes, reproduction agencies and, indeed, governments) will take advantage of individuals and misuse sensitive genetic information.

In looking forward, appropriate and well balanced regulation would ensure that genetic information is protected and that a genetic underclass does not become a reality in society. Engaging transatlantic perspectives on this issue offers relevant insights as to how the US has responded and how the ethical and legal issues have been addressed and framed. It highlights the choice of regulatory framework adopted in the US and the non-discrimination approach taken.

On consideration of the potential for abuse and the fundamental human rights at stake, as well as the evident gaps in protection in the EU, this volume explores the need for an appropriate regulatory response at EU level to protect the privacy of genetic information and to prevent genetic discrimination. It offers insights as to the shape that this response might take, as well as the legal bases for such action.

A clear and specifically tailored EU-level response would contribute towards enhancing public confidence at an early stage, as well as facilitating and allowing further advances in genetic science and technology. From an economic perspective, the progression of science and technology are keys to growth of the EU economy and the EU's economic interaction with other jurisdictions. It is acknowledged, however, that any EU legislative action is likely to be a lengthy process and the issue is at an early stage of discussion. Although such an EU-level response requires further debate and consultation with all stakeholders, as well as the collation of the necessary empirical evidence, such an approach merits consideration and discussion.

The insights given and proposals made in this book are a small element in the longer journey towards effectively grappling with the myriad of regulatory, policy and other challenges presented as the law addresses sweeping scientific and technological advances. Accordingly, one challenge of the twenty-first century will be to find new and innovative ways to close the gap between law and technology, and acknowledge emerging legal and ethical concerns (as well as commercial interests), while at the same time allowing science and technology to flourish for the benefit of all.

# Index